A GUIDE TO THE IDENTIFICATION
AND NATURAL HISTORY
OF THE SPARROWS OF
THE UNITED STATES AND CANADA

D0107939

DEDICATIONS

Jim Rising wishes to express his deep gratitude for the help and encouragement he has received from his family, Myra and Jesse, Dean and John Edward, Trudy, and David and John Torin, and dedicates this book to them, with love.

David Beadle would like to dedicate this book to the memory of his parents Joan and Arthur — 'for trusting me to follow my own path'.

Ken Seyffert

A GUIDE TO THE IDENTIFICATION AND NATURAL HISTORY OF THE SPARROWS OF THE UNITED STATES AND CANADA

James D Rising
Department of Zoology
University of Toronto, Toronto, Canada

Illustrated by David D Beadle

ACADEMIC PRESS
Harcourt Brace & Company, Publishers
SAN DIEGO   LONDON   NEW YORK
BOSTON   SYDNEY   TOKYO   TORONTO

This book is printed on acid-free paper.

Copyright © 1996 ACADEMIC PRESS
Text © 1996 James D Rising
Illustrations © 1996 David D Beadle

All rights reserved.

No part of this publication may be reproduced or transmitted in any form or by any means, electronic or mechanical including photocopying, recording, or any information storage and retrieval system, without permission in writing from the publisher.

Academic Press, Inc.
525 B Street, Suite 1900, San Diego
California 92101-4495, USA

Academic Press Limited
24–28 Oval Road
London NW1 7DX, UK

ISBN: 0-12-588970-4 (hbk)
        0-12-588971-2 (pbk)

Library of Congress Cataloging-in-Publication Data

A catalogue record for this book is available from the British Library

Typeset by Selwood Systems Typesetting, Bath, Avon
Printed in Great Britain by The Bath Press, Bath, Avon

96 97 98 99 00 01 EB 9 8 7 6 5 4 3 2 1

CONTENTS

LIST OF SPECIES COVERED

LIST OF PLATES

ACKNOWLEDGMENTS

I am indebted to the following persons who kindly criticized portions of this book: George Barrowclough (*Junco*), James Dick, Kimball Garrett, Brian Henshaw, Dan Kozlovic, Richard Knapton (*Spizella*), Alvaro Jaramillo, Ned Johnson (*Amphispiza*), Tony Lang, Joe Morlan, Tom Parsons, Van Remsen, Trudy Rising, Tom Shane (Lark Buntings), and Bob Zink (*Passerella*). I am especially grateful to Gene Hess, Dan Gibson, and Van Remsen who kindly gave me information, much of it yet unpublished, on Delaware, Alaskan, and Louisiana sparrows. Also many thanks to Andrew Richford and Roopa Baliga of Academic Press who have encouraged us and assisted us in every step along the way. I also benefited from many comments and observations posted on the e-mail group, birdchat.

James D Rising

The artwork for this guide would not have been possible without the use of material from the following institutions: The Royal Ontario Museum, Toronto (ROM); The Academy of Natural Sciences, Philadelphia (ANSP); The Canadian Museum of Nature, Ottawa (CMN) and the University of Western Ontario (UWO).

At the ROM I am particularly indebted to James A Dick, not only for arranging loan of study skins but for his unwavering support and taxonomic expertise. I would also like to thank Ross James and Glen Murphy for much help and understanding. At ANSP I owe much to David Agro for friendship and advice and for photographing some key skins from the collection. Michel Gosselin at CMN kindly arranged access to the collection and was very supportive of the project. Likewise Sandy Jonsson arranged the loan of several skins from the bird collection at the department of Zoology at UWO.

Many people kindly provided photographic material which was of great use throughout the project. I thank: David Agro, Tim Bagworth, Nigel Bean, Peter Burke, Jochen Dierschke, Dan Gibson, Phill Holder, Tony Lang, Nadine Litwin, Doug McRae, Michael Richardson, Jim Rising, David Shepherd and George Wallace.

Specialized information was gleaned from many people. In particular I wish to thank the following people: Dan Gibson for much help regarding Asian Buntings in Alaska and for supplying a superb series of transparencies depicting McKay's Buntings from the collection of the University of Alaska Museum. Theodore Tobish provided useful notes on Common Reed Buntings in Alaska. In addition Peter Burke, Brian Henshaw, Alvaro Jaramillo and Paul Prior provided much useful comment.

Long days were spent in the field in an attempt to get to know my subjects a little better. I would like to thank many people (too numerous to mention) whose companionship and expertise in the field helped to make this aspect of the research most enjoyable. However, I should single out the staff and research volunteers at both Long Point Bird Observatory, Ontario and Point Reyes Bird Observatory (SE Farallon contingent), California for some truly memorable times. In addition Jon Curson, Paul Prior and David Shepherd have enlivened many hours tramping through field and brush in search of sparrows.

My work on this project would not have been possible without the support and encouragement of Doug and Lois Thomas and, indeed, the whole Thomas family in Toronto — my thanks to them all. Peter Thomas was particularly helpful in supplying much sonic assistance. I thank my sisters Rosemary, Jenny and Lynn in England for cheerfully entertaining me on my numerous trips 'home'.

At Academic Press Andrew Richford has been an enthusiastic supporter of the project since the beginning. I thank him for his guidance and faith in my abilities to complete the task.

Finally, I thank Katie for tremendous support, encouragement and ever-ready wit throughout this long project. As well as being a super birding companion on numerous research trips she provided much invaluable assistance on several aspects of the project.

David D Beadle

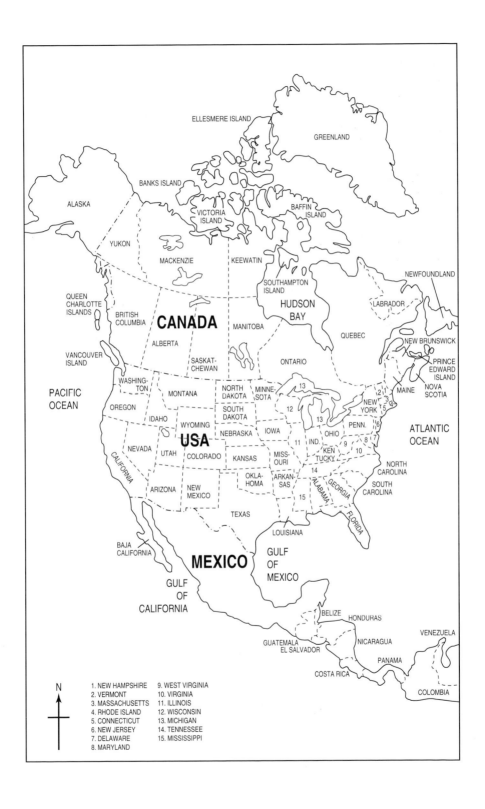

INTRODUCTION

I am often asked why I like 'boring little brown birds.' In part, it's because I don't find them boring. Neither, I suspect, do you, or you wouldn't be reading this. Although brown is a common color among sparrows, not all are brown, and even the brown ones are subtly beautiful. Another reason, I think, that I am so fond of these small, generally inconspicuous birds is an environmental one. As a young teenager, I started birding in the mid-west — Kansas City — where, in winter, sparrows and ducks dominated the birdlife. Duck identification was less of a challenge to me than the sparrows. Often hard to see, sparrows usually require stalking, spishing, and other forms of active pursuit. Each winter, my older brother and I took the 'Parkville Bottoms' route on the Christmas Bird Count — an area with dense brush along the Missouri River — excellent wintering sparrow habitat. Our objective became to get all of the sparrows, and more of each species than any other party — not science, but good fun! After learning all the common species, we started looking for challenging ones. We spent hours on cold, damp March mornings chasing migrating flocks of Lapland Longspurs through hilly pastures trying to pick a Smith's, McCown's, or Chestnut-collared out of the lot — alas, without success. Henslow's, Sharp-tails, and Baird's remained similarly elusive.

At university I largely abandoned bird watching as a hobby, but my interest in birds certainly did not wane. My research on birds, initially on oriole hybridization, and later on geographic variation took me to virtually all parts of North America, all of the United States, all of the Canadian provinces and territories, north to the Arctic Ocean, Hudson Bay, and the Ungava Peninsula, and most of Mexico. Much of this research involved studies of sparrows, especially Savannah Sparrows and Sharp-tailed Sparrows, but also grassland sparrows in general. In the course of this work, I have seen every species of sparrow that breeds north of Mexico in the New World, with the exception of McKay's Bunting and the White-collared Seedeater in their natural breeding habitat north of Mexico. Fortunately, I have seen the seedeaters in Mexico and Costa Rica, and 'hybrid' Snow and McKay Buntings in the Pribilof Is., Alaska.

Several years ago, a colleague asked me why I didn't write a guide to sparrow identification. The idea intrigued me, but this was before the first of the 'expert guides' appeared, and I wondered if there would be a niche for or any interest in such a book. Nonetheless, I kept the idea in the back of my mind, and a few years ago, Andrew Richford of Academic Press/Poyser Books asked me if I was interested in writing just such a book. The need for a good artist was paramount, of course, and it was my good fortune that my graduate student Alvaro Jaramillo recommended David Beadle. When Dave and I met, he brought with him a couple of sample plates, one of *Zonotrichia* sparrows and the other of Savannah Sparrows. Looking at these, I attempted to identify them all — to region — this is a Savannah Sparrow from the northeast; this from the prairies (I've spent 25 years studying Savannah Sparrows); etc. I got them all right, which made us both happy. I had a test of my ability to identify these birds correctly, and he had a test of his ability to paint them in a way that they could be identified by someone who knew the birds.

Dave Beadle is originally from Kent, in the United Kingdom, but has now settled in Toronto, Ontario with his wife, Katie. A birder for twenty years or so, he has always been interested in identification of the 'difficult' groups of birds. After spending much of the 1980s working at bird observatories in the UK and North America, David decided to concentrate full-time on his other main interest — bird art. It seemed a natural progression to combine the two.

Ever since he first started birding, David has had a certain fascination with buntings and sparrows. Their subtle, sometimes complex plumage patterns and often cryptic behavior were very appealing. On first visiting Canada (to work at Long Point Bird Observatory) in 1986, David was captivated by the North American sparrows and it was always in the back of his mind to one day illustrate a book on the subject of their identification and geographical variation. It was fate indeed that Alvaro put David in contact with me, and the book became a reality.

David has always thought it essential to get to know in life the birds one is to portray and has made much effort to do this. Despite quite extensive travel across North America, David realizes he has barely scratched the surface of what is a very complex and enigmatic group of birds. There is always more to learn!

While writing this book I have learned a great deal, have been humbled by how much I didn't know, how much I still don't know, and by how much appears not to be known. David has related that he feels the same. We hope this book stimulates us all to be better observers; we hope that you will help us correct misinterpretations, and that you will communicate new information to me, on behalf of both of us for including in possible future editions.

ABOUT THIS BOOK

This book is a guide to the identification of sparrows that have been recorded in the United States and Canada. For each species you will find an account, and one or more color illustrations. There are also range maps for those species that breed north of Mexico. When possible, the accounts are provided in the sequence given in the 7th edition of the American Ornithologists' Union (AOU) Check-List of North American Birds (1996), a sequence that places together species that are thought to be closely related to each other. This list identifies several changes in the species-level taxonomy for North American sparrows, including several that will not be known to people familiar with current editions of field guides. For example, the 'Rufous-sided' Towhee is split into the Eastern and Spotted towhees, the 'Brown Towhee' into the Canyon and California towhees, and the Sharp-tailed Sparrow into Nelson's Sharp-tailed and Saltmarsh Sharp-tailed sparrows. I have followed the species-level classification English vernacular names of the AOU Check-List with a few exceptions: I thus split the Sage Sparrow into two species — the coastal Bell's Sparrow and inland Sage Sparrow — and the Fox Sparrow into three — the eastern and northern Red Fox Sparrow, the northwestern Sooty Fox Sparrow, and the western Slate-colored Fox Sparrow. The AOU Check-List committee has yet to recognize these changes, pending the publication of work in progress. Once this work is published, however, it is probable that these splits will be recognized. In any event, the forms described here can be readily identified in the field. For other, similarly variable groups, such as the Savannah Sparrows, Nelson's Sharp-tailed Sparrows, and Dark-eyed Juncos, additional taxonomic revision seems less imminent; I have treated these as single species, though separate accounts are given for each of the clearly-identifiable forms. In total, 62 species and 69 forms are treated in detail here.

THE TEXT

Preceding the species accounts, you will find a short summary of some of the general characteristics of the species in that genus, and some indication of which other genera are thought to be their closest relatives, unless the genus is represented north of Mexico by only one species (or two very similar species, e.g. *Plectrophenax*).

Each species is introduced by its common name, its scientific name and number, in square brackets, assigned to it by the AOU. This number is often used by ornithologists, especially banders, for ease of reference.

Each **species account** is divided into the following sections:

IDENTIFICATION: This is a statement of the most conspicuous features of the species, emphasizing both physical and behavioral features that characterize it. Following this, is a section on **Similar species**, a brief description of the features that best separate the species from the others that it most closely resembles. This is followed by detailed descriptions of the plumages of the species, starting with the adult (Basic) plumage. The format of these descriptions varies, to accommodate the many different patterns found in sparrows.

VOICE: The songs and various calls and notes of the species are verbally described. When possible, they are likened to those of other species, and differences that will aid in field identification are stressed.

HABITS: The general behavior or mannerisms of the species are described; features that aid in field identification are stressed.

HABITAT: This section contains a description of the characteristic habitats used, in summer, winter and migration. Although in migration, a bird may be found in uncharacteristic habitat, all species have specific habitat preferences, and knowing these is invaluable to the person looking for a particular species. For example, in summer juncos tend to be found in coniferous woods, and longspurs in fields, tundra, or shortgrass prairie.

BREEDING: The placement of nest, its structure, number of eggs laid and general breeding biology are discussed; these facts will help to identify nests found.

RANGE: This section contains a detailed statement of the breeding and wintering ranges of the species, and, where appropriate, notes on where the species may be seen in migration. The distributional data have been taken from regional bird lists (see **RANGE REFERENCES**), and from personal experience.

HISTORY: For species that breed north of Mexico, there is a section detailing the discovery, and original description and naming of the species. When possible, I quote early naturalists' accounts of its abundance and behavior, and contrast them with contemporary accounts. The empasis in this section is, 'now and then,' since the available information is variable, the reader will find these reports in only some of the accounts.

GEOGRAPHIC VARIATION: Many of the species discussed in this book differ geographically, that is, the species varies in coloration and size from one part of its range to another. If such variation exists in the species, major patterns of variation are discussed in this section. If geographically variable species have been divided into two or more **subspecies**, some of these and their characteristics are described. For most species treated here, each of the subspecies from north of Mexico that has been generally accepted is mentioned, with comments on its distinctiveness; however, most of these cannot be individually identified in the hand, let alone in the field. For species in which many subspecies have been described, all **subspecies groups**, but not all subspecies, are described here (particularly when the number of subspecies is large, and their distinctiveness is small), because many of these are poorly differentiated or they have not been adequately described. The English names for subspecies have not been standardized; I have used those that are commonly used, but in some instances no such commonly used name is available. With a few exceptions, I discourage people from trying to identify subspecies in the field. This only perpetuates the notion that these identifications can be made with reasonable accuracy, which is usually not the case. I have tried to identify cases where I think field identification is possible.

MEASUREMENTS: Measurements of each species are given in millimeters (figures in parentheses represent mean values). These are taken from a variety of sources, and thus the measurements as well as the quality of information given varies from account to account. Measurements of wing (the length of the unflattened wing, from the bend to the tip of the longest primary feather), tail (length of the longest tail feather, from its base), tarsus (length of the tarsus — unfeathered part of the leg — from the middle of the ankle joint to the middle of the joint between the tarsus and the middle toe), and exposed culmen (length of the upper bill, from the edge of the feathers to its tip), are given for each species. Data for both sexes are given, to give an indication of sexual differences in size, and when possible, data from different populations, to give an indication of geographic variation in size.

REFERENCES: Some references are given at the end of each account. These are sources that are particularly helpful. Many other sources were also consulted for each species. These include the many regional faunal lists and breeding bird atlases listed at the end of this book, in addition to the life histories in *Life Histories of North American Cardinals, Grosbeaks, Buntings, Towhees, Finches, Sparrows and Allies* (Austin 1968), *Taxonomic and Adaptive Features of the Juvenal Plumage in North American Sparrows* (Graber 1955), *Identification Guide to North American Passerines* (Pyle *et al.* 1987), and *The Birds of North and Middle America* Part 1 (Ridgway 1901). These standard sources were used in each account, when appropriate, but not specifically acknowledged at the end of the accounts.

COLOR PLATES: The 27 plates illustrate all of the distinctive plumages of each species, including, when possible, the juveniles. For most species, several different poses are shown, to emphasize different plumage characteristics that aid in field identification. For geographically variable species the most distinctive subspecies are illustrated. Species have been shown in habitats that are characteristic. Line drawings in the species accounts illustrate behavior and other features.

RANGE MAPS: The range maps delimit the breeding and wintering ranges of each species. Within the areas indicated, each species will generally be found only in characteristic habitat. Thus species, such as juncos, that occur in coniferous woods, are widely distributed throughout the west, but habitat suitable for them in most regions occurs only in mountains; we have not attempted to identify each mountain range in these maps, only to give an indication of usual general distribution of the species. The description of the range in the text is more detailed. In the verbal description of the range, I have abbreviated compass directions when used as adjectives: thus northern is n, sw is southwestern and e-c is east-central.

Map colors:
Red: Areas where the species may be found nesting in suitable habitat.
Blue: Areas where the species may be found more or less regularly in winter.
Purple: Areas where the species may be found throughout the year.

BREEDING ABUNDANCE MAPS: Recently, Jeff Price *et al.* (1995) have published maps showing centers of abundance of birds in summer, based on breeding bird surveys. They have generously made these available to us, and we have reproduced relevant ones here. The breeding bird survey data do not take into account all records, and are most reliable where there are roads (thus they cut off much of Canada).

SPARROW TOPOGRAPHY: In writing the plumage descriptions, I have used the terms shown in the figures below. These terms are those most often used in contemporary ornithological literature.

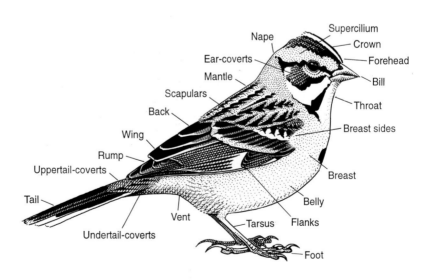

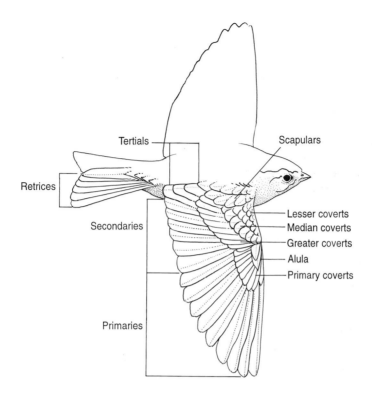

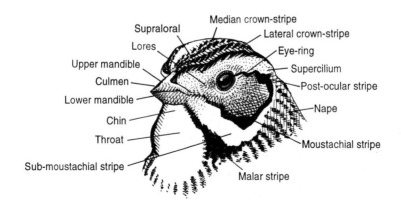

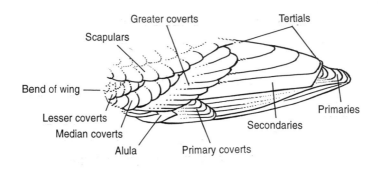

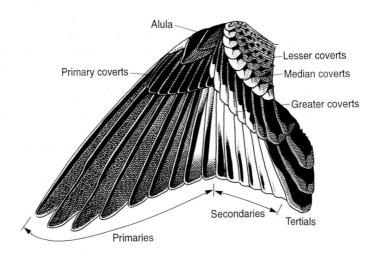

WHAT ARE SPARROWS?

*"All birds look like sparrows to me. There are big
sparrows, small sparrows and gaily colored sparrows. But
they all look like sparrows. Last summer I realized this
was a know-nothing attitude, so I bought two bird books.
They were filled with every conceivable kind of sparrow."*

—ANDY ROONEY

INTRODUCING THE SPARROWS

The name sparrow has its origin in the Anglo-Saxon word *spearwa* which literally
means 'flutterer.' In England the name is used for three different species of small
brown birds, the House Sparrow and European Tree Sparrow (Family Passeridae),
and the unrelated Hedge Sparrow (today more commonly known as the Dunnock,
Family Prunellidae). The name sparrow was applied by English-speaking colonists in
the Americas to many of the small brown birds that they found to be common in the
New World, the 'sparrows' in this book (Family Emberizidae). The American
'sparrows,' however, are not closely related to the English birds with the same name.

The Old World birds that are most closely related to the American sparrows are
usually called buntings in the English vernacular (for example, Reed Bunting and
Corn Bunting). The name 'sparrow,' of course, was only one of many English
vernacular names that were applied to New World birds that resembled Old World
birds that were not close relatives. Others include 'warbler' (the New World warblers
or wood-warblers [Parulidae or Emberizidae] are not closely related to the Old World
warblers [Sylviidae]); 'blackbird' (in England, a thrush [*Turdus merula*], closely
related to the American Robin [*T. migratorius*], which is not closely related to the
European robin [*Erithacus rubecula*]); 'grosbeak' (some American grosbeaks, such as
the Evening and Pine grosbeaks are closely related to the European grosbeaks, but
others, such as the Rose-breasted and Black-headed grosbeaks are not); and
'bunting' (the New World buntings, with the exceptions of Snow and McKay's
buntings, are closely related to the cardinals).

Putting all common name confusion aside, the sparrows found in the Americas
belong to a large group of songbirds known as the nine-primaried oscines. The
oscines are one of the two subdivisions of the avian order Passeriformes, the so-called
'perching birds,' which in turn contains about 60% of the over 9000 living species of
bird currently recognized. Oscines are divided into the nine- and ten-primaried

oscines. The nine-primaried oscines are divided into several large groups, New World blackbirds, New World wood-warblers, tanagers, cardinals, and sparrows or buntings. Most contemporary classifications consider the American sparrows to be in a subfamily (Emberizinae) in a much larger family (Emberizidae) that also contains the American blackbirds, wood-warblers, Bananaquit, tanagers, and cardinals. To date, we know of no characteristics that can be used to distinguish clearly among these various subgroups, but in general they differ in bill shape and feeding habits. The wood-warblers generally have thin bills and feed mostly on insects; the tanagers have thicker bills and feed mostly on fruit; and the sparrows and finches have conical bills and mostly eat seeds, at least in winter. Some classifications place the New World sparrows in an even more comprehensive family (Fringillidae) that also includes the fringillid finches (such as goldfinches, siskins, crossbills, and Pine and Evening grosbeaks).

Of the nine-primaried oscines, the fringillids are found naturally in North and South America, Eurasia, and Africa; the Hawaiian Honeycreepers probably also belong in this group. The blackbirds (Icterinae), wood-warblers (Parulinae), cardinals (Cardinalinae), Bananaquit (Coerebinae), and tanagers (Thraupinae), on the other hand, are found only in the New World.

The New World sparrows (Emberizinae) like the finches (fringillids) are found in the Americas, Eurasia, and Africa. However, they show their greatest diversity in the New World, where the group almost certainly originally evolved. Of approximately 156 species recognized, only 44 occur regularly in the Old World, and almost all of these (38) are in a single genus *Emberiza*. By contrast, more than 50 species in 16 different genera breed in North America north of Mexico. As previously indicated, this book is a guide to the identification of these species, plus an additional nine Eurasian or Central American species that occur occasionally in North America north of Mexico.

General Features of Sparrows

Sparrows are generally small to medium-sized brown birds with streaks. Some, however, are not brown. In some plumages the longspurs, Eastern and Spotted towhees, and Lark Bunting are brightly colored, and the Snow and McKay's buntings are predominantly white. Many of the Central American sparrows are predominantly green, and of these the Olive Sparrow is found north into southern Texas. The Green-tailed Towhee of the west is also predominantly green.

Sparrows have conical bills, which are used to shell seeds, an important component of their diet, especially in winter. However, most sparrows eat insects when available and also other animal foods, and these comprise the greatest part of the diets of sparrows in the breeding season; fruits of various sorts, when available, are also eaten by sparrows.

In most species there is little difference in appearance of males and females (sexual dimorphism), the conspicuous exceptions being the longspurs, Snow and McKay's buntings, Lark Bunting, the Eastern Towhee, the seedeaters (only one of which regularly occurs north of Mexico and the West Indies), and the Palearctic buntings, all of which occur rarely in North America. In the sexually dimorphic species, the males have a bright breeding plumage. Some other species, though not conspicuously dimorphic, can usually be sexed in the field (e.g. juncos, Harris's Sparrow, Black-chinned Sparrow). The breeding (or alternate) plumage and winter (or basic) plumage are similar in most species, and the prebasic molt, which takes place after breeding, though variable in the group, is generally complete. The spring, prealternate, molt is absent or incomplete. In dimorphic species, much of the brightness of the male breeding plumage is acquired through wear.

Juvenal plumage is a bird's first plumage. All juvenile North American sparrows (in juvenal plumage) are streaked, with the exception of the seedeaters (*Sporophila*). Juvenal plumage is often kept for only a short time and is replaced by the first basic plumage in late summer or early autumn. Young in the first basic plumage generally resemble adults (adult females in dimorphic species), but usually are no so brightly colored and often have a yellowish or buffy cast. In a few species (e.g., White-crowned Sparrow) there is a distinctive first basic plumage.

Male sparrows are on average larger than females, but differences are generally not obvious, and there is considerable overlap in size between sexes in each sparrow species.

Habitat and Distribution

Sparrows are characteristically birds of open country — tundra, prairies, desert shrub, old-fields, marshes, and dune-grass. Many species, such as the Chipping, Fox, and White-throated sparrows and the juncos, however, breed in woodlands, and frequent weedy fields or woodland edge in migration and winter. Towhees are almost always found in brush.

Sparrows as a group are hardy, and conspicuous in many northern habitats. Although sparrows that breed in the north are highly migratory, most do not winter south of the United States or northern Mexico, and none migrate south to the Neotropics (there are, however, many resident Neotropical species). In some species, such as eastern Dark-eyed Juncos and western White-crowned Sparrows, males tend to winter farther north than females, but this is not so for some others, such as Savannah Sparrows (see individual species accounts for details).

Habits

Although most species of sparrows are territorial during the breeding season, many are gregarious in winter, when they are often found in flocks. Flocks of sparrows in open country commonly contain only individuals of a single species, but, in brushy old-field habitats where species diversity is generally higher, mixed flocks are more usual. Although flocks are generally small, huge flocks of some species, especially longspurs, can be found. Sparrows can be difficult to see, even in habitats where the grass is very short.

Sparrows usually forage on the ground where they may scratch among litter for food, but they also glean insects, and pick seeds and fruits from standing plants.

Winter Snow Buntings foraging on beach

Vocalizations

Most sparrows have complicated and often melodious songs. Characteristically, territorial males sing persistently from song perches which may or may not be exposed. Females rarely sing. In winter full song is uncommon, but occurs regularly in some species; winter songs may be different from songs given in the breeding season. Some sparrow songs have an insect-like quality. This seems to be particularly true of the songs of some of the grassland or marsh dwelling species (e.g., Grasshopper, Savannah, LeConte's, Henslow's, Sharp-tailed and Seaside sparrows), and some of these songs are very short (LeConte's and Henslow's sparrows). Nocturnal singing is fairly common in the sparrows as a group, and is frequent in

McCown's Longspur in song flight

some species, again particularly in the grassland and marsh dwelling species (especially LeConte's, Henslow's and Sharp-tailed sparrows).

Flight singing is common and characteristic of several species, such as Seaside, sharp-tailed (especially prairie and northern populations), and Cassin's sparrows, Lark Bunting, Snow Bunting, and the longspurs. Even LeConte's Sparrow has a flight song. These flight songs, and the behaviors associated with them, are often a great aid in identification. In Lark Buntings and McCown's Longspurs, the flight song is given while the male performs a stiff winged 'butterfly' display. Occasional flight singing occurs in some of the other species (e.g., Bachman's, Savannah, and Song sparrows).

Sparrow call notes are characteristically short, high *chips* or *seeps*. Although calls of many species are superficially similar to each other and are difficult to describe, most are species specific. Some calls, such as those of the Song and Swamp sparrows, are easily learned, and serve as an important aid in field identification (skulking sparrows are more often heard than seen). Most sparrows call in flight, especially as they take off. Longspurs and Snow Buntings give distinctive flight calls, and these calls are an important aid to identification.

Breeding Behavior

Typically, sparrows are territorial, and males defend territories by singing and by chasing rivals. Escalated fighting often takes place as territorial boundaries are established. Both sexes or the female alone build the nest which, in most species, is placed on or near the ground. The female alone incubates the eggs, although males may sit on the nest on occasion. Males characteristically bring food to their mates, and play a significant role in feeding the young once the eggs hatch. Males may

White-throated Sparrow feeding nestlings

accompany the young as females initiate second broods, and males commonly play a larger role than females in attending fledged young.

Most sparrows are assumed to be monogamous (although extrapair copulation is common), but many species have not been closely studied. In some, such as the Savannah Sparrow, males in some populations may have two mates whose broods are staggered, so that the male can attend the first brood before the second hatches, then attend the second one later. Male Swamp Sparrows may also have two mates. When this occurs, each of the females appears to have a sub-territory on the territory occupied by the male, which appears to assist both. Male Lark Buntings with two mates help only the first with the care of the brood. Probably a small percentage of the males in many other species also have two mates.

The breeding system of the sharp-tailed sparrows is atypical. Sharp-tailed sparrows are not territorial, and although males sing, they are not aggressive toward other males. Females alone build the nest, and when they are laying, solicit matings from males, and mate promiscuously. Males play no role in parental care. The breeding biology of Smith's Longspur appears to be similar.

Conservation of Sparrows

The greatest danger faced by the sparrows of North America is the same danger facing all wildlife — habitat destruction. I cannot be emphatic enough about this problem. Certainly there are other threats to sparrows. Pet cats kill migrating sparrows and other songbirds, and thousands are killed by flying into lighted (often needlessly lighted) buildings during their nocturnal migration, but these are relatively minor problems, that almost certainly have no longterm effects on population sizes.

If habitat is preserved, the sparrows will flourish. Many sparrows, such as the American Tree Sparrow, Harris's Sparrow, Snow Bunting, and Smith's and Lapland longspurs, breed in the far north in habitats that have been little disturbed by humans. These species probably occur today in numbers equivalent to those that existed in pre-colonial times. Some, indeed, may have benefited by the clearing of forests in the east, which in certain cases has created field or brush and second-growth habitats that are the preferred wintering habitat of many species; feeders are also a valuable source of winter food for many sparrows. Other species, especially those that live in marsh habitats or in southwestern grasslands, have not been so fortunate. One well-marked population of the Seaside Sparrow, the 'Dusky' Seaside Sparrow, was driven to extinction, perhaps partly by pesticide use and wildfires, but primarily because of the destruction of its saltmarsh habitat for mosquito control. These sparrows were both genetically and phenotypically distinct, and today would almost surely have been recognized as a distinct species. Botteri's Sparrow is on the verge of being driven from southern Texas as a consequence of habitat destruction, and the decline in Bachman's Sparrow is attributable to the forestry practices in the southeastern states, that is, clearcutting the pines, then replanting in dense pine plantations. More details on the conservation of many species are given in the 'History' sections of the species accounts.

Taxonomic Relationships among the Sparrows

The relationships among the genera of sparrows are not clearly understood, and there has to date been no detailed phylogenetic analysis of the group. It is generally argued that only closely related species can hybridize, and evidence from interspecific hybrids has influenced our speculation about relationships among species, and in some cases genera. In a few cases, modern biochemical studies have elucidated relationships. Nonetheless, in many others the relationships implied by the order in which species are listed has been established by tradition, with the actual reasons for placing species together intuitive or obscure.

It is conventionally thought that the longspurs (*Calcarius*) and snow buntings (*Plectrophenax*) are, of the American sparrows, those that are most closely related to the Eurasian buntings (*Emberiza*). The Lark Bunting (*Calamospiza melanocorys*) may belong with these as well. The Fox Sparrow, generally placed in the genus *Passerella*, is probably closely related to *Melospiza* (Song, Swamp, and Lincoln's sparrows). These, in turn, are generally placed with the crowned sparrows (*Zonotrichia*) and juncos (*Junco*); there are several known hybrids between White-throated Sparrows (*Z. albicollis*) and Dark-eyed (Slate-colored) Juncos (*J. hyemalis*). The relationship of *Spizella* (e.g., Chipping and Field sparrows) to other groups is not clear. It has been suggested that they are close to both *Aimophila* (e.g., Cassin's and Rufous-crowned sparrows) or to *Junco*; the Black-chinned Sparrow does superficially resemble a junco, but this is not compelling evidence. *Spizella* may be close to *Zonotrichia*.

Many of the grassland sparrows are thought to be closely related. The Savannah Sparrow (*Passerculus sandwichensis*) is conventionally thought to be most closely related to Baird's (*Ammodramus bairdii*) and Grasshopper sparrows (*A. savannarum*); there are records of hybrids between Savannah and Grasshopper sparrows. The sharp-tailed (*A. caudacutus* and *A. nelsoni*) and Seaside (*A. maritimus*) sparrows seem to be closely related, and they, in turn, to the LeConte's Sparrow (*A. leconteii*); there is a record of a hybrid between LeConte's and Nelson's Sharp-tailed Sparrow, and mating between a sharp-tailed and Seaside sparrow has been observed.

In the past, some authors have placed LeConte's and Henslow's (*A. henslowii*) sparrows in a separate genus (*Passerherbulus*), but hybridization and biochemical analyses suggest that LeConte's is more closely related to the Sharp-tailed Sparrow than to Henslow's Sparrow, which in turn may be most closely related to Baird's or Grasshopper sparrows; at present, most classifications place all of these in *Ammodramus*. The Vesper Sparrow (*Pooecetes gramineus*) may belong with the other grassland sparrows, but is generally placed in the monotypic genus *Pooecetes*.

The relationships of the large genus *Aimophila* likewise are not clear. As mentioned above, they may be close to *Spizella*. Some include the genus *Amphispiza* (Black-throated, Five-striped, and Sage sparrows) in *Aimophila*. The Lark Sparrow (*Chondestes grammacus*) may be close to *Amphispiza*.

Of the sparrows found north of Mexico, the Olive Sparrow (*Arremonops*) is the only species of a large Central American group that is probably closely related to the towhees (*Pipilo*).

The White-collared Seedeater (*Sporophila torqueola*) and the Yellow-faced and

Black-faced grassquits (*Tiaris*) likewise are the only species representative of a large Neotropical group that occur north of Mexico and the West Indies. Many ornithologists consider these to be more closely related to the cardinal-grosbeaks (Cardinalinae) than to the sparrows, underscoring the difficulty in defining these groups precisely.

Subspecies

This guide will describe geographical variation in many species. Most of the sparrows treated here show some detectable geographic variation; in fact, some sparrow species are among the most variable of North American birds: some 30 subspecies of Song Sparrows (*Melospiza melodia*) and 12 subspecies of Savannah Sparrows *(Passerculus sandwichensis)* from north of Mexico are commonly recognized. In discussing geographic variation, we frequently will refer to subspecies. *A subspecies is a named population or race or group of populations, of a species that are geographically separate from other subspecies when breeding, and that can be morphologically distinguished from other populations.* Subspecies have three-part Latin names instead of two. For example, *Passerculus sandwichensis princeps* is the Latin name for a subspecies of the Savannah Sparrow, and *Melospiza melodia saltonis* is the name for a subspecies of Song Sparrow. Because there is a great deal of disagreement about how morphologically distinct a population must be to warrant a subspecific name, there is a great deal of variation in the number of subspecies that different ornithologists recognize.

In this guide only subspecies or groups of subspecies (subspecies groups) that can be readily and reliably identified in the field are discussed in detail. As a general rule, subspecies that were listed in the 5th edition of the AOU Check-List of North American Birds (1957) are mentioned, but, in a few species, poorly differentiated subspecies are omitted when it is felt that their mention would only confuse and mislead. For example, the western Savannah Sparrows tend to be paler and smaller than eastern ones, but it is not possible to identify a given individual, especially in the field, as being either a 'western' or 'eastern' Savannah Sparrow, and within each of these regions several subspecies that differ virtually imperceptibly from each other have been named. On the other hand, it is easy to tell any 'Large-billed' Savannah Sparrow from any 'typical' Savannah Sparrow, or any 'Ipswich' Savannah Sparrow from any typical Savannah Sparrow. One could say that there are 'good' subspecies, and 'bad' ones, and here we discuss and illustrate only those we think can be reliably identified in the field, at least under favorable circumstances. When possible, it is important to record information about them that specifically differentiates them from others of their species. Many have distinct molt patterns, migration dates and tendencies, and mating biology. Many, indeed, may be found to be different species when fully studied. Subspecies that are not found in the United States and Canada are not described.

In many instances, when subspecies or groups of subspecies can be easily identified in the field, English vernacular names that are associated with them are used. For example, Belding's, Large-billed, and Ipswich sparrows are at present considered to be subspecies of Savannah Sparrows; Slate-colored, Oregon, Pink-sided, White-winged, and Gray-headed juncos are subspecies of the Dark-eyed Junco that can be readily identified in the field. In some other instances, for example the Fox Sparrows, some of the distinct subspecies do not have well established vernacular names. For these species, we use the English names given in Austin (1968).

1 **Olive Sparrow** *Arremonops rufivirgatus* [586]   PLATE 1

IDENTIFICATION: 13.5–15 cm (*c.* 5.5–6 in), males slightly larger; sexes similar in coloration.

The Olive Sparrow, the only species of this genus found north of Mexico, is a fairly large and stout, dull olive-green sparrow with faint rusty brown lateral crown-stripes; the throat and belly are dull whitish.

Similar species: The Green-tailed Towhee is somewhat larger, and in adult plumage much more brightly colored, with a rusty cap, grayish side of face, and whitish throat. Botteri's Sparrows, which may occur in the same area as Olive Sparrows, are much browner in appearance, and have a streaked back. Juvenile Green-tailed Towhees are very similar to juvenile Olive Sparrows, but Olive Sparrows are smaller, with some-what whiter throat and belly, and less ventral streaking. The breeding ranges of the two species do not overlap.

Adult—*Head:* lateral crown-stripes variable, but usually dull rusty brown; median crown-stripe greenish olive; supercilium grayish; eye-stripe and lores olive-brown; thin whitish eye-ring; ear-coverts greenish olive; throat grayish, often with a thin, dull malar stripe; ***back:*** nape, mantle and ***rump*** dull brownish olive-green; ***tail:*** green-ish olive; ***wing:*** greenish olive, with yellow in the bend; ***underparts:*** throat grayish white, breast and flanks buffy grayish; ***bill:*** upper mandible dusky brown; lower mandible paler; ***legs*** and ***feet:*** light brownish; ***iris:*** light brown.

First-winter (after Sept) resemble adults, but are usually duller in coloration; coverts may be tipped with brownish yellow, forming two indistinct wing-bars.

Juveniles (June–Sept) brownish, with brown streaking on the crown, nape, mantle, throat, breast, and flanks.

VOICE: The song is a distinctive accelerating ***chip chip chip chip-chip-chip-chipchipchip***, or ***chip chip chip chi chi chi pitpitpitpitpit*** on a single pitch. Singing is most frequent in March through July. The call notes are an insect-like buzz, or a squeak.

HABITS: Males most commonly sing from a hidden perch close to the ground, but may sing from a fairly high, exposed place. They run, and scratch for food on the ground.

HABITAT: Olive Sparrows are resident in scrubby chaparral and weedy thickets in southern Texas. They are found most commonly in thorny shrubs such as mesquite, Texas ebony, and huisache, but may be found in streamside thickets of ash, cane, and live oak.

BREEDING: ***Nests*** are placed in low, usually dome-shaped bushes, usually less than a meter high. The nest is a rather bulky cup of twigs and grasses, lined with finer grasses and sometimes hair. Nests are often placed in cacti. Nesting begins in early May and continues through September. The species is apparently double-brooded with the first brood raised in May and June, and the second in August and September. ***Eggs***, 3–5, usually 4–5, are glossy white and unspotted. ***Incubation***, no information. Olive Sparrows are sometimes parasitized by Bronzed Cowbirds.

RANGE: ***Resident*** from s Texas (north to Karnes Co., east to Nueces Co., and northwest to Val Verde and Uvalde cos.), south through Coahuila, Nuevo León, eastern Mexico, Yucatan, n Guatemela and Belize, and along the Pacific Coast of Mexico from c Sinaloa south to c Oaxaca; n and c Costa Rica. Commonest south of Sabinal, Beeville, and Rockport, Texas. Recorded in fall west to Brewster Co., Texas.

HISTORY: The Olive Sparrow was first described by George N. Lawrence in 1851 from a specimen collected near Brownsville, Texas, where it is still common today. Its numbers in Texas, however, have diminished since the mid-1930s as a consequence of clearing of scrubby brush for the purpose of expanding range for livestock grazing. It, nonetheless, remains locally common in suitable habitat in southern Texas.

GEOGRAPHIC VARIATION: Although there are several Central American subspecies, only the nominate race, *A. r. rufivirgata* occurs north of Mexico.

MEASUREMENTS: (7 males): wing 62–67 (66), tail 62–70 (65), tarsus 23.1–25.4 (23.9), exposed culmen 12.2–14.0 (13.0), depth of bill at base 6.9–7.6 (7.1); (6 females): wing 59–62 (61), tail 57–64 (60), tarsus 22.9–24.6 (23.4), exposed culmen 11.9–13.2 (13.0), bill depth 6.4–7.4 (7.10) (Ridgway 1901).

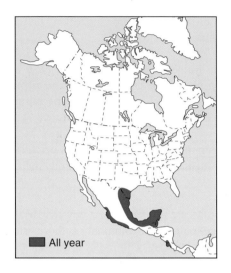

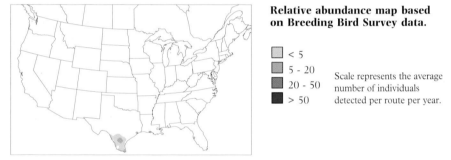

Relative abundance map based on Breeding Bird Survey data.

☐ < 5
▨ 5 - 20
▧ 20 - 50
■ > 50

Scale represents the average number of individuals detected per route per year.

Mass: (N=14), 23.6 g (18.8–29.5) (Dunning 1993).

Genus *Pipilo*

The genus *Pipilo* contains nine species, six of which occur north of Mexico. These are large, long-tailed sparrows (the tail is usually longer than the wing), with stout feet. They are unstreaked as adults. Some of the species are sexually dimorphic in plumage. They generally forage on the ground, scratching for food, with a distinctive 'double scratch,' in which the bird remains stationary while scratching backward simultaneously with both feet. Although this is a rather widespread emberizid behavior, it is nonetheless particularly characteristic of the towhees.

The relationships of the towhees to other sparrows are not clear, although they are generally placed close to several other similarly proportioned tropical American genera (e.g., *Pezopetes*, *Atlapetes*, *Arremon*, *Arremonops*, and *Melozone*). Some ornithologists argue, in fact, that the 'brown' towhees (California, Canyon, and Abert's) are more closely related to *Melozone* than to the other towhees. The Rusty-crowned Ground-Sparrow (*M. kieneri*) of western Mexico, which is mostly brown (although it has a white throat), with some rust in the crown, nape, and sides of neck, is especially similar in coloration. Also, the songs, call notes, egg color and pattern, and choice of nest-site suggest that the brown towhees are closer to *Melozone* that to the other towhees, indicating that perhaps the brown towhees should be put with these rather than the other *Pipilo*.

2 **Green-tailed Towhee** *Pipilo chlorurus* [590]   PLATE 1

P.BEADLE.

IDENTIFICATION: 16–18 cm (*c.* 6–7 in), males slightly larger; sexes similar in coloration, although the female may be slightly grayer on the back, with a duller crown.

The Green-tailed Towhee is a large rusty-capped sparrow with a greenish back and tail, black malar stripe and white throat.

Similar species: Although the Green-tailed Towhee is distinctive, a dull individual could be confused with the smaller Olive Sparrow, but the larger size, rusty cap, and white throat of the towhee are usually apparent. Juveniles of these two species are similar, but the Olive Sparrow is less extensively and less strikingly streaked below, is more buffy in hue, and has a buffy supercilium.

Adult—*Head:* crown rusty or cinnamon-rufous; forehead, lores, and malar stripe gray to dark gray; supraloral and submoustachial stripes, and chin and throat white; face otherwise gray or greenish gray; ***back:*** nape, mantle and ***rump*** greenish gray or greenish brown, with centers of mantle feathers somewhat darker; ***tail:*** greenish, tinged with yellowish olive; ***wing:*** greenish olive with a yellow bend in the wing (carpal edge); ***underparts:*** chin and throat white, usually contrasting sharply with the gray breast; flanks grayish to whitish; belly white; undertail coverts whitish beige; ***bill:*** upper mandible blackish; lower mandible grayish to bluish white; ***legs:*** brownish; toes darker; ***iris:*** cinnamon.

First-winter (after Aug) resemble adult, but have duller crowns on average.

Juveniles (June–Aug) crown, back, breast and flanks heavily streaked with dark brown; throat whitish, and contrasts with dark brown malar stripe; tail and wings have a greenish cast.

VOICE: The Green-tailed Towhee's song is a lively Lark Sparrow-like warbled ***wheet clur cheeewee-churr***, or a rapid wheezy ***eet-ter-te-te-te-te-ti-si-si-si-seur***. In California, the song can sound very like that of the Slate-colored Fox Sparrows; perhaps song mimicry is involved. The call note is a sharp ***keek***, or a plaintive cat-like ***me-u*** or a plaintive ***see-u-wee***. The species sometimes sings at night.

HABITS: Male Green-tailed Towhees sing from the top of shrubs. If alarmed, towhees dive into a bush, or drop to the ground without opening their wings, and when flushed from a nest they run rapidly along the ground with their tail up. They scratch backward with both feet (double-scratch) when feeding.

HABITAT: In the Great Basin, Green-tailed Towhees are associated with dense shrubs, usually sagebrush and antelope brush, dense montane chaparral, on dry slopes, in higher valleys and foothills (up to 2400 m). They may be found in chaparral. In winter, they are found at lower elevations in mesquite and other dry brush, and sometimes in urban areas. In California they are in montane thickets (*Ceanothus*, willow).

BREEDING: *Nest* is placed on or close to the ground, to 70 cm high, in or at the base of a bush (sagebrush, waxberry, snowbush, scrubby oak, *Ceanothus*), and occasionally in cactus. The nest is a rather large cup of twigs and grasses, lined with finer material, including hair. Nesting begins in May and continues through July, with most nesting activity in June. *Eggs*, 3–5, usually 4, are white, heavily spotted with reddish brown; female alone incubates, but both parents feed the young; incubation period and fledging age not known. This species is parasitized by cowbirds.

RANGE: *Breeds* from s-c and c Oregon (n to Grant County), se Washington, s Idaho, s-c and sw Montana, Wyoming, and possibly w-c South Dakota (summer records), south through California (south to Sacramento Valley, and principally east of the Sierras, and in mountains of sw California), Nevada (except extreme south), n and c Arizona (Kaibab Plateau, San Francisco and White mountains), w-c and ne New Mexico through c and w Colorado, w Oklahoma (one nesting record), sw Texas (Chisos Mountains, McKittrick Canyon).

Winters from s California (rare), s Nevada, c Arizona, c New Mexico, and Texas, south to s Baja California, Jalisco, Guanajuato, Querétaro, Morelos, Hidalgo, and Tamaulipas; they winter occasionally north to c and w Colorado, Wyoming, Kansas and Missouri. Most common in winter in sw Texas west to s Arizona.

Casual or accidental north to British Columbia, Saskatchewan, Ontario and s Quebec, and east to Nova Scotia, Massachusetts (vagrant, but several records), New York, New Jersey, Delaware, Virginia, Georgia, Florida and Louisiana.

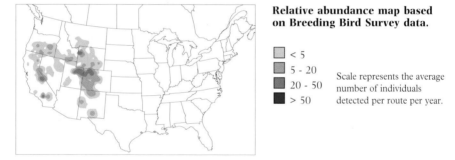

Relative abundance map based on Breeding Bird Survey data.

□ < 5
□ 5 - 20
■ 20 - 50   Scale represents the average
■ > 50   number of individuals
                   detected per route per year.

HISTORY: When Audubon described the Green-tailed Towhee in 1839 he called it *Fringilla chlorura*, thus placing it in the group of birds that contains the siskins, Pine and Evening grosbeaks, and crossbills. Subsequently, ornithologists have generally placed it in the American sparrows, but have debated its position within that group, different workers having placed it in as many as nine different genera. For many reasons, it appears to be close to the towhees: the juvenal plumage is very like that of the other towhees, and the basic plumage, though different from the other northern towhees, is reminiscent of that of the Collared Towhee of Mexico, which interbreeds with the Spotted Towhee. The calls are also somewhat reminiscent of the Spotted Towhee.

GEOGRAPHIC VARIATION: None described; has hybridized with Spotted Towhee.

MEASUREMENTS: (11 males): wing 76–83 (80), tail 80–87 (84), tarsus 22.6–25.4 (24.1), exposed culmen 12.2–13.0 (12.7), depth of bill at base 8.1–8.6 (8.4); (8 females): wing 71–79 (76), tail 74–85 (81), tarsus 21.8–24.6 (23.6), exposed culmen 11.4–13.0 (12.5), bill depth 8.1–8.6 (8.4) (Ridgway 1901).

Mass: (N=68), 29.4 g (21.5–37.3) (Dunning 1993).

3 **Eastern Towhee** *Pipilo erythrophthalmus* [587]   PLATE 2

IDENTIFICATION: 17–20.5 cm (*c.* 7–8 in), males slightly larger; sexes differ in coloration.

The Eastern Towhee is a large, long-tailed sparrow. Males have a black head, breast, back, wings, and tail, bright rusty flanks, and white bases to the primaries and in the sides and corners of the tail; females are similarly patterned, but a rich light, somewhat reddish brown where males are black.

Similar species: The western Spotted Towhee is similar, but scapulars and wing coverts are tipped with white, giving the back a spotted appearance, and the Spotted Towhee lacks the white bases to the primaries. The tertials are white edged in both species. Female Spotted Towhees resemble male Spotted Towhees, but are dark gray or dull black instead of black—not brown like female Eastern Towhees. Both the songs and calls of Spotted Towhees differ from those of Eastern Towhees.

Juvenile towhees are streaked below, and have a pale buff submoustachial stripe; juvenile Spotted Towhees have lighter buffy tips to their scapulars and coverts than juvenile Eastern Towhees.

Adult males—*Head:* nape, mantle; ***rump,*** throat, and breast black; ***tail:*** black, with outer web of lateral rectrix white, and tips of outer three rectrices white-tipped; ***underparts:*** breast black; flanks cinnamon-rufous; belly white; undertail-coverts

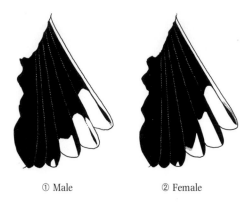

① Male   ② Female

buffy; ***wing:*** black, with bold white bases to the primaries and white edges to the primaries; tertials broadly edged with white; ***bill:*** black in summer; lower mandible horn colored in winter; ***legs:*** light brownish; toes usually darker; ***iris:*** color variable, ruby red in most populations, but orange or orangish white in coastal Georgia and northern Florida, and yellowish white in Florida.

Adult females similar to males, but brown where males are black, and bill brownish horn color.

First-winter males similar to adults, but primary coverts brownish, contrasting with darker secondary coverts, wing feathers dark brown to blackish, and eye color gray-brown (in fall).

First-winter females similar to adults, but primary coverts brownish, and eye color gray-brown.

Juveniles (May through Aug) forehead and crown blackish brown, inconspicuously streaked with light brown, with brown streaking becoming more conspicuous on the nape and mantle. Ear-coverts blackish brown, often with some brown; submoustachial stripe buff; malar stripe and throat blackish brown. Wings black, with coverts and tertials edged with buff. Underparts buffy, with dark brown streaks. Tail blackish brown with pale edges. The bill is dusky above, and flesh colored below, and the iris is dark brown. There is sexual dimorphism in this plumage as in the adults, with females brown where males are blackish-brown. This plumage is held for rather a long time.

VOICE: The song of the Eastern Towhee is a distinctive, loud, ringing ***drink your teeeeee***, or ***drink teeeeee***. The '***teeeeee***' is usually higher than the other elements, and the '***your***' lower. The song has an introductory syllable, and a trill. Individual males may use a variety of different introductory syllables, and several (usually one

Breeding
Winter
All year

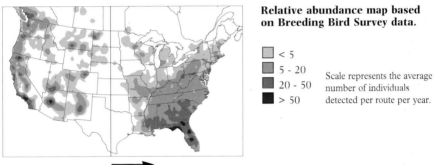

Relative abundance map based on Breeding Bird Survey data.

◻ < 5

◻ 5 - 20

◼ 20 - 50   Scale represents the average
                   number of individuals
◼ > 50   detected per route per year.

to three) are used in a song, such as ***drink your***. The song is highly variable. The call note is an emphatic ***chee-wink***, ***joree***, or simply ***wink***.

HABITS: Males may sing from a conspicuous perch in a small tree or shrub. Females incubate closely, and often run from the nest giving a broken-wing distraction display if disturbed. During courtship, males may pursue females in short flights. They jerk their tails in flight. Although large and noisy sparrows, towhees can be difficult to see. They do not form large flocks or mix closely with other species, but do respond to *spishing*.

HABITAT: Towhees are birds of dense deciduous or mixed thickets, often second-growth thickets, young jack pines, and edges of oak forests. Southern birds may be found in scrub palmetto. In winter they are found in dense thickets, with well-developed understory, and may be found in residential areas at feeders.

BREEDING: *Nest* is usually built in a depression in the ground under a bush, fallen branches or a log, or occasionally in a shrub, vine or small tree, rarely to 5.5 m high. It is a well-hidden large cup of bark strips, grasses, lined with fine grass, conifer needles, or hair. The female alone builds nest. Nesting begins in early April (Alabma, South Carolina), early May (Kansas, Ontario) to late May (Vermont) through mid-August. *Eggs*, 2–6, usually 3–4, are creamy or grayish white, speckled or spotted with brown or reddish brown. *Incubation*, 10–12 days; female along incubates, but both parents feed the young; young leave the nest after 8–10 days; double- and probably sometimes triple-brooded. This species is parasitized by cowbirds.

RANGE: *Breeds* from s Manitoba (Treesbank, Winnipeg) and probably west to se Saskatchewan (Round L.), east through s Ontario (L. of the Woods, Manitoulin I., North Bay), s Quebec, Vermont (absent in northeast), New Hampshire (absent in north), c Maine, s New Brunswick (Bocabec; rare), south through ne North Dakota, se South Dakota, c and se Minnesota, Iowa, c Nebraska, e Kansas, ne Oklahoma, Arkansas (west to Sebastian, Garland, and Union counties), e Louisiana (southwest to L. Charles), the Gulf Coast and Florida (absent in the Keys).

Winters from e Nebraska (Lincoln), Iowa, Minnesota (rare), Wisconsin (occasional), extreme s Ontario (rare), s Quebec (rare), Maritime Provinces (occasional) south to s Florida, the Gulf Coast, and through e Kansas, c Oklahoma to Texas (absent in southwest). Most common in winter south of se Pennsylvania, s Ohio, s Illinois, and se Missouri, to e-c Texas. Casual north to n Ontario, Newfoundland, and west to Colorado. Accidental in Britain (June).

HISTORY: The Eastern Towhee was originally described on the basis of Mark Catesby's 'towhee-bird.' He called it '. . . a solitary Bird; and one seldom sees them but in Pairs.'

Clearing of the eastern deciduous forests apparently benefited this species. Audubon noted that towhees were generally common in the United States in the early 1800s, and especially common in '. . . the Barrens of Kentucky.' He said that they did not occur in Mississippi and Louisiana, where they can be found today following the extensive clearing of mature forests. In New England they are now declining in numbers as old fields are reverting to forests.

Because of the rather extensive hybridization between Eastern and Spotted towhees in the Great Plains (especially central Nebraska), they were merged in the mid-1950s into a single species, the Rufous-sided Towhee. However, because a substantial number of non-hybrid individuals can be found in all hybrid populations, and because of significant differences in both their songs and call, ornithologists have recently decided to split them again. Eastern Towhees have also been called Red-eyed Towhees, but the name 'Eastern' is more appropriate as many of the towhees of the southeast have orangish or whitish eyes.

GEOGRAPHIC VARIATION: Four subspecies are generally recognized: the northeastern Red-eyed Towhee (*P. e. erythrophthalmus*); *P. e. rileyi*, which breeds from western Florida east to southeastern Georgia and north to coastal North Carolina; *P. e. alleni* of Florida; and *P. e. canaster*, which breeds from Louisiana into southern Tennessee, across northern Alabama and Georgia, into south-central North Carolina. *P. e. erythrophthalmus* is large with a relatively small bill, and a bright red eye. *P. e. rileyi* is medium sized, large billed and with variable eye color; it has less white in the tail than *P. e. erythrophthalmus*. *P. e. alleni* is small, with intermediate bill size, pale eyes, and little white in the tail. *P. e. canaster* is large, large billed, pale eyed (not so pale as *P. e. alleni*), and has an intermediate amount of white in its tail.

MEASUREMENTS: *P. e. erythrophthalmus*, (345–359 males): wing 80–96 (88), tail 82–104 (93), tarsus 24.8–29.5 (27.4), exposed culmen 13.1–16.0 (14.5), length of tail spot on inner web of outer rectrix 24–55 (37); (90–95 females): wing 77–90 (83), tail 78–97 (88), tarsus 24.0–29.0 (26.6), exposed culmen 13.0–15.4 (14.5), tail spot 25–45 (33).

P. e. alleni, (80–82 males): wing 73–89 (80), tail 78–102 (91), tarsus 24.7–29.1 (26.8), exposed culmen 13.9–16.1 (15.1), tail spot 6–28 (20); (26 females): wing 73–82 (77), tail 79–92 (85), tarsus 24.2–28.0 (25.9), exposed culmen 13.1–15.5 (14.7), tail spot 6–20 (16).

P. e. canaster, (136–145 males): wing 78–93 (87), tail 86–105 (95), tarsus 25.2–31.0 (28.2), exposed culmen 14.5–17.0 (15.4), tail spot 18–44 (32); (27–31 females): wing 80–87 (83), tail 84–96 (90), tarsus 25.6–29.5 (27.9), exposed culmen 14.0–16.5 (15.2), tail spot 19–36 (27).

P. e. rileyi, (84–100 males): wing 80–92 (86), tail 87–103 (95), tarsus 25.3–30.6 (28.3), exposed culmen 14.1–17.0 (15.6), tail spot 17–34 (26); (23–38 females): wing 73–85 (80), tail 81–97 (90), tarsus 25.4–29.6 (27.5), exposed culmen 14.5–16.5 (15.3), tail spot 20–30 (23) (Dickinson 1952).

Mass: (84 males) 42.1 g (37.8–50.0) (Pennsylvania, March–Oct); (113 females) 39.1 g (32.1–52.3) (Pennsylvania, April–Oct) (Clench and Leberman 1978).

References: Borror (1975), Dickinson (1952), Sibley and West (1959).

4 **Spotted Towhee** *Pipilo maculatus* [588]   PLATE 2

D. BEADLE.

IDENTIFICATION: 17.5–21 cm (*c.* 7–8 in), males slightly larger; slight sexual dimorphism in color.

Spotted Towhees are large, long-tailed sparrows. Males have a black head, breast, back, wing, and tail, with distinct white spotting on the wings and mantle, and lack white bases to their primaries. Females are similarly colored, but dark gray to almost black (Pacific Coast) or grayish brown rather where the males are black. Both sexes have bright rusty flanks, and a white belly.

Similar species: See Eastern Towhee.

Adult males—*Head:* nape, mantle, and ***rump,*** throat, and breast black with some white streaking on the mantle; ***underparts:*** breast black; flanks cinnamon-rufous; belly white; undertail-coverts buffy, but the same color as the flanks in northwestern birds; ***wing:*** black, with edges of primaries white; scapulars and coverts boldly tipped with white, making the wings and the back appear spotted; ***bill:*** black, with lower bill paler in winter; ***legs*** and ***feet:*** light brownish; ***iris:*** bright red.

Adult females similar to males, but the black of the head, throat and breast is duller and more sooty, or in some populations (Great Plains, northwest coast) dull brownish gray.

First-winter males similar to adults, but duller, the dark areas being sooty gray instead of black, and primary coverts brownish and eye color gray-brown.

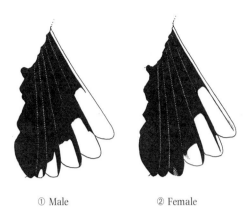

① Male   ② Female

First-winter females similar to first-winter males, but browner.

Juveniles (May through Aug) forehead and crown dark blackish brown or brownish, inconspicuously streaked with light brown; nape mantle colored like crown, but with more streaks; mantle dark brownish, mottled with buff or light brown, and white in the scapulars. Wings dark brown to blackish, with coverts and tertials edged in buff. Underparts buffy and streaked. Females are browner in color than males.

VOICE: The song consists of 1–5 notes followed by a trill that is usually higher than the introductory notes, a ***chup chup chup zeeeeeee***, ***chup zreeeeeeee***, or ***clip-clip-cheee***; the introductory note is often not given. The song is harsher and less musical than that of Eastern Towhees, and shows a great deal of geographic variation. The song of Pacific Coast birds is reduced to a dry buzz, often lacking introductory notes. The call is catbird-like ***pshew*** or ***meeew*** or a quiet ***tseep.***

HABITAT: Spotted Towhees are found in brushy thickets and ravines, canyons, open woodlands and chaparral, and locally in urban gardens. They prefer stiff-branched shrub thickets such as manzanita and *Ceanothus* chaparral, or oak brush with rank understory. In coastal British Columbia, they frequent forests with dense understory of salal, shrubs and ferns; in California, they are primarily birds of scrubland or riparian edge. In the northern plains they nest in rank, deciduous streamside thickets. In winter, they are found in thickets or gardens.

HABITS: Territorial males sing persistently from a shrub, sometimes the top of the shrub, or from thickets. Like other towhees, Spotted Towhees double-scratch. When flushed from the nest the female runs across to cover, and could be mistaken for a rodent.

BREEDING: *Nest* is placed on the ground in a depression dug by the bird, or low in a bush. It is a well-concealed bulky cup of bark strips, small twigs, weed stalks, dried

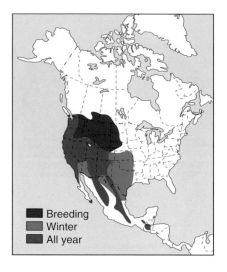

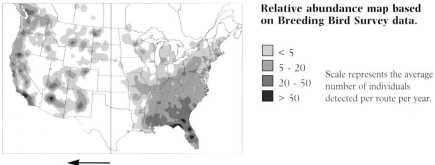

Relative abundance map based on Breeding Bird Survey data.

☐ < 5
☐ 5 - 20
■ 20 - 50   Scale represents the average
■ > 50   number of individuals
                   detected per route per year.

leaves and grasses, lined with finer grasses and rootlets. The female alone apparently builds the nest, and incubates. Nesting begins in mid-April and continues through July. *Eggs*, 3–5, usually 3–4, are pale olive-gray, finely speckled with brown, or splotched with brown or gray. *Incubation*, probably 12–13 days; female alone incubates, but both parents feed with young; age at fledging apparently not known; double-brooded. This species is parasitized by cowbirds.

RANGE: *Breeds* from s British Columbia (Comox, Lillooet, Okanagan Valley, Elko), s Alberta (north to Camrose, Wainright), and s Saskatchewan (north to Elbow, east to Fort Qu'Appelle) south through c North Dakota (east to Wells Co.), c South Dakota (mainly west of the Missouri R.), n Nebraska (Niobrara R.), nw Colorado (Crook), nw Kansas (uncommon; hybrids), c and se Colorado, New Mexico (except in east), w Texas (Guadalupe, Davis, and Chisos mountains), and the highlands of Mexico south to Oaxaca and s Sinaloa, and nw Baja California. There are isolated resident populations in Chiapas, Guatemala, the Cape region of Baja California, and the Revillagigedo Is.

Winters s British Columbia, Washington, Oregon (mainly west of the Cascades), s Idaho, Utah (common in south), sw Wyoming, Colorado (uncommon in north), s Nebraska, Kansas, Oklahoma (commoner in west), and w Missouri (uncommon), south through Oklahoma (commoner in west), Texas, w Louisiana (rare), to Tamaulipas, Nuevo León, Coahuila, Chihuahua, Sonora, and Baja California. Most common in winter along the Pacific Coast and in central Texas. Rare or casual east to Minnesota, Iowa, Illinois, Pennsylvania, New York, Ontario, Quebec, New Brunswick and Massachusetts, and north to Alaska (Juneau, Oct–Dec).

HISTORY: The Spotted Towhee is one of many new species of bird originally described by William Swainson in 1827, on the basis of specimens collected in Hidalgo, Mexico. Swainson was a prominent English ornithologist and artist-naturalist of the early 20th century. As a young man, Swainson collected birds, plants, insects, and fish in Brazil, then returned to England. Later in life he went to Australia and New Zealand, where he died in 1855.

The Spotted Towhee hybridizes commonly with the dissimilar-looking Collared Towhee (*P. ocai*) in Jalisco, but in some other places in Mexico where they are found together, hybridization is rare. Spotted and Eastern towhees hybridize commonly in the Great Plains, especially in Nebraska.

GEOGRAPHIC VARIATION: Like many species that are found in the montane west, many different subspecies of Spotted Towhee have been described. Nine of the most commonly recognized of these are found north of Mexico. The Arctic Towhee (*P. m. arcticus*), breeds from the Canadian prairies south into central Nebraska, and perhaps rarely in northwestern Kansas; the Spurred Towhee (*P. m. montanus*), breeds from eastern California, Utah, and Colorado south into northwestern Mexico; the Texas Towhee (*P. m. gaigei*) breeds in southeastern New Mexico and western Texas; the Nevada Towhee (*P. m. curtatus*) breeds from central southern British Columbia south to northeastern California and central Nevada; the Oregon Towhee (*P. m. oregonus*) breeds along the Pacific Coast from British Columbia to California; the Sacramento Towhee (*P. m. falcinellus*) is resident from southwestern Oregon south through the northern interior coast ranges, western and southeastern slopes of the Sierra Nevada, in the Great Valley south to Kings and Tulare counties; the San Francisco Towhee (*P. m. falcifer*) is resident along the coasts of northwestern and central western California; the San Diego Towhee (*P. m. megalonyx*) is resident in southwestern California and northwestern Baja California; and the San Clemente Towhee (*P. m. clementae*) is resident on larger Channel islands.

P. m. arcticus is most similar in appearance to *P. m. montanus*, but tends to have more dorsal spotting, and the females a more olivaceous (brownish) head and back. *P. m. gaigei* is like *P. m. montanus*, but smaller and on average paler. *P. m. curtatus* is like *P. m. montanus*, but has shorter wings and is slightly darker colored. *P. m. oregonus* is the darkest and least spotted of the Spotted Towhees; the head and back of females may be brownish black. *P. m. falcinellus* is like *P. m. megalonyx* but has a shorter hind claw, and somewhat more white markings, and a grayish or olivaceous rump, which is black in adult male *P. m. megalonyx*; female *P. m. megalonyx* are blackish. *P. m. falcifer* is intermediate between *P. m. oregonus* and *P. m. megalonyx* in back coloration, and has a smaller claw than the latter. *P. m. clementae* is like *P. m. megalonyx*, but has an even larger claw, and is grayer on the back. Probably only a few extreme spotted Towhees can be identified to subspecies in the field.

MEASUREMENTS: *P. m. arcticus*, (16 males): wing 85–91 (88), tail 91–104 (97), tarsus 25.4–28.2 (26.9), exposed culmen 11.9–14.0 (13.0); (13 females): wing 79–91 (84), tail 86–104 (92), tarsus 25.4–27.9 (26.7), exposed culmen 12.2–14.0 (12.7).

P. m. montanus, (50 males): wing 84–93 (86), tail 90–112 (100), tarsus 26.4–29.2 (27.7), exposed culmen 12.2–14.7 (13.5), bill depth at base 9.7–11.2 (10.4); (26 females): wing 80–88 (84), tail 87–106 (96), tarsus 25.9–28.2 (27.2), exposed culmen 12.5–15.0 (13.7), bill depth at base 9.4–10.9 (10.2).

P. m. megalonyx, (11 males): wing 82–90 (86), tail 94–102 (98), tarsus 26.4–29.2 (28.2), exposed culmen 13.0–15.0 (13.7), bill depth 9.9–10.9 (10.4).

P. m. oregonus, (13 males): wing 82–88 (85), tail 87–98 (94), tarsus 26.9–29.0 (27.9), exposed culmen 13.7–15.0 (14.5), bill depth 9.7–11.7 (10.9); (9 females): wing 77–86 (81), tail 84–98 (91), tarsus 24.9–28.5 (27.2), exposed culmen 13.2–14.7 (14.2), bill depth 10.4–11.2 (10.7) (Ridgway 1901).

Mass: (27 males) 40.0 g (35.0–48.0); (5 females) 40.3 (34.3–46.7 (laying)) (Saskatchewan, June) (Rising, unpublished).

References: Borror (1975), Sibley (1950), Sibley and West (1959).

5 **California Towhee** *Pipilo crissalis* [591.1]   PLATE 3

IDENTIFICATION: 21–24 cm (*c.* 8.5–9.5 in), males slightly larger; sexes similar in coloration.

The California Towhee is a large, long-tailed, nearly uniformly brown sparrow, with a rusty brown face, throat, and undertail-coverts, and orangish iris..

Similar species: Canyon and Abert's towhees are similar in size and coloration. Canyon Towhee usually are shorter tailed, paler, grayish brown on the head and underparts, with a necklace of brownish spots and a faint central breast spot and a pale, rusty crown. Note also differences in songs and calls. Abert's Towhees are washed with cinnamon-brown and have a black face that contrasts with their light-colored bill. Juveniles of these species are similar to adults, but streaked below; California Towhees are darker than Canyon Towhees; juvenile Abert's have the dark face, are washed with cinnamon-brown, and are only faintly streaked below.

Adult males—*Head:* crown dark cinnamon-brown; side of face brown, with buff in front of eye, and indistinctly around eye; submoustachial area buffy, thinly streaked with brown; malar stripe thin and brown; ***back*** and ***rump:*** dark brown, contrasting slightly with crown, and unstreaked; ***underparts:*** chin and throat cinnamon-brown, with a thin crescent-shaped necklace of brown spots; breast and flanks buffy cinnamon-brown to grayish olive-brown; belly pale olive-brown, becoming buffy cinnamon posteriorly; undertail-coverts cinnamon-brown; ***wing:*** brown and unmarked; ***tail:*** long, brown, and unmarked, or with thin cinnamon-brown tips to outer 2 or 3 rectrices; ***bill:*** brown, lower mandible paler; ***legs:*** pale brownish; ***iris:*** orangish-brown.

First-winter (after Oct) like adults, but retain juvenile wing and tail feathers, which are duller in color.

Juveniles (Mar–Sept) like adults, but less cinnamon or buffy in hue, and heavily streaked brown on breast and flanks.

VOICE: The song is a series of staccato notes, getting faster toward the end, *tss tss tss tsurr tsurr tsurr*, or *chip chip chip chip chip*, or *tic-tic-tic-ti-ti-ti-ti-ti* all on one pitch. Some sing *tss tss it tsss*, *chi chi chi chi chi*, *chuchu chee*, *tsee tsee*, on different pitches, first falling, then rising at the end. The first notes are soft and can be heard only at short range. Singing apparently is principally for attracting mates, so only unmated males sing with any frequency. They tend to sing in the evening. The call notes are a high-pitched, sharp *tsip* or *chip*, or a more emphatic *chink*. The locative note is a high, thin *seep*.

HABITS: Males sing infrequently, and mostly in the evening after they are mated; persistently singing birds are probably unmated males. California Towhees are highly territorial, and territorial defense involving chases and fighting is most pronounced in the spring. Members of pairs commonly occur together, foraging on the ground, and communicating through *seep* notes. They scratch less vigorously than Spotted Towhees.

HABITAT: The California Towhee is characteristically a bird of brushy hillsides, shrubby thickets, streamside thickets, chaparral (especially chamise and ceanothus), dry upland chaparral, dense willow thickets (Argus Mountains), and parks and gardens with suitable cover. They are often found in brushy sides of trails, clearings or gardens.

BREEDING: *Nest* is placed in bushes or trees, usually within 1–4 m of the ground, but up to 12 m; rarely on the ground. The nest is usually supported by several branches, and placed in the densest part of a shrub or tree; sometimes in eucalyptus. The nest is a deep, bulky cup of grasses and twigs, lined with finer grasses, rootlets, and horse hair. Nesting takes place in mid-Apr through June. *Eggs*, 2–5, usually 4, are pale blue, with black or purplish brown spots; they are indistinguishable from those of Abert's Towhee. *Incubation*, 11 days; the female alone builds the nest and incubates, but both parents feed the young; the young leave the nest after about 8 days; double-brooded. This species is parasitized by cowbirds.

RANGE: *Resident* from se Oregon (Rogue Valley, lower Klamath R. canyon, s Douglas Co.) and n-c California (Berwick, Hornbrook, Edgewood), and nw California (Humboldt and Trinity cos.) south through w California (absent in San Joaquin Valley; isolated population in Argus Mountains of e California) and Baja California (absent along ne coast).

HISTORY: The California Towhee was originally described in 1839 by the British ornithologist Nicholas A. Vigors on the basis of a specimen collected near Monterey, California. At least as early as 1872, Elliott Coues, in his *Key to North American Birds*, considered it to be a subspecies of the Brown Towhee. Although many have noted

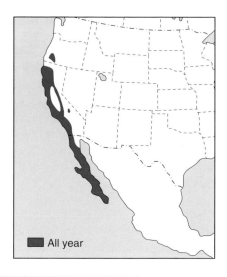

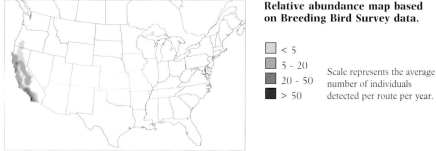

Relative abundance map based on Breeding Bird Survey data.

◻ < 5

◻ 5 - 20

◼ 20 - 50   Scale represents the average
              number of individuals
◼ > 50   detected per route per year.

many differences between California and Canyon towhees, including differences in appearance, songs, singing behavior, call notes and nests, it is curious that most ornithologists continued to consider these two conspecific until morphological and particularly allozyme studies published in 1988 indicated that the California and Abert's towhees are actually mutually closest relatives ('sister species') and that the White-throated Towhee of central Mexico is the sister species of the Canyon Towhee.

Although much of the natural habitat used by California Towhees has been destroyed, they have been able to adapt to a certain extent to exotic vegetation, and are, for the most part, reasonably common throughout their range. There is, however, an isolated population in the Argus Range of California that probably numbers fewer than 150 individuals.

GEOGRAPHIC VARIATION: Six subspecies of California Towhees are generally recognized from north of Mexico. The Oregon Towhee (*P. c. bullatus*) is found in southwestern Oregon and in the Shasta valleys of north-central California. On average these are darker on the crown and back, and grayer on the flanks than towhees from central California. The range of *P. c. bullatus* does not overlap that of the Sacramento Towhee (*P. c. carolae*), which is found in California east of the humid coastal region. *P. c. carolae* is grayer on the back, sides, and flanks, with a less rufescent crown than the north coastal San Francisco Towhee (*P. c. petulans*), and slightly larger than the coastal *P. c. crissalis* of the central coast, south to Santa Barbara. *P. c. crissalis* also has a slightly paler cap and is slightly browner in color. The southern Anthony's Towhee (*P. c. senicula*) is darker and browner in color than the other subspecies. The isolated Argus (or Inyo) Towhee (*P. c. edremophilus*) is browner and has a longer bill than *P. c. carolae*, and is paler and larger than *P. c. senicula*. There is a great deal of overlap in coloration, partly due to age and wear, and these subspecies probably cannot be safely identified in the field.

MEASUREMENTS: Oregon and n-c California (20–32 males): wing 97–104 (100), tail 109–119 (112), tarsus 27.1–30.3 (28.6), bill length from nostril 10.2–11.9 (11.0), bill depth at anterior edge of nostril 8.0–8.8 (8.5); (11–20 females): wing 92–98 (95), tail 104–112 (109), tarsus 27.1–29.1 (28.3), bill length 10.1–11.6 (10.8), bill depth 8.0–8.8 (8.3).

East side of Sacramento Valley, California (28–41 males): wing 95–103 (100), tail 109–117 (113), tarsus 27.4–30.5 (28.6), bill length 10.3–12.1 (11.1), bill depth 8.2–9.0 (8.6); (11–27 females): wing 90–98 (93), tail 106–114 (108), tarsus 26.8–28.9 (28.1), bill length 10.2–11.7 (10.9), bill depth 7.9–8.7 (8.3).

Alameda and Contra Costa cos., California (14–27 males): wing 94–101 (98), tail 107–115 (110), tarsus 27.6–29.5 (28.5), bill length 9.8–11.4 (10.5), bill depth 7.8–8.5 (8.1); (13–31 females): 92–96 (93), tail 106–111 (108), tarsus 26.5–29.4 (28.1), bill length 9.8–11.1 (10.4), bill depth 7.4–8.6 (8.0).

Salinas R. Valley east to San Joaquin Valley, California (25–45 males): wing 95–103 (99), tail 108–118 (112), tarsus 27.0–29.9 (28.4), bill length 9.9–11.0 (10.4), bill depth 7.9–8.7 (8.2); (19–27 females): 89–97 (93), tail 104–115 (108), tarsus 27.2–29.8 (28.1), bill length 9.8–10.8 (10.2), bill depth 7.4–8.2 (7.9).

Los Angeles Co., California (42–71 males): wing 86–96 (93), tail 100–109 (104), tarsus 24.3–28.8 (26.7), bill length 9.4–10.6 (10.0), bill depth 7.5–8.3 (7.9); (42–57 females): wing 85–94 (89), tail 96–107 (102), tarsus 24.4–28.1 (26.3), bill length 9.2–10.8 (9.7), bill depth 7.3–8.5 (7.9) (Davis 1951).

Mass: (21 breeding males, *P. c. carolae*) 55.8 g (49.6–60.2); (17 breeding females, *P. c. carolae*) 55.4 g (48.8–61.7); (19 breeding males, *P. c. crissalis*) 51.5 g (48.6–55.6); (19 breeding females, *P. c. crissalis*) 51.1 g (46.3–61.2); (21 breeding males, *P. c. senicula*) 43.8 g (39.6–47.8); (9 breeding females, *P. c. senicula*) 41.5 g (37.0–44.5) (California) (Davis 1951).

References: Davis (1951), Marshall (1964b), Zink (1988).

6 **Canyon Towhee** *Pipilo fuscus* [591]   PLATE **3**

D.BEADLE 94.

IDENTIFICATION: 18.5–22 cm (*c.* 7.5–8.5 in), males slightly larger; sexes similar in coloration.

The Canyon Towhee is a large, brownish sparrow, with a pale throat that is outlined with thin brown spots or streaks, and a breast spot (not always distinct). The crown often appears pale rusty brown, contrasting slightly with the brownish gray back.

Similar species: (see California Towhee).

Adult—***Head:*** forehead brown; crown pale rusty-brown; lores and supraloral spot buffy; ear-coverts brown, flecked with buff; post-auricular stripe buffy; submoustachial stripe and throat buffy; malar stripe thin and brown; ***back*** and ***rump:*** brown and unmarked, contrasting slightly in color with crown; ***wing:*** brown and unmarked; ***underparts:*** chin and throat pinkish buff, sometimes slightly flecked with brown, with a crescent-shaped necklace of brown spots extending from the malar stripe across the upper breast; breast brown, flecked with beige and darker brown, often with a central spot; flanks brown; belly beige, becoming pinkish beige posteriorly; undertail-coverts rufous-beige; ***tail:*** brown, with rectrices (especially outer ones) indistinctly tipped with buff; tail darker than rump and back; ***bill:*** brownish, lower mandible paler; ***legs:*** light brown, toes lighter; ***iris:*** brown.

First-winter (after Oct) like adults, but juvenal wing and tail feathers retained.

Juveniles (Apr–Oct) like adults, but crown lacks rust, throat, breast, and flanks brown spotted, and edges of coverts tipped with pinkish buff, forming one or two indistinct wing-bars.

VOICE: The song of the Canyon Towhee is a musical tinkling, typically a series of 6 or 7 evenly spaced double syllables, ***chili-chili-chili-chili-chili-chili***, ***chur chee-chee-chee ch***, with the middle elements higher, or a thinner junco-like ***chip-chip-chip-chip-chip-chip***; the song may change tempo in the middle. Mated pairs sometimes sing a duet, ***squeal-churrrr***. The call note is a two syllable ***tscheddap*** or ***sheddap***. The locative call is a thin high-pitched ***see*** or a soft ***tic***.

HABITS: Territorial males advertise their territories by song, and fight with encroaching neighbors, but fighting is uncommon. Unmated males sing almost constantly, usually from a low tree, bush, or rock. They run or hop on the ground. Canyon Towhees double-scratch when feeding, but do so less frequently than Spotted or Green-tailed towhees; they like to feed under things. Females breed closely.

HABITAT: Canyon Towhees are found in rocky, semi-arid country, in scrub oak, juniper, piñon pine, manzanita, mountain mahogany, ceanothus, cholla, mesquite, and catclaw. They are also found in brushy pastures, and streamside thickets, and on the Edwards Plateau of Texas, in oak savannah, juniper breaks, and 'shinnery' oak, and in brushy urban areas and around ranch buildings.

BREEDING: ***Nest*** is a well-constructed cup of small twigs, grasses, and weeds, lined with leaves, fine strips of bark, and animal hair. It is generally placed 1–3 m high, against the main trunk of a small tree (mesquite, hackberry; in Oklahoma in piñon or juniper), tall bush (elderberries), or cholla, and concealed by dense vegetation. Nesting may begin in early March and continues into early July, and Sept (Oklahoma). ***Eggs***, 2–6, usually 3, are pale bluish white, or light gray (rarely pure white), and are sharply spotted with dark brown, or blotched with brown. ***Incubation***, probably about 11 days; the female alone incubates, but both parents feed young; the fledging period is not known; two broods, and maybe more are attempted. Brown Towhees are parasitized by cowbirds.

RANGE: ***Resident*** from Arizona (north to Mohave Mountains, Lupton), New Mexico (absent in northwest and extreme east, except for northeast), se Colorado (north to El Paso County probably Boulder Co.), and nw Oklahoma (Cimarron Co., Texas Co. in Sept), and sw Kansas (Morton Co.; rare) south through sw Texas and c Texas (Edwards Plateau) and Mexico to n Chiapas and e to Puebla, sw Tamaulipas, and c Nuevo León. Some wander in winter to sw Oklahoma (Greer and Comanche cos.), the Texas Panhandle and to se Texas (to Aransas Co.); it has been reported at the Grand Canyon, Arizona.

HISTORY: The Canyon Towhee, like the Spotted Towhee, was first named by Swainson. He described the species on the basis of a specimen collected in the Mexican state of México. The type specimen was probably collected in 1826 by the son of William Bullock, a friend of Swainson who named Bullock's Oriole in his honor, and given to Swainson by the elder Bullock to describe. Until recently the

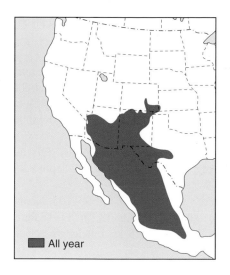

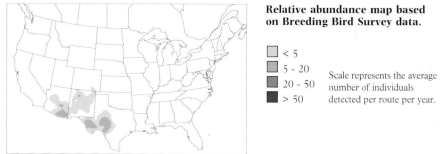

Relative abundance map based on Breeding Bird Survey data.

◻ < 5
▨ 5 - 20
▨ 20 - 50
■ > 50

Scale represents the average number of individuals detected per route per year.

Canyon and California towhees have been considered to be a single species, the Brown Towhee. See the account of the California Towhee for a discussion of reasons for the change in classification.

GEOGRAPHIC VARIATION: Of the 10 or so subspecies of Canyon Towhees commonly recognized, four occur north of Mexico. *P.f. mesoleucus* is found through most of Arizona and New Mexico. It differs from *P.f. relictus* of northeastern New Mexico, southeastern Colorado, and the western Panhandle of Oklahoma, by having a darker cap, and a grayer back and flanks and a shorter wing. *P.f. relictus* of the Harquahala Mountains of west-central Arizona is supposedly darker, but the two overlap considerably in coloration. *P.f. texanus* of southwestern Texas is relatively short-tailed, and darker and grayer than *P.c. mesoleucus.* The variation in this species is slight, and clinal, and individuals cannot reliably be assigned to subspecies in the field.

MEASUREMENTS: Pima Co., Arizona (25–46 males): wing 92–99 (94), tail 98–111 (104), tarsus 24.5–27.8 (25.9), bill length from nostril 9.8–12.0 (10.7), bill depth at anterior edge of culmen 8.4–9.4 (9.1); (24–37 females): wing 86–93 (89), tail

95–107 (100), tarsus 24.0–26.3 (25.2), bill length 9.6–11.5 (10.5), bill depth 8.5–9.2 (8.9).

Harquahala Mountains, Yuma and Maricopa cos., Arizona (15–20 males): wing 91–98 (94), tail 100–111 (104), tarsus 24.9–27.4 (25.6), bill length 9.7–11.2 (10.6), bill depth 8.2–9.2 (8.8); (7–13 females): wing 87–92 (89), tail 100–104 (101), tarsus 25.2–27.4 (26.0), bill length 9.7–11.2 (10.6), bill depth 8.2–9.2 (8.8).

Colorado and Oklahoma (4–14 males): wing 98–101 (99), tail 99–111 (104), tarsus 24.8–27.7 (26.1), bill length 10.0–10.6 (10.4), bill depth 8.4–9.3 (8.7).

West Texas (24–38 males): wing 92–100, tail 95–105, tarsus 24.1–27.0 (25.4), bill length 10.0–11.9 (10.8), bill depth 8.1–9.3 (8.9); (11–18 females): wing 87–93 (90), tail 91–99 (94), tarsus 24.0–26.8 (25.1), bill length 9.7–11.0 (10.5), bill depth 8.2–9.1 (8.7) (Davis 1951).

Mass: 44.4 g (36.6–52.5) (Arizona) (Dunning 1993).

References: Davis (1951), Marshall (1964a), Zink (1988).

7 **Abert's Towhee** *Pipilo aberti* [592]   PLATE 3

IDENTIFICATION: 20–23 cm (*c.* 8–9 in), males slightly larger; sexes similar in coloration.

Abert's Towhee is a large, plain pinkish-brown sparrow with a long tail, a black face, and a pale bill.

Similar species: (see California Towhee).

Adult—*Head:* brown, with blackish lores, supraloral spot between the eye and the bill forming a black mask; ***back*** and ***rump:*** brown, not contrasting in color with crown; ***wing:*** brown and unmarked; ***underparts:*** chin and throat brown, tinged with cinnamon and thinly streaked with dark brown; breast and flanks brown; belly buffy-brown, tinged with cinnamon; undertail-coverts rusty or cinnamon-brown; ***tail:*** brown and unmarked; ***bill:*** pale grayish brown; ***legs:*** pale brownish with toes darker; ***iris:*** tan.

First-winter (after Oct) like adults, except that juvenal wing and tail feathers are retained through the first year.

Juveniles (Apr–Sept) like adults, but somewhat paler in color, with thin streaks on the flanks and belly, and with cinnamon-brown coverts.

VOICE: The song of Abert's Towhee is a rather sharp series of notes, a ***peep peep chee-chee-chee***, ***sleep sleep cha cha cha***, or ***chi chi chi chur chur chur chz***. Like the song of the California Towhee, the song tends to accelerate at the end, often ending in rapid notes at a lower pitch. Also like California Towhees, mated males sing little, the song apparently not used in territorial defense. Mated pairs sing a duet. Unmated males may start singing before dawn and sing through the day. The call notes are a sharp *peep* or *huit huit*, or a loud *cut*. The locative call is a thin high-pitched *tic* or *seep*.

HABITS: Abert's Towhees forage on the ground in dense brush, often using the double-scratch. They either run or hop along the ground. Flights are generally short and low to the ground, from one bush to the next or to the ground. Fights with other pairs are fairly frequent, and may involve short chases and *cut* notes. In the non-breeding season, floaters are tolerated in the territory. Males often sing from a bush, but not from an exposed perch.

HABITAT: Abert's Towhees inhabit dense brush, especially cottonwoods and willows along desert rivers, and mesquite woodland with dense understory. Recently, they have moved into suburban gardens in central Arizona. They are found at relatively low elevations, below 1300 m. Abert's and Canyon towhees tend to be found together only in sparse mesquite brush.

BREEDING: *Nest* is a bulky cup of leaves and bark of mesquite, salt cedar, cottonwood, weeds, and even newspaper, placed in a small mesquite, shrub (such as Mexican elderberry, willow), or mistletoe, 1½ to 2½ m high. The female alone builds the nest and incubates the eggs. Nesting begins in March and continues through September. *Eggs*, 1–4, most commonly 3, are pale blue, with sparse but well-defined dark brown markings; they are indistinguishable from those of the California Towhee. *Incubation*, 14 days; female alone incubates, but male helps feed young after they are one day old; young fledge in 12–13 days; the species is apparently usually double-brooded, but up to 6 broods may be laid if nests are destroyed. The species is frequently parasitized by cowbirds.

RANGE: *Resident* in the Colorado and Gila river valleys, from sw Utah (Virgin R. Valley, St. George), s Nevada, w and s Arizona, extreme nc Sonora (San Pedro and Santa Cruz rivers), west along the Gila R. to se New Mexico, and west to se California (Colorado R. south of Needles, west to Palm Springs), south to ne Baja California (Colorado R. Delta). Abert's Towhee has been collected in El Paso Co., Texas, but the specimens have been lost.

HISTORY: During and following the Mexican War, the US Army sent a number of well-trained officers to the southwest to survey the territory that they had obtained. One of these was James William Abert who in 1846–1847 spent some time in what is now the State of New Mexico. While there, he collected a number of birds that were subsequently studied by Spencer Fullerton Baird. Among these apparently was the first specimen of Abert's Towhee, which Baird named after Abert. It seems probable, however, that Abert never saw this species alive as his travels did not take him to the present-day range of the species, and he makes no mention of the towhee in his notes. The specimen no longer exists. Although the type locality of the species is not known, it seems probable that it was collected west of New Mexico in Arizona, and the specimen passed on to Abert, who in turn gave it to Baird.

Relative abundance map based on Breeding Bird Survey data.

◻ < 5
◻ 5 - 20
■ 20 - 50   Scale represents the average
■ > 50   number of individuals
              detected per route per year.

Much of the streamside vegetation that forms suitable habitat has been destroyed, resulting in the fragmentation of the range of Abert's Towhee, and a decline in numbers in many areas, probably especially in southwestern Utah and the lower Colorado R. Nonetheless, the species' range seems to be expanding in south-central Arizona, along the Santa Cruz R. and Sonoita Creek, and up Oak Creek in central Arizona. To a limited extent it has adapted to suburban gardens in central Arizona.

GEOGRAPHIC VARIATION: Three subspecies have been described, *P. a. dumeticolus*, *P. a. aberti*, and *P. a. vorhiesi*. These seem to be poorly defined, and populations are variable, perhaps in part a result of wear and sun-bleaching. Their ranges are uncertain, and they cannot be separated in the field.

MEASUREMENTS: Colorado Desert, California (17–28 males): wing 88–96 (92), tail 108–119 (113), tarsus 27.2–28.8 (28.1), bill length from nostril 10.0–11.2 (10.6), bill depth at anterior edge of nostril 8.3–9.1 (8.8); (18–30 females): wing 83–89 (86), tail 102–110 (107), tarsus 26.0–28.6 (27.3), bill length 9.4–10.8 (10.2), bill depth 8.2–8.7 (8.5).

Colorado R., California (45–56 males): wing 87–96 (93), tail 108–121 (113), tarsus 27.0–29.4 (28.3), bill length 9.7–11.5 (10.5), bill depth 8.3–9.5 (8.7); (31–41 females): wing 83–91 (88), tail 103–113 (109), tarsus 26.9–28.9 (27.7), bill length 8.9–10.8 (10.1), bill depth 7.9–9.0 (8.5).

Nevada and Utah (11–21 males): wing 92–95 (93), tail 107–117 (112), tarsus 27.3–29.7 (28.5), bill length 10.1–11.5 (10.8), bill depth 8.4–9.5 (8.9); (5–12 females) wing 86–90 (88), tail 104–111 (107), tarsus 27.5–28.8 (28.1), bill length 10.0–11.0 (10.4), bill depth 8.4–8.8 (8.6) (Davis 1951).

Tucson, Arizona (114 males): wing 80–98 (92); (57 females): wing 78–96 (87) (Tweit and Finch 1994).

Mass: (69 males) 47.5 g (40.0–55.6); (44 females) 44.7 g (38.9–51.0) (Tucson, Arizona, Mar–Aug) (Tweit and Finch 1994).

References: Davis (1951), Marshall (1964a), Tweit and Finch (1994), Zink (1988).

8 **White-collared Seedeater**   PLATE **4**

Sporophila torqueola [602]

IDENTIFICATION: 9.5–11 cm (*c.* 4–4.5 in), males slightly larger; sexes differ in coloration.

Seedeaters are the smallest North American sparrows, with blunt, curved bills. Adult males have a blackish crown and side of face, with a beige collar, blackish tail and wings, with two variable white wing-bars, and white bases to the primaries, a whitish throat and variable, thin blackish breast-band (usually incomplete in Texas birds) and buffy underparts. Texas birds do not have conspicuous white collars. Females are buffy overall, with two indistinct buffy wing-bars. Males in the first winter resemble females, but may have some black feathers in the crown, tail, and especially wing.

Similar species: Seedeaters are variable in plumage, perhaps because the males do not obtain full plumage in their first summer. Nonetheless, they do not resemble other sparrows, and their small size and blunt, distinctly curved bill separate them from female and first-winter buntings (*Passerina*). Female Yellow-faced Grassquits are greenish in tone, with a straight bill, and dull yellowish supercillium.

Adult males—*Head:* crown and side of face black, often flecked with brown; thin white crescent under eye; malar region and throat white, perhaps flecked with black; side of neck whitish buff; ***back:*** nape and mantle grayish brown, variously flecked with black; ***rump:*** light buffy; ***tail:*** uppertail-coverts and rectrices blackish, edged with buff in unworn individuals; ***underparts:*** throat whitish, sometimes flecked with black; breast variable, but with some black, sometimes with a thin black crescent breast band; flanks, belly, and undertail-coverts rich buffy; ***wing:*** coverts and tertials black, edged with white, forming two wing-bars; bases of primaries and secondaries white, forming a white wing-stripe in flight and a white rectangle on the closed wing; ***bill:*** black in breeding season, dusky otherwise; ***legs:*** dusky brownish; ***iris:*** dark.

Adult females—*Head:* crown and side of face pale olive-brown; ***back:*** pale olive-brown, not contrasting with head; *rump:* somewhat paler than back; *tail:* the same color as the back and unpatterned; *underparts:* throat, breast, flanks, and belly pale, buffy olive-brown, somewhat paler on belly; *wing:* coverts and tertials olive-brown, tipped with pale buff, forming two dull wing-bars; *bill:* yellowish olive-brown; *legs:* dusky brownish; *iris:* dark.

First-winter males (after Oct) resemble adult females, but often with some darker feathers, especially in the coverts.

First-winter females resemble adult females.

Juveniles (Apr–Sept) apparently like first-winter birds.

VOICE: The song is high pitched and variable, a loud clear *sweet sweet sweet cheer cheer cheer*, or *sweet sweet sweet cheer cheer cheer chee swee swee r r r r r.* The flock note is a double *tick tick.* The call is a soft *che.*

HABITS: Males sing from a perch on top of a low bush or tall weed or grass. Males sing rather frequently from Mar through July, and sometimes into Sept. Territorial defense is not particularly vigorous, but males will chase intruders out of their territory. Females are difficult to see as they feed in the grass most of the time. In winter they form loose flocks, formerly of 100 or more individuals. Seedeaters typically cling to the thinnest of grass stems as they extract seeds, a behavior made possible by their small size.

HABITAT: Seedeaters are found in open grassy areas, including pastures, weedy fields, roadsides, and in Texas especially near marshlands with cattails, coarse grass, sunflowers, and giant ragweed with scattered low bushes (such as retama and huisache). They are most often found along the Rio Grande, irrigation ditches, ponds, and at the edges of fields.

BREEDING: *Nest* is placed in a weed, commonly giant ragweed, shrub, or old vine 1–3 m high. The nest is a delicate cup of very fine, dried grasses, with a few leaves and hairs. Nesting begins mid-Mar and may continue into Sept. *Eggs*, 2–5, usually 3–4, are pale blue or bluish white, and finely mottled with light brown. *Incubation*, about 13 days; female alone incubates, but both parents feed the young; young leave the nest after 10–11 days. This species is parasitized by cowbirds.

RANGE: *Apparently resident* from the lower Rio Grande Valley of Texas northwest to Zapata, San Ygnacio, and Laredo, and along the coast to Corpus Christi, south through e Mexico to nw Panama; along the west coast of Mexico, they are resident from c Sinaloa, south to w Oaxaca. Recently, most records in Texas are from San Ygnacio and Zapata. Apparently wanders in winter.

HISTORY: There are three groups of White-collared Seedeaters. The *S. t. sharpei* group of northwest Mexico and southeast Texas intergrade in Veracruz into the *S. t. morelleti* group of eastern Mexico and Central America. The ranges of the seedeaters

of western Mexico, *S. t. torqueola*, apparently do not overlap those of eastern Mexico, and some workers consider them to be different species. Although this species was originally described on the basis of birds from western Mexico, 'Sharp's' Seedeater of southeastern Texas and northeastern Mexico was first named in 1889 by the American ornithologist George Lawrence on the basis of four females from Lomita, Texas. This locality was probably La Lomita Mission, in southern Hidalgo Co., along the Rio Grande R., and the mission after which Mission, Texas was named.

The clearing of woods and brush in the Rio Grande Delta during the early 20th century for agricultural purposes, although greatly reducing the numbers of many Neotropical species whose range makes it just that far north, benefited the little White-collared Seedeaters. They were reasonably common in that area until the 1950s when cotton replaced citrus growing as the principal form of agriculture. The cotton fields were sprayed with DDT and other insecticides, as well as weed killers. This change in agricultural practice well correlated with the decline of seedeaters in southeastern Texas. Cowbird parasitism may also have affected their numbers there.

GEOGRAPHIC VARIATION: None north of Mexico. See comments in HISTORY.

MEASUREMENTS: (47 males): wing 48–55 (51), tail 40–47 (44), tarsus 14.2–16.5 (15.5), exposed culmen 8.1–9.1 (8.6), bill depth at base 6.4–8.1 (7.4); (10 females): wing 48–51 (50), tail 39–45 (42), tarsus 15.2–16.0 (15.5), exposed culmen 8.1–8.9 (8.6), bill depth 7.4–8.1 (7.6) (specimens from Texas, eastern Mexico, and Central America; there appears to be little geographic variation in size) (Ridgway 1901).

Mass: 8.7 g (6.3–12.0) (specimens from Mexico) (Dunning 1993).

Reference: Oberholser (1974).

9 **Yellow-faced Grassquit** *Tiaris olivacea* [603.2]   PLATE 4

D.BEADLE .

IDENTIFICATION: 9.5–11 cm (*c.* 3.5–4.5 in), males slightly larger; sexes differ in coloration.

The Yellow-faced Grassquit is a small, olive-green sparrow with a bright yellow supercilium and throat, and gray belly. Adult males have a dark gray breast. Young birds and females have less yellow in their throat and supercilium than adult males, and may show none at all.

Similar species: See Black-faced Grassquit. Males distinctive. Females may closely resemble female Black-faced Grassquits, but appear greener in hue, and may show a thin yellow supercilium, yellowish on the throat, and yellow in the bend of the wing. Female White-collared Seedeaters have a distinctly curved bill, and are brownish in tone.

Adult males—*Head:* crown olive-green; ear-coverts olive-green or black (Mexican); forehead, lores, and submoustachial stripe black; supraloral spot and supercilium bright yellow, broad toward bill becoming narrow behind eye; yellow crescent under eye; ***back, rump,*** and ***tail:*** olive-green, not contrasting in color with crown; ***wing:*** greenish olive and unpatterned, with slight yellow on the alula; ***underparts:*** chin and throat bright yellow; breast black; flanks gray or grayish olive; belly and undertail-coverts grayish to olive-green, often (especially birds from Mexico) with black on upper belly; ***bill:*** black; ***legs:*** brownish; ***iris:*** dark.

Adult females similar to males, but duller in color, and lacking black; the yellow on the face is variable, but may be absent (probably young individuals).

Young males (any time of year) resemble adult males, but yellow reduced, and black on breast and throat reduced or absent, and chin grayish white or dull yellowish. Older young males have a dark malar stripe outlined by a thin yellow sub-moustachial stripe and yellow throat.

Young females similar to adult females, but probably duller, without yellowish or whitish on throat.

VOICE: The song is a series of thin, high trills, varying in speed and pitch, *tsi-tsi-tsi-tsi*. In the West Indies the song resembles that of a Worm-eating Warbler. The call is a soft *tek*, or *tssip*.

HABITS: Courting males hover with rapidly vibrating wings near females while singing. In their range, they are usually found in pairs or small flocks.

HABITAT: Yellow-faced Grassquits are found in weedy fields, roadsides, and edges of clearings in fairly open country.

RANGE: *Resident* from s Tamaulipas south along the coast of Mexico (including Yucatán), Guatemala and Belize, and long both coasts of Honduras, the Caribbean slope of Nicaragua, and both coasts of Costa Rica and Panama. Also in the Greater Antilles (east to Puerto Rico), and in the Cayman Is. A singing adult male at Homestead, Dade County, Florida, 7–12 July 1990 was apparently an individual from the Greater Antillean subspecies. There is also a record of a first-year bird from 20–25 Apr 1994 from the Dry Tortugas, Florida, and a record of a male from the Santa Ana Refuge, se Texas, 22–24 Jan 1990, probably of the Mexican subspecies.

GEOGRAPHIC VARIATION: There are several subspecies of Yellow-faced Grassquits. The two that are most likely to appear in the area covered by this book are *T. o. olivacea*,which is resident in Cuba, Jamaica, the Cayman Is., and Hispaniola, and *T. o. pusilla*, which is resident in eastern Mexico (north to Tamaulipas) south to Colombia. The Mexican Yellow-faced Grassquits have more black ventrally than the Caribbean ones, and in full adults the ear-coverts are black rather than green.

MEASUREMENTS: *T. o. olivacea* (24 males): wing 51–56 (54), tail 39–44 (42), tarsus 15.8–18.5 (17.0), exposed culmen 8.9–10.2 (9.4), depth of bill at base 7.4–7.9 (7.6); (11 females): wing 50–55 (52), tail 38–41 (40), tarsus 16.3–17.8 (17.0), exposed culmen 9.1–10.2 (9.7), bill depth 7.1–7.6 (7.4).

T. o. pusilla (31 males): wing 48–54 (52), tail 36–43 (40), tarsus 16.3–18.0 (17.3), exposed culmen 8.9–10.2 (9.4), bill depth 6.4–7.4 (6.9); (13 females): wing 48–52 (50), tail 36–40 (38), tarsus 15.0–17.8 (16.3), exposed culmen 8.4–9.4 (8.9), bill depth 6.4–6.6 (6.5) (Ridgway 1901).

Mass: (N=21) 8.9 g (Panama) (Dunning 1993).

10 **Black-faced Grassquit** *Tiaris bicolor* [603]   PLATE 4

IDENTIFICATION: 9.5–11 cm (*c.* 4–4.5 in), sexes nearly the same size; sexes differ somewhat in coloration.

The Black-faced Grassquit is a small, drab sparrow. Adult males are dark, with a black head, bill, throat, and breast, and dark olive-green back, tail, wings, and belly that could appear black in poor light. Females are olive-green above and grayish beige below, and lack any distinctive markings. Young males tend to be pale bellied, with a paler bill.

Similar species: The Yellow-faced Grassquit is about the same size, and the females are similar in coloration. Female Yellow-faced Grassquits tend to be darker and more olive-green below, and *may* have a trace of the male facial markings. Female buntings (*Passerina*) are larger; female and young Painted Buntings are greenish or bluish green; female Indigo Buntings are browner, and faintly streaked below. No other small sparrow found north of Mexico is blackish like the male, although the Blue-black Grassquit, which is glossy black, is found north to southern Tamaulipas. In flight, these often show a bit of white in the wing.

Adult males—*Head, throat, breast* and upper ***belly:*** flat black; ***back, rump, wings, tail,*** and lower ***belly:*** dark olive-green; ***bill:*** black; ***legs:*** brownish; ***iris:*** dark.

Adult females—*Head, back, wings* and ***tail:*** dull, grayish olive-green; ***throat*** and ***breast:*** grayish; ***flanks:*** grayish, and sometimes washed with dull olive; ***belly:*** whitish gray; ***bill:*** brownish, with lower bill paler than upper; ***legs:*** brownish; ***iris:*** dark.

Young males (may occur in any season) like adult male, but paler, especially on flanks and belly, and with a pale lower bill.

Young females like adult.

VOICE: The song is a weak, but emphatic buzzing *tik-zeeee*, *tik-tik-zeeeeee*, or *dik-zeezeezee*. The call note is a soft *tsip*.

HABITS: Black-faced Grassquits often occur in small groups or in pairs. Displaying males fly a short distance, slowly, with rapid wing-beats, while singing.

HABITAT: In their usual range, Black-faced Grassquits are birds of the edges of fields, roadsides, and thickets in fairly open country.

RANGE: *Resident* throughout the West Indies (except Cuba), islands in the western Caribbean Sea (Providencia, Santa Catalina, San Andrés), Netherlands Antilles east to Trinidad and Tobago, and n Colombia and Venezuela. Very rare in winter (Oct–May) to the coast of se Florida and the Keys. The Florida birds are probably from the Bahamas.

MEASUREMENTS: Bahamas, (24 males): wing 50–56 (54), tail 39–44 (42), tarsus 15.8–18.5 (17.0), exposed culmen 8.9–10.2 (9.4), bill depth at base 7.4–7.9 (7.6); (11 females): wing 50–55 (52), tail 38–41 (40), tarsus 16.3–17.8 (17.0), exposed culmen 9.1–10.2 (9.7), bill depth 7.1–7.6 (7.4) (Ridgway 1901).

Mass: (N=59) 9.7 g (7.8–11.2) (Dunning 1993).

Genus *Aimophila*

The genus *Aimophila* contains 13 species, five of which breed north of Mexico. They are medium-sized sparrows with rather long, often rounded tails and rather short, rounded wings. Most ornithologists feel that *Aimophila* is a heterogeneous and probably not a natural genus, but rather contains at least three distinct groups of birds, with separate evolutionary histories, and perhaps should be split into three genera. Representatives of each of these groups are found north of Mexico.

The first group contains Bachman's, Botteri's, and Cassin's sparrows. These three species are difficult to distinguish in the field, and almost certainly closely related to each other. They are found in open weedy fields, have dull plumages, and have yellow in the bend of the wing. The second group of *Aimophila* is represented north of Mexico only by the Rufous-winged Sparrow. It has a relatively simple song and bright plumage, with the juvenal plumage much like that of the adult. Members of the third group, which includes the Rufous-crowned Sparrow, probably evolved in the pine–oak woodlands of the southwest and Mexico, distinguishing them from other *Aimophila*, which probably evolved in grasslands.

The relationships of the *Aimophila* to other sparrows are not clear, although they are often thought to be closely related to sparrows in the genus *Amphispiza* (Black-throated, Sage, Bell's, and Five-striped sparrows), and indeed these two genera are commonly merged in classifications. The Lark Sparrow (*Chondestes*), in turn, on the basis of plumage similarity appears to be closely related to the Sage Sparrow (*Amphispiza belli*).

11 **Bachman's Sparrow** *Aimophila aestivalis* [575]   PLATE 6

IDENTIFICATION: 12–16 cm (*c.* 5–6 in), sexes similar in coloration, males slightly larger.

Bachman's Sparrow is a fairly large, large-billed, round-tailed sparrow with reddish brown lateral crown-stripes, streaked scapulars and back, gray chin and throat, and unstreaked, buffy breast.

Similar species: Botteri's Sparrow is very similar in appearance, and both vary geographically. In practice, the very different songs and habitat preferences facilitate the field identification of these two, which have non-overlapping ranges. Western Bachman's Sparrows have a distinct brown eye-stripe, and are more rufescent in color than eastern Botteri's Sparrows. Botteri's may have rusty crown-stripes. The two central tail feathers of Cassin's Sparrows are pale brown, contrasting with the others, which are dark, and are distinctly barred; the lateral tail feathers are edged and tipped with dull white. Cassin's Sparrow is grayer in appearance.

Adult (eastern)—**Head:** median crown-stripe buffy gray; lateral crown-stripes dull rusty; supercilium and side of head buffy gray, with a narrow rusty post-ocular stripe, nape buffy gray, narrowly streaked with chestnut or chestnut-brown; **back:** streaked with chestnut or chestnut-brown, the feathers often with blackish centers;

rump: grayish brown with chestnut-brown centers; *tail:* dull brown, rounded, and slightly longer than wing, may show pale tips and faint bars, central ones paler than others; *wing:* coverts chestnut-brown, without conspicuous wing-bars, marginal coverts pale yellow; *underparts:* chin and throat very pale dull gray or buffy white, deepening on chest, sides, and flanks, surrounding paler buffy white belly; females may have small black spots on breast; a dusky submalar streak sometimes present; *bill:* stout, upper mandible dusky, lower mandible paler; *legs* and *feet:* pale brownish buffy or dull yellow; *iris:* brown.

First-winter (Sept–Feb) resemble adults, but are less rufous on the back, and the breast often has blackish spots.

Juveniles (May–Sept) crown and back dark brown or black, with mantle and scapulars edged with buffy or reddish brown, but less rufous than adults, and heavily streaked with brown; greater coverts edged with rust to form a slight wing-bar; underparts whitish or cream; chin, sides of neck, throat, breast, and flanks streaked with brown.

VOICE: The song is highly variable but distinctive, and generally consists of a long, sweet note followed by a clear trill; sometimes there is a third element. Each individual sings several different songs differing in pitch or tempo, often repeating one several times, then switching to another. The song is similar to that of the eastern Rufous-sided Towhee, with the second element, the trill, often like Swamp Sparrow, but shorter and less emphatic. Birds sing all day, usually from an exposed perch well off the ground. Countersinging is frequent. A bubbling and exuberant flight-song has also been described. The call note is a thin, high *chip* or *pseet*, much like that of Chipping Sparrow.

HABITS: On the breeding grounds, males sing persistently and often all day from an exposed perch, generally less than 3 m from the ground. Otherwise, however, these sparrows are secretive and hard to observe, and may run, rather than fly when pursued. When flushed, they commonly drop again into the understory vegetation, and they do not 'spish' up readily.

HABITAT: During all seasons, Bachman's Sparrow is characteristically found in open pine woods, with fairly rank understory of wiregrass, palmettos, and weeds. It also occurs in oak-palmetto scrub and in grasslands away from pine woods. In Indiana, it occurs in overgrown old fields (degraded pastures), with broomsedge, deciduous shrubs, and red cedar.

BREEDING: *Nest* is placed on the ground, usually but not always in dense cover; some nests are domed and all concealed by vegetation. The nest is rather bulky, and primarily made of coarse grasses. Apparently the female alone builds the nest. Nesting takes place from mid-Apr through July, with a peak in early June; probably double-brooded. *Eggs*, 2–5, usually 4, smooth and glossy, white and unmarked.

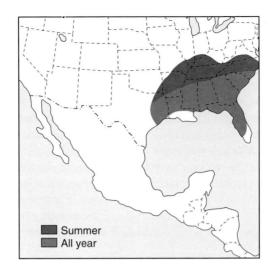

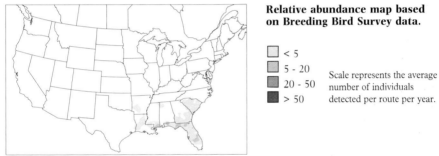

Relative abundance map based on Breeding Bird Survey data.

- < 5
- 5 - 20
- 20 - 50
- > 50

Scale represents the average number of individuals detected per route per year.

Incubation, 12–14 days; female alone broods, but both parents feed the young; young fledge in 9–10 days. The species is parasitized by the Brown-headed Cowbird.

RANGE: *Breeds* from s-c Missouri (Caney Mountain, Ozark Co., local and declining), e and c Oklahoma, e Texas, Arkansas, se Illinois, s-c Indiana (especially in south, declining), sw Kentucky (declining), and West Virginia (formerly?), s-c Virginia (Brunswick Co., declining), south to the Gulf Coast and s-c Florida. Formerly bred in c Ohio, sw Pennsylvania, and c Maryland.

Winters from se North Carolina south to the Gulf states, and s Florida.

Has been reported in ne Kansas, Michigan, Ontario, New York and New Jersey, but found less regularly north of normal range than in the past.

HISTORY: Audubon first met John Bachman in the fall of 1831, and the two quickly became lifetime friends. By that time, Bachman already had a strong interest in natural history, and had earlier interacted with Alexander Wilson. Later, each of

Audubon's two sons married one of Bachman's daughters. The two naturalists collaborated in the production of *The Viviparous Quadrupeds of North America* (1827–1838). Among the birds Bachman sent to Audubon, several were new to science, including the now extinct Bachman's Warbler. Audubon believed that the '. . . humble . . . Finch' that Bachman collected in Apr, 1832, near Parker's Ferry, on the Edisto R., South Carolina was new as well, and named it *Peucaea Bachmanii*, Bachman's Pinewood-finch. However, the species had been described in 1832 by Heinrich Lichtenstein, on the basis of a specimen collected in Georgia, and named *Fringilla aestivalis*. Although frequently called the Pine Woods Sparrow, the name Bachman's Sparrow has become established. Bachman, in writing to Audubon, noted that 'This bird appears to be rarer in Carolina than it really is. It is in fact often-er heard than seen. When I first heard its notes, they so nearly resembled those of the Towhee Bunting, that I took it to be that bird . . .'. These were perceptive comments, and I suspect that the species is still overlooked, especially in winter.

Since the 1930s, Bachman's Sparrow has inexplicably declined, and now is apparently extirpated from the northern part of its range, even though suitable habitat still exists in that area. As the species leaves the northern part of its range in winter, destruction of suitable wintering habitat in the south may have caused this decline. Certainly resident populations in the deep south have suffered significantly as a consequence of the loss of open pine woods with grassy understory. Bachman's Sparrow is found in the habitat preferred by Red-cockaded Woodpeckers, and has locally benefited from efforts to save that species.

GEOGRAPHIC VARIATION: Three subspecies are generally recognized: Bachman's Sparrow (*A. a. bachmani*), which breeds from Virginia south to South Carolina and Alabama; Pine Woods Bachman's Sparrow (*A. a. aestivalis*), which breeds southern South Carolina, Georgia and Peninsular Florida; and the Illinois Bachman's Sparrow (*A. a. illinoensis*), which breeds in Indiana, Illinois, and Missouri, south to central Louisiana and east Texas. *A. a. bachmani* and *A. a. aestivalis* are very similar in appearance, the latter being darker and less rufous than the former. *A. a. illinoensis* are on average paler in color, but more rufous on the back than eastern birds, with little or no dorsal black streaking. Variation appears to be clinal, and reliable subspecific identification is probably not possible.

MEASUREMENTS: Pine Woods Sparrow (*A. a. aestivalis*) (11 males): wing 57–62 (60), tail 61–65 (63), tarsus 18.3–19.8 (19.1), exposed culmen 10.2–12.7 (11.9); (4 females): wing 57–58 (57), tail 58–61 (60), tarsus 18.3–19.8 (19.1), exposed culmen 11.4–12.2 (11.7).

Bachman's Sparrow (*A. a. baehmani*) (28 males): wing 58–64 (61), tail 61–67 (64), tarsus 18.3–20.3 (19.3), exposed culmen 10.9–13.2 (12.2); (5 females): wing 58–60· (59), tail 61–66 (64), tarsus 18.5–20.8 (19.6), exposed culmen 10.9–12.5 (11.7) (Ridgway 1901).

Illinois Sparrow (*A. a. illinoensis*) (males): wing length (N=45) 57-66 (60), tail (N=31) 59–67 (63), tarsus (N=48) 18.5–21.5 (20.0), culmen length from nostril (N=48) 7.3–8.7 (8.0), bill depth at anterior edge of nostril (N=48) 5.2–6.2 (5.6); (females): wing length (N=22) 55–62 (58), tail (N=16) 57–66 (61), tarsus (N=36) 18.1–20.5 (19.5), culmen length (N=36) 7.2–8.7 (7.9), bill depth (N=32) 5.1–6.1 (5.6) (Wolf 1977).

Mass: (12 males) 20.2 g (18.4–22.6) (Wolf 1977).

References: Harrison (1978), Kaufman (1990), Mengel (1965), Wolf (1977).

12 **Botteri's Sparrow** *Aimophila botterii* [576]   PLATE **5**

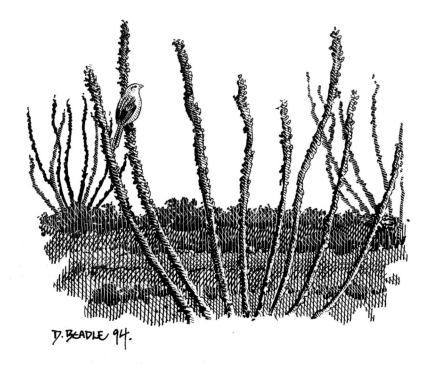

D. BEADLE 94.

IDENTIFICATION: 13–16 cm (*c.* 5–6 in), males slightly larger; sexes similar in coloration.

Botteri's Sparrow is a fairly large, rather large-billed, round-tailed sparrow without conspicuous markings.

Similar species: Botteri's Sparrow is very similar in size and coloration to Bachman's Sparrow. Western Botteri's may appear slightly warmer rusty buff ventrally than eastern Bachman's Sparrows, and Bachman's usually shows some rusty on the crown; western Bachman's Sparrows are more rufescent in color than eastern ones, and have a distinct brown eye-stripe. Eastern Botteri's Sparrows are paler and grayer in overall color than western ones, and may show some rust in the crown. Botteri's Sparrow can be told from the similar Cassin's Sparrow in several ways: the central two tail feathers of Cassin's Sparrow are pale brown (contrasting with others, which are darker) with distinct barring, and the lateral ones are edged and tipped with dull white (which may not be obvious in worn individuals), whereas the tails of Botteri's and Bachman's sparrows are brown with the edges of the feathers paler brown; the mantle and scapular feathers of Botteri's are brown with dark brown centers, whereas the back feathers of Cassin's are paler brown with subterminal dark

① Fresh plumage   ② Worn plumage

spots and pale fringes, giving them a scaly appearance (except in very worn birds); overall, Cassin's Sparrow has a grayer appearance than Botteri's, especially western Botteri's; there are distinct dark brown spots on the lower flank of Cassin's Sparrow. The bouncing ball song of Botteri's Sparrow can sound like that of the Olive Sparrow, which can occur in adjacent habitats..

Adult—Head: brown, with centers of crown feathers dark brown; supercilium and lores pale buffy brown, and eye-stripe somewhat darker; **back:** brown, with centers of mantle and scapular feathers dark brown; **rump:** dark brown, with centers of feathers somewhat darker; **tail:** brown, with darker centers; **wing:** brown with yellowish alula and lesser coverts, and edges of median and greater covers somewhat lighter; **underparts:** chin, throat, breast and flanks buffy brown, somewhat paler on belly; undertail-coverts buffy brown with dark brown centers; **bill:** brownish gray, upper bill darker than lower bill, with pale bluish gray tomial edge; **legs:** dull pinkish; **iris:** dark brown. Females may have more streaking on the crown and neck, and perhaps faint streaking on flanks.

First-winter (July–Dec) similar to adult, but sometimes with light brown spots on breast.

Juveniles (June–Aug) crown, back and rump feathers with large dark centers; underparts dull white to buffy on breast, heavily streaked on throat, breast and flanks; edges of greater coverts rusty and tipped with buff; undertail-coverts buffy orange without dark centers.

VOICE: The song is loud and clearly whistled, slightly canary-like, and characteristically consists of two **che-lick** elements (like Horned Lark flight calls, or Western Kingbird calls), followed by a variable series of notes, **wit-wit-wit-wit-t-t-t-t tseeoo wit wit**, becoming more rapid, like a bouncing ball; or **che-lick che-lick wit wit** (lower pitch) **wit-wit-wit-wt-t-t-t-t**, sometimes dropping in pitch at the

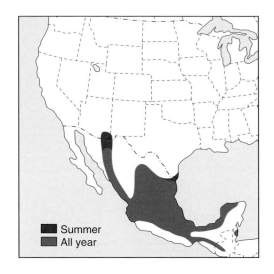

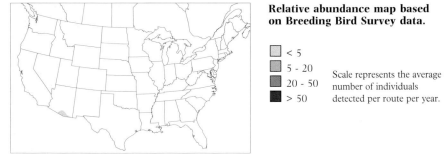

Relative abundance map based on Breeding Bird Survey data.

< 5
5 - 20
20 - 50
> 50

Scale represents the average number of individuals detected per route per year.

end. The song is highly variable; individuals also frequently vary their songs. The song carries well, and can probably be heard up to 200 m. The note is a ***chip***, ***pit*** or ***tsip***.

HABITS: Territorial males sit in low bushes (mesquite, ocotillo), trees (oak) or a fence to sing, but otherwise Botteri's Sparrows spend most of their time on the ground, and can be very difficult to see. When flushed, they fly to the nearest bush or fence, or may drop back into the grass. In Texas, singing occurs from May through July, and occasionally into Sept. Occasionally sings in horizontal flight.

HABITAT: In Arizona, Botteri's Sparrows are found in fairly tall grass (esp. sacaton), mixed with mesquite, ocotillo and oaks. In Texas, they are found in saltgrass (*Spartina*), mixed with mesquite, palo verde, yucca, and prickly pear, or in bunch. grass (20 cm tall or more) growing among scattered mesquite or huisache bushes.

BREEDING: ***Nest*** is placed on or near the ground, in tall grass, or at the base of a tuft of grass, sometimes under a mat of grass. The nest is a roundish cup of grass, lined with finer grasses. Nesting takes place in May through July. *Eggs*, 3–5, usually 4, pure white and unmarked. *Incubation*, unknown.

RANGE: *Breeds* from se Arizona (formerly north to Oracle), sw New Mexico (probably) south to Chiapas and locally to Costa Rica, and north along the Gulf Coast of eastern Mexico into coastal s Texas (formerly north to Corpus Christi) and the lower Rio Grande Valley.

Winters, probably, from northern Mexico south through its breeding range.

HISTORY: Matteo Botteri was a Dalmatian naturalist who in 1854 traveled to Mexico to collect plants for the Royal Horticultural Society of London. He established his residence at Orizaba, Veracruz. He so liked the area and its people that he spent the rest of his life there. In 1857 he sent a collection of birds that were examined by Philip Sclater, who identified 120 different species, including two new ones. One of these he named *Zonotrichia botterii*, Botteri's Sparrow, in honor of its collector. Botteri's Sparrow was not found north of Mexico until Henry Henshaw collected several in southeastern Arizona in the 1870s.

When not singing, Botteri's Sparrow is both difficult to find and to identify. Thus, its status in the past is uncertain. Nonetheless, Henshaw, and other early ornithologists found the species in many places in Arizona, indicating that prior to the general overgrazing of the late 1800s it was more common in Arizona than today. The habitat destruction in southern Texas that has occurred after World War II has greatly decreased the numbers of Botteri's Sparrows there, but they are still locally common where conditions suitable for them exist. It seems probable that most of the birds that breed in the United States retire to Mexico in winter.

GEOGRAPHIC VARIATION: Several subspecies have been described, and two occur north of Mexico, the Arizona Botteri's Sparrow (*A. botterii arizonae*) and the Texas Botteri's Sparrow (*A. b. texana*). The Texas Botteri's Sparrow is generally pale and gray, with a whiter belly than the Arizona Botteri's Sparrow, which appears to be pale reddish in contrast. In the field, however, the apparent overall coloration of individuals is often significantly modified by dust bathing.

MEASUREMENTS: Arizona Botteri's Sparrow (21 males): wing 63–69 (65), tail 58–69 (63).

Texas Botteri's Sparrow (45 males): wing 65–71 (68), tail 57–68 (63) (data from Webster 1959).

Botteri's Sparrow (males): wing (N=55) 57–68 (63), tail (N=41) 56–71 (65), tarsus (N=54) 20.6–23.3 (21.9), culmen length from anterior edge of nostril (N=53) 7.6–9.0 (8.1), depth of bill at anterior edge of nostril (N=43) 5.2–6.2 (5.5);

(females) wing (N=41) 56–66 (61), tail (N=21) 58–71 (63), tarsus (N=41) 20.6–23.0 (22.0), culmen length (N=38) 7.3–8.8 (8.0), bill depth (N=29) 5.0–6.2 (5.5) (Wolf 1977).

Mass: (21 males) 22.2 g (16.4–25.2); (6 females) 21.6 (19.2–23.5) (Wolf 1977). (6 males) 19.8 g (18.3–21.6) (Arizona, July) (Rising, unpublished).

References: Kaufman (1990), Oberholser (1974), Webster (1959), Wolf (1977).

13 **Cassin's Sparrow** *Aimophila cassinii* [578]   PLATE 5

IDENTIFICATION: 13–15 cm (*c.* 5–6 in), males slightly larger; sexes similar in coloration.

Cassin's Sparrow is a fairly large, grayish sparrow of dry grasslands, that lacks conspicuous markings. In flight, the white tips to the tail feathers are apparent. The song is distinctive, and an aid to identification.

Similar species: Cassin's Sparrow is similar in size and markings to Botteri's Sparrow, but generally paler gray in coloration, with white along the outer edges of the outer two tail feathers and white tips to lateral tail feather, and central two tail feathers distinctly barred; the bill is slightly smaller than Botteri's Sparrow. On the breeding grounds, Cassin's Sparrow frequently gives a conspicuous flight-song and this along with the distinctive song is the best way to separate it from Botteri's Sparrow; Cassin's has streaked hind flanks.

Adult—*Head:* brown streaked with gray and dark brown; supercilium buff; thin dark brown submoustachial stripe; ***back:*** mantle and scapulars brown, feathers with dark brown subterminal spots and edged with buff, giving a scaly appearance; ***rump:*** and uppertail-coverts with brown spots; ***wing:*** brown, with secondary coverts edged in buff, forming an indistinct wing-bar; alula pale yellow; ***tail:*** middle rectrices light brownish gray with narrow brown bars; lateral two rectrices edged and tipped with white (not distinct in worn specimens); ***underparts:*** chin, throat, and breast gray; flanks gray with black streaks posteriorly; belly whitish; undertail-coverts sometimes buffy; ***bill:*** brownish gray, with upper mandible

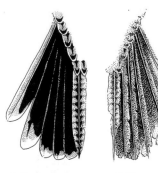

① Fresh plumage   ② Worn plumage

darker, with pale bluish gray tomial edge and lower mandible; **legs:** dull pinkish; **iris:** dark brown.

First-winter (July–Mar) like adult, but some with dark spots on breast.

Juveniles (May–Aug) similar to adult, but back brown, feathers with buffy tips and darker brown central streaks, greater coverts edged with white, and light streaking on breast and throat..

VOICE: The song is a clear usually descending sweet, liquid trill, followed by two notes, the second usually higher than the first; this is preceded by two soft notes that are seldom heard: *ti ti tzeeeeeeeeeee tay tay*. Song is often given in flight, as the male jumps into the air to a height of about 6 m, sets his wings, and floats back to a low bush. There is also a *chitter* flight song, that is a rapid series of *chips* that become a warbled sound at the end. *Chip* calls are given by adults when around young and probably when alarmed; *sip* (soft) calls are given by young.

HABITS: Territorial males sit in low bushes, commonly sage, juniper or mesquite (west Texas), or grass, or on ground to sing, and often give spectacular flight-songs. When flushed, they fly to a bush or fence, or may drop back into the grass. Singing may begin on warm days in Feb, and persists through the summer into Sept. Males commonly sing at night.

HABITAT: In the central plains (western Kansas, Colorado), Cassin's Sparrows live in shortgrass interspersed with sagebrush and rabbitbrush. In the south and southwest they are found in shortgrass interspersed with other bushes (mesquite, hackberry, yucca, oaks, cactus, ocotillo); along the Texas Gulf Coast, both Cassin's and Botteri's sparrows live in bunch grass, but the latter is more closely tied to saltgrass associations in this part of its range. In Arizona, both species occur in grassland admixed with acacias, ocotillo and oaks. In winter they occur in similar habitat in the

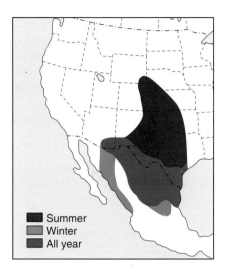

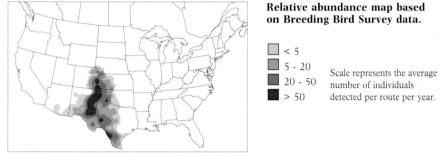

**Relative abundance map based
on Breeding Bird Survey data.**

< 5
5 - 20
20 - 50
> 50

Scale represents the average
number of individuals
detected per route per year.

southern part of their U.S. range. The species' occurrence is irregular, and it may be
absent from many areas in the northern and eastern parts of its range during years
when rainfall promotes good grass growth.

BREEDING: Nest is placed on or near the ground, in grass or bunch grass, near the
base of a bush or in grass, often under or in *Opuntia* cactus. The nest is a cup of
weeds and grasses, lined with fine grasses, hair or rootlets. Nesting takes place March
(Texas) through early Sept (Arizona). Nesting appears to take place in early summer
in coastal Texas, Kansas, Colorado and northeastern New Mexico, and in late summer (after the rains) in southeastern Arizona; perhaps some individuals are double-
brooded, raising one brood in the plains in early summer and another late in the summer in Arizona, but there is no direct evidence of this. ***Eggs***, 3–5, usually 4, white or
white tinged with greenish blue, and unmarked. ***Incubation***, unknown; both parents
feed young. Parasitized by Brown-headed Cowbirds.

RANGE: Breeds from c Wyoming (Torrington, Midwest; probable), sw South
Dakota (Fall R. Co.; one record), sw Nebraska (Garden Co.; rare), w Kansas (east

to Rice Co.), and e and c Colorado south through w-c Kansas and c Oklahoma, and e New Mexico to s Texas (Corpus Christi), s Arizona, and n Sonora, and south on the Mexican Plateau through Chihuahua, Durango, Coahuila, and Tamaulipas to s Tamaulipas, Zacatecas, and San Luis Potosí. Territorial males have been seen in lush years in s California (San Diego and San Bernardino counties.).

Winters from se Arizona, s New Mexico (rarely), w and s-c Texas, south to s Nayarit, Guanajuato, San Luis Potosí and Tamaulipas.

In **migration**, a rare and erratic spring migrant in California (early May to mid-July), and very rare fall transient (mid-Sept to early Oct); reported as occasional in e Nevada, with a specimen from May (Lincoln Co.).

Casual in Ontario (Point Pelee, Marathon; May, Sept), Nova Scotia (Seal I.; May), Missouri (unconfirmed; May), Illinois (Chicago; May–June), Indiana, and New Jersey.

HISTORY: Cassin's Sparrow was first found by the naturalist Dr. John Woodhouse, who collected a male near San Antonio, Texas, in April, 1851. He named it *Zonotrichia Cassinii* '. . . in honor of my friend Mr. John Cassin . . . to whose inde-fatigable labor in the department of Ornithology [at the Academy of Natural Sciences in Philadelphia] we are so much indebted.' Cassin was a prominent American ornithologist in the 19th century, and named nearly 200 species of birds himself, including 26 that are found in North America north of Mexico.

In Texas, since the 1930s, Cassin's Sparrow increased in abundance at least through the 1970s as a consequence of programs to clear brush and establish grasslands in the western part of the state. Replacement of native grasses with foreign species, however, may hurt this sparrow. In Kansas, the eastern edge of its breeding range varies from year to year. There, it is generally commonest in the far west and south of the Arkansas R., but in some years occurs into the central part of the state.

GEOGRAPHIC VARIATION: None described.

MEASUREMENTS: (males): wing (N=43) 62–67 (64), tail (N=13) 64–71 (68), tar-sus (N=45) 18.5–21.4 (19.9), culmen length from anterior of nostril 6.8–8.3 (7.7), bill depth at anterior edge of nostril 4.5–5.5 (4.9); (females): wing (N=16) 59–66 (62), tail (N=13) 62–71 (66), tarsus (N=37) 18.8–21.4 (19.8), culmen length 7.0–8.2 (7.5), bill depth 4.5–5.1 (4.8) (data from Wolf 1977).

Mass: (11 males) 17.8 g (16.9–18.5) (Kansas, June) (Rising, unpublished).

References: Kaufman (1990), Oberholser (1974), Wolf (1977).

14 **Rufous-winged Sparrow** *Aimophila carpalis* [579] PLATE 6

IDENTIFICATION: 12–14 cm (*c.* 5–5.5 in), males slightly larger; sexes similar in color.

The Rufous-winged Sparrow is a medium sized bird of flat, dry grass scattered with thornscrub. It has rusty lateral crown and eye-stripes, and dark moustachial and malar stripes.

Similar species: The Rufous-winged Sparrow does not closely resemble other species, although it is vaguely similar to the slimmer, adult Chipping Sparrow. The rusty shoulders are not conspicuous in the field. Rufous-crowned Sparrows are darker, especially in the neck, throat and breast; these tend to be brownish in Rufous-crowned Sparrows and grayish in Rufous-winged Sparrows.

Adult—*Head:* broadly streaked with rufous, sometimes with an indistinct median crown-stripe; supercilium buffy gray; lores and eye-stripe rusty; ear-coverts buffy gray; moustachial and malar stripes dark brown; submoustachial stripe and chin pale buffy gray; ***back:*** including uppertail-coverts and tail brownish gray or light grayish brown, the mantle and scapular feathers with dark brown oblong centers, giving a streaked appearance; ***wing:*** brown, with rusty lesser coverts; median and greater coverts edged with buff, forming one or two indistinct wing-bars; ***underparts:***

grayish white, with breast slightly darker and flanks buffy gray, undertail-coverts light buff; **bill:** upper mandible brown; lower mandible flesh colored with a dusky tip; **legs** and **feet:** brownish; **iris:** light brown.

First-winter (Aug–Nov) similar to adult; wing and tail feathers are usually retained from juvenal plumage.

Juveniles (May–June) crown and back light brown heavily streaked with dark brown; submoustachial stripe suggested; underparts whitish with brown spotting on throat and breast, and flanks streaked with brown; margins of coverts buff.

VOICE: The song is a rapid series of notes, often with one or two introductory notes, followed by a series of **chip** or **tsip** notes, such as **chip burr chip-ip-ip-ip-ip-ip-ip**, or **tsee chip-ip-ip-ip-ip**, the first note higher than the following trill, resembling the song of Canyon or Abert's towhees. Also an accelerating **cha cha cha chi chi chi ci ci ci c c c c**. The note is a distinctive high-pitched **seep**. Although the species may sing at any time, the main season is June or July through Sept.

HABITS: Males usually sing from a bush, not far from the ground. Rufous-winged Sparrows are rather easy to see. When flushed, they usually fly up to a bush or small tree, and watch the observer. Do not flock.

HABITAT: The Rufous-winged Sparrow is found in flat desert grasslands in desert scrub, with desert hackberry, palo verde, and chollas, usually along washes.

BREEDING: Nest is built in the edge of a bush (commonly desert hackberry), 0.6 to 2.5 m above the ground. The nest is a conspicuous cup of dead plant stems, lined with fine grass and usually with hair. Nesting takes place in late Apr through mid-Sept, but nesting is triggered by summer rains. **Eggs**, 2–5, usually 4, pale bluish white and unmarked. **Incubation**, by female; young fed by both parents. The species is sometimes parasitized by cowbirds.

RANGE: Resident from s-c Arizona (Oracle) and se Arizona (Tucson area), west to Papago Indian Reservation (Ventana Ranch and Menager's Dam), south through c and se Sonora to c Sinaloa.

HISTORY: The Rufous-winged Sparrow was first described by Eliot Coues in 1873 on the basis of specimens collected by Major Charles Bendire along Rillito Creek near Tucson, Arizona, where it was, at that time, abundant. It and Bendire's Thrasher were the last two distinctive bird species to be first discovered in the United States, and both were originally obtained by Bendire, one of the best 19th century ornithologists in the U.S. military.

By 1884, however, Rufous-winged Sparrows had disappeared from the Tucson area, presumably as a consequence of the severe overgrazing that occurred in that area in

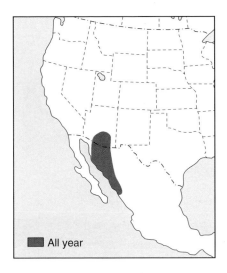

the late 1800s and early 1900s. Although Rufous-winged Sparrows were, to a certain extent, probably overlooked, their numbers were doubtlessly greatly reduced, and there were only scattered records from the state until the mid-1950s when there appeared to be an irruption of the species. Today they can usually be seen in suitable habitat.

GEOGRAPHIC VARIATION: None described north of Mexico.

MEASUREMENTS: (males): wing (N=62) 53–64 (59), tail (N=42) 58–69 (63), tarsus (N=58) 17.9–21.4 (19.1), culmen length from anterior edge of nostril (N=58) 6.8–8.1 (7.4), depth of bill at anterior edge of nostril (N=56) 5.1–6.3 (5.6); (females): wing (N=38) 53–65 (57), tail (N=32) 57–67 (61), tarsus (N=14) 17.6–20.0 (18.8), culmen (N=50) 6.7–7.7 (7.3), bill depth (N=43) 4.9–5.7 (5.4) (data from Wolf 1977).

Mass: (44 males) 15.0 g (12.6–17.5); (24 females) 15.0 g (13.0–16.9) (Wolf 1977).

Reference: Wolf (1977).

15 Rufous-crowned Sparrow

Aimophila ruficeps [580]

PLATE 6

D. BEADLE.

IDENTIFICATION: 13–15 cm (*c.* 5–6 in), males slightly larger; sexes similar in coloration.

The Rufous-crowned Sparrow is a fairly large, round-tailed sparrow with rusty crown, gray supercilium, distinct dark malar stripe, rather prominent eye-ring, and unmarked grayish or buffy gray underparts.

Similar species: No other sparrow closely resembles the Rufous-crowned Sparrow. American Tree Sparrows are somewhat smaller, with a yellow lower bill, and distinct breast spot, and lack the dark brown malar stripe. Chipping Sparrows are slimmer, with a white supercilium and black eyeline stripe. See the Rufous-winged Sparrow. Juveniles resemble juvenile Botteri's Sparrows, but are somewhat darker in color.

Adult (interior)—***Head:*** crown rusty, thinly outlined with black above the bill, sometimes with an indistinct gray median crown-stripe and with a thin median stripe just above the bill; supercilium gray posteriorly, becoming brighter or white between the eye and bill and narrowly edged with black; eye-stripe gray; eye-ring white; supraloral spot pale; ear-coverts blackish around eye and grayish brown posteriorly; submoustachial stripe thin and dark; lores dark gray; ***back:*** grayish brown, with rusty or brownish centers of mantle and scapular feathers; ***rump:*** and uppertail-coverts brown and more or less unmarked; ***tail:*** brown with faint darker brown barring; ***underparts:*** unmarked gray-brown, paler on belly than on breast and flanks; ***wing:*** brown, with centers of greater coverts dark brown, and no wing-bars; ***bill:*** upper mandible dusky brown becoming pale yellow on cutting edge; lower mandible pale yellow; ***legs*** and ***feet:*** pale brownish or dull yellow; ***iris:*** brown or tan.

First-fall (June–Nov) resemble adults, but are more buff colored.

Juveniles (May–Oct) crown brown with brown streaks; side of face brown without distinctive markings, but distinct dark brown malar stripe; breast and flanks thinly streaked with dark brown; belly perhaps with some streaking.

VOICE: The song is variable, but generally a series of 6–9 jumbled bubbling or staccato notes, resembling the song of House Wren, such as ***tchee-dle tchee-dle tchee-dle tchee-dle tchee-dle tchee-dle***, often slightly ascending then slightly descending; sometimes the song is followed by a series of ***chur*** notes. Males may sing from a perch or the ground, and occasionally they will sing while flying, especially during chases. A singing male may repeat the same song one to several times, then switch to another song. Pairs occasionally duet. The call note is a distinctive nasal ***dear***, nearly always a series of ***dear dear*** calls; the alarm call is an upward-slurred ***tzit***.

HABITS: Territorial males often sing from fairly exposed perches in bushes, but they spend most of their time on the ground, often running rather than flying from one patch of cover to another. Many individuals will respond to spishing.

HABITAT: The Rufous-crowned Sparrow is characteristic of xeric rocky hillsides and canyons, with rocks interspersed with shrubs and grass (they are sometimes called Rock Sparrows). It lives on or near the ground in rocky and hilly semi-arid grassland, interspersed with clumps of small junipers, piñon, oaks, acacias, or other shrubs; along the coast, it is most frequently found in sage scrub (including sagebrush, buckwheat, and taller plants such as yuccas); it avoids dense, continuous chaparral but will occupy post-burn chaparral for several years.

BREEDING: ***Nest*** is placed on or near the ground, often wedged among rocks or the branches of a low bush or shrub, and partially covered by vegetation. The nest is a compact cup of grasses, lined with finer grasses and sometimes hair. Nesting takes place from mid-Mar through Aug; the timing of the nesting is influenced by rains. ***Eggs***, 2–5, usually 3–4, pure white or pale bluish white and unmarked. ***Incubation***, by female alone. The species is occasionally parasitized by Brown-headed Cowbirds.

RANGE: ***Breeds*** from c California (north to Glenn and Sonoma cos., including Santa Cruz, Anacapa, and (formerly) Santa Catalina Is.), deserts of e California (New York and Providence Mountains), s Nevada (rare), sw Utah (Zion Canyon, Virginia; rare), nw and c Arizona, and c New Mexico, northeast to se Colorado, sw Kansas (scarce, Morton Co.; has been recorded from Comanche Co.), e-c and se Oklahoma (east to Sequoyah, Heskell and Pittsburg cos.), and w-c Arkansas (Magazine Mountains), south through c Texas to n Baja California, and south in Mexico on both slopes to Oaxaca and w-c Veracruz. The species is most common in c and w Texas, sw New Mexico, se Arizona and parts of coastal California.

Breeding
All year

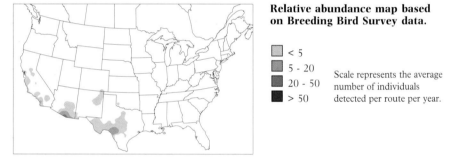

Relative abundance map based on Breeding Bird Survey data.

< 5
5 - 20
20 - 50
> 50

Scale represents the average number of individuals detected per route per year.

Winters from c California (sedentary), s-c Colorado, ne New Mexico, n Texas, and s-c Oklahoma, south throughout the breeding range; reported in winter in e-c Kansas (Junction City) and se Texas. Most common in winter in w and c Texas and se Arizona.

HISTORY: The Rufous-crowned Sparrow was described and named by John Cassin, of the Philadelphia Academy of Science, on the basis of specimens collected by Adolphus Lewis Heerman, in 1852. In the same paper, Cassin named Heermann's Gull in honor of Heermann, a surgeon and naturalist who served in the U.S. military for 31 years. In his notes, Heermann wrote that Rufous-crowned Sparrows were '. . . quite abundant on the Calaveras R. [east of Stockton, California] . . .' from which Cassin apparently came to the erroneous conclusion that they '. . . live in the vicinity of the shores of the ocean and the margins of streams of fresh water.'

Although not much is known about changes in the abundance of the Rufous-crowned Sparrow, the preferred breeding habitat of Rufous-crowned Sparrows has probably not been much affected by human activities. That there has been a recent increase in the number of records of this species from southwestern Kansas and west-central Arkansas may indicate an increase in range. However, it seems more likely that it reflects better coverage of these areas.

GEOGRAPHIC VARIATION: Several subspecies have been described. The California Rufous-crowned Sparrow (*A. r. ruficeps*) is resident on the western slopes of the Sierra Nevada in central California; the Ashy Rufous-crowned Sparrow (*A. r. canescens*) is resident from Santa Barbara south into Baja California; the Santa Cruz Rufous-crowned Sparrow (*A. r. obscura*) is resident on Santa Cruz, Anacapa, and formerly Santa Catalina Is.; the Rock Rufous-crowned Sparrow (*A. r. eremoeca*) is found in the southern Great Plains south to northeastern Mexico, west to southwestern New Mexico, where it is replaced by Scott's Rufous-crowned Sparrow (*A. r. scottii*), which is found west to eastern California. *A. r. ruficeps* is similar to *A. r. scottii*, but the back colors and tail are darker and more rufous, ear-coverts, side of neck and underparts are brown rather than gray-brown or gray. *A. r. obscura* is very like *A. r. ruficeps*, though is said to average darker. *A. r. eremoeca* has relatively gray back, with brown rather than rufous centers to mantle and scapular feathers, which are characteristic of *A. r. scottii*, and crown averages more brightly colored than *A. r. scottii*; there appears to be clinal variation, with birds from central Texas and Tamaulipas being relatively grayer, and those from Arizona and New Mexico being more rufous on their backs, with a rusty crown, often with little trace of gray in the median crown-stripe; coloration may be significantly affected by dust bathing.

MEASUREMENTS: (males): wing (N=55) 58–70 (63), tail (N=48) 62–79 (68), tarsus (N=60) 18.5–22.5 (20.7), culmen from anterior of nostril (N=60) 6.7–9.4 (8.1), bill depth at anterior edge of nostril (N=58) 4.5–5.7 (5.2); (females): wing (N=48) 56–67 (63), tail (N=38) 57–73 (65), tarsus (N=58) 18.5–22.3 (20.6), culmen length (N=57) 6.7–9.3 (8.0), bill depth (N=55) 4.5–5.7 (5.1) (Wolf 1977).

Mass: (59 males) 19.3 g (16.0–23.3), (39 females) 18.1 g (15.2–20.3) (Arizona) (Dunning 1993).

References: Oberholser (1974), Wolf (1977).

Genus *Spizella*

The seven species of sparrows in the genus *Spizella* are all found north of Mexico, although one, Worthen's Sparrow, has been recorded there only once. *Spizellas* are small, semi-arboreal sparrows, with small, conical bills that are relatively deep at the base, and with long tails. In most species the lateral rectrices are longer than the middle ones (that is, the tail is notched), but in the Black-chinned Sparrow the middle ones are the longest. Adults have unstreaked breasts; the Tree Sparrow has a central breast spot. The sexes are alike in most species, although males may be more brightly colored on average; female Black-chinned Sparrows have much less black on the chin and throat than males.

As a general rule, *Spizellas* are sparrows of brushy, open habitats, but not grasslands without many bushes. The Chipping Sparrow, however, is an exception, and breeds in open woodlands, parks, urban areas, and coniferous forests. Again with the exception of the Chipping Sparrow, they characteristically place their nests on or near the ground, commonly near the base of a small shrub or tree. Their flight is direct and fast, and with the exception of some Field and Worthen's sparrows, they are migratory.

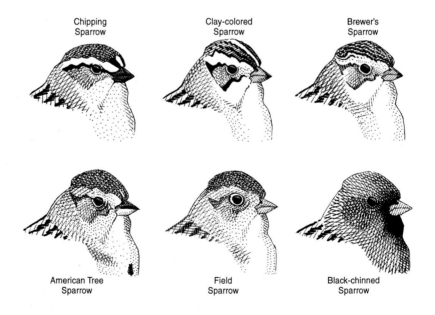

Chipping Sparrow   Clay-colored Sparrow   Brewer's Sparrow

American Tree Sparrow   Field Sparrow   Black-chinned Sparrow

16 **American Tree Sparrow** *Spizella arborea* [559]   PLATE 7

D·BEADLE 95.

IDENTIFICATION: 13–15 cm (*c.* 5–6 in), males slightly larger; sexes similar in coloration.

The American Tree Sparrow is a medium-sized sparrow with a rufous crown, a black spot in the center of its unstreaked grayish breast, a rusty shoulder, a rusty line back from the eye, and a yellow lower mandible.

Similar species: The Chipping Sparrow is slimmer, has a dark beak, white supercilium, and no spot in the breast. The Rufous-crowned Sparrow is browner, with black malar stripe. Field Sparrows have pink bills and no breast spot.

Adult—*Head:* cap rusty, often with a grayish median crown-stripe; supercilium gray; eyeline rusty; lores gray; malar stripe thin; ***back:*** rusty brown with dark streaks; ***rump:*** brown; ***wing:*** brown with rusty brown coverts and two distinct wing-bars; ***underparts:*** chin, throat and upper breast gray; breast with a distinct rusty spur that extends down on the breast just anterior to the bend of the wing, with lower flanks and belly fading to a warm rusty beige; upper belly white with a conspicuous black central spot next to the gray chest; ***tail:*** brown, with outer feathers somewhat paler; ***bill:*** upper mandible dark; lower mandible yellow with a dusky tip; ***legs:*** brown; ***iris:*** dark brown.

Young fall (July–Oct) similar to adults, but may have streaks on their crown, nape, and upper breast, traces of which may remain through Oct.

Juveniles (June–Sept) resemble adults, but have streaked brown (perhaps tinged with rusty) crown, nape and side of neck, and underparts (except for lower belly) heavily streaked with blackish brown, often with a distinct breast spot. Most resemble adults by fall migration, although hints of the streaking may remain.

VOICE: The song is clear, sweet and musical: *tsee tsee-a tsi tsi tsi* or *tsee-a tsee tsi tsi tsi*, with the '*a*' and final *tsi* lower in pitch than the other elements. Rarely sings in mid-winter, but singing increases in frequency by Feb. The call notes, *tseet*, and in feeding flocks a musical *teedle eet* call, are distinctive.

HABITS: On the breeding grounds, males sing from exposed perches on dwarf birch, willow, or small conifer, usually not more than a meter above the ground. They sing persistently throughout the day, but night singing is infrequent (there is not much night where they breed). In winter, they are generally found in loose flocks or small groups, sometimes in mixed species flocks. When flushed from the ground or grass, they commonly fly up into a small nearby tree where they can be easily observed. They readily respond to spishing.

HABITAT: On the breeding grounds, they are found in open shrubby vegetation, most commonly in shrubby deciduous trees, but occasionally in dwarf conifers (spruce; tamarack), generally in bogs, or north of the limit of trees or above timberline in mountains. In winter, they are found in weedy fields, hedgerows, low brush, or the edge of deciduous or mixed woodlands. American Tree Sparrows readily come to feeders.

BREEDING: *Nest* is placed generally in tussocks of sedge or depressions in the ground at the base of a small deciduous tree, commonly birch or willow, or in depressions in peat hummocks. A few nests are placed up to over 1.5 m high (5ft) in small willows, birches or dwarf spruce. The nest is a neatly woven cup of dead sedges or grasses, weed stems, rootlets, bits of lichen, lined with finer grasses, feathers, or hair. The female alone builds the nest. Nesting takes place from early June through July, with the peak in mid- to late June; single-brooded. *Eggs*, 3–6, usually 5, white to pale greenish, but heavily spotted with reddish brown. *Incubation*, 11–13 days; female alone broods, but both parents feed the young; young fledge in 8–10 days. The species is apparently monogamous. Parasitism by cowbirds has not been reported.

RANGE: *Breeds* from the Alaska Peninsula (west to Port Heiden) east across Yukon, perhaps on Banks I., n Mackenzie, c Keewatin, n and c Alberta (uncommon and local), n Manitoba and Ontario, n Quebec and Labrador south to s Mackenzie, extreme nw Alberta, n Saskatchewan, n Manitoba (Southern Indian L., Churchill), n Ontario (Winisk, Cape Henrietta Maria, Attawapiskat, Akimiski I.), c Quebec (Schefferville) and s Labrador. Reported in June from the Chukchi Peninsula, Siberia.

Winters from s British Columbia (rare along coast), s Alberta, sw Saskatchewan, s Ontario, sw Quebec, New Brunswick, Prince Edward I., and Nova Scotia south to North Carolina (northwest and mountains; rare), Tennessee (irruptive), Arkansas. (common in northwest), Texas (rare south of 32nd parallel), c New Mexico, n Arizona, and s California (rare but regular along coast). In winter it is especially abundant in the central States. It has been reported south to the Rio Grande Delta,

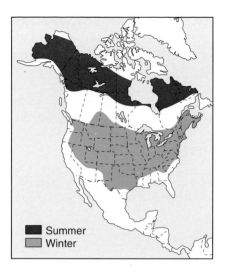

Summer
Winter

w Louisiana, n Alabama (mountain region), South Carolina (Hilton Head), and Georgia.

HISTORY: Alexander Wilson, the father of American ornithology, named this species in 1810 *Fringilla arborea* on the basis of a specimen from eastern Pennsylvania. Although Audubon called the species the Canada Bunting (*Emberiza canadensis*), apparently others called it the Tree Sparrow because of its supposed superficial resemblance to the European Tree Sparrow. More recently, the English name has been standardized as the American Tree Sparrow, to avoid confusion with the other tree sparrow. Audubon correctly recognized that this was a bird that winters in the northern and middle states, and noted that he had never seen one in the Carolinas. He writes that it was the commonest wintering sparrow around Boston.

Because the breeding habitat of the American Tree Sparrow has been little damaged by mining and other activities, it is unlikely that it has declined in numbers. Destruction of the forests of the east may indeed have increased wintering habitat for the species, although increased clearing and cultivation of the prairies may have decreased suitable habitat in the mid-west.

GEOGRAPHIC VARIATION: Two subspecies are generally recognized: the Western American Tree Sparrow (*S. a. ochracea*), which breeds Alaska, Yukon, and nw Mackenzie south to nw British Columbia, and the Eastern American Tree Sparrow (*S. a. arborea*), which breeds elsewhere. *S. a. ochracea* averages slightly, but not significantly larger, and paler than *S. a. arborea*, but differences cannot be seen in the field.

MEASUREMENTS: (50 males from Yukon, NWT, Manitoba, Ontario, Quebec): wing 71–79 (75), tail 59–72 (65), tarsus 17.7–22.0 (20.6), exposed culmen 7.8–11.1

(9.9), longest toe (N=35) (15.5–21.0 (17.1), mass (N=64) 14.9–27.7 (18.6); (44 females): wing 66–77 (71), tail 57–70 (64), tarsus 18.3–22.8 (20.0), culmen 8.3–10.5 (9.5), longest toe (N=29) 15.6–20.0 (17.3), mass (N=40) 12.6–20.8 (17.1).

Mass: (64 males) 18.6 g (14.9–27.7); (40 females) 17.1 g (12.6–20.8) (Yukon, NWT, Manitoba, Ontario, Quebec) (Naugler 1993).

References: Harrison (1978), Naugler (1993).

17 **Chipping Sparrow** *Spizella passerina* [560]   PLATE 8

D.BEADLE 95.

IDENTIFICATION: 12–14 cm (*c.* 4.5–5.5 in), males slightly larger; sexes similar in coloration.

The Chipping Sparrow is a small slim sparrow with a long notched tail; adults have a rusty cap, white superciliary stripe, black line through the eye, and a gray rump. In the first fall, the cap may be brown, and the superciliary stripe is less distinct. Only juveniles have a streaked breast.

Similar species: Clay-colored and Brewer's sparrows are similar in shape, but lack the rusty cap, white superciliary stripe and black eyeline stripe; juveniles and first-winter birds are very similar, but Chipping have a somewhat more distinct eyeline stripe that goes to the bill; all three have striped crowns, but Clay-colored has a more distinct median crown-stripe. American Tree Sparrows are larger, have a broad gray supercilium and rusty eyeline stripe, a central black spot on the breast, and a yellow lower mandible. Field Sparrows have an indistinctly marked, gray face, eye-ring, and pink bill. Other sparrows with rusty crowns (Rufous-crowned and Swamp) are larger and not so slim, and lack the distinct superciliary and eyeline stripes.

Adult—*Head:* crown rusty or chestnut, sometimes with a small medial pale spot (especially in winter) above the bill; forehead black; supercilium and supraloral spot white; eye-stripe and lores black; ***back:*** rusty brown with dark brown streaking; ***rump:*** gray; ***wing:*** greater and middle coverts rusty, edged with white or beige, forming one or two wing-bars; ***tail:*** moderately long, notched and brown; ***under-parts:*** gray; breast and flanks gray or grayish brown and unstreaked; belly dull white; ***bill:*** conical, small, black in breeding individuals, pale brownish lower mandible in non-breeding individuals; *legs:* straw colored or light brown; *iris:* black. *In fall and winter:* (Aug–Mar) adults with duller colors, the chestnut of the cap being partially or wholly obscured by buffy feather.

First-fall and winter (June–Aug in east; Aug–Mar in west) resemble non-breeding adults, but cap is dark beige, finely streaked with dark brown or black, especially late in the season, with some rusty in the cap; the thin, dark eyeline goes all the way to the bill; rump is brown and finely streaked at first, but becomes gray; ear-coverts are brownish, contrasting with the grayish throat (but not so clearly outlined by a thin, dark brown fringe as in Clay-colored Sparrows); streaking on breast and flanks.

Juveniles (June–Oct) have a brown crown, with thin dark streaks; buffy throat and breast with thin, dark brown streaks on throat and flanks; back brown with dark brown streaks; tertials edged rusty; lower mandible pale yellow. Western birds are paler than eastern ones. The first prebasic molt occurs later in western birds than eastern ones, sometimes after migration.

VOICE: The song is a dry rattle or trill on one pitch; may closely resemble the song of the Pine Warbler or Dark-eyed Junco. The note is a thin, clear *tseep*, or a dry *chip*.

HABITS: In spring and summer, males sing persistently from a tree, not generally from an exposed perch. They forage both in trees and on the ground; in migration, they frequently occur in large, loose flocks feeding in short grass, and sometimes in trees. The flight is fairly strong, fast and direct. They are apparently monogamous.

HABITAT: Characteristically breeds in dry, open woodlands or woodland edge with grassy understory, orchards, parks, golf courses; in coniferous, deciduous, or mixed woods.

BREEDING: *Nest* is placed in a bush or tree, commonly a conifer, often in an open grassy area, from 1–19 m (3–56 ft) high (usually less than 6 m), and rarely on the ground. The nest is a neatly woven cup of dead grasses, rootlets, and weed stems, lined with finer grasses, hair or rootlets; nests are commonly placed along lateral branches rather than near the trunk. The female alone builds the nest. Nesting takes place March (in the south) through July. Commonly double-brooded, but may raise up to three broods in the south. *Eggs*, 3–5, usually 4, light blue, sparsely spotted with brown, blackish, or sometimes lavender, or rarely without spotting. *Incubation*, 11–14 days; young fledge at 9–12 days. Commonly parasitized by cowbirds.

RANGE: *Breeds* from e-c and se Alaska and c Yukon (Dawson) east to Great Bear L. and se to n Saskatchewan (L. Athabasca, Reindeer L.), Manitoba (very rare north to Churchill), n Ontario (north to Big Trout L., Moosonee; rare north to Fort Severn, Attawapiskat), Quebec (north to Eastmain, Mingan), and sw Newfoundland (Codroy Valley), south to c and sw Georgia, the Panhandle of Florida (irregular), Louisiana, ne Texas and the Edwards Plateau, c Oklahoma, and c Kansas, Nebraska

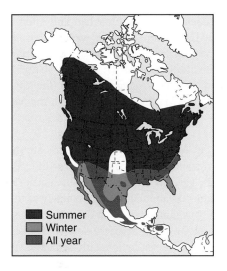

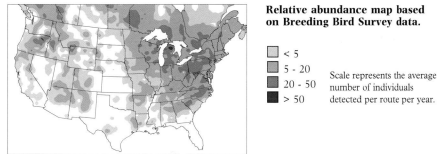

**Relative abundance map based
on Breeding Bird Survey data.**

☐ < 5
☐ 5 - 20
■ 20 - 50
■ > 50

Scale represents the average
number of individuals
detected per route per year.

(except for the southwest), and in the west, south through British Columbia (except on the Queen Charlotte Is.) to northern Baja California, and in the highlands through c Colorado and c New Mexico, and Mexico to n-c Nicaragua, e Guatemala, and Belize.

Winters from c California, s Nevada, c Arizona and New Mexico, n Texas, s Oklahoma, Arkansas, Tennessee, Virginia, Maryland, rarely north to Nova Scotia and s Ontario, Minnesota, Idaho, Nebraska, south to c Mexico. Most common in winter in s Arizona, s New Mexico, c Texas, and the southeast (but rare in the southern Peninsula of Florida). Casual to n Alaska (Barrow, St. Lawrence I.), n Newfoundland (St. Anthony), Costa Rica, Bermuda, the n Bahama Is.

Resident in n Baja California, the Mexican highlands (south to Chiapas and Oaxaca), Belize, Guatemala, e Honduras, and nw Nicaragua.

HISTORY: In 1810, when the American ornithologist Alexander Wilson named the Chipping Sparrow, he called it *Fringilla socialis*, the social 'sparrow', a fitting name for this little sparrow which is easily approached and often closely associated with human habitations. (The Latin name 'fringilla' was used by a Roman poet for a small bird, perhaps the European Robin (*Erethacus*) or House Sparrow (*Passer*), and now generally associated with the Chaffinch (*F. coelebs*).) Unbeknownst to Wilson, the species had been named in 1798, *Fringilla passerina* (the 'sparrow-like sparrow') by the German biologist Johann Matthaeus Bechstein on the basis of a specimen from Quebec City.

Of the Chipping Sparrow, Audubon wrote, 'Few birds are more common throughout the United States than this gentle and harmless little Bunting. It inhabits the towns, villages, orchards, gardens, borders of fields, and prairie grounds . . . The Chipping Sparrow is almost as abundant in our country as the Domestic Sparrow is in Europe, and it is nearly as familiar, though otherwise different in its habits.' Not a bird of the deep woods, the Chipping Sparrow doubtless benefited substantially from the clearing of the forests in the east by the early settlers. Today, although still common in cities and towns in some parts of its range, the Chipping Sparrow is apparently less common than it was in Audubon's time.

GEOGRAPHIC VARIATION: Three subspecies from north of Mexico are generally recognized: the Eastern Chipping Sparrow (*Spizella p. passerina*), Canadian Chipping Sparrow (*S. p. boreophila*), and the Western Chipping Sparrow (*S. p. arizonae*). *S. p. boreophila*, which breeds in the north and northwest east to Manitoba and western Ontario, is supposedly larger and more grayish than *S. p. passerina*, but differences, if any, are slight. *S. p. arizonae*, of the west, is slightly larger and paler in coloration than *S. p. passerina*, but these differences cannot be safely determined in the field.

MEASUREMENTS: *Eastern Chipping Sparrows* (9 males): wing 67–71 (69), tail 53–60 (57), tarsus 15.8–16.8 (16.3), exposed culmen 8.9–9.7 (9.4), bill depth at base 5.3–5.8 (5.6); (9 females): wing 63–71 (67), tail 51–60 (55), tarsus 15.5–16.8 (16.3), exposed culmen 8.6–9.6 (9.1), bill depth 5.3–5.6 (5.4).

Western Chipping Sparrows (18 males): wing 67–76 (72), tail 54–65 (61), tarsus 16.0–18.0 (17.0), exposed culmen 9.1–10.4 (9.7), bill depth 5.3–5.8 (5.6); (14 females): wing 67–76 (72), tail 54–61 (59), tarsus 16.3–17.5 (17.0), exposed culmen 8.9–10.2 (9.7), bill depth 5.3–5.8 (5.6) (Ridgway 1901).

Mass: (58 adult males) 12.0 g (10.5–14.6); (22 adult females) 12.2 g (10.5–14.6) (Pennsylvania, May–June) (Clench and Leberman 1978).

Reference: Kaufman (1990).

Fall Chipping, Clay-colored, and Brewer's sparrows at a glance

Characteristic	Chipping	Clay-colored	Brewer's
Crown	Medium brown, some-times with some red; thin black streaks; median stripe indistinct or missing	Buff brown; with thin brown streaks; median stripe paler buff; usually visible	Buff brown; thin brown streaks; median stripe usually missing
Supercilium	Distinct; pale whitish buff	Distinct; buffy	Indistinct; grayish buff
Lores	Dark	Pale	Pale
Post-ocular Stripe	Dark & broad	Dark & broad	Thin & indistinct
Ear-coverts	Brown; moustachial stripe indistinct	Light brown; darkly outlined; moustachial distinct	Pale grayish brown; moustachial indistinct
Malar	Pale grayish buff; indistinct	Buff; distinct	Whitish; indistinct
Nape	Brown; dark streaks	Often grayish; paler streaks	Light brown; thin streaks
Side of neck	Gray; contrasts with ear-coverts	Gray; contrasts with ear-coverts	Grayish buff or gray; contrasts with ear-coverts
Tertials	Edged with rusty brown	Edged with pale rusty brown	Edged with pale rusty brown
Breast	Pale grayish brown	Pale buff	Pale grayish buff
Rump	Grayish; often washed brown	Buffy-brown	Buffy-brown

18 **Clay-colored Sparrow** *Spizella pallida* [561]   PLATE **8**

D. BEADLE 95.

IDENTIFICATION: 12.5–14 cm (*c.* 5–5.5 in), sexes similar in coloration; males slightly larger.

The Clay-colored Sparrow is a small, slim sparrow with a long, notched tail, unstreaked breast, buffy brown ear-coverts, broad white supercilium, and whitish median crown-stripe.

Similar species: The light brown ear-coverts, distinctly outlined by a dark brown fringe, relatively bright whitish buff supercilium, and thin pale central crown-stripe usually separate the Clay-colored Sparrow from the similar Brewer's Sparrow. Juvenile and first-winter Clay-colored, Brewers, and Chipping sparrows are similar. The facial pattern of juvenile Clay-colored Sparrows is generally more distinct than that of Brewer's: the supercilium of Brewer's Sparrow is grayish whereas it is buffy on Clay-colored; the moustachial stripe and outline of the ear-covert are less distinct in Brewer's than in Clay-colored. Juvenal Chipping Sparrows usually lack rufus in the crown, but have a distinct, thin stripe from the eye to bill; juvenile Clay-colored Sparrows have an indistinct median crown-stripe.

Adult—*Head:* streaked, dark brown crown with a distinct pale central stripe, a broad, brownish or grayish white supercilium, pale lores that contrast little with the supercilium, brown ear-coverts that are distinctly outlined by a thin, dark brown fringe and a dark brown moustachial stripe, thin but distinct moustachial malar stripes, side of neck gray; **back:** brown with distinct dark brown stripes; **rump:** brown; **wing:** brown with middle and lesser coverts edged in beige forming two indistinct wing-bars; **tail:** long, thin, notched, unstreaked; **underparts:** chin and throat unstreaked, white, breast and flanks pale, warm beige, belly whitish; **bill:** pale reddish brown with a dusky tip, upper mandible darker than lower; **legs** and **feet:** pale brownish or pinkish; **iris:** dark reddish brown.

First-winter (Aug–Apr) resemble adults, but buffier, brown streaks on crown thinner making the central stripe less distinct, nape gray; some may retain some flank streaking.

Juveniles (July–Sept) similar to adults, but crown streaked with blackish and median stripe buffy, nape gray, throat and flanks with distinct, thin brown streaks and spots; rump brown and uppertail-coverts buffy with thin brown streaks; supercilium indistinct, but pale dull buff, the dark fringe around the ochre-brown ear-coverts and richer brown color separate it from Brewer's Sparrow; both species molt before migration.

VOICE: The song is a series of 2–8 (usually 2–3) short (about 2 s each), low-pitched, loud insect-like buzzes, **zee-zee-zee** or **buzz-buzz-buzz** or **bzztt-bzztt-bzztt**. The note is a sharp **tsip**, **seep** or **chip** or a weak **tsip-tsip**.

HABITS: In spring and summer males may sing persistently, and singing birds may be readily approached. Males sing from a perch, generally 0.3–2 m high, occasionally up to 6 m. They sing throughout the day, but most persistently during the morning, and only occasionally at night. Chases are common during pair formation. The birds forage on the ground or in bushes, hop but do not run. Territories may be small, and local densities high, giving the impression that they are loosely colonial; often feed off territory.

HABITAT: Clay-colored Sparrows breed in open, uncultivated brushy areas, where bushes are interspersed with grassy areas. In the northern prairies, where they breed commonly, they are characteristically found in rose, snowberry or wolfberry thickets, often along a stream or near the edge of a pond. They also occur in alder, willow, birch, or poplar parkland. They have recently expanded their breeding range east through central Ontario into southern Quebec and New York where they are often found in abandoned fields with scrub and small trees, burns, or young conifer plantations. Where Brewer's and Clay-colored sparrows co-occur, Clay-colored Sparrows appear to occupy areas of denser and more diverse vegetation. In migration they occur in mesquite and other desert shrubs, thickets, weed patches, open woodlands and parks. They generally arrive on their breeding grounds rather late, in mid- to late May.

BREEDING: *Nest* is placed low (near ground to over 1 m [4½ ft], but mostly below

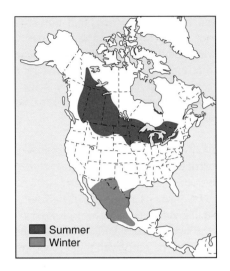

Summer
Winter

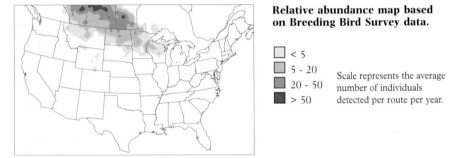

Relative abundance map based on Breeding Bird Survey data.

☐ < 5
☐ 5 - 20   Scale represents the average
■ 20 - 50   number of individuals
■ > 50   detected per route per year.

0.3 m) in a bush or small conifer. In the Canadian prairies, most nests are placed in snowberry. The nest is a woven cup that closely resembles that of the Chipping Sparrow. Eggs are laid 22 May through 7 July; most clutches are completed in late May or the first half of June. Replacement clutches are laid, and the species is sometimes double-brooded. Females generally build the nest, but sometimes males assist. *Eggs*, 3–5, usually 4, light blue, sparsely spotted with brown or blackish, are similar to those of the Chipping and Brewer's sparrow. *Incubation*, 10–14 days; both parents brood young; young fledge at 7–9 days. Clay-colored Sparrows are apparently monogamous. The species is commonly parasitized by cowbirds. Has been reported to hybridize with Chipping and Brewer's Sparrows.

RANGE: *Breeds* from w-c and s Mackenzie (north to Norman Wells), e British Columbia (Fort Nelson, Okanagan Landing), Alberta, nw and c Saskatchewan, across Manitoba and Ontario (irregularly n to Hudson and James bays) into s Quebec (rarely to Gaspé Peninsula), south to New York (irregular, but increasing), Michigan (rare in south), s Wisconsin, and possibly rarely to n Indiana and n Illinois, Minnesota, nw Iowa (formerly?), ne South Dakota, possibly n Wyoming (no breeding records), and perhaps irregularly south to Nebraska, and perhaps w Kansas and e Colorado (recorded breeding from those states may be based on late migrants or refer instead to Brewer's Sparrows), Montana and e Washington (Spokane Valley, possible).

Winters from s Texas south to Veracruz, Oaxaca, Chiapas, and rarely to Guatemala, and (mostly in highlands) to w Mexico and Baja California (uncommon).

Migrates primarily through the Great Plains from the Rocky Mountains east to the Mississippi Valley; occurs regularly, but uncommonly in s California in fall, and east to New York, Pennsylvania, Massachusetts, Delaware (mostly in fall), and the Carolinas and Florida. Has been recorded north to Alaska (mouth of Stikine R.; Camden Bay, North Slope; Haines).

HISTORY: The first specimen of the Clay-colored Sparrow was collected by the English naturalists John Richardson and Thomas Drummond at Carlton House, on the North Saskatchewan River, on 14 May 1827. Of this species, Richardson wrote, 'This Buntling [*sic*] which is even smaller than the Field Sparrow of the United States, visits the Saskatchewan in considerable numbers. It frequents the farmyard at Carlton House, and is as familiar and confident as the common House Sparrow of England.'

Clay-colored Sparrows formerly bred south to northwestern Iowa, but the conversion of brushy prairie into croplands destroyed suitable habitat there. More recently, however, the species has extended its range eastward, through northern Illinois, Michigan, and southern Ontario, where it breeds in abandoned land and Christmas tree farms.

GEOGRAPHIC VARIATION: No geographic variation has been described.

MEASUREMENTS: (8 adult males): wing 59–63 (61), tail 55–62 (58), tarsus 17.5–18.0 (17.8), exposed culmen 8.6–9.9 (9.4), bill depth 5.1–5.8 (5.6); (8 females): wing 58–64 (60), tail 53–61 (57), tarsus 16.8–18.0 (17.5), exposed culmen 8.6–9.9 (9.4), bill depth 5.3–5.8 (5.6) (Ridgway 1901).

Mass: (8 breeding males) 11.7 g (9.8–12.8) (Minnesota and Alberta); (10 breeding females) 12.2 g (10.8–14.5) (Minnesota and Michigan) (Knapton 1994).

References: Houston and Street (1959), Kaufman (1990), Knapton (1994).

19 **Brewer's Sparrow** *Spizella breweri* [562]   PLATE 8

IDENTIFICATION: 12–13 cm (*c.* 5 in), males slightly larger; sexes similar in coloration.

Brewer's Sparrow is a small, slim sparrow with a long, notched tail. The finely streaked, brown crown, dull gray supercilium, obvious thin white eye-ring and generally duller coloration, separate Brewer's Sparrow from the similar Clay-colored Sparrow.

Similar species: See Clay-colored Sparrow.

Adult—*Head:* the streaked brown crown lacks a distinct pale central stripe (although some birds appear to have the hint of a stripe); supercilium pale dull gray to dull whitish (usually not as bright as in Clay-colored); lores pale; eye-ring thin and white; ear-coverts brown, not outlined by a dark fringe; moustachial and malar stripes thin and brown (less distinct than those of Clay-colored); side of neck grayish-brown or brownish and faintly streaked; ***rump:*** brown; ***back:*** brown with dark brown streaks or rows of spots; ***wing:*** brown, median and greater coverts edged with buff forming two poorly defined wing-bars; ***tail:*** long, notched and brown; ***underparts:*** throat pale and unstreaked; breast and flanks dingy gray; belly dull white; ***bill:*** conical, small, pale brown with a dusky tip; ***legs*** and ***feet:*** pale pinkish or pale horn color; ***iris:*** dark.

Young in first-fall (June–Aug) similar to adults, but less sharply streaked above, buffier above, and wing-bars buffy and more distinct.

Juveniles (July–Aug) similar to adults, but less streaked above and with breast and flanks narrowly streaked with black triangular marks. Less rufous in scapular region than Chipping Sparrow, which it resembles. Chest, upper belly and flanks of 'Timberline Sparrow' (*S. b. taverneri*, see below) *heavily* streaked, making these separable from Brewer's Sparrows (*S. b. breweri*).

VOICE: There are two distinct songs. The long song is varied and sustained with a variety of buzzing, bubbling, wheezing, and 'canary-like' trilling on different pitches. The short song is a ***bzzzzzzz chip-chip-chip-chip . . .***, the second part on a slightly lower pitch than the buzz; the first part of the song is like that of a Clay-colored Sparrow, the second like Chipping Sparrow. Individuals often engage in flock singing, especially on the breeding grounds, but even in migration and in winter. The note is variously described as a weak ***tsip***, ***chip***, or ***seep*** (very like Clay-colored Sparrow).

HABITS: Brewer's Sparrows are unusually gregarious when not breeding, when they often can be found in fairly large and surprisingly vocal flocks. They forage on or near the ground, characteristically in sagebrush. On the breeding ground they can be quite inconspicuous, and do not flush easily when on nests. They may breed in fairly high densities, and are perhaps loosely colonial.

HABITAT: Throughout most of their range, Brewer's Sparrows are closely associated with sagebrush at a wide range of elevations. They are, however, sometimes found in mountain mahogany, rabbitbrush, piñon–juniper woodlands or in bunch grass prairie; the isolated northern populations (the 'Timberline Sparrow') is found in balsam–willow or dwarf birch habitat at or above timberline. In migration, they occur in a variety of habitats, including weeds and brush, agricultural, and urban areas. In winter they can be found in creosote bush deserts and in other low, xeric vegetation.

BREEDING: *Nest* is placed on or near the ground (rarely 3.25 m) in a sagebrush or other low bush (dwarf birch). The nest is a compact cup of grass and weed stems lined with fine grass and sometimes hair. Nesting takes place mid-Apr to early Aug. Replacement clutches are produced, and the species is occasionally double-brooded. *Eggs*, 3–5, usually 3–4, light blue, sparsely spotted with brown or blackish, and resemble those of the Chipping and Clay-colored sparrows. *Incubation*, 10–12 days; young fledge at 7–9 days; young are brooded by both parents. Brewer's Sparrows are occasionally polygynous. The species is commonly parasitized by cowbirds.

RANGE: *Breeds* from extreme e-c Alaska (Nutzotin Mountains), sw Yukon (Kluane region) the interior of nw British Columbia and w Alberta (Jasper Park) (Timberline Sparrow), and from c Alberta southeast to sw Saskatchewan (Cypress Hills) and sw North Dakota and south (generally east of the Cascades) through se British Columbia, sw Saskatchewan and nw North Dakota, w South Dakota, w Nebraska, w Kansas (locally), w Oklahoma (Cimarron Co., rare), Colorado, nw New Mexico, and Utah, to c Arizona, e and s California (east of the Sierra Nevada, Modoc Plateau, scattered mountains in south), and n Baja California.

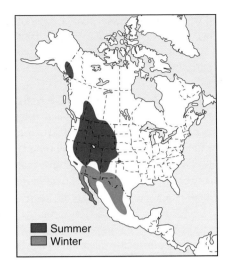

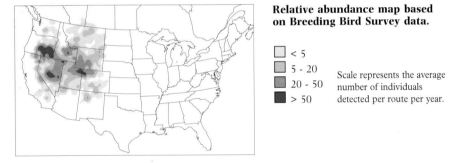

Relative abundance map based on Breeding Bird Survey data.

☐ < 5
☐ 5 - 20
■ 20 - 50
■ > 50

Scale represents the average number of individuals detected per route per year.

Winters from c and s interior (rare on coast) California, s Nevada, c Arizona, and c and w Texas south to s Texas, in the Mexican highlands to Jalisco and Guanajuato, the Pacific lowlands of c and n Mexico, and s Baja California.

Migrates east through e Colorado and rarely to w Kansas and Oklahoma, and along the coast of California.

HISTORY: After studying specimens in the collection at the Philadelphia Academy of Science, in 1856 John Cassin separated Brewer's Sparrow from the similar Clay-colored Sparrow, and named it in honor of Thomas Mayo Brewer, a Boston physician, naturalist, and politician. His father, Colonel James Brewer, participated in the Boston Tea Party. Although his contemporary Elliott Coues once referred to Brewer as a 'cantankerous old ass,' he clearly was one of the foremost American naturalists of the 19th century, writing, among other things, 'North American Oölogy; being an Account of the Habits and Geographical Distribution of the Birds of North America during their Breeding Season,' and contributing to Baird, Brewer, and Ridgway's 'A

History of North American Birds.' He was, however, one of the few ornithologists who supported the introduction of the House Sparrow into North America.

GEOGRAPHIC VARIATION: Two subspecies are generally recognized: Brewer's Sparrow (*S. b. breweri*) and the Timberline Sparrow (*S. b. taverneri*). The Timberline Sparrow, which breeds in mountains from Alaska, Yukon, and northwestern British Columbia south locally to south-central Alberta and eastern British Colombia is slightly larger and darker than *S. b. breweri*, although the difference is subtle and it is not yet clear whether or not they can be recognized in the field. Where their ranges overlap, *S. b. breweri* breeds at lower elevations, in sagebrush. There are winter specimens of Timberline Sparrows from southern California, Arizona, New Mexico, and west Texas; most specimens from southern California and Arizona are *S. b. breweri*. There is genetic divergence between these two subspecies, which may soon be separated into two species. Brewer's Sparrows may hybridize occasionally with Clay-colored Sparrows.

MEASUREMENTS: *S. b. breweri* (10 males): wing 61–65 (62), tail 59–67 (61), tarsus 16.6–18.0 (17.2), exposed culmen 8.0–8.5 (8.2); (10 females): wing 58–60 (59), tail 58–60 (59), tarsus 16.2–17.5 (17.1), culmen 8.0–8.8 (8.4).

S. b. taverneri (6 males): wing 62–66 (64), tail 63–68 (65), tarsus 17.0–18.0 (17.3), exposed culmen 7.0–8.5 (7.8); (3 females): wing 60–62 (61), tail 57–62 (60), tarsus 17–18 (17.6), exposed culmen 8.0–8.5 (8.2) (Swarth and Brooks 1925).

References: Graber (1955), Harrison (1978), Kaufman (1990), Swarth and Brooks (1925).

20 **Field Sparrow** *Spizella pusilla* [563]   PLATE 7

IDENTIFICATION: 12–14 cm (*c.* 5–5.5 in), males slightly larger; sexes similar in coloration, though males may be slightly brighter and darker.

The Field Sparrow is a slim bird, with rusty cap, pink bill, thin but distinct eye-ring, gray face, rusty on upper flank by the bend in wing, and unmarked underparts.

Similar species: Worthen's Sparrow, which has only once been reported north of Mexico, is similar (especially to western Field Sparrows), but lacks the eye-ring and any rust on the upper flank, near the bend of the wing; there is no rust in the post-ocular stripe of ear-coverts of Worthen's, but this can be faint on western Field Sparrows; Worthen's has darker, usually blackish, legs. American Tree Sparrow is larger, has a more distinctly patterned face, a dark upper mandible and yellow mandible, and a distinct dark central breast spot. Adult Chipping Sparrows have a darker rusty crown, and distinct white supercilium and eyeline stripe. Juveniles can be separated from other *Spizellas* by their pink bills.

Adult—*Head:* pinkish rusty cap, sometimes with a faint, grayish median stripe (more prominent in west); side of head light gray with a white eye-ring and a small rusty eye-stripe (less prominent in west); ***back:*** pinkish rusty nape; back rusty brown with darker brown streaking; ***rump:*** unstreaked or slightly streaked light-brown; ***wing:*** brown, rusty coverts and two whitish wing-bars; ***tail:*** moderately long, dark brown and notched, and edged with light gray; ***underparts:*** gray, with rufous wash on breast and flanks (rufous less prominent in west); ***bill:*** pink; ***legs:*** pale brown or pinkish yellow; ***iris:*** brown. ***Fall and winter*** birds may appear buffier than summer ones.

First-fall (July–Oct) resemble adults, but usually with indistinct streaking on the breast and sides..

Juveniles (July–Sept) similar to adults without rusty colors. Crown dull gray to brown, and breast and flanks with light dusky streaks.

VOICE: The song is a series of from 2 to several clear, plaintive, run-on whistles that accelerate and ascend into a trill, and can be written ***swee-swee-swee-swee-wee-wee-wee-wee***. The note is a ***tsip***, ***zweep***, or sharp ***chip***. Field Sparrows begin to sing early in the morning, and may sing at night.

HABITS: On the breeding grounds, males sing persistently, often from an exposed perch in a bush in an old field. Singing rate decreases markedly after pair formation. They are solitary or occur in small flocks (often of mixed species composition) in winter. They are not generally difficult to see, and respond to spishing.

HABITAT: Field Sparrows breed in old fields with scattered bushes, blackberry tangles, sumac, deciduous thickets, and small trees (commonly hawthorn and pines), and brushy fencerows. In the mid-west, Field Sparrows are particularly common in all seasons in broomsedge fields interspersed with small trees.

BREEDING: ***Nest*** is placed on the ground or low in vegetation up to 1 m; early nests are usually placed on the ground in a clump of grass or weed clumps, but later ones are often higher (up to 1 m) in a dense bush (blackberry, hawthorn, small trees, etc.). The nest is a cup of woven grasses, lined with finer grasses and often hair. Nesting takes place from mid-Apr to early Aug, and the species is frequently double-brooded. ***Eggs***, 2–5, usually 3–4, are white or pale bluish, and speckled with small brown dots. ***Incubation***, 11–17 days (11.6 average in Michigan); female alone broods, but both parents feed the young; young fledge in 7–8 days. The species is usually monogamous, but occasionally polygynous. Frequently parasitized by cowbirds.

RANGE: ***Breeds*** from s Manitoba (local), nw and se Montana, c Minnesota, Michigan (uncommon and local in the Upper Peninsula), s Ontario, sw Quebec and s New Brunswick south to Georgia (except in the extreme southeast), n Florida and the Florida Panhandle, the Gulf Coast, west to c Texas, Oklahoma (rare in the Panhandle), e Colorado (local), South Dakota (except for Black Hills).

Winters from Massachusetts, s Ontario (rare), s Michigan, s Wisconsin, Ohio, Indiana, Illinois, Missouri, and Kansas (rare in west) south through Texas (rare in west), se New Mexico to n Mexico (Coahuila, Nuevo León, Tamaulipas), the Gulf coast and s Florida.

HISTORY: The Field Sparrow was first described and named by Alexander Wilson, on the basis of birds from around Philadelphia, Pennsylvania. In pre-colonial times, it was probably less common in the northeast than today, as much of that area was

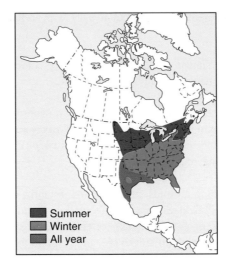

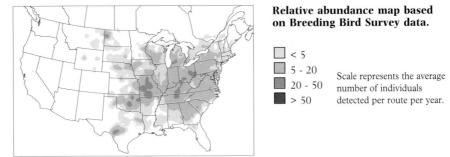

Relative abundance map based on Breeding Bird Survey data.

☐ < 5
☐ 5 - 20   Scale represents the average
☐ 20 - 50   number of individuals
■ > 50   detected per route per year.

covered by heavy forest. Initially, the clearing of the land little benefited the species because the cultivation was intense. However, when marginal farms were abandoned, they reverted to old-fields, and Field Sparrows flourished. In the 1800s, Audubon wrote that 'In South Carolina they are met with along every hedgerow and in every briar-patch, as well as in the old fields slightly covered with tall slender grasses, on the seeds of which they chiefly subsist during the inclement season. Loose flocks, sometimes of forty or fifty, are seen hopping along the sandy roads, picking up particles of gravel.' During the latter part of the 19th century and the first half of the 20th century, the species became abundant in the northeast in the summer, but has declined in the last 20–30 years, as the trend of pastures reverting to old-fields has slowed.

GEOGRAPHIC VARIATION: Two subspecies are generally recognized: the Eastern Field Sparrow (*S. p. pusilla*), which breeds west to the Great Plains, and the Western Field Sparrow (*S. p. arenacea*), which breeds east to Minnesota, central Kansas and Oklahoma (where the two subspecies intergrade). *S. p. arenacea* is similar to *S. p. pusilla*, but wings and especially the tail are longer, the coloration is grayer, the cap usually has a gray median stripe, the rusty eyeline usually lacking or less obvious, and rusty colors are paler.

MEASUREMENTS: (males from Pennsylvania): flattened wing (N=117) 62–70 (66), tail (N=22) 55–67 (62), tarsus (N=22) 16.0–18.0 (17.1), exposed culmen (N=22) 8.0–12.0 (10.5), longest toe (N=22) 14.0–17.0 (15.5); wing (N=141) 59–65 (62), tail (N=26) 55–65 (60), tarsus (N=27) 15.0–18.0 (16.4), culmen (N=27) 8.0–11.0 (9.6), toe (N=27) 14.0–16.0 (15.0) (Carey *et al.* 1994).

Mass: (15 breeding males) 13.1 g (11.5–14.3); (17 breeding females) 13.0 g (11.4–14.0) (Pennsylvania) (Carey *et al.* 1994).

Reference: Carey *et al.* (1994).

21 **Worthen's Sparrow** *Spizella wortheni* [564]   PLATE 7

D. BEADLE.

IDENTIFICATION: 13–14 cm (*c*. 5–5.5 in), males slightly larger; sexes similar in coloration.

Worthen's Sparrow is a small, slim bird, with a pink bill, light rusty crown, no wing-bars, and a gray, unpatterned side of face, breast, flanks, belly, and dark legs.

Similar species: Worthen's Sparrows resemble the Field Sparrows, particularly western Field Sparrows. See that species' account.

Adult—*Head:* crown rusty; forehead gray or rusty gray; side of face gray, with a thin white eye-ring; ***back:*** pale brown with dark brown streaking; ***rump:*** brownish gray, with centers of some feathers light brown; ***wing:*** brown, with two indistinct buffy wing-bars; ***underparts:*** breast light gray with rust anterior to the bend of wing, throat and belly whitish; ***tail:*** brown, edged with pale gray; ***bill:*** pinkish orange; ***legs:*** black or horn colored; ***iris:*** dark.

First-winter probably like adults.

Juveniles are similar to juvenal-plumaged Field Sparrows, but differ by '. . . possessing a prominent, pale buffy eye-ring and a more prominent and more buffy post-ocular stripe' (Webster in Austin 1968).

VOICE: The song is a ***peee churrrrr***, with the initial note slurred and generally but not always on a lower pitch, or a dry rattle, resembling that of the Chipping Sparrow.

HABITS: In the breeding season males sing persistently from dawn through mid-morning from a low perch. Worthen's Sparrows generally feed on the ground. In winter, they usually occur in single-species flocks (commonly of about 10 birds) that usually stay in tall grass, but will enter shortgrass (grazed) areas to feed. Pair formation occurs in Mar.

HABITAT: This little-known bird apparently breeds in weedy, overgrown fields and in open, dry shrubby desert, from 1200 to 2450 m. In Zacatecas it is found in mesquite grassland near the edge of the pine–oak forest, between 2350–2450 m; in Coahuila it is found in fairly tall grassland interspersed with *Yucca* and small junipers.

BREEDING: *Nest* is placed near to the ground (within 15 cm) near the base of a shrub. The nest is a woven cup of grasses lined with finer fibres or hair. Nesting records are from 4 May through 15 July. *Eggs*, 3–4, bluish, speckled, spotted or blotched with brown.

RANGE: *Resident* in Coahuila, Nuevo León (probable), Chihuahua (probable), southwestern Tamaulipas and Zacatecas; also recorded from San Luis Potosí, Puebla, and Veracruz; most recent records are from Zacatecas and bordering states. Although there is some post-breeding wandering, the species probably is not migratory.

HISTORY: The type specimen of Worthen's Sparrow was collected by Charles Kimball Worthen, a naturalist, collector, and artist, on 16 June 1882, near Silver City, New Mexico. The species was described by Robert Ridgway, and named in honor of Worthen. Interestingly, the species has not been reported from New Mexico since the original collection. Doubtlessly the species formerly bred north into southern New Mexico and Arizona, but was extirpated by habitat alterations. There may also be, or have been, local populations in Pueblo, Veracruz, and central Chihuahua. Many consider Worthen's Sparrow to be a subspecies of the Field Sparrow.

GEOGRAPHIC VARIATION: None described.

MEASUREMENTS: (7 males): wing 67–70 (69), tail 60–64 (62), tarsus 17.5–18.5 (18.0), exposed culmen 9.4–9.9 (9.7), bill depth 5.3–5.8 (5.6); (2 females): wing 65–68, tail 58–64, tarsus 17.0–17.5, culmen 8.9–9.1, bill depth 5.3 (1 measurement) (Ridgway 1901).

Reference: Wege *et al.* (1993).

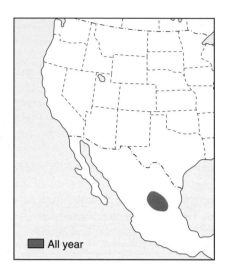

All year

22 **Black-chinned Sparrow** *Spizella atrogularis* [565] **Plate 7**

IDENTIFICATION: 12–14 cm (*c.* 5–5.5 in), males slightly larger; males usually have a darker face than females.

The Black-chinned Sparrow is a small, slim, dark gray sparrow with a long tail, striped brown back, and pinkish bill.

Similar species: Black-chinned Sparrows do not closely resemble any other sparrows; they look like slim 'Gray-headed Juncos,' without white in the tail..

Adult male—*Head:* gray, with black around the base of the bill; ***back:*** rusty or cinnamon-rufous brown, streaked with black; ***rump:*** gray or olive-gray; ***tail:*** long, dark grayish brown and unpatterned; ***wing:*** brown or rusty brown with indistinct wingbars; ***underparts:*** gray, with dull white belly; ***bill:*** pink; ***legs:*** deep brown or dusky; ***iris:*** dark.

Adult female like adult male, but usually with the black of the chin less extensive, duller, or missing.

First-fall and winter (Aug–Mar) like adult females, but the chin and throat without black, not contrasting with the breast and often brownish gray instead of gray, and with streaks on the back narrower and less sharply defined, edges of wing coverts more rusty, and underparts paler, indistinctly streaked with light gray.

Juveniles (June–July) similar to adult females, without black on the face, and back streaks narrower, tertials broadly edged with pale rust, and chest gray, becoming nearly white on belly, indistinctly streaked (variable) with light gray.

VOICE: The song is canary-like or Field Sparrow-like, a clear trill that begins with a series of 2 or 4 emphatic clear slurred notes and ends with a gradually descending or ascending trill, ***sweet sweet sweet te te te te te***, or ***cheet cheet trrrrrrrr***. The note is a single thin ***seep***, ***cheep***, or ***tsweet***.

HABITS: This is not generally a conspicuous species, although territorial males sing persistently from an exposed perch. It feeds both in bushes and on the ground, and flight is generally near the ground.

HABITAT: Characteristically breeds in dry chaparral in the foothills of coastal California, and similar brushy habitats (commonly in tall and fairly dense sagebrush, greasewood, or open juniper woodlands) in rugged, rocky country. It is a local species, generally not widespread and uncommon even within its usual range, although in good habitat local densities may be high. It may be loosely colonial.

BREEDING: ***Nest*** is placed in a bush (commonly sagebrush) less than 1 m high, but off the ground. The nest is often a loose cup of grasses and plant fibers, lined with finer grasses, feathers or hair. Nesting takes place from late Apr through May. ***Eggs***, 2–5, usually 2–4, light blue, with little or no spotting. ***Incubation***, no information; both parents attend young. Parasitized by cowbirds.

RANGE: ***Breeds*** from c California (San Francisco region), the southern Sierra Nevada south to n Baja California, and east across s Nevada and Utah, c and se Arizona, c New Mexico, and w Texas (Chisos and Guadalupe mountains), south in the Mexican highlands to Guerrero, Oaxaca, and Puebla.

Winters from coastal California (casually), extreme se California, s Arizona and New Mexico, w Texas, and Nuevo León south to s Baja California and highlands of Mexico.

HISTORY: The German ornithologist Jean Louis Cabanis discovered the Black-chinned Sparrow in Mexico in 1851, and named it *Spinites atrogularis*. Cabanis was the founder and long-time editor of the prestigious *Journal für Ornithologie*. It is not certain where Cabanis obtained his specimen, but it probably was near Mexico City. The Black-chinned Sparrow seems to be relatively uncommon wherever it is found, and little appears to be known about long-term trends in abundance.

GEOGRAPHIC VARIATION: North of Mexico, three subspecies are generally recognized: *S. a. caurina*, which breeds in the coastal ranges of central western California (Oakland south to San Benito Mountains); *S. a. cana*, which breeds in the mountains of south-central and south-western California, south to northern Baja California; *S. a. evura*, which breeds east of the Sierra Nevada, south and east to southern Arizona

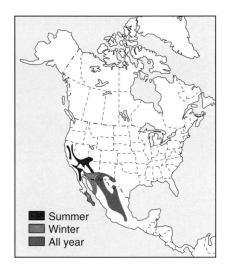

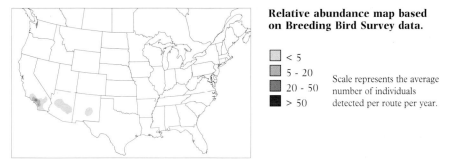

Relative abundance map based on Breeding Bird Survey data.

☐ < 5
☐ 5 - 20
■ 20 - 50   Scale represents the average
■ > 50   number of individuals
                 detected per route per year.

and New Mexico, and west Texas. *S. a. evura* averages larger and paler than the Pacific coastal forms, which are poorly differentiated. These cannot reliably be differentiated in the field.

MEASUREMENTS: (15 males): wing 60–70 (64), tail 61–74 (68), tarsus 17.5–20.3 (18.8), exposed culmen 8.6–10.2 (9.4), bill depth at base 5.8–6.1 (6.0); (13 females): wing 60–65 (61), tail 60–70 (65), tarsus 18.0–19.8 (18.8), exposed culmen 8.6–9.9 (9.1), bill depth at base 5.8–6.1 (6.0) (Ridgway 1901).

S. a. cana (30 males): wing 59–65 (63), tail 62–69 (67), tarsus 17.3–19.5 (18.3), culmen 8.2–8.9 (8.5).

S. a. caurina (5 males): wing 61–65 (64), tail 69–70 (70), tarsus 17.3–19.7 (18.3), culmen 7.8–8.7 (8.3) (Miller 1929).

Reference: Miller (1929).

23 **Vesper Sparrow** *Pooecetes gramineus* [540]   PLATE 9

D. BEADLE 94.

IDENTIFICATION: 13.5–15 cm (*c.* 5–6 in), males slightly larger; sexes similar in coloration.

Vesper Sparrows are fairly large, have a streaked breast, notched tail with distinct white edges to the outer tail feathers, a rusty shoulder (lesser coverts), conspicuously streaked back, and a thin, but distinct eye-ring.

Similar species: The Savannah Sparrow, which may occur in the same habitat, is smaller, shorter-tailed, has a distinct median crown-stripe, a yellow supercilium, and lacks the eye-ring and rusty shoulder. Vesper Sparrows generally appear paler than Savannah Sparrows. Baird's Sparrows have conspicuous yellow-ochre head markings, have large bills, and appear to be flat-headed. Juvenile Grasshopper and LeConte's sparrows are streaked below, but are noticeably smaller than Vesper Sparrows, and have short tails. Wintering Lapland and Smith's longspurs also have white edges to the lateral tail feathers; Lapland Longspurs have rusty greater coverts. Longspurs in general are chunkier, shorter-tailed birds than Vesper Sparrows, and unlike Vesper Sparrows are often found in flocks, often with Horned Larks or Snow Buntings. Song Sparrows are usually much more heavily streaked below, with a central breast spot, and a long, rounded tail; only a few Vesper Sparrows will have a breast spot.

Adult male—*Head:* crown and nape grayish brown, conspicuously streaked with dark brown; supercilium and submoustachial stripes grayish or buffy, paler than other facial markings, but not distinct; thin white eye-ring; ear-coverts pale in center, but dark toward the back; moustachial and malar stripes brown; throat pale, with

① Pooecetes g. gramineus   ② Pooecetes g. confinis

indistinct spotting; ***back:*** nape and mantle grayish brown, with dark centers to feathers, making the back conspicuously streaked; ***rump:*** less conspicuously streaked than back; ***tail:*** brown, with outer web and tip of outermost (6th) rectrix white, 5th variable, but usually with some white in the outer web; ***wing:*** brown, with tips of median and greater coverts, and tertials edged buffy or buffy white, forming one or two indistinct wing-bars; lesser coverts rusty; ***underparts:*** throat buffy or buffy white and indistinctly spotted; breast and flanks narrowly streaked with brown; belly white; undertail-coverts whitish; ***bill:*** upper mandible dusky brown; lower mandible pinkish or flesh colored; ***legs:*** pinkish or flesh colored; ***iris:*** light brown or brown.

First-fall (July–Oct) resemble adults, but are perhaps less brightly colored, with less rusty lesser coverts.

Juveniles (May–Aug) resemble adults, but are much darker on back, feathers with blackish centers, narrowly edged in pale beige; ventral streaking darker and more extensive; rusty lesser coverts indistinct.

VOICE: The song of the Vesper Sparrow is sweet and musical, generally starting with two long clear notes, often downward slurs, followed by shorter flutelike trills, often rising then falling in pitch; sometimes the long notes at the beginning are the highest, with the remainder of the song declining in pitch. The song reminds one of that of the Song Sparrow, but is sweeter and more plaintive. The name notwithstanding, Vesper Sparrows sing throughout the day, as well as after sunset. Rarely, a flight song is given. The call note is a sharp ***chirp***.

HABITS: Vesper Sparrows nest in sparse, open fields with song perches. Although territorial males sometimes sing from the ground, they usually seem to prefer a high perch, often in a tree at the edge of a field, or the top of a shrub. They walk or run along the ground, and sometimes use a double-scratch when feeding. Females incubate closely, and often perform a broken-wing distraction display when flushed from the nest. In migration and winter, Vesper Sparrows are usually found in small, loose

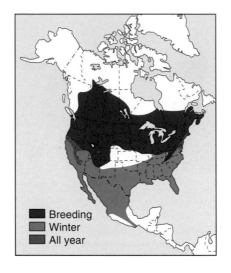

Breeding
Winter
All year

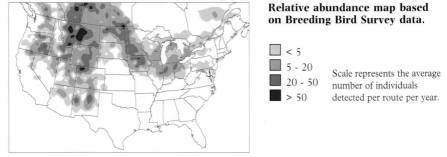

Relative abundance map based on Breeding Bird Survey data.

< 5
5 - 20
20 - 50
> 50

Scale represents the average number of individuals detected per route per year.

flocks of up to 10 individuals. When flushed, they typically fly to a nearby tree or bush, and perch in the open. They commonly take dust baths.

HABITAT: In the east, Vesper Sparrows are found in sparse pastures and cultivated land (often nesting in corn stubble of the previous year), gravelly, well-drained areas, and fairly dry pastures. Suitable singing perches appear to be an important part of a territory. In the west, Vesper Sparrows are characteristic of sagebrush–grass habitats of higher elevations; dry, open ponderosa–pine parkland, and sometimes in sagebrush in piñon–juniper; and alpine and subalpine shortgrass meadows. In winter they are found in weedy or grassy pastures, prairies, old burned areas, or woodland clearings.

BREEDING: *Nest* is placed on the ground, often in a depression dug by the birds, at the base of clump of grass, thistle, or even a clod of dirt. The nest is often near patches of bare ground, or where vegetation is sparse. The female alone probably builds the nest. Nesting begins in late Mar (Kentucky), mid-Apr (Michigan) to mid-May (British Columbia), and continues through mid-Aug. *Eggs*, 2–5, usually 3–4, are creamy white or pale greenish white, with brownish spots or blotches. *Incubation*, 11–13 days; both parents will incubate and feed the young; young leave the nest after 7–12 days; the species is double-brooded. Vesper Sparrows are frequently parasitized by cowbirds.

RANGE: *Breeds* from c and s British Columbia (Victoria, rare), Peace R. parklands, s Mackenzie (probably Fort Smith and Fort Simpson), Alberta (rare in north), Saskatchewan (north to Lake Athabasca, Wollaston L.), Manitoba (north to Thompson), c and s Ontario (north to Sioux Lookout and Moose Factory), s Quebec (north to Lac Saint-Jean; Gaspé Peninsula), New Brunswick, Prince Edward I., Nova Scotia (except Cape Breton) south to s California (San Bernardino Mountains), c Nevada (Elko Co., Reno, Eureka), Utah, c and ne Arizona (south to Mogollon Plateau), c New Mexico (Zuñi and Sangre de Christo mountains), w and c Colorado, w Kansas (summer records from Morton and Russell cos.), Nebraska, n Missouri (north of Missouri R.), Illinois (rare in south), Indiana (uncommon in south), Ohio, n-c Kentucky (local; not reported recently), West Virginia (except southwest), Virginia (mountains), e Tennessee, North Carolina (south to Buncombe and Haywood cos.), Maryland (uncommon), and Delaware (uncommon; declining).

Winters se Oregon (Willamette and perhaps Umpqua and Rogue valleys; rare), sw Utah (rare), c and s Arizona, s New Mexico, Texas, s Oklahoma (rare), Kansas (very rare), Missouri (rare), Arkansas (irregular in north), Louisiana, Tennessee, Kentucky (rare), s Ontario (rare), and along the Atlantic Coast from Nova Scotia (rare), Massachusetts (rare), New York (rare), and Maryland (uncommon), south to Florida, Guerrero, Oaxaca, n Veracruz, and s Baja California. Most common in winter in c California, s Arizona, New Mexico, Texas, and n and c Florida (rare in s Florida).

Casual or accidental in Yucatán, Chiapas, Guatemala, the Bahamas, and Bermuda.

HISTORY: Audubon, and other early American ornithologists, called this species the 'Bay-winged Bunting,' a name far more appropriate than 'Vesper Sparrow,' given to these birds because some thought that its '. . . song was sweeter and more impressive toward evening.' Vesper Sparrows have declined in abundance in the east in this century, probably reflecting changes in agricultural practices. In some regions, the 19th and early 20th century habit of leaving one-quarter of the fields fallow each year would have benefited the Vesper Sparrow, as they nest readily in short fields; in others, the abandonment of marginal, sandy farmlands has resulted in the loss of the shortgrass habitat, with exposed sand and rocks, that the species prefers. Today, it is endangered in Rhode I. and New Jersey.

GEOGRAPHIC VARIATION: Three subspecies are generally recognized: the Eastern Vesper Sparrow (*P. g. gramineus*), Western Vesper Sparrow (*P. g. confinis*), and the Oregon Vesper Sparrow (*P. g. affinis*). *P. g. confinis* is slightly larger than *P. g. gramineus*, with a narrower bill, paler and grayer back coloration, and reduced and thinner breast and flank streaking. *P. g. affinis* is like *P. g. confinis*, but smaller in size, with ground coloration tending to be buffy brown rather than grayish brown. Vesper Sparrows cannot reliably be identified to subspecies in the field; *P. g. affinis* and *P. g. confinis* probably cannot be separated consistently in the hand.

MEASUREMENTS: Eastern Vesper Sparrow (14 males): wing 77–84 (81), tail 59–66 (61), tarsus 20.3–22.1 (21.1), exposed culmen 10.7–12.2 (11.2), bill depth at base 7.9–8.9 (8.4); (13 females): wing 73–81 (77), tail 55–62 (59), tarsus 20.1–21.3 (20.6), exposed culmen 10.4–11.7 (10.9), bill depth 7.6–8.1 (7.9).

Western Vesper Sparrow (11 males): wing 79–87 (84), tail 63–69 (66), tarsus 20.8–22.1 (21.6), exposed culmen 10.9–11.7 (11.2), bill depth 7.4–8.4 (7.6); (14 females): wing 76–84 (80), tail 58–68 (62), tarsus 19.8–22.4 (21.3), exposed culmen 10.4–12.5 (11.2), bill depth 7.1–8.1 (7.6).

Oregon Vesper Sparrow (7 males): wing 74–80 (77), tail 53–60 (58), tarsus 19.8–21.6 (20.6), exposed culmen 10.2–11.4 (10.9), bill depth 6.4–7.6 (7.4) (Ridgway 1901).

Mass: (28 males) 26.5 g, (15 females) 24.9 g (Michigan) (Dunning 1993). (10 males) 25.8 g (24.3–27.2), (4 females) 24.9 g (21.3–28.9) (Saskatchewan and North Dakota, June and early July) (Rising, unpublished).

24 **Lark Sparrow** *Chondestes grammacus* [552]   PLATE **9**

D·BEADLE 95.

IDENTIFICATION: 14–16 cm (*c.* 5.5–6.5 in), sexes similar in coloration; males slightly larger.

The Lark Sparrow is a fairly large sparrow with a brightly colored chestnut, black and white face, conspicuous white in the tail, and an unstreaked breast with a prominent breast spot, and a long, rounded tail.

Similar species: This is a distinctive sparrow. In head patterning, it resembles the slightly smaller Sage Sparrow, which also has an unstreaked (or slightly streaked) breast and a prominent breast spot, but the Sage Sparrow lacks rusty or chestnut marking on the face and obvious white in the tail, and is grayish rather than brownish in general hue. Young and juvenile Lark Sparrows have a lightly streaked breast and flanks, but a white throat and conspicuous white in the corners of the tail.

Adult—*Head:* white or light beige median crown-stripe, rusty or chestnut lateral crown-stripes, becoming blackish near bill; white supercilium; thin black eyeline stripe; wide white crescent under eye; chestnut ear-coverts with a white spot at the posterior; white submoustachial stripe; prominent black malar stripe that becomes broader toward the neck, and a white throat; ***back:*** nape warm brown, slightly streaked with darker brown; mantle brown with conspicuous brown stripes; ***rump:*** brown and unstreaked; ***tail:*** brown with outer 3–4 rectrices boldly tipped with white and outer two edged laterally with white; ***wing:*** brown, with bases of primaries

Chondestes grammacus strigatus

conspicuously whitish (producing a rather distinct band); primary coverts dark; median coverts dark brown, boldly tipped in white (forming a wing-bar); **underparts:** throat white; breast pale beige with a bold, brown breast spot; flanks pale beige; belly dull white; undertail-coverts dull white, slightly spotted with light brown; **bill:** yellowish, or pinkish gray, paler below; **legs:** dull flesh color; **iris:** sepia or brown.

First-winter (July–Nov) resemble adults but head marking duller, and brown streaking on the breast and flanks.

Juveniles (May–July) underparts heavily streaked; head has brown lateral, not rusty, crown-stripes and ear-coverts, and whitish submoustachial stripes.

VOICE: The song is musical and variable, a broken series of clear notes, **twee twee trerere trerere twee twee twee**, introduced with one or two clear **twee** notes, followed by some gurgly and rough buzzy notes, and one to three more clear notes. An individual singing bird may vary his song in a singing bout. The call note is a sharp, distinctive, warbler-like **tsip**, or a metallic **chip** or **cheep**, often given in flight.

HABITS: Lark Sparrows breed in open, dry woodland, or at the edge of dry woodland. They are easily flushed, and often will fly to a fence or low branch; they often fly high and for long distances. Males sing persistently from an exposed perch, up to 3–4 m, often from a cottonwood tree in a field or at the edge of woods. On the ground they either walk or hop; grasshoppers are a major food. In migration and winter they generally occur in flocks, which often consist only of Lark Sparrows, but sometimes other sparrows as well.

HABITAT: Lark Sparrows are common in open cottonwood woodland, especially along rivers, scrubland, mesquite, or oak savannah, piñon–juniper woodland, and ponderosa pine interspersed with bunch grass. In winter they may be found in agricultural areas or large suburban gardens, oak woodlands, chaparral, and mesquite and acacia mixed with grassland.

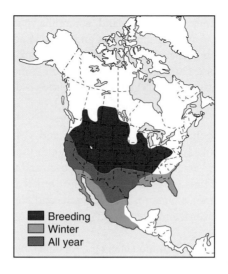

Breeding
Winter
All year

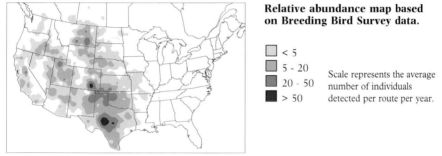

Relative abundance map based on Breeding Bird Survey data.

☐ < 5
◻ 5 - 20
◼ 20 - 50   Scale represents the average
◼ > 50   number of individuals
                   detected per route per year.

BREEDING: *Nest* is placed on the ground, often at the base of bunch grass, or a small cactus, thistle, or bush (sagebrush, rabbitbrush) to up to 3 m high in a tree (live oak, cottonwood, sycamore, mesquite — sometimes in mistletoe). The nest is a cup of grass, twigs, rootlets, and bark fibers lined with finer grass, leaves and sometimes hair. The female alone builds the nest. Nesting begins in mid-Apr, and continues through July. *Eggs*, 3–6, usually 4 or 5, are white, bluish white, or brownish white, lined or speckled with dark brown or reddish or purplish brown. *Incubation*, 11–12 days; female alone incubates, but both parents feed the young; young leave the nest after 6 days; may be double-brooded. This species is frequently parasitized by cowbirds.

RANGE: *Breeds* from w Oregon (Rogue and Umpqua valleys), e Washington, s interior British Columbia (Okanagan and Similkameen valleys, Richter Pass, north to Kamloops), se Alberta (north to Big Valley and Czar), Saskatchewan (north to Nipawin and Battleford), s Manitoba, w Minnesota (south to Clay Co.), e-c and se Minnesota (Minnesota and Mississippi river valleys), w and c Wisconsin, s Michigan (extirpated?), sw Ontario (north to Bruce Co., Durham; rare, probably extirpated), and formerly east to Pennsylvania, Maryland, w Virginia (one record), and possibly North Carolina, south to West Virginia (rare and local; Pendleton, Hampshire and Jackson cos.), nw and w-c Alabama, nw and n-c Louisiana, Texas, n Tamaulipas, Nuevo León, Zacatecas, Durango, s Chihuahua, ne Sonora, and s California. Breeding east of the Mississippi Valley, where the species is declining in numbers, is local and irregular.

Winters from sw Oregon, California, s Nevada, c and s Arizona, s Utah, s New Mexico (rare), Oklahoma (casual), c and e Texas, south through Mexico to s Baja California, Chiapas and Veracruz, along the Gulf Coast, and uncommonly along the Atlantic Coast from Virginia (rare) to s Florida. Has wintered north to Alberta (Red Deer), Wisconsin (Racine), s Ontario, Massachusetts and New York. Most common in winter in Texas, s Arizona, and California (Central Valley).

In migration regular, but uncommon along the Atlantic Coast, especially in the fall; very rare along the coast of British Columbia. Casual or accidental in Alaska (Scottie Creek), n Saskatchewan, Manitoba, Ontario, se Quebec, the Maritime Provinces, and Newfoundland, and south to Yucatán, Guatemala, El Salvador, Honduras, Cuba, and the Bahamas. Recorded twice in England (Suffolk, June–July; Norfolk, May).

HISTORY: The Lark Sparrow was first collected near St. Louis, Missouri on the Long expedition to the Rocky Mountains. Thomas Say named the species *Fringilla grammaca*. In colonial times, the Lark Sparrow was strictly a western bird, found east to Illinois. However, in the 19th century, species extended its range eastward, as the forests were cleared for farms. After becoming common in many places west of the Allegheny Mountains by the 20th century, Lark Sparrows have again declined in the east, and today they are rare or local there. For example, the first record for Ohio was 1861; their population there peaked in the first 10 years of the 20th century, by 1935 they were local, and today they are rare. In Pennsylvania, the species was first reported breeding in 1893, but has not been reported breeding since 1931. In West Virginia the Lark Sparrow was first recorded in 1900, and became abundant there between 1910 and 1925; today it is rare and local. The decline in the east probably occurred as marginal farms reverted to second-growth forest.

GEOGRAPHIC VARIATION: Two subspecies are generally recognized: the Eastern Lark Sparrow (*C. g. grammacus*) and the Western Lark Sparrow (*C. g. strigatus*). Eastern Lark Sparrows, which breed from Minnesota, eastern Kansas and northeastern Texas eastward, are slightly darker in coloration, with darker chestnut markings on the head and wider streaks on the back. They are very similar, and cannot be reliably separated in the field, and probably not in the hand.

MEASUREMENTS: Eastern Lark Sparrow (8 males): wing 82–94 (87), tail 65–78 (70), tarsus 19.8–20.3 (20.1), exposed culmen 10.4–12.2 (11.4), bill depth at base 7.6–8.1 (7.9).

Western Lark Sparrow (48 males): wing 81–92 (87), tail 64–76 (70), tarsus 19.3–21.6 (20.3), exposed culmen 10.4–13.7 (11.9), bill depth 7.6–8.9 (8.1); (32 females): wing 79–89 (84), tail 61–71 (68), tarsus 18.8–20.8 (20.3), exposed culmen 10.7–13.0 (12.2), bill depth 7.6–8.4 (7.9) (Ridgway 1901).

Mass: (N=49) 29.0 g (24.7–33.3) (California) (Dunning 1993). (12 males) 30.1 g (27.2–33.0), (8 females) 30.7 g (25.5–32.6) (Kansas, June) (Rising, unpublished).

Genus *Amphispiza*

The genus *Amphispiza* contains four species, all of which breed north of Mexico. They are small to medium-sized sparrows with rather long tails and pointed wings, relatively small bills, are unstreaked or slightly streaked below, and have striking white superciliary and sub-moustachial stripes, and a black breast or breast spot. They live in dry shrub or chaparral habitats in the Great Basin, southwest and northern Mexico.

The relationships of the *Amphispiza* to other sparrows are not clear, although they are often thought to be closely related to sparrows in the genus *Aimophila*. The Lark Sparrow (*Chondestes*), in turn, may also be a close relative.

25 **Black-throated Sparrow**

PLATE 10

Amphispiza bilineata [573]

D. BEADLE 94.

IDENTIFICATION: 12–14 cm (*c*. 5–5.5 in), males slightly larger; sexes similar in coloration.

Black-throated Sparrows are medium-sized sparrows with a prominent white supercilium, white malar stripe, and black throat and breast. Their back and wings are sandy brownish, tail brownish black with white tips to the outermost feathers (in unworn bird), and belly grayish to pale grayish brown.

Similar species: The bold, black throat and breast separate the Black-throated Sparrow from others; the white markings on the face are more extensive than those on Sage and Five-striped sparrows which are also larger in overall size. Juveniles resemble juvenile Sage Sparrows, but the supercilium on Black-throated is longer, extending well behind eye, and brighter. The crown is not spotted or streaked, and crown and back somewhat darker.

Adult—*Head:* crown and ear-coverts brown or grayish brown, supercilium long, extending to nape, and white, sometimes partially thinly bordered with black dorsally; lores and throat black, malar stripe white, with a thin white eye-ring under the eye; ***back:*** sandy brownish, becoming grayish brown toward nape; ***rump:*** brownish; ***tail:*** blackish, with the tips of the outermost rectrix white (often inconspicuous in worn individuals), and outer webs of lateral feathers whitish; ***underparts:*** chin, throat, and breast black, with the black terminated in a black 'v' on the breast, the black bordered by grayish white, becoming darker and browner on the flanks and

① Amphispiza b. bilineata   ② Amphispiza b. deserticola

belly, undertail-coverts light beige and unpatterned; ***wing:*** brown, with feathers edged with pale brown, coverts, scapulars, and tertials edged with buff; ***bill:*** dark gray, with lower mandible paler bluish gray; ***legs:*** dark gray; ***iris:*** dark brown.

First-fall and winter (Apr–Nov) similar to adults, but without any distinct black markings on the head, the supercilium, chin and throat white, the throat sometimes flaked with grayish, the breast more or less distinctly streaked, the coverts and tertials edged with buffy brownish, and the back with obscure dusky streaks. First-year birds apparently migrate before completing their prebasic molt.

Juveniles (Mar–July) crown dark gray-brown, lores and ear-coverts gray, partial white eye-ring, supercilium white, not extending to nape, nape and upper back tinged with brown-gray, rump grayish or brownish gray, uppertail-coverts brown, darker than back, rectrices black, outer ones tipped with white and white on outer webs; throat mottled with gray, breast, upper belly, and flanks finely streaked with gray, lower belly and undertail-coverts light buffy, wings blackish (not as dark as tail), with coverts and tertials edged with light rusty brown.

VOICE: The song is a short pleasant, tinkling, rapidly repeated ***tchi-tchi twrrr*** or ***tsp tsp tsp tsp churrrrr***, or ***pip chip churrrrr***, or ***wut wut zeeeee*** with initial notes quick and distinct and the last a prolonged silvery trill, often on a different pitch than the introductory elements; also ***chee-whee whit wherrrrr cha cha cha*** or ***che cha cherrrr chee***. There is a great deal of variability in the song, both within a population and in the repertoire of a single individual. The call is a low ***chip*** or tinkling notes.

HABITS: Males sing from an exposed perch on a low shrub, and chases are common when territories are being established. On the ground, the species moves in short hops or occasionally runs; it is not difficult to see. In winter it gathers in small flocks, often mixed flocks, including Brewer's, Chipping, Sage, and White-crowned sparrows, or Cactus Wrens and Verdins.

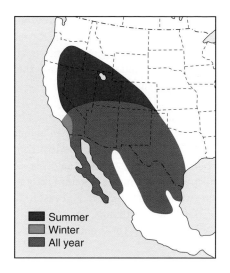

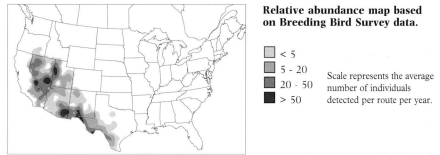

**Relative abundance map based
on Breeding Bird Survey data.**

■ < 5
■ 5 - 20   Scale represents the average
■ 20 - 50   number of individuals
■ > 50   detected per route per year.

HABITAT: The Black-throated Sparrow is a bird of sparse xeric shrubs of the southwest, most commonly found on hillsides, where ocotillo, cactus, mesquite, cat-claw and other thorny plants predominate, or in saltbush, greasewood, canotia, and creosote, interspersed with taller plants (e.g., Joshua trees); in some areas they are found in sagebrush, antelope brush, and rabbit brush, perhaps interspersed with piñon–juniper. It can be found from below sea level (Death Valley) to over 2200 m, but below 1500 m in the northern part of their range. In winter it may occur in riparian areas.

BREEDING: *Nest* is loose cup of fine grasses, stems, twigs, and plant cotton, lined with finer grasses and often fur, hair, wool, or feathers. Nests are placed at the base of a cactus or bush (usually canotia or creosote bush in Arizona), or in a tuft of grass, on or near the ground (occasionally to 2 m), in a bush. Nesting takes place from Feb through mid-Aug, with most records from Apr–June. *Eggs*, 2–4, usually 3–4, are bluish white or greenish white and usually unmarked, but occasionally slightly spotted with brown. *Incubation* and fledging times are not reported. Parasitized by cowbirds.

RANGE: *Breeds* from s-c and se Oregon (n and w to Wheeler and Klamath cos.; uncommon), Idaho, sw Wyoming (Farson and Green R.; rare), south to nw and s Colorado (uncommon), w Oklahoma (Black Mesa; uncommon), Texas (e to Armstrong, Young and Nueces cos.), and through e California to s Baja California, c Sinaloa, Hidalgo, Querétaro, Guanajuato and n Jalisco.

Winters from s California, s Nevada, sw Utah, c Arizona, s New Mexico, Oklahoma (Kenton; very rare), and c and s Texas (rarely n to the Panhandle) south through the breeding range, and rarely to coastal s California. Most common in winter from s Texas, s New Mexico, c and s Arizona, and se California, southward. Casual in w Canada (British Columbia, Alberta; summer), South Dakota (Dec), Nebraska (winter and summer), Kansas (winter and summer), and east to Minnesota (Sept), Ohio (summer), Wisconsin (Oct–May), Illinois (Sept–Apr), Ontario (Oct), and Massachusetts (Apr), Virginia (Oct–Apr), and south to w Florida (Feb) and Louisiana.

HISTORY: The Black-throated Sparrow was first described by the American ornithologist John Cassin, on the basis of specimens from Rio Grande R. in Texas, where the species is common today. The clearing of brush on rangeland has decreased the abundance of this species, and their numbers declined both in Texas and the southwest during the 1970s. Nonetheless, it is widespread and remains one of the commonest of desert birds.

GEOGRAPHIC VARIATION: Three subspecies are generally recognized north of Mexico, *A. b. bilineata* (c Texas south into Mexico), *A. b. opuntia* (w Oklahoma, s Colorado, south through w Texas and New Mexico), and *A. b. deserticola* (Oregon, Wyoming, and w Colorado south to Mexico). These are poorly marked, and cannot be separated in the field. *A. b. bilineata* is smaller on average, is darker, and has a larger spot on the lateral rectrix, than *A. b. opuntia* or *A. b. deserticoln*. None of these are well marked, and the species needs more study.

MEASUREMENTS: (6 males from Texas and ne Mexico): wing 62–66 (63), tail 58–63 (59), tarsus 18.0–19.8 (18.8), exposed culmen 9.7–9.9 (9.9), bill depth at base 6.1–6.4 (6.4); (6 females from Texas and ne Mexico): wing 60–66 (62), tail 55–62 (58), tarsus 17.5–18.5 (18.0), exposed culmen 9.7–10.2 (9.9); (7 males from sw US): wing 64–71 (67), tail 61–68 (64), tarsus 18.0–19.8 (19.1), exposed culmen 9.9–10.7 (10.2), bill depth 5.6–6.4 (6.1); (9 females from sw US): wing 62–66 (64), tail 59–63 (60), tarsus 17.0–18.8 (18.3), exposed culmen 9.9–10.7 (10.2), bill depth 5.6–6.4 (6.1) (Ridgway 1901).

Mass: (89 birds from Arizona) 13.5 g (10.2–16.4) (Dunning 1993).

26 **Bell's Sparrow** *Amphispiza belli* [574]   PLATE 10

D. BEADLE.

IDENTIFICATION: 12.5–14.5 cm (*c.* 5–6 in), males slightly larger; sexes similar in coloration.

Bell's Sparrow is a medium-sized sparrow with a conspicuous white supraloral spot and submoustachial stripe, a broad black malar stripe, and a conspicuous black breast spot.

Similar species: The Sage Sparrow is like Bell's Sparrow in general pattern and coloration, but paler. The back of Bell's Sparrow is deep gray-brown, contrasting little with the tail, whereas the tail of Sage Sparrow is noticeably darker than the back. The dorsal striping of Bell's Sparrow is indistinct; because the back of Sage Sparrow is paler, the streaking is more conspicuous. The facial markings are blackish and more striking, and the flank and breast streaking generally somewhat less extensive on Bell's Sparrow. Bell's Sparrow is also significantly smaller than Sage Sparrow, and this can sometimes be detected in the field.

Adult—see Sage Sparrow.

First-fall and winter (June–Aug) is similar to Sage Sparrow, but darker.

Juveniles (Apr–July) are similar to Sage Sparrows, but darker.

VOICE: The vocalizations of Bell's Sparrows are like those of Sage Sparrows, but persons familiar with them can detect differences. The song is a thin, tinkling, but musical *tweesitity-slip*, *tweesitity-slip*, *swer* or *tst twzeee-twzeee-do twzeey-twzu* or a sing-song *chappa-chee*, *chip-chippa-chee* with the song lasting 2–3 s. The call note is a high, thin *tik* or *tik-tik*.

HABITS: Males are conspicuous when they sing from the top of a bush, but otherwise Bell's Sparrows are difficult to see. Like Sage Sparrows, they hop or run beneath bushes, but they appear to run less frequently, and are more difficult to see because of their denser habitat.

HABITAT: Bell's Sparrows are generally found in chaparral dominated by dense chamise (greasewood), but may also be found in baccharis and coastal sagebrush, and in brush mixed with cactus in arid washes.

BREEDING: *Nest* is a cup of weed fibers, lined with finer fibers, fur, or cottony seed heads, placed 15–60 cm high in dense brush. Nesting takes place mid-Mar (San Clemente I.), or Apr through June (usually Apr and May). *Eggs*, 3–5, usually 4, are like those of Sage Sparrow in color.

RANGE: *Resident* in California and Baja California from the inner Northern Coast Range from Shasta and Trinity cos., south to coast in Marin Co., and along coast and in foothills south to Bahia Ballenas, Baja California; also in the western Sierra Nevada from El Dorado Co. south to Mariposa Co. Some wander in winter, rarely to se California. An isolated population on San Clemente I., California was endangered because of habitat destruction by goats, but the goats have been removed and the habitat is recovering.

HISTORY: Like the Black-throated Sparrow, Bell's Sparrow was named by John Cassin in 1850. Cassin named the species in honor of its collector, John Graham Bell, who collected specimens at Sonoma, and later at San Diego, California. Bell was a taxidermist from New York whom Audubon employed to accompany him on his expedition to the Upper Missouri in 1843. On that trip, Bell along with Edward Harris collected several new species, including Sprague's Pipit, Bell's Vireo, Baird's Sparrows, and Smith's Longspur. After returning to New York, Bell went westward to collect specimens in the newly acquired territory of California, where in addition to Bell's Sparrow he collected the first specimens of White-headed Woodpecker, Williamson's Sapsucker, and Lawrence's Goldfinch. Although Bell's Sparrow has been 'lumped' with Sage Sparrow in recent times, it is a distinctive bird and the ranges of the two do not overlap when both are breeding.

GEOGRAPHIC VARIATION: Three subspecies, two found north of Mexico, are recognized. The San Clemente Sage Sparrow, *A. b. clementeae*, found only on San Clemente I., is weakly differentiated, but has a longer bill and lighter juvenal plumage than *A. b. belli*. The Gray Sage Sparrow, *A. b. cinerea*, is similar in size to *A. b. belli*, but paler in color. It is found from latitude 29° south to latitude 26°.

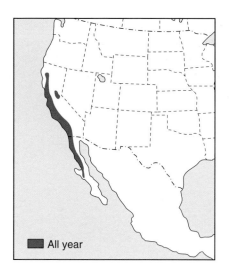

MEASUREMENTS: See table.

Reference: Johnson and Marten (1992).

Measurements (averages in mm) of Male Sage and Bell's Sparrows[a]

Locality (N)	Wing L	Tail L	Bill L	Bill D	Bill W	Tars + Toe	Mass (g)
Amphispiza b. belli							
Coulterville, CA (15)	64.6	66.0	7.39	5.62	3.89	33.8	14.8
Beegum, CA (12)	65.9	65.6	6.88	5.66	3.77	32.9	15.0
Lake Co., CA (11)	66.3	66.8	7.06	5.82	3.91	33.7	15.2
Monterey, CA (8)	65.7	65.7	7.08	5.58	3.75	33.3	15.0
Pozo, CA (12)	66.4	66.4	6.97	5.53	3.67	33.4	15.1
Castaic, CA (14)	67.6	68.2	7.20	5.59	3.77	33.6	15.6
Barona Mesa, CA (8)	67.7	67.0	7.02	5.27	3.64	33.4	14.7
Sacatone Spring, CA (8)	68.1	68.3	7.11	5.30	3.56	33.1	14.4
Amphispiza nevadensis canescens							
Panoche Hills, CA (12)	68.7	69.1	7.55	5.53	3.79	34.3	16.1
Carrizo Plains, CA (16)	68.6	69.0	7.68	5.50	3.71	34.4	16.5
Jawbone Canyon, CA (11)	70.6	69.0	7.37	5.35	3.68	33.7	16.5
Coso Junction, CA (8)	71.2	69.0	7.48	5.44	3.78	33.7	16.8
Squaw Flat, CA (8)	71.2	68.2	7.61	5.40	3.81	33.5	16.7

Amphispiza n. nevadensis

Chalfant Valley, CA (7)	76.4	71.4	8.10	5.69	4.14	35.3	18.1
Benton Valley, CA (12)	76.1	70.7	7.96	5.72	4.07	35.5	17.8
Queen Valley, CA (15)	77.0	72.2	8.04	5.65	4.32	35.1	18.0
Mono Lake, CA (14)	76.9	72.1	8.15	5.75	4.15	35.6	18.7
Rattlesnake Flat, NV (25)	77.1	71.4	8.12	5.72	4.14	35.1	18.2
Paradise Range, NV (12)	76.8	71.5	8.02	5.63	4.38	35.4	18.7
Pioche, NV (14)	76.7	70.2	8.22	5.91	4.18	34.5	18.7
Denio, NV (15)	77.1	70.8	8.28	5.83	4.22	35.1	18.7
Plush, OR (13)	77.3	73.6	8.45	5.80	4.33	35.9	18.4

[a]from Johnson and Marten 1992

27 **Sage Sparrow** *Amphispiza nevadensis* [574.1]   PLATE 10

IDENTIFICATION: 13.5–16 cm (*c.* 5.5–6.5 in), males slightly larger; sexes similar in color.

The Sage Sparrow is a medium-sized bird with a gray-brown head, sandy brown back, with faint streaking on the back and flanks, a bold white supraloral spot, white eye-ring, and a conspicuous white submoustachial stripe, often outlined with a dark malar stripe — which is usually much darker in birds from the interior of California (*A. n. canescens*) than in birds from the Great Basin (*A. n. nevadensis*) — and a dark breast spot.

Similar species: Bell's Sparrow, of western California, is similar in coloration and pattern, but conspicuously darker and somewhat smaller; the dorsal streaking is usually distinct in Sage Sparrow, and indistinct in Bell's. The Five-striped Sparrow, of southern Arizona, is similar in pattern, but darker, with a wide black malar stripe, and unstreaked gray breast and flanks. Juveniles can be told from Black-throated Sparrows by their less distinct supercilium, pale or white only in front of eye (white extends behind the eye in Black-throated), and streaked crown. The tail is noticeably darker than the back in Sage Sparrow, whereas it is nearly the same color as the back of Bell's Sparrow.

Adult—*Head* and ***nape:*** gray-brown; crown faintly streaked; white supraloral spot and sometimes some of the supercilium; white eye-ring; lores dark; ear-coverts gray;

① Amphispiza nevadensis   ② Amphispiza belli

moustachial stripe dark brown; submoustachial stripe pale buff to whitish; malar stripe dark; **back:** mantle pale brownish with thin dark brown streaking; **rump:** brown; **tail:** dark brown, with outer web and tip of lateral rectrices white in unworn individuals; **wing:** brownish, with scapulars, tertials, and greater coverts broadly edged in buff; **underparts:** throat buffy white; breast slightly darker, often with a necklace of thin, dark stripes; breast spot dark brown; flanks buffy white and thinly streaked; belly dull white; **bill:** dark brown, paler below; **legs:** dark yellow brown; **iris:** dark brown.

First-winter (after Aug) resemble adults.

Juveniles (May–Sept) grayish brown, heavily streaked with brown on crown, nape, and mantle, and undersides, with pale white supercilium in front of eye.

VOICE: The song is a weak, plaintive, high-pitched series of tinkling notes, lasting 3–4 s: *tsit tsit, tsii you, tee a-tee,* or *tsit-tsoo-tseeetsay,* the third note high and accentuated, or *chip-si ship-si-do chip-si-do shu-zup,* with the *do* and *zup* slightly lower. Individual males tend to sing only a single song pattern. Calls are a rapidly repeated, high *te te te te,* or *tse tse tse.* The alarm notes is a thin *tsip,* similar to that of juncos, but weaker.

HABITS: In the Great Basin, Sage Sparrows often arrive on their breeding grounds paired. At that time males sing from the top of sagebrush or other vegetation, twitching the tail while singing. When not singing, they are difficult to detect as they forage on the ground, amongst xeric shrubs. Characteristically, they run rapidly along the ground with tail cocked. Females are difficult to flush from nests, and when flushed, usually run from the nest. Post-breeding birds form loose flocks that may move to higher elevations later in the season.

HABITAT: Sage Sparrows breed in cold desert (saltbush) or semi-desert (big sagebrush) where they are characteristically found in sagebrush, saltbush (Shadscale),

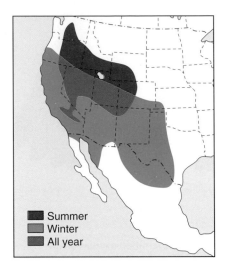

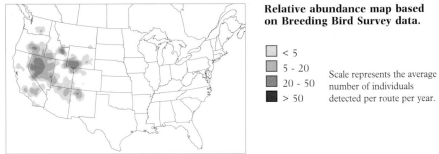

**Relative abundance map based
on Breeding Bird Survey data.**

□ < 5
□ 5 - 20
■ 20 - 50
■ > 50

Scale represents the average
number of individuals
detected per route per year.

antelope brush, and (uncommonly) rabbit brush, from about sea level to nearly 2000 m, generally in places where sagebrush or saltbush are dominant, and in some places where sagebrush is interspersed with scattered juniper or piñon. After breeding, some individuals move to shrubs at higher elevation, and in winter northern birds move south into sagebrush grasslands, into coastal chaparral (chamise). In southeastern California, in winter, they are commonly found in weedy scrub (especially *Suaeda*), often near water (especially in dry years).

BREEDING: *Nest* is built in a depression in the ground, or more commonly low to the ground (10 cm–100 cm; average *c.* 40 cm). The nest is a cup of small sticks, grasses, and shredded bark, often lined with fine shreds of bark, fine grasses, fur, wool, hair, or feathers. Nesting takes place from March through July; later broods are probably replacement clutches. ***Eggs***, 3–5, usually 3–4, are pale blue or bluish white, speckled, spotted, or blotched with brown or occasionally black. ***Incubation***, 13 days; female alone probably broods, but both parents feed; nestling period is not known. Parasitized by cowbirds.

RANGE: ***Breeds*** from east of the Cascade range in c-e Washington and west of the Rocky Mountains in s Idaho, sc and sw Wyoming (Rawlins, Green R. Basin) south to w Colorado, nw New Mexico, ne Arizona, Utah, and west to e-c California (Mono Lake) and c California (Owens and San Joaquin valleys)

Winters from sw Kansas (rare), w Oklahoma (Kenton; rare) w Texas (uncommon), s Colorado (rare), and uncommonly north to Utah, c Nevada and sw Oregon, south to n Chihuahua, n Sonora and n Baja California. Casual in Montana, sw British Columbia, and Nova Scotia (Nov).

HISTORY: Although specimens of *Amphispiza belli* collected in New Mexico, Arizona, and Utah in the 1850s almost certainly were of this species, the type of the Sage Sparrow was designated in 1873 by Robert Ridgway, with the type locality designated as the West Humboldt Mountains, Nevada.

GEOGRAPHIC VARIATION: Two subspecies are commonly recognized, the Northern Sage Sparrow, *A. n. nevadensis*, and California Sage Sparrow, *A. n. canescens*. *A. n. canescens*, which is confined to central California is smaller than *A. n. nevadensis*, and generally slightly richer in coloration; the two cannot be reliably separated in the field. These two probably intergrade in the Owens Valley in east-central California; *A. n. nevadensis* breeds in the Mono Lake, Queen Valley region of east-central California. Bell's Sparrow (*A. belli*) (which see) is often considered conspecific, and the two together called Sage Sparrow (*Amphispiza belli*).

MEASUREMENTS: See table.

Reference: Johnson and Marten (1992).

28 **Five-striped Sparrow**

PLATE 10

Amphispiza quinquestriata [584.2]

IDENTIFICATION: 13–14.5 cm (*c.* 5–6 in), males slightly larger; sexes similar in coloration.

The Five-striped Sparrow is a dark, gray sparrow, with a dark, rusty brown back, and with white superciliary and submoustachial stripes, and bold black malar stripes, outlining the white throat (the fifth stripe). A black central breast spot is not conspicuous, but the white belly stands out.

Similar species: Sage and Bell's sparrows have similar plumage pattern, but are much paler in coloration; Black-throated Sparrow is paler, smaller, with white in the tail and a black throat.

Adult—*Head:* crown, nape, and side of face brownish gray; supercilium, submoustachial stripe, eye-ring, and throat white; malar stripe wide and black; ***back:*** dark rusty gray, without conspicuous marking; ***rump:*** brownish; ***tail:*** dark brown, with light edges; ***wing:*** dark brown, with paler edges to coverts and scapulars; ***underparts:*** chin and throat white; breast and flanks dark gray, with a black breast spot; belly white; undertail-coverts gray with pale edges; ***bill:*** blackish, with lower mandible paler bluish gray; ***legs:*** dull pinkish flesh; ***iris:*** dark.

First-winter (Oct–May) resemble adults, but retain some juvenal wing and tail feathers and coverts; belly yellowish.

Juveniles (July–Sept) crown and back brown, spotted with darker brown, lower back and rump without streaking, tail dark with tips of lateral rectrices white; underparts yellowish and brownish breast and flanks; wings dark, with primaries edged whitish, and secondaries and coverts edged with rust, undertail-coverts brown, tipped yellowish.

VOICE: The song is staccato and brief, lasting just over a second, and is usually composed of an introductory note followed by several note complexes, each usually repeated two or three times, *tsi-gp tsi-gp twsee tweep*, or *chip chip chip pt pt pt*, the second series of elements higher or lower in pitch than the first. Calls are described as *chuck, pip*, and *seet*.

HABITS: On the breeding grounds males sing persistently from the top of ocotillo, mesquite, or other plants. Birds take short flights from bush to bush. On the ground, they generally take short hops, but will run when pursued. In winter they may form small, loose flocks.

HABITAT: Five-striped sparrows are found on steep hillsides, on either side of a wash, with water present year round. The hillsides are covered with fairly dense vegetation, including hackberry, ocotillo, yuccas, acacias, mesquite, and trumpet bush, and, at higher elevations, oak and juniper. In Arizona they are found from 1000–1200 m altitude. They are difficult to find in winter, but some are probably present all year.

BREEDING: *Nest* is a deep cup of grass and stems, lined with fine grass and fur (javelina or horse), built low in dense vegetation. Nesting takes place from June through early Sept (mostly in July and Aug) in Arizona; in Mexico a second brood may be raised in late Aug and Sept. *Eggs*, 3–4, are dull, white and unmarked. *Incubation*, 12–13 days, young fledge after 7 days (?); the female alone incubates and builds the nest, but both parents feed the young. They are commonly parasitized by cowbirds.

RANGE: *Resident* in the Sierra Madre Occidental of n and w Mexico and se Arizona (Pajarito and Santa Rita mountains; Sonoita Creek) and ne Sonora south through sw Chihuahua, e Sinaloa and w Durango. A southern population is found in n Jalisco, s Zacatecas, and w Aguascalientes. Arizona birds may move south in some winters.

HISTORY: The Five-striped Sparrow was first described in 1868 on the basis of a specimen collected in Jalisco, Mexico. Until 1957, this species had not been recorded north of Mexico. Populations in south-central Arizona, although small, appear to be stable and well established; breeding was first documented there in 1969. The status of the Five-striped Sparrow in Mexico is uncertain, and the northern population (Sonora and Arizona) and southern one (southwestern Zacatacas, western Aguascalientes, and northern Jalisco) may not be connected by breeding populations in Sinaloa, although the species occurs there in winter.

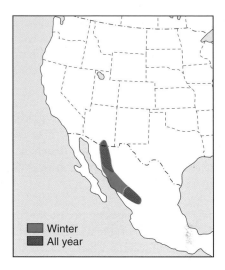

GEOGRAPHIC VARIATION: Only one subspecies nests north of Mexico. Five-striped Sparrows are often put in the genus *Aimophila*, but their placement there is questionable, and their plumage pattern and general ecology more closely resemble *Amphispiza*.

MEASUREMENTS: (16 males): wing 65–74 (71), tail 66–72 (68), tarsus 19.6–20.8 (20.3), exposed culmen 11.4–12.7 (12.2), bill depth at base 6.9–7.1 (6.9); (11 females): wing 64–71 (67), tail 62–72 (68), tarsus 19.1–21.1 (20.3), exposed culmen 11.4–12.5, bill depth 6.9 (1 specimen) (Ridgway 1901).

Mass: (23 males) 19.3 g (17.1–21.7), (4 females) 18.8 g (17.9–19.5) (Dunning 1993).

References: Groschupf (1992), Wolf (1977).

29 **Lark Bunting** *Calamospiza melanocorys* [605]   **PLATE 9**

IDENTIFICATION: 14–18 cm (*c.* 5.5–7 in), males slightly larger; strongly sexually dimorphic in color.

In summer, male Lark Buntings are large, black sparrows with conspicuous white patches in wing, and white corners to tail. Females are large, heavily streaked with chocolate-brown, whitish buff in wings and white corners to tail. Males in winter resemble females, but with black and white on wings, and usually some black on throat and breast.

Similar species: No other species closely resembles the male Lark Bunting. At all seasons, it may be found in the same fields as McCown's and Chestnut-collared longspurs, and female longspurs resemble female or young Lark Buntings. Both longspurs, especially Chestnut-collared, have noticeably smaller bills. The patterns of white in the tail differ: the two longspurs have white toward the bases of the outer tail feathers; Lark Bunting has white tips to the tail feathers (except the central ones). Lapland and Smith's longspurs have white in the outer tail feathers (more pronounced in Lapland than in Smith's); male Lapland in winter has a rusty collar, and male Smith's may have white in the lesser coverts. The scapulars of female and wintering male Lark Buntings are conspicuously edged in pale buffy white.

Adult male in summer—*Head, back,* and *underparts:* black, sometimes flecked with white on the belly; ***wing:*** black, with primaries narrowly edged with white, secondaries tipped in white, and tertials boldly edged in white, coverts white; ***tail:*** outer web white, inner webs of outermost five rectrices tipped with white; ***bill:*** large, conical and bluish, paler below; ***legs:*** brownish, feet darker; ***iris:*** reddish brown.

① Adult female   ② Adult male   ③ Winter male molting

Adult female—*Head:* crown and nape brown, streaked with darker brown; supercilium and lores pale brown; ear-coverts brown, but paler in the center, and with a pale spot on the back edge; moustachial and malar stripes dark brown; submoustachial stripe and throat pale brown; ***back:*** brown, and streaked with darker brown; ***wing:*** brown, with coverts and scapulars broadly edged with very pale brown; ***underparts:*** pale brown, broadly streaked on the neck and flanks; ***tail:*** brown, with all but central rectrices tipped with dull white, especially on the inner webs; undertail-coverts pale brown, with dark brown centers; ***bill:*** dark horn colored; ***legs:*** legs and feet horn colored.

Adult males in winter (Aug–Mar) like adult females, but with varying amounts of white in the face, throat, breast, and belly, remiges, and coverts, and scapulars with broad, whitish edges.

First-winter (Aug–Mar) like adult females; hatching year males obtain some black feathers in a prealternate molt starting in March.

Juveniles (June–Aug) similar to adult females, but with a yellowish cast, and broad, buffy edges to the neck and back feathers, and scapulars, giving a scaly impression; large, pale buffy patch evident on the wings.

VOICE: The song is a musical mixture of short notes and slurred phrases, ***kazee kazee kazee kazee zizizizizi zoo quit quit quit quit trrrrrr too wewewewewew tur tur tur quit quit quit quit***, or ***sweet sweet sweet sweet sweet sweet toot toot toot toot toot chug chug chug tr-r-r-r-r***, often given in a stiff-winged display flight. The call note is a gentle ***who-ee-ee***, ***whee-ta-wer*** or ***hoo-ee***.

HABITS: On the breeding grounds, these are conspicuous birds, with males frequently giving a stiff-winged flight display, rising to 10 m, then floating back to the ground at the end of the display. The birds forage on the ground, and males follow

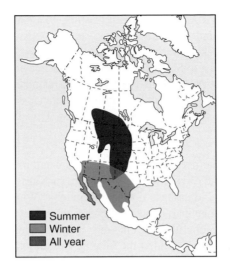

Summer
Winter
All year

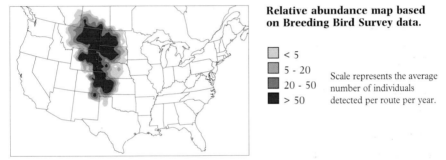

Relative abundance map based on Breeding Bird Survey data.

☐ < 5
☐ 5 - 20
■ 20 - 50
■ > 50

Scale represents the average number of individuals detected per route per year.

females as they forage when they are off the nest. They often seem to breed in loose colonies, in dry grasslands. Locally, their numbers fluctuate greatly from year to year, and in dry years they may nest commonly east of their usual breeding range. In winter they are found in flocks, often large ones.

HABITAT: Lark Buntings breed in shortgrass prairie, sometimes interspersed with sage or other shrubs, as well as stubble fields and alfalfa. In winter, they are found in brushless, weedy dry grasslands, and open farmland.

BREEDING: *Nest* is placed on the ground often near the base of a small shrub or in taller vegetation where it is protected from the afternoon sun. The nest is a simple cup made of grasses and slender plant fibers, often lined with finer grasses, plant cotton, or hair. Nesting takes place from mid-May through mid-July; probably sometimes double-brooded. *Eggs*, 3–7, usually 4–5, are light blue in color and unmarked. Female alone probably builds nest and incubates; males may have two mates. *Incubation*, 12 days; both parents attend young. Parasitized by cowbirds.

RANGE: ***Breeds*** from s Alberta (north to Castor), s Saskatchewan (irregular), sw Manitoba (Lyleton, Brandon), North Dakota (rare in east) and sw Minnesota (casual), s through South Dakota (rare in extreme east), Nebraska (western two-thirds), Kansas (sporadically east to Shawnee and Franklin cos.), e and rarely nw Colorado, w Oklahoma (rare eastward), Texas (irregular in Panhandle, casual in central and southwest), and e New Mexico, and through c Montana, south through Wyoming (less common in west) to nw Colorado and se Utah (Unitah Co.); has bred in wet years in e California.

Winters from s Nevada (irregular), s California (rare and irregular), c Arizona, and s New Mexico and s and e Texas, regularly north to sw Kansas (Morton Co.) and se Colorado (Baca Co.), and casually north to Manitoba (Winnipeg) and Minnesota (Winona), south to Tamaulipas, Jalisco and Baja California. Very rare or casual n (in every season) to Oregon, Washington, and British Columbia, and east to se Louisiana, Wisconsin, Ontario and to the Atlantic Coast, from Nova Scotia south to Florida.

Migrates through California (commoner in fall).

HISTORY: The first specimens of the Lark Bunting were collected by the Philadelphia naturalist, John Kirk Townsend, who accompanied Thomas Nuttall on his journey to the Columbia R. in 1833. On the plains of the Platte R. in western Nebraska, and later in southeastern Wyoming, Townsend saw hundreds of these distinctive, black sparrows. Lark Buntings are among the least philopatric of the sparrows, appearing and breeding commonly in a place one year, only to be absent there the next. It is thus difficult to assess changes in their populations. Nonetheless, they appear to have been increasing slightly in numbers in recent years in their breeding range, but have declined significantly in numbers in California. They are a species that would benefit from efforts to preserve shortgrass and bunch grass prairies. The affinities of the Lark Bunting are uncertain. Like longspurs, it is highly sexually dimorphic in color, and gathers in large flocks in winter (like blackbirds). The male's 'butterfly flight' display is longspur-like (especially like McCown's), but many birds, such as chats and mockingbirds, have similar displays.

GEOGRAPHIC VARIATION: None has been described.

MEASUREMENTS: (6 males): wing 85–92 (88), tail 66–71 (69), tarsus 22.9–25.9 (24.4), exposed culmen 13.2–14.7 (14.0), bill depth at base 10.7–11.9 (10.7); (6 females): wing 82–85 (83), tail 60–69 (66), tarsus 22.4–25.2 (23.9), culmen 12.7–13.2 (12.7), bill depth 10.2–11.9 (10.7) (Ridgway 1901).

Mass: (40, both sexes, from Arizona) 40 g (29.5–51.5) (Dunning 1993).

Reference: Shane (1974).

30 **Savannah Sparrow** *Passerculus sandwichensis* [542] PLATE 11

IDENTIFICATION: 11–15 cm (*c.* 4.5–6 in) males slightly larger; sexes similar in coloration.

Typically, Savannah Sparrows are brown or dark brown streaked both on their back and breast, have pink legs, a yellow (usually) supercilium, whitish median crown-stripe, and a medium to rather short, notched tail with no white. Their flight is direct, and they generally are not difficult to see. Variable (see below).

Similar species: The Song Sparrow is larger than the Savannah Sparrow, with a longer, rounded tail and larger bill; the crown-stripe is less distinct than in the Savannah Sparrow, and it lacks yellow in the supercilium (as do some Savannah Sparrows). Both species, however, are highly variable, and habitat and behavior are useful aids to identification. Savannah Sparrows are found in open fields or the edges of fields, and when flushed their flight is direct. Song Sparrows are found in edge or brush habitats and when flushed their flight is slightly undulating, with their long tail flopped slightly to one side. The central breast spot, often said to be a good field mark for Song Sparrow, is often present on Savannah Sparrows. Vesper Sparrows are larger and longer-tailed, with a thin but conspicuous eye-ring, no median crown-stripe or yellow in the supercilium, and they have rusty shoulders (lesser coverts); in flight, they show white in their outer tail feathers (Savannah Sparrows may have pale, but not white outer feathers). Baird's Sparrow appears flat-headed and large-billed; the entire head is washed with yellow ochre, and with a buffy ochre crown-stripe; territorial Baird's Sparrows are rather easy to see, but otherwise they are secretive and hard to flush, unlike Savannah Sparrows. Juvenile Grasshopper Sparrows have streaked breasts, but are short-tailed and flat-headed.

Typical Savannah Sparrow (most of North America): Adult—(medium-sized, 11.2–13.7 cm; larger in Aleutians); ***head:*** lateral crown-stripes brown, streaked with

dark brown; median crown-stripe whitish; supercilium yellowish; supraloral spot yellow; eyeline dark brown; moustachial and malar stripes dark brown; submoustachial
stripe whitish, ear-coverts brown to grayish brown, darker on the back margin; **back:**
dark (especially in the northeast) to pale (especially in the west) brown, streaked with
scapulars and back feathers with dark centers and pale edges; **rump:** brown and
streaked; **tail:** brown, slightly notched, with outer webs of feathers somewhat paler,
but not white; **wing:** brown with indistinct beige wing-bars; **underparts:** white to
buff, variably streaked with brown on flanks and breast (commonly coalescing into a
central dot), flanks, and less extensively streaked on the chin, throat, and belly; **bill:**
upper mandible brownish or horn colored; lower mandible paler, yellowish brown;
legs and **feet:** pink; **iris:** dark brown.

Young in fall (July–Sept) resemble adults, but crown-stripes flecked with pale, buff
feathers, making these stripes less distinct than in adults, the supercilium is thinner
and yellower (in east) or very pale (in west), ear-coverts chestnut, breast and belly
buffy with heavier streaking, wing feathers and coverts broadly edged with rufous or
buff. They are difficult to separate from adults after mid-Sept.

Juveniles resemble adults, but crown with brown streaks, and narrow, indistinct yellowish or beige median stripe, wing-coverts with broad beige edges, and throat and
belly beige, and extensively streaked with dark brown.

Ipswich Sparrow (North Atlantic Coast): Adults resemble typical Savannah
Sparrows in pattern, but are substantially larger (13.5–15.4 cm) and conspicuously
paler overall, appearing grayish, with supercilium pale yellow or white, breast and
sides decidedly less brown streaked than typical Savannah Sparrows, and white belly.
They breed on Sable I., Nova Scotia (rarely on adjacent mainland), where they nest
commonly in dunes stabilized by marram grass and beach peas, and (rarely) in similar habitats on the adjacent coast of Nova Scotia. In winter they are rarely found
away from coastal dune grass.

Belding's Savannah Sparrow (California saltmarshes): Adults are more heavily
streaked and darker brown than typical Savannah Sparrows, and have a brown
(although sometimes pale) median crown-stripe; supercilium and, especially,
supraloral spot yellow. Their bill is relatively longer and more slender than that of
other Savannah Sparrows.

First-fall and juveniles resemble adults, but lack yellow in supercilium.

Large-billed Savannah Sparrow (Salton Sea; coastal southern California):
Adults average larger (length 13.0–14.5 cm vs. 11.5–14.0 cm) than either Belding's,
or typical Savannah Sparrows, and have a large bill. They resemble other Savannah
Sparrows in general plumage pattern, but are generally paler brown or brownish gray
(especially in contrast with Belding's sparrows); supercilium pale beige or yellowish
beige; crown-stripe indistinct; back with indistinct streaking; underparts less heavily

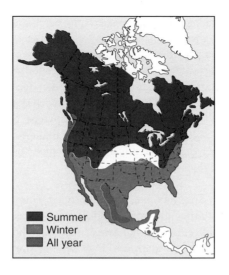

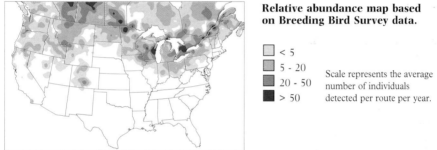

Relative abundance map based on Breeding Bird Survey data.

☐ < 5
☐ 5 - 20
☐ 20 - 50
■ > 50

Scale represents the average number of individuals detected per route per year.

streaked than Belding's or typical Savannah Sparrows; throat white with few indistinct brown flecks; legs horn-coloured; bill horn-coloured or grayish brown, with lower mandible paler.

First-fall and juveniles resemble adults, but generally paler in color and with no yellow in the supercilium; crown lacks a distinct median stripe; rump usually unstreaked.

VOICE: The song of the typical Savannah Sparrow is generally a lisping ***tzip-tzip-tzip ztreeeeeeeee-ip***, usually uttered from a perch, but sometimes in flight. At a distance the initial ***tzip*** notes, generally 3–5 in number, may not be heard; the terminal ***ip*** or ***zip***, which may not be uttered, is lower than the buzzy ***zrteeee . . .*** element. The song of Belding's sparrow is similar, but may be slightly higher, and the ending is often more emphatic. The song of the large-billed and Ipswich sparrows are likewise similar. During the breeding season, males occasionally sing at night. The call is a thin ***seet***, ***chip*** or ***tzip***; sometimes a rapid emphatic ***chip-chip-chip***, given by a female around a nest, or a ***buzt-buzt-buzt*** given by a subordinate in an aggressive encounter.

HABITS: On the breeding grounds, males sing persistently, generally from an exposed perch (top of a weed, in a small tree or shrub, etc.). Chases are common. Incubating females may flush directly from nests, or perform *rodent-run* distraction displays. Savannah Sparrows generally feed on the ground, but they may glean larval insects from branch tips. In the breeding season they feed alone or in pairs, and in winter alone or in loose flocks. They (especially Ipswich sparrows) sometimes feed at the tide line on sandy beaches and among beach wreck. Savannah Sparrows are generally not difficult to see, and flush readily. Their flight is strong and direct; when flushed from the ground, they frequently alight in a small bush or tree. They are not usually found in mixed flocks.

HABITAT: Savannah Sparrows are birds of open country. Typical Savannah Sparrows are found in grassy meadows, cultivated fields (especially alfalfa), lightly grazed pastures, roadside edges, coastal grasslands, sedge bogs, at the edge of saltmarshes, and tundra. Ipswich sparrows at all seasons are virtually restricted to marram grass, often mixed with other plants, along the coast. Although Savannah Sparrows avoid areas with extensive tree cover, they are generally found in fields with some herbaceous plants or weeds, and at the northern edge of their range, they are almost always associated with dwarf willows or birches; in the more arid parts of their range, they are generally restricted to irrigated areas or to the grassy margins of ponds.

Belding's and Large-billed sparrows in all seasons are found in saltmarshes and coastal estuaries where *Salicornia* (pickleweed), *Allenrolfea*, *Suaeda* (sea blite), *Atriplex*, and *Distichlis* (saltgrass) are dominant plants. Non-breeding large-billed sparrows were formerly found in a variety of habitats in southern California including beaches, wharves, and city streets, in addition to marshes.

BREEDING: *Nest* is a cup of woven coarse grass, lined with fine grass, or other fine material. It is built in a hollow scratched into the ground, with the rim at ground level, generally well concealed by a dome of grass or a shrub. In typical Savannah Sparrows, nesting takes place from mid-Feb (coastal California) through early Aug, and commences later at higher latitudes; 2–3, usually 2, broods are raised except at high latitudes where only a single brood is produced. ***Eggs***, 2–6 (usually 4–5 in typical Savannah Sparrows and Ipswich sparrows). Clutch size varies with latitude; the largest clutches are laid in the north, and the smallest in Baja California. The eggs are very pale greenish or bluish or cream white, heavily speckled with brown; markings are most dense at the large end of the egg. ***Incubation***, 9–15 days (usually about 12) (12.5 average on Sable I.); females alone incubate, but both parents feed the young; young fledge in 8–13 days (usually 10–12), and young stay with one parent for about 15 days. Nests of Belding's sparrows are placed in saltgrass or pickleweed, and may be 15 cm above the ground. Where their ranges overlap, the Savannah Sparrow is frequently parasitized by cowbirds.

RANGE: *(Typical Savannah Sparrow) Breeds* from Alaska, west to the Aleutian

Is. (Amukta I.), Canada, south of the Arctic Archipelago and ne Keewatin, south to West Virginia (in mountains), e Kentucky and Tennessee and n Georgia, s Ohio, c Indiana, c Iowa (formerly or irregularly south to sw Missouri and nw Arkansas), c Nebraska, and locally (in damp montane meadows, irrigated hayfields, and marsh edged) in Colorado, Utah, Nevada, Arizona, and e California, south to Oaxaca and perhaps w Guatemala.

Winters east of the Appalachian Mountains from Massachusetts south, and s Kentucky, s Tennessee, s Missouri, s Kansas, c New Mexico, n Arizona, and s British Columbia south to the Bahamas, Cuba and the Isle of Pines, Grand Cayman I., Swan Is., and throughout most of Mexico, Belize and south to n Honduras. Found, especially at feeders, rarely north to n United States, Nova Scotia, s Ontario and Alaska. In migration, found throughout North America. In winter, especially abundant from Florida west through s Mississippi, c Texas, and s New Mexico, Arizona, and California.

Both Ipswich and typical Savannah Sparrows have been recorded from Britain. Savannah Sparrows are very rare to accidental in the Canadian Arctic (Pelly Bay, Southampton, Victoria, Seymour and Cornwallis Is.), the Chukchi Peninsula (Uélen), Bol'shoi Diomede, and Wrangel Is. (June, Sept), southern Ussuriland, Japan, Hawaii (Kure), and Costa Rica (Cocos I.). This species probably breeds occasionally in ne Siberia.

(Belding's Sparrow) Resident along the Pacific Coast of California probably from San Francisco Bay south to Magdalena Bay, Baja California. Many sources suggest that only resident birds found from Santa Barbara southward are Belding's Sparrows, but those breeding in Morro Bay are as well, and it may be best to put the dark Savannah Sparrows that breed in saltmarshes in the San Francisco Bay area in this group as well, whereas birds in other habitats in that area are probably typical Savannah Sparrows. It is not clear whether or not these intergrade, but they can be found in close proximity.

(Large-billed Sparrow) Breeds and probably generally resident from the Delta of the Colorado R. (formerly?) south on the coast of Sonora and Sinaloa, Mexico; postbreeding and winter visitor to the Salton Sea and the s California coast, north and west (formerly, at least) to San Luis Obispo Co. and the Channel Is.; has decreased in California, probably as a consequence of drying of marshes in which they breed in the Colorado Delta. However, in recent years they have again increased and are fairly common at Salton Sea.

HISTORY: The Savannah Sparrow was first described by the British ornithologist, John Latham, in his *General Synopsis of Birds* (1790). He called it the 'Sandwich Bunting', as the specimens he had were from Sandwich Bay, Unalaska I. (Aleutians), Alaska. Latham felt that Latin names were unnecessary; thus it fell to the German ornithologist Johann Gmelin, in his 13th Edition of Linnaeus's *Systema naturae*

(1987) to give it the name *Emberiza sandwichensis*. The English vernacular name comes from Alexander Wilson's *Fringilla Savanna*, from Savannah, Georgia. Audubon noted that 'This is one of the most abundant of our Finches,' and it remains so today. In the east, it has doubtless benefited greatly from the clearing of the closed forests; this certainly must have facilitated its spread southward in the Appalachian Mountains. However, there was a great amount of suitable habitat, especially in the north, for Savannah Sparrows in pre-Columbian times. In the prairies, cultivation of moist grasslands, particularly in the northern prairies, has reduced habitat, and doubtless numbers, but in recent years, numbers appear to have been stable throughout their range.

When C.J. Maynard collected the first specimen of an 'Ipswich' Sparrow in 1868 in the dune grass near Ipswich, Massachusetts, he initially mistook it for a Baird's Sparrow, reflecting his lack of familiarity with both birds. Maynard later recognized it as a new form, which he called *Passerculus princeps*. The residents of Sable I., Nova Scotia, where the Ipswich Sparrow breeds, call it the 'gray bird.' Although there has been a great deal of destruction of their wintering habitat along the east coast, numbers of Ipswich Sparrows have been stable in recent years, as somewhat over 2000 birds return to nest annually on Sable I.

'Belding's' Sparrows were named by Robert Ridgway in honor of Lyman Belding, who collected this species at Bahia San Quintin, Baja California, and many other birds in California, and Baja California. The widespread destruction of *Salicornia* saltmarshes in southern California has greatly reduced the number of Belding's Sparrows. Their numbers seemed to increase in the 1970s, and in 1988 there were an estimated 2274 breeding pairs in 27 marshes in California, with the largest numbers at Mugu Lagoon, Upper Newport Bay, Anaheim Bay, and Tiajuana Marsh (Zembal *et al.* 1988).

GEOGRAPHIC VARIATION: Up to 12 subspecies from the United States and Canada are recognized; of these, two are resident or partially migratory in coastal saltmarshes in California, *P. s. beldingi* and *P. s. alaudinus*. Resident birds from Humboldt and Morro bays are conventionally called *P. s. alaudinus*, but we feel that the latter are better placed with *P. s. beldingi*, whereas the former are typical Savannah Sparrows.

Large-billed Savannah Sparrows (*P. s. rostratus*) are easily identifiable in the field. They are now uncommon to fairly common in winter in southern California, their decline in numbers probably attributable to the extensive destruction of their breeding habitat in the mouth of the Colorado River.

The large, pallid Ipswich sparrows (*P. s. princeps*) are also readily identifiable in the field.

Although there is geographic variation, especially in coloration, among typical

Savannah Sparrows, this is clinal, one subspecies grading into another, and they can not be safely identified in the field. Birds breeding on the Alaska Peninsula, Aleutian Is., and Middleton I., Alaska (*P. s. sandwichensis*) are substantially larger than those from the Alaskan mainland; they are nearly the same size as Ipswich sparrows. These winter along the Pacific coast from southern British Columbia south to central and western California, and could be safely identified in the hand by size.

There are a number of substantial differences between large-billed sparrows and typical Savannah Sparrows, and certainly there can be little interbreeding among large-billed, Belding's and typical Savannah Sparrow (Zink *et al.* 1991). Additional research may show that they are best treated as three separate species. Although there is occasional hybridization between Ipswich and typical Savannah Sparrows, and the two are apparently interfertile, Ipswich sparrows breed on the mainland only rarely, as do typical Savannah Sparrows on Sable I. (Stobo and McLaren).

MEASUREMENTS: See table.

References: Bradley (1977), Dixon (1978), Potter (1972), Rising (1988), Stobo and McLaren (1975), Van Rossem (1947), Weatherhead (1979), Wheelwright and Rising (1993), Zembal *et al.* (1988), Zink *et al.* (1991).

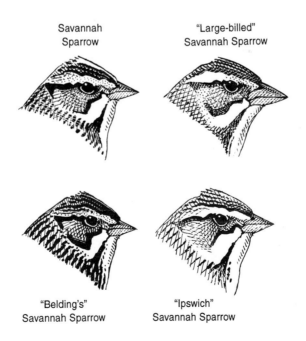

Savannah Sparrow

"Large-billed" Savannah Sparrow

"Belding's" Savannah Sparrow

"Ipswich" Savannah Sparrow

Measurements of Male Savannah Sparrows from 14 Localities

Locality	N	Wing Length		Tail Length		Tarsus Length		Culmen Length[a]		Mass	
		Mean	Range	Mean	Range	Mean	Range	Mean	Range	Mean	Range
Sable I., NS	24	77.9	73.3–83.4	59.3	56.1–63.0	22.6	21.7–23.5	6.4	5.6–7.0	28.2	24.0–32.5
Kuujjuaq, QUE	20	70.2	66.9–72.7	52.9	50.7–54.5	20.7	20.0–21.5	6.0	5.5–6.6	19.2	17.6–20.5
Preston Co., WV	24	69.0	65.2–71.2	53.3	50.1–55.5	20.2	18.7–21.3	5.9	5.4–6.5	19.0	17.5–20.5
Peel Co., ONT	42	69.7	64.3–78.2	53.5	48.9–57.7	20.4	19.1–21.5	5.9	5.4–6.5	19.9	17.3–22.8
Moosonee, ONT	43	70.0	66.3–72.7	52.6	48.2–57.9	20.2	18.4–21.6	5.9	5.3–6.4	19.7	17.2–22.0
Sheridan, WY	31	71.4	68.0–76.4	54.0	50.4–57.4	19.7	18.3–21.0	5.8	5.1–6.3	18.1	16.9–19.4
Coppermine, NWT	30	70.6	66.2–73.6	53.9	49.5–57.1	20.3	19.3–21.1	5.9	5.2–6.6	20.2	17.9–23.6
Umnak I., AK	26	75.6	73.4–78.3	56.0	53.5–59.5	22.1	20.7–23.2	6.7	6.0–7.2	25.1	22.0–28.0
Cold Bay, AK	15	74.8	71.9–76.9	55.3	52.6–58.0	21.7	20.3–22.8	6.6	6.1–7.1	23.6	20.1–25.4
Wasilla, AK	26	72.4	68.8–76.8	55.6	52.9–57.9	20.0	18.9–21.0	5.7	5.3–6.2	18.7	17.0–20.1
Creston, WA	33	71.2	67.3–74.5	54.3	50.8–58.8	19.9	18.9–20.7	5.5	4.9–6.2	18.1	15.6–19.6
Owens L., CA	18	70.6	67.6–73.8	53.6	50.5–56.6	20.3	19.2–21.9	5.5	5.2–5.9	17.8	16.5–19.0
San Diego, CA	19	65.2	61.3–68.9	47.6	41.9–50.3	20.0	18.5–20.9	6.1	5.6–6.8	17.8	16.5–19.0
Kino Bay, SONORA	18	70.4	65.1–73.4	55.0	52.8–57.7	21.6	19.6–22.6	7.6	6.6–8.4	22.7	21.0–25.2

[a] measured from the anterior edge of the nostril; measurements in mm; mass in g. (Wheelwright and Rising 1993)

Genus *Ammodramus*

The genus *Ammodramus* contains nine species, seven of which breed north of Mexico, the other two in South America. They are small to medium-sized sparrows with relatively short, thin tails and wings, with the 9th primary shorter than the 7th. Ecologically, *Ammodramus* are found both in wet grasslands (LeConte's Seaside, and the sharp-tailed sparrows) and dry grasslands (Grasshopper, Henslow's and Baird's Sparrows).

Despite their superficial similarities, this is a diverse group, and at various times the North American *Ammodramus*, as delimited here, have been split into as many as four genera, *Ammodramus* (Grasshopper Sparrow), *Centronyx* (Baird's Sparrow), *Ammospiza* (Seaside and the sharp-tailed sparrows), and *Passerherbulus* (LeConte's and Henslow's sparrows). Some authors include the Savannah Sparrow (*Passerculus sandwichensis*) in this genus. Within *Ammodramus*, Baird's and Grasshopper sparrows have very similar juvenal plumages and appear to be closely related; biochemical analyses suggest that Henslow's Sparrow is probably close to these two. Seaside, LeConte's and the sharp-tailed sparrows appear to be closely related, not only in general appearance but also biochemically. Biochemical evidence also indicates that the Savannah Sparrow (Passerculus) should be placed in the genus, probably close to the Baird's – Grasshopper – Henslow's group.

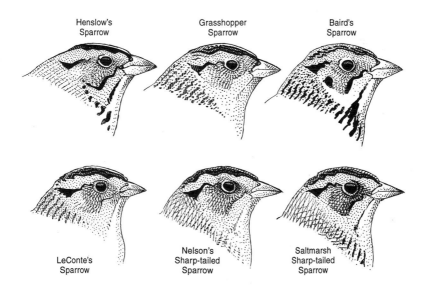

Henslow's
Sparrow

Grasshopper
Sparrow

Baird's
Sparrow

LeConte's
Sparrow

Nelson's
Sharp-tailed
Sparrow

Saltmarsh
Sharp-tailed
Sparrow

31 **Baird's Sparrow** *Ammodramus bairdii* [545]   PLATE 12

IDENTIFICATION: 12–14 cm (*c.* 5–5.5 in), males slightly larger; sexes similar in coloration.

Baird's Sparrow is medium-sized, rather short-tailed grassland sparrow, with a necklace of small, dark brown spots on the breast and upper flanks, pale ochre supercilium and ear-coverts, and ochre in the crown and nape streaked with dark brown; head markings are generally indistinct. The feathers on mantle and back are dark brown, broadly edged with pale ochre, giving them a scaly appearance. The pale lateral tail feathers are sometimes apparent in flight. In profile, Baird's Sparrow appears flat-headed, with no appearance of a crest.

Similar species: The Savannah Sparrow is similar in size, but more extensively streaked below, has more distinct facial markings, and often has a yellow supercilium, but otherwise lacks buffy median crown-stripe and the yellowish cast on the head that is characteristic of Baird's Sparrow; Savannah Sparrow may have a bit of a crest. The Grasshopper Sparrow averages slightly smaller, and either lacks or has indistinct ventral streaking. Its mantle, back and rump feathers are rusty brown or brown, and edged with grayish brown or pale brown, contrasting less distinctly than on Baird's Sparrow. The crown has a distinct pale beige (not ochre) median crown-stripe. Juvenile Grasshopper and Baird's sparrows are very similar in appearance, but the juvenile Baird's Sparrow, like the adult has a yellow-ochre cast to its head and a scaly back; juvenile Baird's Sparrows have a pale ochre median crown-stripe, whereas the stripe is grayish on Grasshopper Sparrows. Some juveniles of either species apparently migrate in juvenal plumage, but this is apparently commoner in Baird's than Grasshopper sparrows. LeConte's Sparrows are noticeably smaller than Baird's Sparrows, with distinct facial and crown markings, streaked flanks, and no streaking on the breast. Juvenile LeConte's Sparrow have a buffy head and could be confused with Baird's Sparrows, but Baird's have heavier breast streaks and dark moustachial and malar stripes.

Adult—*Head:* ochraceous; crown heavily streaked with dark brown spots, with a more or less distinct buffy-ochre median crown-stripe that tends to become wider toward the nape; supercilium buff or ochre and indistinct; ear-coverts buffy or ochre, edged posteriorly with dark brown and a thin dark brown moustachial stripe; sub-moustachial stripe buffy or ochre; malar stripe thin and dark brown; throat pale buff; ***back:*** nape ochre or buffy, boldly streaked with thin black spots; mantle and back dark brown with feathers distinctly edged with pale buff; ***rump:*** and uppertail-coverts brownish and darker centers; ***wing:*** brown with coverts and scapulars bold-ly edged with ochre; often slightly rusty in color; ***tail:*** dark brown with pale edges, outermost rectrix pale, especially at the tip; ***underparts:*** breast and flanks pale to pale buffy ochre, thinly streaked with small dark brown spots; belly and undertail-coverts pale and unmarked; ***bill:*** brownish, with lower mandible pale flesh color; ***legs:*** pale flesh color; ***iris:*** brown.

First-winter (after Aug–Sept) resemble adults, but may be somewhat buffier below.

Juveniles (July–Sept) crown and nape buffy-ochre, heavily speckled with brown, mantle, back and scapulars brown, broadly edged with buffy-ochre, breast and flanks more heavily spotted than adults.

VOICE: The song is ***zhe zhe she zurrrrrrrrr, zhe zhe zhe ze chrrrrrrrrrrrrr***, or ***zip zip zip z-r-r-r-r-r***, or ***zee zee zee zee zee zee ze-lit***, with the last trill or note on a lower pitch. The song most commonly has a melodious trill at the end, which carries well. The song lasts only 2–3 seconds; actively singing birds will repeat it every 10–15 seconds. Although the song is variable, individuals tend to sing the same song repeatedly. They may give a whining ***meeerr***, perhaps repeated ***meeerr meeerr meeerr*** if agitated, or a sharp ***kee-keep***; the alarm note is a repeated ***chip***.

HABITS: Territorial males sing from a conspicuous perch on a tussock of grass or small shrub, or from the ground. Singing is most frequent in the morning and evening. Although aerial displays are not common, territorial males fly up with a series of upward flights, to perhaps as high as 15 m, and flight-singing has been recorded. Otherwise, these are difficult birds to see. The female incubates closely, not flushing until immediately threatened. Breeding birds appear to be loosely colonial. In winter they may be solitary, and rarely sing. They often run mouse-like through the grass. In winter when flushed they flutter in zig-zag flight, low to the grass, like a Grasshopper Sparrow, before dropping into the grass; Baird's are among the most difficult spar-rows to see well in winter. The Savannah Sparrow's flight is higher and more direct.

HABITAT: Baird's Sparrow breeds in ungrazed or lightly grazed grassland, inter-spersed with scattered clumps of grass and low shrubs (wolfberry, snowberry, buck brush, rose) with tangled, matted grass on the ground, or in grasses in dry, shallow ponds or sloughs. In some areas it shows a strong preference for native grasses such as northern and western wheat grass, Junegrass, and needle grass, whereas in other regions it may also be common in introduced grass species such as crested wheat

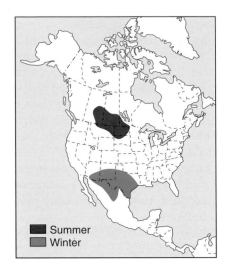

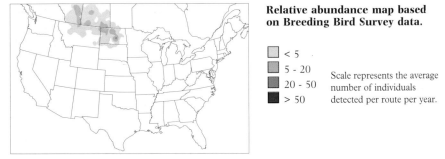

Relative abundance map based on Breeding Bird Survey data.

☐ < 5	
☐ 5 - 20	Scale represents the average
☐ 20 - 50	number of individuals
■ > 50	detected per route per year.

grass, fescue, and Russian wild rye, as well as alfalfa. The wintering ecology is not well known, but it is found in dense reddish plains grassland in southeastern Arizona, and grasslands and overgrown fields in Texas.

BREEDING: *Nest* is a cup placed in a tuft of grass, a depression in the ground, or supported by a small shrub, sometimes under an overhanging tuft of grass, with only a small entrance hole at the side, made of grasses, and lined with finer grasses. The nest is generally well concealed. Nesting takes place from early June through mid-July; generally two broods are produced in a year, and the female may mate with a second male for the second brood. *Eggs*, 3–6, usually 4–5, are white or faintly tinged with blue, with reddish brown, or occasionally black or lavender, spots and blotches, especially around the wider end. *Incubation*, 11–12 days, and the young fledge after 8–10 days. The female alone incubates, but both parents feed the young. They are parasitized by cowbirds.

RANGE: *Breeds* from se Alberta (to Lake Isle, Mayerthorpe, Elk I. Park, Banff), c Saskatchewan (Saskatoon, Last Mountain L.), south to sw Manitoba (Swan R., Winnipeg), nw Minnesota (formerly?), North Dakota (rare in east), nw South

Dakota (to Dewey, Haakon, Meade cos.), ne and n-c Montana, and perhaps e Wyoming (Van Tassel, Cheyenne).

Winters from se Arizona, New Mexico (Roswell; rare) and n-c Texas (scarce and local west of the 96th meridian; casual east of there to the upper Gulf coast), south to ne Sonora, Durango, Chihuahua, and n Zacatecas. Reported in November and December in Tulsa Co., Oklahoma, and in November in Oklahoma Co., Oklahoma. Migrates through Nebraska, Kansas (rarely east to Topeka), Colorado, New Mexico, Oklahoma (probably regularly in western Panhandle), Texas, nw Arkansas, and probably Missouri (very rare) (Apr–May; Aug–Oct). Very rare in Minnesota, Wisconsin, Ohio, Illinois (Apr–June) and casual in California (San Diego Co., Oct; southeast Farallon I., 2 records, Sept; Ft. Dick, Del Norte Co., Sept); accidental in New York (Montauk Point, Long I., 13 Nov, 1899). Formerly an abundant migrant in se Arizona and sw New Mexico, but now very rare. This species should be identified with caution.

HISTORY: Spencer Fullerton Baird was one of the most prominent American ornithologists of the 19th century, long-time Secretary of the Smithsonian Institution, and author of (along with Brewer, Ridgway, and Coues) the three-volume *A History of North American Birds* (1874). Baird introduced himself to Audubon at the age of 17, and he immediately impressed the aging naturalist, who asked Baird to accompany him on his trip to the headwaters of the Missouri R. Because of concerns about his health, Baird declined the invitation. Perhaps had he not done so, he would have been the first person to collect Baird's Sparrow, as Audubon's party collected the first two specimens on 26 July 1943 near Old Fort Union, North Dakota. Audubon described this new species, and named it Baird's Bunting (*Emberiza Bairdii*) '. . . after my young friend Spencer F. Baird, of Carlisle, Pennsylvania.' Although Baird's Sparrow has a fairly limited breeding range, it apparently was locally quite common in the past. In the plains of the Dakotas, Elliott Coues found it in 1873 'In some particular spots . . . outnumbered all the other birds together.' Much of their habitat, however, has been destroyed by the conversion of prairie to cultivated fields, and today Baird's Sparrow is local, and generally not common.

GEOGRAPHIC VARIATION: None described.

MEASUREMENTS: (8 males): wing 71–73 (72), tail 52–53 (53), tarsus 20.3–21.1 (20.6), exposed culmen 10.4–10.9 (10.7), bill depth at base 6.6–6.9 (6.7); (5 females): wing 66–69 (68), tail 48–53 (52), tarsus 19.3–20.3 (19.8), exposed culmen 10.2–10.7 (10.4), bill depth 6.6–7.4 (6.9) (Ridgway 1901).

Mass: (*N*=21) 17.5 g (15.0–20.3) (Arizona) (Dunning 1993); (19 breeding males) 19.5 g (17.3–21.5) (North Dakota and Saskatchewan) (Rising, unpublished).

Reference: Cartwright, Shortt, and Harris (1937).

32 **Grasshopper Sparrow**   PLATE 12
Ammodramus savannarum [546]

D. BEADLE.

IDENTIFICATION: 10.5–13 cm (*c.* 4–5 in), males slightly larger; sexes similar in plumage.

The Grasshopper Sparrow is a small- to medium-sized grassland sparrow, with a short tail. Adults are unstreaked, or at most faintly streaked, below, brownish and mottled above; the crown has a distinct pale median crown-stripe, and wide, dark brown lateral crown-stripes. Grasshopper Sparrows appear to be rather flat-headed, with large bills.

Similar species: Adult LeConte's Sparrows lack streaking on their breast, but have streaked flanks, a distinct, broad ochre superciliary stripe, and are smaller. Baird's Sparrows have a thin, but distinct necklace of dark brown spots on their breast, their heads are suffused with buffy or ochre, with rather indistinct markings, and are slightly larger. Juvenile Baird's are very similar (see Baird's Sparrow). Juvenile Henslow's Sparrows show ochre rather than buffy or whitish tones; the pale areas on the side of face and nape of juvenile Grasshopper Sparrows are thinly streaked with dark brown, whereas on juvenile Henslow's these are olive and unstreaked or at least not obviously streaked.

Adult—*Head:* lateral crown-stripes dark brown, with edges of feathers lighter in unworn birds, and a pale buffy median crown-stripe; lores buffy yellowish; supercilium buffy yellowish in front of eye, grayish white behind eye; side of face otherwise grayish brown, with posterior edge of ear-coverts edged with dark brown; ***back:*** nape and side of neck grayish buff, with centers of feathers rusty chestnut; mantle feathers with dark centers, edged with pale buff or rusty; ***rump:*** rump and upper-tail-coverts mottled with rust; ***tail:*** brown, with feathers edged in pale grayish brown, outermost feathers broadly edged and tipped in grayish white; ***wing:*** brown, with feathers edged in pale brown; tertials and coverts with dark brown centers, tipped in rusty chestnut, and tipped in pale buff in unworn birds; ***underparts:*** throat pale buffy; breast and flanks buffy white and unmarked or faintly marked (especially in west); belly whitish; undertail-coverts pale buffy; ***bill:*** pale horn colored, lower mandible pinkish; ***legs*** and ***feet:*** pinkish; ***iris:*** brown.

First-winter (after July–Oct) like adult.

Juveniles (July–Oct) crown, nape, back and rump dark brown, with edges of feather pale buff or rusty brown; median crown-stripe indistinct and grayish brown; breast and flanks whitish or buffy, streaked with brown spots; belly and undertail-coverts pale buffy or whitish and unmarked. Some individuals complete the first prebasic molt after migration.

VOICE: The song is thin, high, and insect-like, and starts with 2–3 high notes followed by a high trill, ***chip chip scheeeeeeeeeeee, tzick tzick tzrrrrrrr***, or a ***chit zhu zeeeeeeeeeeeeeeee***, with the trill on a higher pitch; sometimes a more musical ***zeeee sic-a-zeedle sic-a-zeedle sic-a-zeedle-zeeee*** is given; the call is a weak ***tillic***. During the breeding season (Mar–July) they sometimes sing at night.

HABITS: Territorial males frequently sing from a conspicuous perch, at the top of a tall weed or bush or from a fence wire, or from the ground. At other times, they can be inconspicuous, frequently running rather than flying when approached. The flight is a weak zig-zag, low over the ground, after which the birds drops to the ground, often out of sight. The female incubates closely, and when disturbed, she generally runs away from the nest, before perhaps taking off for a short flight.

HABITAT: Grasshopper Sparrows breed in wet or dry grassy pastures, interspersed with sparse shrubs or weeds; in some parts of their range, they are found in alfalfa or clover, hayfields, and seasonally wet meadows. Where they are found together, Grasshopper, Baird's and Savannah sparrows can be found in the same fields, at times apparently in the same habitat. However, Grasshopper Sparrows tend to favor more xeric habitats, and Baird's in more mesic ones, than the others. In Florida, Grasshopper Sparrows are resident in small stunted saw palmetto and dwarf oaks, interspersed with sparse grass and bare ground. In winter they are generally found in rather dense grass.

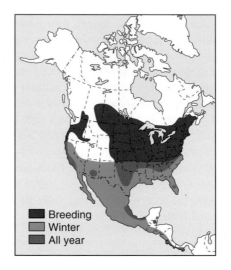

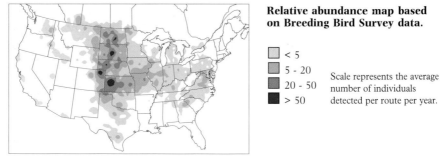

**Relative abundance map based
on Breeding Bird Survey data.**

☐ < 5
☐ 5 - 20
■ 20 - 50
■ > 50

Scale represents the average
number of individuals
detected per route per year.

BREEDING: ***Nest*** is a cup of grass, lined with fine grass and sometimes hair, usually placed in a clump of grass, the lip of the cup at ground level; the nest is frequently overhung by vegetation. In Florida, nests may be in palmettos or tussocks of dead
wire grass. Nesting takes place from early April through July. ***Eggs***, 3–6, most commonly 4 or 5, are white, or slightly tinged with green or brown, and spotted with reddish or dark brown, with the spotting most dense at the wider end of the egg.
Incubation, 11–12 days, and young fledge after 9 days; newly fledged young run
well, but perhaps cannot fly. The female alone incubates, but both parents feed the
young. They are probably double-brooded. Grasshopper Sparrows are occasionally
parasitized by cowbirds.

RANGE: ***Breeds*** from s-c British Columbia (Okanagan Valley), s Alberta, s
Saskatchewan (probably n to Saskatoon; uncommon), s Manitoba, w Ontario (Lake
of the Woods), e Ontario (mostly s of the Canadian Shield), Michigan (uncommon
in north), sw Quebec (rarely north to Lac Saint-Jean), and s New Brunswick
(Waweig, Grand Manan I.; rare), south to c Georgia (s to Burke and Sumter cos.),

c Alabama (s to Bullock, Lowndes, and Sumter cos.), Tennessee (uncommon in west, Shelby Co.), Arkansas, Texas (except along Coast, in Rio Grande Valley, and west of the Pecos R.), se Colorado, ne New Mexico (probable), e Wyoming, c and nw Montana, and in the west from s-c British Columbia (Okanagan Valley; rare) south to n Idaho, eastern Washington, Oregon (north to Lincoln Co.), nw Utah (Box Elder Co.; rare), n Nevada (Elko and Humboldt cos.), and south along the coast from n Oregon to s California (San Diego; local) and nw Baja California and locally in c California (Sacramento Valley, Central Valley). In most places in the west and the northern plains the status varies greatly from year to year.

Local *resident* populations in s-c Arizona (Pima, Cochise, Santa Cruz, and Graham cos.); in c Florida (Osceola, Polk, Highlands, Okeechobee, and Glades cos.); in the state of Mexico, Veracruz, Oaxaca, Chiapas, Guatemala, Belize, Honduras, ne Nicaragua, nw Costa Rica, and Panama; Jamaica, Hispaniola, Vieques I., and Puerto Rico; w Colombia and w Equador; and the Netherlands Antilles (Curaçao, Bonaire).

Winters from e North Carolina, Tennessee, Arkansas (Fayetteville), Oklahoma (rare), c Arizona and c California (rare), south through Mexico to northern Central America and n-c Costa Rica, Belize, Quintana Roo (Cozumel I.), Cuba, the Isle of Pines, Caymen Is., Swan I., and the Bahamas. Most common in winter along the Gulf Coast, and along the Atlantic Coast from South Carolina to Florida. Very rare in winter n to Nova Scotia, Massachusetts, Ohio, Illinois, Missouri, Kansas, and Oregon.

Has been recorded west to the west coast, from sw British Columbia (Saanach) southward and in Newfoundland, Nova Scotia (mostly in fall), and Prince Edward I.

HISTORY: The Grasshopper Sparrow was named *Fringilla Savannarum* by the German biologist Johann Gmelin in 1789 on the basis of material from Jamaica. In 1818, the species was described for the first time in North America by the French ornithologist Louis Pierre Vieillot, who examined specimens from *Etat de New Yorck* (New York). Audubon wrote that the 'Yellow-winged Bunting' (Grasshopper Sparrow) was 'found in considerable numbers' from Maryland to Maine, and was 'not uncommon' in Pennsylvania, New Jersey, New York, and Connecticut. It seems likely that Grasshopper Sparrows spread eastward after 1800, following the clearing of the forests of the northeast. It was much more common in Connecticut during the late 19th century than it is today, and is currently designated 'Endangered' in that state. Throughout much of the rest of the east, Grasshopper Sparrows seem to be declining in numbers, but they are locally common in some areas; there are only about 200 resident individuals in Florida.

GEOGRAPHIC VARIATION: The Grasshopper Sparrow is one of the most widespread of the sparrows, with populations in North, Central, and South America, and in Jamaica, Hispaniola, Puerto Rico, Curaçao, and Bonaire. Four subspecies from north of Mexico are recognized. The Eastern Grasshopper Sparrow (*A. s.*

pratensis) breeds west to Wisconsin and eastern Oklahoma; the Western Grasshopper Sparrow (*A. s. perpallidus*) breeds in western North America, south central Texas, central Arizona, and southwestern California; the Arizona Grasshopper Sparrow (*A. s. ammolegus*) breeds in southeastern Arizona and northern Sonora; and the Florida Grasshopper Sparrow (*A. s. floridanus*) breeds in central peninsular Florida.

On average Western Grasshopper Sparrows appear to be more pallid than Eastern Grasshopper Sparrows, with more rusty brown and less dark brown or black on the back, and a slightly smaller bill. These cannot be reliably separated in the field. *A. s. ammolegus* is paler and more rusty still, with rust often appearing as faint streaking on the breast. Florida Grasshopper Sparrows have darker backs than Eastern Grasshopper Sparrows, with feathers dark brown or blackish, edged with grayish, and virtually no brown or rust; they are paler and less buffy below than Eastern Grasshopper Sparrows.

MEASUREMENTS: (12 males, western U.S.): wing 57–66 (62), tail 43–51 (46), tarsus 18.3–20.3 (19.6), exposed culmen 10.2–11.7 (10.9), depth of bill at base 5.6–6.9 (6.4); (8 females from west): wing 61–64 (62), tail 43–51 (46), tarsus 18.5–19.8 (19.1), exposed culmen 10.2–11.2 (10.9), bill depth 5.6–6.9 (6.4) (Ridgway 1901).

Mass: (33 males from New Jersey) 20.7 g (18.0–23.1), (14 females from New Jersey) 17.8 g (15.3–19.0) (Dunning 1993); (11 males from North Dakota, Saskatchewan, and Kansas) 17.8 g (16.9–18.5); (2 females from Kansas) 15.6, 19.2 g (Rising, unpublished).

Reference: Sutton (1935).

33 **Henslow's Sparrow** *Ammodramus henslowii* [547] **PLATE 12**

IDENTIFICATION: 10–13 cm (*c.* 4–5 in), males slightly larger; sexes similar in coloration.

Henslow's is a small, short-tailed sparrow, with thin, dark stripes on the breast, and a slightly olive-greenish cast to the face; there is usually a dark brown spot on the posterior margin of the ear-coverts. The edges of the coverts, scapulars, and tertials are generally reddish, unlike those of other short-tailed, grassland sparrows. Henslow's Sparrow appears large-billed and flat-headed.

Similar species: Henslow's Sparrow most closely resembles Baird's, Grasshopper, and LeConte's sparrows. Baird's Sparrow is larger, has rich yellow-ochre median crown-stripe, supercilium, and ear-coverts, and a scaly-looking back. Adult Grasshopper Sparrows lack breast streaks (these can be faint on Henslow's), has distinct crown-stripes, rusty stripes on the nape, and is paler in general appearance. Grasshopper Sparrows are also generally much more easily seen than the other short-tailed grassland sparrows. The streaking on the breast of LeConte's Sparrow is restricted to the flanks, and LeConte's has a dark lateral crown-stripe and eyeline stripe, accentuated by a bright yellow-ochre supercilium, a pale median crown-stripe, and a rusty, streaked nape. LeConte's Sparrow appears paler and much more yellowish than Henslow's Sparrow.

Juvenile *Ammodramus* sparrows are difficult to identify. Henslow's differs from the others by having a greenish cast to the median crown-stripe, supercilium, and ear-coverts, which are edged with brown posteriorly, thin dark malar and post-ocular streaks, and by the rusty edging to the greater coverts and tertials. Henslow's Sparrow molts into First Basic Plumage before migrating.

Adult—*Head:* lateral crown-stripes dark brown and streaked with buffy olive; median crown-stripe buffy olive; supercilium broad and buffy olive; lores and ear-coverts buffy olive; posterior margin of ear-coverts dark brown; side of neck buffy olive, often with a greenish hue; eye, moustachial and malar stripes dark brown, and fairly thin; ***back:*** nape buffy olive, streaked with dark brown; mantle feathers dark brown, edged with buff; ***rump:*** buffy olive feathers, with dark brown centers; ***tail:*** middle rectrices dark brown with broad rusty brown edges; lateral rectrices brown, with darker centers; rectrices pointed; ***wing:*** brown, with scapulars, tertials and sometimes secondaries edged with rust; bend of wing yellow; ***underparts:*** throat pale buff and unstreaked; breast and flanks darker buff than throat and with thin dark brown streaks; belly whitish buff; undertail-coverts buffy; ***bill:*** upper mandible brown, lower mandible flesh colored; ***legs*** and ***feet:*** flesh colored; ***iris:*** dark brown.

First-fall and winter (after Sept) resemble adults, but are perhaps somewhat buffier on the head, breast, and flanks.

Juveniles (June through Sept) similar to adults, but buffier, and lacking moustachial and malar stripes, and with little or no streaking on the breast and flanks.

VOICE: The song is an unobtrusive insect-like, short ***tsi-lick***, or ***flee-sic***. The song carries surprisingly far, perhaps up to 100 m on a calm day. Rarely, a longer flight-song, ***sis-r-r-rit-srit-srit***, is given. The call note is a ***tsip***. The species is apparently silent in the winter, but males are singing when they arrive on their breeding territories.

HABITAT: Henslow's Sparrow is a grassland species, characteristically found in wet meadows, neglected fields, wet hay fields, grassy swamps, and in some areas in dry upland prairies, often dotted with small shrubs. However, they avoid fields with a lot of woody vegetation, and abandon fields that have been mowed. They prefer fields with a lot of standing dead vegetation, and matted dead grass on the ground. Burnt fields are unsuitable for Henslow's Sparrows for one or two years, but fires reduce woody vegetation, ultimately enhancing the suitability of these fields for this species.

In winter, Henslow's Sparrows are found in dense grass and weedy areas in humid open country, or in grassy areas in pine woods.

HABITS: Territorial males sing persistently from the ground or from a perch in a bush or tall grass, often an exposed place on the top of a weed or a small tree. They commonly start singing at dawn and sing through the night; singing rate slows down

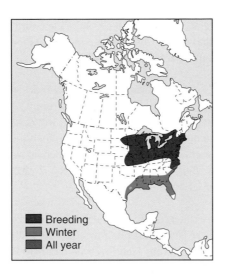

Breeding
Winter
All year

late in the day. Henslow's Sparrows occasionally make short flights from weed to weed; their flight is low and jerky, and they twist their tails as they fly. Females rarely fly, and run mouse-like, rather than fly off the nest. They often appear to be loosely colonial, but this may be because they may nest at high density in limited suitable habitat. In winter, flushed Henslow's Sparrows tend to fly short distances, then drop to the grass and run. A persistently flushed bird, however, may perch in an exposed place. Henslow's Sparrows are solitary, and do not associate with other species of sparrows. Migrants are reluctant to flush, and can be approached closely.

BREEDING: *Nest* is placed on or near the ground (up to 50 cm high), occasionally in a small depression, and often at the base of a clump of grass (*Spartina*, bluestem), and sometimes domed over. The nest is a neatly woven cup of grass, lined with finer grass. Apparently the female alone builds the nest. Nesting begins in mid-May and continues through early Sept. *Eggs*, 4–5, are creamy white or pale greenish white, speckled or blotched with reddish brown. *Incubation*, 10–11 days; female alone incubates, but both parents feed the young; young leave the nest after 9 or 10 days; probably double-brooded. This species is parasitized by cowbirds.

RANGE: *Breeds* from South Dakota (east of the Missouri R.), w Minnesota (casual north to Norman and Mahnomen cos.), se Minnesota (Winona Co.), c Wisconsin, Michigan (Menominee and Delta cos. southward), s Ontario (north to Bruce Co., Kingston), sw Quebec (formerly?), New York (declining, especially in southeast; absent from Adirondack Mountains), c Vermont (declining), and se New Hampshire (declining), and Massachusetts south through e Kansas (increasing), ne Oklahoma (near Bartlesville; possible) to e Texas (Harris Co.; rare), c and w Missouri, s Illinois (rare and local), Indiana (rare and local), c and w Kentucky (irregular), West Virginia (irregular, and apparently declining recently), Delaware (extirpated), Virginia (declining), and irregularly south to North Carolina (Dare and Beaufort cos., west to Chapel Hill), and South Carolina (Greenville Co.).

Winters from coastal ne North Carolina (scarce), and coastal South Carolina, c Alabama, Louisiana, and e Texas, south to Florida (rarely south to Lee and Martin cos.), the Gulf Coast, and s Texas. Most common in winter along the Atlantic Coast, from North Carolina to northern Florida, and along the Gulf Coast from Northern Florida to Corpus Christi, Texas. Has been recorded in winter rarely north to c Oklahoma, c Missouri, Illinois (probably declining), Indiana, Kentucky, Virginia, Massachusetts, and Nova Scotia (Oct).

HISTORY: The first specimen of Henslow's Sparrow was collected by Audubon in Kentucky, across the river from Cincinnati in 1820. In 1829 he named it *Emberiza Henslowii*, in honor of John Stevens Henslow who had helped him on one of his visits to England to sell subscriptions to his *Birds of North America*. Henslow, though not an ornithologist, was a prominent naturalist and geologist, and a professor of Botany at Cambridge University. It was he who recommended Charles Darwin to accompany Captain FitzRoy on the famous voyage of the *Beagle*. Audubon considered Henslow's Sparrow to be abundant in New Jersey, where it is '. . . found in ploughed fields . . .', and in winter he found it '. . . in great numbers in all the pine barrens of the Floridas.'

From what is known of the ecology of the species, I speculate that it was once abundant in the unplowed and periodically burnt tallgrass prairie that originally grew from Illinois west into central Kansas and Nebraska. Today, Henslow's Sparrow is declining in numbers throughout the northeast, but apparently increasing in eastern Kansas and western Missouri where remnants of the prairie are being protected or re-established. The declines in the east probably reflect the widespread draining of wetlands, and the destruction of the southern pine woods.

GEOGRAPHIC VARIATION: Two subspecies are generally recognized: the Western Henslow's Sparrow (*A. h. henslowii*), which breeds east to central West Virginia, and the Eastern Henslow's Sparrow (*A. h. susurrans*). Eastern Henslow's Sparrows have larger bills, on average, than Western Henslow's Sparrows. Ridgway (1901) gives the following measurements: Western (N=17): exposed culmen, 10.7 mm, bill depth, 7.1; Eastern (N=34): exposed culmen 12.6 mm, bill depth 8.1 mm. Eastern Henslow's Sparrows are said to be slightly darker than Western Henslow's Sparrows, with slightly more yellow at the bend of the wing. These differences would not be evident in the field.

MEASUREMENTS: (34 males): wing 51–57 (54), tail 44–53 (49), tarsus 15.8–18.5 (17.3), exposed culmen 10.2–14.0 (11.9), depth of bill at base 6.6–8.6 (7.9); (17 females): wing 49–55 (53), tail 44–51 (48), tarsus 15.2–18.0 (17.0), exposed culmen 10.4–12.7 (11.7), bill depth 6.6–8.4 (7.6) (Ridgway 1901).

Mass: (12 breeding males) 12.9 g (11.4–14.9); (6 breeding females) 13.1 g (11.1–14.8) (Michigan, Ohio, Ontario) (Hyde 1939).

Mass: Hyde (1939), Pyle *et al.* (1987), Schulenberg *et al.* (1994), Sutton (1935), Zimmerman (1988).

34 **LeConte's Sparrow** *Ammodramus leconteii* [548]   **PLATE 13**

D. BEADLE.

IDENTIFICATION: 10.5–12.5 cm (*c.* 4–5 in), males slightly larger; sexes similar in coloration.

LeConte's is a very small, sharp-tailed sparrow, with a bright ochre supercilium, pale whitish median crown-stripe, broad dark brown lateral crown-stripes, and purplish-chestnut streaks on the nape. The eye-stripe is dark brown, and becomes broader toward the neck, making it wedge-shaped. The breast is usually ochre, unstreaked in adults; the flanks are ochre, distinctly streaked with dark brown.

Similar species: In size and behaviour, LeConte's Sparrow most closely resembles Henslow's Sparrow, which however appears to be darker (olive to greenish olive), has a streaked breast, and a reddish cast to the wings (edges of coverts and tertials rusty); LeConte's has a smaller bill, and does not appear to have a large, flat head as Henslow's does. The Grasshopper Sparrow is larger and has a larger bill, and although the head patterning is similar, does not show as much contrast as LeConte's; the nape is not so rusty as LeConte's, and the flanks are unstreaked or sparsely streaked (especially in Florida). Baird's Sparrow is larger, has distinct moustachial and malar stripes and breast streaking, and lacks the chestnut nape. Nelson's Sharp-tailed Sparrows, which are often found in the same marshes as LeConte's Sparrows, are slightly larger, have a grayish median crown-stripe and side of neck, dark, white-streaked back, and little streaking on the flanks.

Juvenile *Ammodramus* sparrows are difficult to identify. Juvenile LeConte's Sparrows have streaking across the breast, are yellowish in hue, especially in the supercilium, nape and breast, and have a distinctive wedge-shaped eye-stripe; they do not have dark moustachial or malar stripes as do juvenile Baird's Sparrows. Apparently, LeConte's Sparrows rather often migrate in this plumage.

Adult—*Head:* median crown-stripe whitish, bordered by two dark brown or blackish lateral crown-stripes; supercilium broad and bright yellow ochre; lores ochre; eye-stripe blackish and wedge-shaped, being narrow at the eye, and broad toward the neck; ear-coverts grayish ochre, thinly edged with brown; submoustachial stripe ochre; throat white; ***back:*** nape feathers rusty or chestnut, edged with ochre; mantle feathers dark brown or blackish, edged with pale buff, giving a scaly appearance; ***rump:*** blackish with light edges to feathers; ***tail:*** feathers narrow and pointed, and dark brown with broad beige edges; ***wing:*** brown, with coverts and tertials edged in light buff; ***underparts:*** throat white and unmarked, breast and flanks ochre with distinct, short black streaks on the flanks; belly white; undertail-coverts pale beige with dark centers; ***bill:*** upper mandible yellowish horn color; lower mandible paler; ***legs*** and ***feet:*** dull flesh color; ***iris:*** brown.

First-fall (after Aug and Sept) similar to adults.

Juveniles (June–Sept) resemble adults, but have a streaked breast, and less ochre, especially in the supercilium and breast, and have reduced or no chestnut in the nape.

VOICE: The song of LeConte's Sparrow is a short (*c.* 1 s) insect-like ***reese-reese***, ***z-z-z-buzz***, or ***tzeek-tzzzz tick*** sounding like the song began and ended by a click of a switch. It frequently sings after dark, and occasionally while hovering up to 6 m high. The flight-song is usually introduced by several ***chips***, followed by an up-slurred note, which is followed by a longer down-slurred one. The call note is a sharp ***chip*** or ***tsip*** or thin ***ssisst***. It calls infrequently in migration or in winter.

HABITS: Territorial males will often sing from near the top of a piece of grass. Otherwise, they can be difficult to see. When flushed, LeConte's Sparrows characteristically fly a short distance, in a jerky flight, close to the grass, before dropping to the ground. Occasionally, they will flush to a bush where they can be seen. In winter they are solitary, although may be found in habitat where there are other sparrows.

HABITAT: LeConte's Sparrows nest in wet freshwater grasslands (cordgrass; whitetop), sometimes mixed with cattail, phragmites, and sourdock, or sedge marshes, often interspersed with small alders, birches, and sweet gale; they also breed in large undisturbed pastures. In migration and in winter they are found in tall, dense grasses, damp weedy fields, stands of broomsedge, cattails or occasionally in overgrown shortgrass prairie.

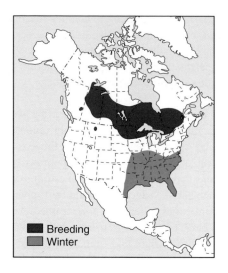

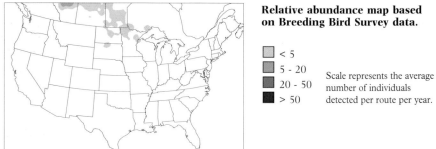

Relative abundance map based on Breeding Bird Survey data.

■ < 5
■ 5 - 20   Scale represents the average
■ 20 - 50   number of individuals
■ > 50   detected per route per year.

BREEDING: *Nest* is placed on the ground, or more commonly near to the ground (up to 20 cm), and occasionally in a depression. The nest is a well-concealed cup of grass or sedges lined with very fine grass and occasionally hair. The female alone builds the nest. Nesting begins in late May and continues through mid-July. *Eggs*, 3–5, usually 4–5, greenish white or grayish white, speckled or blotched with brown. *Incubation*, 11–13 days; female alone incubates, but both parents feed the young. This species is parasitized by cowbirds.

RANGE: *Breeds* from e-c British Columbia (Peace R. parklands, probably the Cariboo), sw and s-c Mackenzie (Fort Simpson, Little Buffalo R.), Alberta (south to Turner Valley, Big Stone), nw Montana (Glacier Park), extreme ne Montana, Saskatchewan (south to Regina, Qu'Appelle Valley), nw and c Manitoba, Ontario (Winisk, Fort Severn; rare), and Quebec (north to Rupert House, east to Saint-Fulgence), south through North Dakota to ne South Dakota, c Minnesota, c Wisconsin, n Michigan (Upper Peninsula) and s (formerly) Ontario (Sudbury, Holland Marsh, Luther Marsh, Ottawa).

Winters from e Kansas (rare), Missouri (rare in north), Illinois (rare in north), s Indiana, possibly Ohio (Lorain Co.; Dec), along the east coast north to Delaware (very rare) and Virginia (very rare), south to s Texas (rare in west), Coahuila, the Gulf Coast, and Florida. Probably most common in winter in east Texas, Louisiana and northern Florida. Reported in winter from s-c British Columbia (Okanagan Valley, Nov; rare) and California (very rare). In migration, LeConte's Sparrow appears rarely in s California and along the Pacific Coast (especially in the fall) and in West Virginia (very rare, Sept).

HISTORY: LeConte's Sparrow was first collected in central Georgia in 1790, and described by the English ornithologist John Latham. The species apparently was not reported again, however, until John Bell, who accompanied Audubon on his Missouri R. expedition, collected one on 24 May, 1843, in what is today south-central South Dakota, near the present-day western edge of its range. Not knowing of the earlier description, Audubon formally described this species in 1844 and wrote, 'I have named this interesting species after my young friend Doctor Le Conte, son of Major Le Conte, so well known among naturalists, and who is, like his father, much attached to the study of natural history.' There were several LeContes that were contemporaries of Audubon, including five naturalists, but John Lawrence LeConte was almost certainly the person after whom LeConte's Sparrow was named. By 1844, J. L. LeConte was already a promising young naturalist. He later served as a physician in the Civil War, and ultimately became best known as an entomologist, especially as an authority on the Coleoptera, He named about 6000 species of insects, but no birds.

Audubon commented that LeConte's Sparrows were common on the 'Upper Missouri prairies,' presumably in South Dakota, where they are today apparently rare in the breeding season. They are, however, locally common as breeding birds in North Dakota, the Canadian prairies, and in sedge meadows in the James Bay Lowlands.

GEOGRAPHIC VARIATION: None described.

MEASUREMENTS: (10 males): wing 49–54 (52), tail 46–52 (49), tarsus 17.8–18.8 (18.3), exposed culmen 8.4–10.2 (9.1), bill depth at base 5.1–5.6 (5.3); (10 females): wing 49–53 (51), tail 46–56 (50), tarsus 17.5–18.8 (18.0), exposed culmen 8.4–9.9 (9.1), bill depth 5.1–5.3 (5.2) (Ridgway 1901).

Mass: (10 Breeding males) 13.8 g (12.6–15.3); (6 breeding females) 13.8 g (12.0–16.3) (late June, early July; northern Ontario); (11 breeding males) 13.1 g (12.4–14.0) (June; North Dakota, Saskatchewan) (Rising, unpublished); (26 males) 13.4 g (12.4–15.2) (North Dakota) (Murry 1969).

References: Murry (1969), Pyle and Sibley (1992).

35 **Saltmarsh Sharp-tailed Sparrow**   PLATE 13
Ammodramus caudacutus [549]

IDENTIFICATION: 11.5–13 cm (*c.* 4.5–5 in), males slightly larger, sexes similar in coloration.

The facial pattern of the Saltmarsh Sharp-tail is striking, with a bold yellow-ochre supercilium, submoustachial stripe, and the posterior margin of the ear-coverts forming a triangle around the gray ear-coverts and lores; thin dark malar stripe separates the pale or whitish throat from the yellow-ochre submoustachial stripe. Saltmarsh Sharp-tails are streaked on both back and breast, have brown lateral crown-stripes, a gray median crown-stripe and side of neck, ochre breast, and short, pointed tail feathers.

Similar species: Nelson's Sharp-tailed Sparrow lacks conspicuous breast streaking, with the back more strikingly streaked, supercilium bright ochre, but ear-coverts, submoustachial and post-auricular stripes more diffuse; the throat is buffy, contrasting little in color with the submoustachial stripe, and the malar stripe is diffuse and absent. 'Acadian' sparrows (included in Nelson's here) are duller and grayer in coloration, with back and breast not conspicuously streaked, yellowish supercilium dull. The Seaside Sparrow is larger, generally darker, with more extensive ventral streaking, and lacks the striking facial pattern; LeConte's Sparrow is smaller, with an unstreaked breast, distinctly ochre streaked back, and white median crown-stripe. Grasshopper Sparrow lacks the distinctive facial pattern, appears scaly backed, and is unstreaked below. Juvenile Saltmarsh Sharp-tailed Sparrows are streaked on the back and flanks, but may not be streaked on the breast; the head and ventral pattern resembles the adults. Juvenile Grasshopper Sparrows are similar, but are paler below and much less ochre in general hue. Juvenile Seaside Sparrows are larger, larger billed, and darker in tones with a distinct supraloral spot that contrasts with supercilium.

Adult—*Head:* median crown-stripe gray; lateral crown-stripes, supercilium, submoustachial, and post-auricular stripes orange-buffy to yellow-orange, with the post-auricular stripe separated from the supercilium by a narrow but distinct brown eye stripe; malar stripe brown; edge of post-auricular stripe narrowly edged with brown, nape grayish brown; ***back:*** mantle and scapular feathers dark brown, narrowly edged in buffy white; ***rump:*** dark brown, with centers of feathers darker; ***tail:*** brown, unpatterned, with lateral feathers shorter than middle ones, and feathers narrow and pointed (sharp); ***wing:*** brown, coverts with dark centers, but no wing-bars, bend of wing edged with pale yellow; ***underparts:*** chin and throat pale yellow; breast and flanks dull whitish yellow, distinctly marked with thin brown streaks; belly whitish; ***bill:*** upper mandible dusky, lower mandible bluish gray, paler toward base; ***legs*** and ***feet:*** pinkish buff to dusky; ***iris:*** brown.

First-winter (Aug–Oct) resemble adults, but more heavily streaked below; may retain some juvenal wing feathers through March.

Juveniles (July–Sept) crown blackish, sometimes streaked with light brownish, with a narrow median crown-stripe; mantle and scapular feathers dark brown broadly edged with buff, producing streaks; underparts buffy, narrowly streaked on breast and flanks, belly nearly white.

VOICE: Males sing a continuous complex whisper song that has a whispery, wheezy quality, and may last for over 1 minute, a ***ts-ts-sssss-tsik***, or ***tsi-lik tsssss-s-s-s-s-s***; it contains phrases like the primary song of Nelson's Sharp-tailed Sparrow, abbreviated trills, and short accented syllables. Songs may be delivered from hidden or more often exposed perches, and may continue in short horizontal flights, or may commence in flight and continue after perching (Nelson's and 'Acadian' Sharp-tailed sparrows have much more elaborate flight-songs). Calls are given by both sexes; females give a soft, toneless ***chic*** call, and a repeated series of ***tsick, chuck,*** or ***chip*** notes. A series of high-pitched ***tic*** calls or a ***tic***-twitter call is given by both sexes, often in response to a predator.

HABITS: On the breeding grounds, males sing persistently from mid-May through early Aug, especially in the morning. When feeding, sharp-tailed sparrows walk or run, or hop slowly to inspect an object. When alarmed, they may climb to the top of vegetation; flight is direct, fairly fast, and slightly undulating; flying birds often drop

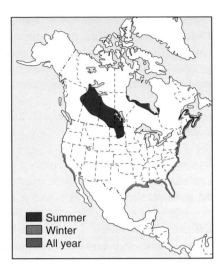

back into the grass, and may run. Females around nests may fly slowly in a jerky manner. Sharp-tailed sparrows are not territorial, but males may supplant other males from perches. In migration and winter, they are found in small, loose feeding groups, and are not usually found in mixed flocks. They apparently sometimes respond to spishing.

HABITAT: Saltmarsh Sharp-tailed Sparrows are found in coastal saltmarshes or wet meadows, where there is dense cordgrass, blackgrass, or saltmeadow grass, or along ditch margins or pool edges; they are usually found in tidal areas. Although usually migratory, they occur in similar habitat in winter. Their inland status is unclear, but most inland records are probably of Nelson''s Sharp-tailed Sparrow; away from the coast, these birds would be most likely found in wet meadows. I know of no inland specimens, but many accounts do not differentiate between the two sharp-tailed sparrows.

BREEDING: *Nest* is usually a simple cup, but occasionally partly domed, of coarse, dry grass or sedge and seaweed, lined with finer grasses. In tidal areas almost all nests are placed off the ground, typically 6–15 cm high, in cordgrass, other grasses, or in a small shrub; in non-tidal areas, nests may be placed on the ground. Nesting takes place from mid-May through early-Aug, with peaks of activity in late May–early June, and mid-July; may be double-brooded. *Eggs*, 2–6, usually 3–5, are greenish white to greenish blue, usually profusely speckled with reddish brown. *Incubation*, 11–12 days; females alone incubate and feed the young. No records of cowbird parasitism.

RANGE: *Breeds* along the coast from s Maine south to the Delmarva Peninsula. (Reported breeding in n North Carolina is almost certainly in error; specimens from there, including the type of *P.c. diversus*, were probably migrants, and recent searches during the breeding season have been unsuccessful.)

Winters in coastal marshes from Massachusetts (rare) and New York south to Florida (rarely in the Keys) and reportedly along the Gulf coast of n Florida, casually west to Louisiana (Mississippi R. Delta) and Texas (Galveston and Refugio cos.). They are commonest on the coast of North Carolina.

HISTORY: The Saltmarsh Sharp-tailed Sparrow was first described by the English physician, John Latham, who called it the Sharp-tailed Oriole. Latham thought that Latin names were superfluous, so he did not assign one to this species. Later, the German biologist, Johann Gmelin, in compiling the 13th Edition of Linnaeus's *Systema naturae* (1788), kept with the oriole concept, naming the species *Oriolus caudacutus*, *Oriolus* being the generic name of many of the Old World orioles. Although locally common today, the Saltmarsh Sharp-tailed Sparrow must formerly have been much more abundant, as Audubon wrote, perhaps with a bit of exaggeration, 'This species and the *Ammodramus maritimus* [Seaside Sparrow] spend the winter among the salt marshes of South Carolina, where I have observed thousands of both in late December, and so numerous are they, that I have seen more than forty of the latter killed at one shot.' These two *Ammodramus* are dependent on coastal saltmarshes at all seasons, and the widespread destruction of this habitat accounts for their decline in numbers.

GEOGRAPHIC VARIATION: Two subspecies are generally recognized, the northern Eastern Sharp-tailed Sparrow (*A. c. caudacutus*) and the Southern Sharp-tailed Sparrow (*A. c. diversus*). These subspecies are not distinct, although the southern birds average darker in back color, with markings perhaps more sharply defined, than the northern ones. Individual specimens cannot be identified to the subspecific level.

MEASUREMENTS: (61 breeding males from Massachusetts, New York, New Jersey, and Delaware): wing 55–64 (60), tail 46–56 (50), tarsus 19.1–22.1 (20.5), culmen from nostril 8.4–10.1 (9.3), toe and claw 12.3–16.1 (14.3); (19 breeding females from the same localities): wing 53–65 (58), tail 44–52 (49), tarsus 18.0–22.4 (20.3), culmen 8.9–10.1 (9.4), toe 13.4–16.2 (15.0) (Greenlaw and Rising 1994).

Mass: (61 breeding males from Massachusetts, New York, New Jersey, and Delaware) 20.3 g (18.2–22.6); (19 breeding females) 19.1 g (16.6–21.7) (Greenlaw and Rising 1994).

References: Greenlaw (1993), Greenlaw and Rising (1994), Woolfenden (1956).

36 Nelson's Sharp-tailed Sparrow   PLATE 13
Ammodramus nelsoni [549.1]

IDENTIFICATION: 11–13 cm (*c.* 4.5–5 in), males slightly larger; sexes similar in coloration.

Sharp-tailed sparrows (Nelson's and Saltmarsh) generally have a distinctive facial pattern with a bold ochre supercilium, moustachial stripe, and posterior edge of the ear-coverts, forming a triangle that surrounds the gray ear-coverts; the color of the submoustachial contrasts little with the throat color. This is somewhat less distinct on Nelson's than on other sharptails. The back of Nelson's is characteristically conspicuously streaked grayish or buffy white; it has an unstreaked or faintly streaked yellowish ochre breast, gray ear-coverts, and a 'sharp' tail. Maritime-breeding populations of this species ('Acadian' sharptails) are much grayer in general appearance than those from the prairies or James Bay lowlands, and have indistinct stripes on back, and faint gray streaks on breast and flanks.

Similar species: The Saltmarsh Sharp-tailed Sparrow has more brightly patterned face and thin, but distinct brown breast streaks. LeConte's Sparrow is smaller, with distinct, white median crown-stripe, and distinct brown streaks on flanks. Grasshopper Sparrow lacks the facial pattern, has a scaly back, and unstreaked breast as an adult; juvenile Grasshopper Sparrows lack yellow in the face and have a streaked breast.

Prairie and James Bay populations. Adult—*Head:* with broad, but not sharply defined median crown-stripe, outlined by brown lateral crown-stripes; yellow-ochre supercilium and supraloral spot; brown eye-stripe; gray ear-coverts; yellowish gray nape and post-auricular stripe; ***back:*** dark brown usually with distinct grayish or buffy white stripes; ***rump:*** brown and unstreaked; ***tail:*** brown, unpatterned, with lateral feathers shorter than middle ones, and feathers narrow and pointed; ***wing:*** brown to chestnut-brown; coverts with dark centers, but no wing-bars; bend of wing (alula) edged with pale yellow; ***underparts:*** chin and throat pale yellow; breast and flanks light yellow-ochre, with faint brown streaks on side of throat and flanks, belly whitish; ***bill:*** horn colored, with lower mandible paler than upper; ***legs*** and ***feet:*** pinkish buff to dusky; ***iris:*** brown.

Maritime populations. Adult*:* As above but somewhat larger and larger billed, lores pale or yellowish slightly contrasting with supercilium, crown and nape grayish, side of throat and flanks gray streaked, and back, grayish brown without stripes.

First-fall and winter (Aug–Oct) resemble adults, but are buffier, and may retain some juvenal wing feathers through Mar.

Juveniles (July–Sept) crown blackish, with broad orange-buff (prairies) or olive-buff (maritimes) median stripe and broad supercilium; nape chestnut (prairies) or rust-buff (maritimes); mantle and scapular feathers dark brown broadly edged with buff, producing streaks; rump and uppertail-coverts slightly streaked (maritimes) or unstreaked; underparts variously streaked, males more so than females in prairies.

VOICE: The song is variously described as a hissing buzz or a choking gasp, or like the sound of water dripped on a hot skillet, a ***pschee-zipt***, or ***pshhh'ipt*** that lasts about 1 s. Males alone sing, and tend to sing in song bouts that may last up to 30 minutes. They often sing from a conspicuous perch, may fly from perch to perch while singing, but may sing from the ground. They also have an elaborate flight-song: males may take off, give a series of ***tic*** notes, fly up to 20 m (about 60 ft), sing, then glide forward and down, sing a second time, then drop back into the vegetation, perhaps 100 m (over 300 ft) from where they originally took off. Singing often occurs at night; this song can be given as ***tictictictictictictektektektek pshhh'ipt***. Calls are like those of the Saltmarsh Sharp-tailed Sparrow.

HABITS: Males sing persistently after arrival on breeding grounds in early June, giving song bouts from perches, the ground, or in a complex aerial display; they commonly sing at night. In migration and winter, they are found in small, loose, feeding groups, and are not usually found in mixed flocks. They do not respond to spishing.

HABITAT: In the prairies, Nelson's Sharp-tailed Sparrows breed in freshwater marshes where cordgrass, squirreltail, whitetop, and phragmites are common. Along the shores of James and Hudson bays, they are found in dense sedge bogs, generally with a few dwarf birch and willow, usually in freshwater above the high tide line and often inland. Along the coast of the St. Lawrence R., they are found in freshwater marshes with bulrushes, cattail, and grasses. In the Maritime Provinces they are found in rank grassland, saltmarshes, and in wet grasslands inland along major rivers

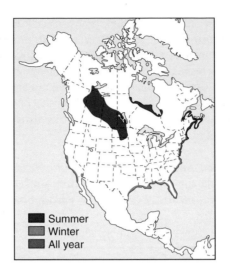

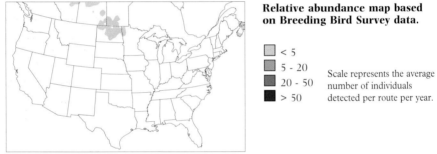

Relative abundance map based on Breeding Bird Survey data.

	< 5
	5 - 20
	20 - 50
	> 50

Scale represents the average number of individuals detected per route per year.

in freshwater habitats, and occasionally at the edge of fields and in dunes adjacent to saltmarshes. In migration they may occur in wet fields and marshes (often in cattail). In winter, they are found along the coast, in both freshwater and saltmarsh habitats, but principally in salt and brackish marshes.

BREEDING: Nest is usually a simple cup of coarse dry grass or sedge, lined with finer grasses. It is placed on the ground, or just above water in marshes. Nesting takes place in June and July. **Eggs**, 4–5, are greenish white to greenish blue, usually profusely speckled with reddish-brown (like those of the Saltmarsh Sharp-tailed Sparrow, but slightly smaller). **Incubation**, probably 11–12 days; females alone incubate; males occasionally help feed the young. Parasitized by cowbirds in the prairies.

RANGE: Breeds locally in marshes from s Mackenzie (sw Great Slave L.), n Alberta, c-e British Columbia (Peace R. parklands), south through sw Alberta (west to Bragg Creek, Standard), extreme ne Montana, c Saskatchewan (Emma L.), sw

Manitoba (north to The Pas), and se North Dakota, n-c South Dakota (Bitter Lake; probable), n Minnesota, w Ontario, and (formerly) to ne Illinois; around James and Hudson bays, from Eastmain, Quebec to Churchill, Manitoba, and probably locally inland in n Ontario; lower St. Lawrence Estuary, locally on the North Shore and on the South Shore from Montmagny to Point-au-Père, on the Gaspé Peninsula from Baie de Gaspé to the head of Chaleur Bay, and the Magdalen Is., Prince Edward I., New Brunswick, Nova Scotia, Maine (south to Sagadahoc Co.), and rarely ne Massachusetts (Essex Co.).

Winters principally along coast from Massachusetts (rare) south to Florida, and along the Gulf Coast to s Texas (mouth of the Rio Grande) and ne Tamaulipas (rare); also regularly, but uncommonly along the Pacific Coast from San Francisco Bay south to Newport Bay, California, and rarely to nw Baja California. In migration reported rarely inland (e California, e Colorado, Kansas, Missouri, Arkansas, Tennessee, and Massachusetts).

HISTORY: Born in New Hampshire, Edward William Nelson made a trip to the Rocky Mountains at the age of 17, accompanied by school friends and the famous paleontologist, Prof. Edward D. Cope. While on that trip, at the age of 18, Nelson collected the first specimens of Nelson's Sharp-tailed Sparrow in Calumet marshes of Chicago, on 17 September 1874; J.A. Allen named the species in his honor. Nelson believed that the sparrows were breeding in Illinois, but the late date suggests that they were migrants; breeding in Illinois has never been substantiated. Jonathan Dwight, who did much pioneering work on avian molts, named and described the distinctive 'Acadian' sharp-tailed sparrow in 1887, on the basis of specimens collected near Hillsborough, Albert Co., New Brunswick. Like their coastal relatives, the Seaside and Saltmarsh Sharp-tailed sparrows, these birds are susceptible to draining of the marshes in which they nest. This has particularly affected prairie-breeding populations of Nelson's Sharp-tailed Sparrow.

GEOGRAPHIC VARIATION: Three subspecies are generally recognized, Nelson's Sharp-tailed Sparrow (*A. n. nelsoni*), the James Bay Sharp-tailed Sparrow (*A. n. alterus*), and the Acadian Sharp-tailed Sparrow (*A. n. subvirgatus*). The first two are virtually identical in appearance, but the James Bay birds average somewhat buffier, and have a grayer median crown-stripe; they are somewhat intermediate in color between *A. n. nelsoni* and *A. n. subvirgatus*. but closer to the former. *A. n. subvirgatus* is less richly colored, with indistinct scapular streaking and more breast streaking, and is slightly larger. There is much confusion about the identity of these birds. Most or all of the inland records of sharp-tailed sparrows are probably *A. n. nelsoni*, whereas most of the records from the east, and probably from the Atlantic Coast are probably of *A. n. subvirgatus* (which can be identified in the field) and *A. n. alterus* (which cannot be told from *A. n. nelsoni* in the field). All of the Pacific Coast records are of 'Nelson's sparrows,' and on geographic grounds it seems likely that they are birds from the prairies. Along the northeastern coast, most of the birds that pass through in migration are apparently *A. n. subvirgatus*.

MEASUREMENTS: (25 breeding males from Saskatchewan and North Dakota): wing 51–58 (56), tail 45–51 (49), tarsus 18.2–21.3 (19.7), culmen from nostril 7.7–9.0 (8.4), toe and claw 12.3–14.8 (13.6); (6 breeding females from North Dakota): wing 52–55 (54), tail 45–49 (48), tarsus 19.6–20.6 (20.0), culmen 8.4–9.0 (8.7), toe 12.9–14.6 (14.0).

(40 breeding males from James Bay): wing 57–65 (60), tail 48–55 (52), tarsus 18.2–22.5 (20.4), culmen 8.0–9.1 (8.5), toe 12.8–15.9 (14.6); (10 breeding females from James Bay): wing 52–62 (58), tail 47–51 (49), tarsus 18.8–21.1 (20.1), culmen 8.1–8.8 (8.5), toe 14.4–18.6 (15.7).

(36 breeding males from Quebec and New Brunswick): wing 55–61 (58), tail 46–57 (53), tarsus 19.4–22.6 (21.1), culmen 7.7–9.1 (8.5), toe 13.8–16.5 (15.1); (3 females from New Brunswick): wing 55–57 (56), tail 49–52 (50), tarsus 20.0–21.2 (20.4), culmen 8.2–8.6 (8.4), toe 15.1–15.9 (15.6) (Greenlaw and Rising 1994).

Mass: (25 breeding males from North Dakota and Saskatchewan) 14.9 g (13.7–16.6); (6 breeding females from North Dakota) 13.9 g (12.8–15.2); (40 breeding males from James Bay) 16.8 g (15.6–18.6); (10 breeding females from James Bay) 16.5 g (15.0–20.0); (36 breeding males from Quebec and New Brunswick) 17.4 g (15.5–20.3); (3 females from New Brunswick) 19.3 g (17.0–20.9) (Greenlaw and Rising 1994).

References: Greenlaw (1993), Greenlaw and Rising (1994), Rising and Avise (1993).

37 **Seaside Sparrow** *Ammodramus maritimus* [550]   PLATE **14**

D. BEADLE.

IDENTIFICATION: 12.5–15 cm (*c.* 5–6 in), males slightly larger; sexes similar in coloration.

The Seaside Sparrow is a geographically variable bird. It is olive-gray to olive-brown in hue, and has a long bill and relative short, sharp tail. The back and breast are streaked, but not always conspicuously so; the facial pattern is distinctive: the supraloral spot and supercilium are yellow from above the eye to the bill, the submoustachial stripe is pale, the malar stripe is dark, and the throat pale.

Similar species: The sharp-tailed sparrows (Nelson's and Saltmarsh), which are conspicuously smaller in size, often occur in the same marshes as Seaside Sparrows. Seaside Sparrows appear dark and dingy, whereas sharp-tailed sparrows are paler, yellowish ochre, with ochre or orangeish ochre on their faces. Nelson's Sharp-tailed Sparrows lack conspicuous streaking on their breast and often show distinct white streaking on their backs. Juvenile Saltmarsh Sharp-tailed Sparrows are yellowish in hue, with the edges of the ear coverts, supercilium, supraloral spot, and breast yellow ochre, and a distinctive wedge-shaped eye-stripe.

Adult—*Head:* lateral crown-stripes brown or dark brown; median crown-stripe gray, streaked with brown; supraloral spot and supercilium yellow to bright yellow from above the eye to the bill, and brown or grayish brown behind the eye where it is usually indistinct; ear-coverts brown, olive-brown, or olive-gray; moustachial stripe sometimes the same color as the ear-coverts, sometimes somewhat darker; sub-moustachial stripe pale, malar stripe dark brown; throat pale and unspotted; ***back:*** olive-gray to brownish, with centers of feathers brown to dark brown, giving the back a streaked appearance in unworn individuals; ***rump:*** brown, uppertail-coverts brown with darker centers; ***tail:*** brown, sometimes faintly barred, with lateral edges of feathers darker than centers, relatively short with pointed feathers; ***wing:*** brown to rusty brown; bend of wing (alula) yellow; greater coverts and scapulars with dark centers; no conspicuous wing-bars; ***underparts:*** breast and flanks olive-gray, whitish or pale ochre, striped with olive-gray, brown, or black; belly grayish to pale buff; undertail-coverts pale with dark centers; ***bill:*** dark horn colored, paler below and near head; ***legs*** and ***feet:*** yellowish brown; ***iris:*** dark brown.

First-winter (after Aug) resemble adults, but may be somewhat buffier below.

Juveniles (June–Aug) crown and back olive-brown streaked with dark brown; mantle feathers with pale edge; face patterned as adults, with supercilium and supraloral stripe pale rather than yellow, and post-auricular stripe sometimes pale; breast and flanks with thin brown streaks or without streaking (southern coastal Texas).

VOICE: The song is a buzzy ***spitsh-sheer, tup tup zee reeeeeeee*** (with the third syllable emphasized), ***cut cut zhe-eeeeeeeee***, ***chur-er eeee***, ***chi eegle eedle zhurr***, or ***oka-che weeeee*** (sounds like a faint Red-winged Blackbird). The song generally lasts about 1–2 s, and is extremely variable. An individual may sing one song repeatedly, then switch to another song. During the height of the breeding season, males may give a flight song of 3–4 s duration. The song of the extinct Dusky Seaside Sparrow was distinctive, and more insect-like than most of the songs of the other Seaside Sparrows. The song of the Cape Sable Seaside Sparrow is also distinctive, and again very insect-like. Seaside Sparrows have a ***chip-chip chip-chip*** alarm note, as well as ***tuck***, ***chrit***, and ***tsip*** notes that are given during aggressive interactions.

HABITS: When singing, males may perch conspicuously near the top of grass or a bush. When approached they either descend into the grass or fly a short distance and drop into the vegetation; their flight is low and direct. On the ground they often run; their large feet facilitate running over soft mud.

HABITAT: In the north, Seaside Sparrows are invariably found in or at the edges of saltmarshes, and they nest in vegetation consisting chiefly of smooth cordgrass, black grass (*Juncus*), cattail, and marsh-elder (*Iva*). They often occupy the wettest, muddiest parts of the marsh. In southern Florida, Cape Sable Seaside Sparrows breed in freshwater habitats, especially in sparse saw grass or *Muhlenbergia* grass prairies, in

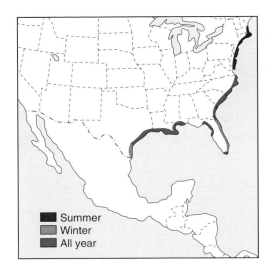

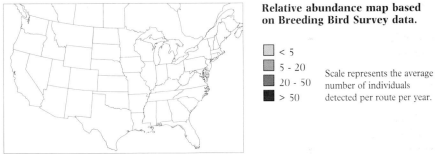

Relative abundance map based on Breeding Bird Survey data.

□ < 5
■ 5 - 20
■ 20 - 50
■ > 50

Scale represents the average number of individuals detected per route per year.

which they are commonest three years after a fire, and in cordgrass prairies; they avoid brushy prairie.

BREEDING: *Nest* is a simple cup of grass, lined with finer grasses, that is placed 18 cm (7 in) to 1 m high in grasses, marsh-elder, or low mangroves, or occasionally as high as 4 m (14 ft). The nest is generally well concealed, and may be domed. Nesting takes place from mid-Mar to late July in Florida, mid-Apr to mid-July in Louisiana and Texas, late May through June in Georgia, mid-May through mid-July in New Jersey, and June through early July in Rhode I. *Eggs*, usually 2–5 (most commonly 3 in south, 4 in north), are pale bluish white or grayish white, and speckled, spotted or blotched with purplish brown. *Incubation*, 11–13 days, and young fledge in 9 days; the female alone incubates, but both parents feed the young. Newly fledged young cannot fly, but run well. Double-brooded or occasionally triple-brooded in the south, but probably generally single-brooded in the north. Cowbird parasitism has not been confirmed.

RANGE: *Breeds* from New Hampshire and ne Massachusetts (Plum I., South Dartmouth, Barnstable marshes, Monomoy) south along the coast to ne Florida (St. Johns R.), s Florida (Everglades National Park, Cape Sable, Ochopee), along the coast of nw Florida (Pasco Co. to Wakulla Co.), and from w Florida (Pensacola Bay) along the coast to extreme s Texas.

Winters from New Hampshire and Massachusetts (rare), but usually south of Delaware, south to s Florida, and s Texas (Río Grande River). Wanders north along the coast in fall and winter to Maine, New Brunswick, and Nova Scotia.

HISTORY: The American ornithologist Alexander Wilson collected the first known specimens of the Seaside Sparrow along the shore of New Jersey, probably near present-day Ocean City, in 1810. He named it *Fringilla maritima*. Early accounts refer to the abundance of Seaside Sparrows (Audubon wrote: 'Having one day shot a number of these birds, merely for the sake of practice, I had them made into a pie, which, however, could not be eaten, on account of its fishy savour.'). Although still abundant in suitable areas, habitat destruction has resulted in substantial decreases in their numbers, and their extirpation in many areas. In Florida, the disjunct and distinctive 'Dusky Seaside Sparrow' (which would probably be treated as a separate species today) was formerly common in the saltmarshes of Brevard Co. By the 1960s, however, most of its habitat on Merritt I. had been destroyed, and its populations declined in the St. Johns Marsh in the 1970s, largely as a consequence of marsh draining; it was effectively extinct by 1980. Another disjunct and distinctive form, the 'Cape Sable Seaside Sparrow,' apparently was formerly limited to the Cape Sable peninsula in southern Florida, where it was believed to have been extirpated by the 'Labor Day' hurricane of 1935. However, it was rediscovered in brackish and freshwater marshes in southern Collier, northern Monroe, and southern Dade cos., and later on Cape Sable. In 1981, it was estimated that their total population numbered 6600 individuals (Robertson and Woolfenden 1992).

GEOGRAPHIC VARIATION: Nine subspecies are generally recognized. Of these, two have at various times been recognized as distinct species, the Dusky Seaside Sparrow (*A. m. nigrescens*) and the Cape Sable Sparrow (*A. maritimus mirabilis*). *A. m. nigrescens* is now extinct. Neither of these are known to have ever overlapped any of the other Seaside Sparrows in breeding range, and both are phenotypically distinct; molecular studies indicate that they are closely related to other Seaside Sparrows.

A. m. maritimus, which breeds from Massachusetts south to the Delmarva Peninsula, is grayish olive above and grayish white below, with indistinct grayish streaking. *A. m. macgillivraii*, which breeds from North Carolina south to the mouth of the St. Johns R., is like *A. m. maritimus*, but darker on average with perhaps more streaking. *A. m. pelonota*, which was very like *A. m. macgillivraii*, was resident from the St. Johns R. south to New Smyrna, in northeastern Florida, but is now extinct (some include the birds from Amelia I. in extreme northeastern Florida in *A. m. pelonota*.) *A. m.*

nigrescens, once resident in marshes in northern Brevard and eastern Orange cos., Florida, is now extinct. It had very dark dorsal striping, was white below, without any buffy wash, and had sharply defined black stripes. *A. m. mirabilis*, the only Seaside Sparrow breeding in southern Florida, is pale whitish below, without any buffy wash, with sharply defined dark brown streaking, olive-brown on the back with dark brown streaks on the crown and usually on the scapulars, and distinct yellow in front of the eye. The Seaside Sparrows breeding on the west coast of Florida, from Pasco Co. to Wakulla Co., have been divided into two subspecies, *A. m. peninsulae* and *A. m. juncicola*, but these are poorly differentiated and grade into each other. They are dark, ash-brown below, with diffuse streaking, and dark on the back, with dark cinnamon-brown centers to feathers. *A. m. fisheri*, which breeds from extreme western Florida, west to San Antonio Bay in east Texas, is washed with bright ochre below, with distinct, thin dark brown stripes; the centers of the scapulars and greater coverts are very dark, edged with pale or rusty in unworn birds. *A.m. sennetti*, which breeds in southern Texas, is similar to *A. m. fisheri*, but paler and less ochre below, greenish gray on the nape and the supercilium (behind the eye), somewhat paler on the back, and with a brown-striped gray median crown-stripe.

MEASUREMENTS: *A. m. maritimus*: (16 males): wing 61–65 (63), tail 51–59 (55), tarsus 22.4–24.1 (23.4), exposed culmen 12.7–14.7 (13.7), depth of bill at base 6.4–7.4 (7.1); (12 females): wing 56–60 (58), tail 50–55 (54), tarsus 22.6–23.4 (22.9), exposed culmen 13.0–14.55 (13.5), bill depth 6.4–6.9 (6.6).

A. m. peninsulae: (7 males): wing 54–62 (59), tail 49–58 (54), tarsus 21.8–23.4 (22.6), exposed culmen 13.0–14.7 (14.0), bill depth 6.6–6.9 (6.7); (13 females): wing 54–61 (57), tail 50–58 (53), tarsus 20.8–23.1 (21.8), exposed culmen 12.5–14.2 (13.5), bill depth 5.8–6.9 (6.1).

A. m. sennetti: (8 males): wing 58–61 (60), tail 49–58 (55), tarsus 20.8–22.9 (22.4), exposed culmen 12.7–13.5 (13.0), bill depth 6.4–7.1 (6.1); (9 females): wing 55–58 (56), tail 51–55 (52), tarsus 21.1–22.9 (22.1), exposed culmen 12.5–13.2 (13.0), bill depth 5.8–6.6 (6.1) (Ridgway 1901).

Mass: (14 males) 24.2 g (21.9–27.4); (3 females) 22.3 g (19.8–24.4) (Dunning 1993).

References: Post and Greenlaw (1994), Quay *et al.* (1983), Woolfenden (1956).

Genus *Passerella*

Sparrows of the genus *Passerella* are large, with strong conical bills, long legs, stout feet with strong claws, rather long wings, slightly rounded or double-rounded tails, and underparts conspicuously streaked with rusty or brown.

Until recently, most ornithologists recognized only one species in the genus *Passerella*, the Fox Sparrow (*P. iliaca*). However, recently published molecular and behavioral (vocal) evidence indicates that these should be divided into as many as 4 species: the Red Fox Sparrow (*P. iliaca*) of the boreal forests from Newfoundland to Alaska; the Sooty Fox Sparrow (*P. unalaschcensis*) of coastal Alaska and British Columbia; the Slate-colored Fox Sparrow (*P. schistacea*) of the Rocky Mountains and Great Basin; and the Thick-billed Fox Sparrow (*P. megarhyncha*) of the California Mountains. Although this revision has not yet been accepted by the AOU Check-list Committee, pending the publication of some work in progress, we are discussing 3 of these fox sparrows separately here, but have combined the Slate-colored and Thick-billed Fox Sparrows (as *P. schistacea*) because of their similarity in appearance.

Fox sparrows are similar to *Melospiza* sparrows in coloration, morphology, song, and nesting habits, and many have combined the two genera. However, molecular evidence indicates that fox sparrows are sufficiently distinct from *Melospiza* and other similar sparrows (*Zonotrichia, Junco*) to warrant their placement in a separate genus.

38 **Red Fox Sparrow** *Passerella iliaca* [585]   PLATE 15

D.BEADLE 95.

IDENTIFICATION: 15–17 cm (*c.* 6–7 in), males slightly larger; sexes similar in coloration.

Red Fox Sparrows are large and rusty red, especially on ear-coverts, back, rump, and tail (which is conspicuous in flight), and have extensive rusty to almost blackish streaking on breast and flanks, and gray and rusty streaking on the back.

Similar species: Other fox sparrows are similar in size, but lack the rust on the head and back, streaks on the back, and have less or no rust on the rump and tail. Red Fox Sparrows have a pale triangular patch above the end of the pale submalar stripe, that is not obvious on other fox sparrows. With the exception of Aleutian populations, Song Sparrows are smaller; eastern Song Sparrows are brown or sometimes rusty brown, but never as rufous as Red Fox Sparrows, and lack the yellowish base of the lower bill and the rusty rump and tail of the Red Fox Sparrow; some western Song Sparrows are rusty brown, but they are always paler and substantially smaller than fox sparrows. The malar stripe of the Song Sparrow is much darker. Swamp Sparrows may have extensive rust in crown, coverts, and tertials, but are substantially smaller. Hermit Thrush also shows a conspicuous rusty rump and tail in flight, but has a thin bill and an unstreaked back.

Adult—*Head:* almost always with a mixture of gray and rust in crown; lores buffy; supercilium dull gray; ear-coverts mixed with buff, rufous and gray; moustachial stripe bold rusty or brownish rusty; submoustachial stripe thin and buffy submoustachial; malar stripe rusty or brownish rusty; **back:** nape and mantle gray or brownish gray with centers of feathers rusty brown, forming streaks; **rump:** brown to rusty brown, uppertail-coverts bright rusty and unpatterned; **tail:** rusty brown and unpatterned; **wing:** rusty brown with extensive rust in scapulars, tertials, and coverts; median and greater coverts narrowly tipped with buff, forming two indistinct wing-bars; **underparts:** chin, throat, and upper breast whitish, speckled with rust; breast with a bold necklace of rusty spots and a darker rusty brown central spot; flanks extensively rusty, spotted with triangular spots; belly white and unspotted; undertail-coverts whitish and usually unspotted; **bill:** upper mandible grayish brown, lower mandible paler, yellowish; **legs** and **feet:** pale brownish or pinkish brown; **iris:** dark brown.

First-fall and winter (July–Sept) resemble adults, but average duller in coloration.

Juveniles (June–July) crown and back brown, with centers of feathers dark brown or rusty brown, rump and tail bright rusty, underparts light buffy, heavily streaked with brown, paler and lightly streaked on belly; coverts and tertials broadly edged with rust. Molt before migrating.

VOICE: A series of over 6 loud, clear, slurred ringing whistles on different pitches, usually ending with a buzzy whistle. Individuals sing the same song repeatedly, but there is much individual variation in song. The alarm note is a loud **smack**, **tchek**, or **chick**.

HABITS: On the breeding grounds, males sing persistently at least until mid-July, usually from a perch 1–3 m high; they occasionally sing in winter. They are generally difficult to see, but respond vigorously to play-back and to spishing. In winter, the birds are usually found in small, loose flocks. Their flight is strong and direct, but when flushed they may fly from bush to bush with a nervous jerking of the tail. They do, however, feed on the ground, often using a double-scratch method; often they can be heard scratching among dried leaves in the winter.

HABITAT: Red Fox Sparrows breed in dense deciduous thickets (commonly alders or willows), in bogs, and dwarf spruce or fir. In migration and winter, they are generally found in low, moist areas with rank, tall brush, and brush piles, often at woodland edge, or in wet woods (such as maple swamps); in the southwest, they are found in chaparral and streamside thickets.

BREEDING: Nest is a bulky cup of twigs, rootlets, lichens, and grasses, lined with finer grasses, fur, and sometimes feathers. Nests are usually placed on the ground, among mosses, grasses or Labrador tea, but less often low (to 2.7 m and rarely to 6 m) in dense trees (e.g. stunted spruce). Nesting takes place from early to late Apr through early July (earliest in the southernmost part of their range). **Eggs**, usually 3–5, are pale green, boldly marked with brown or reddish brown, with markings generally denser at the large end. **Incubation**, 12–14 days, young fledge in 9–10 days;

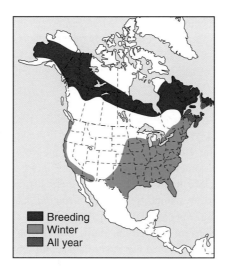

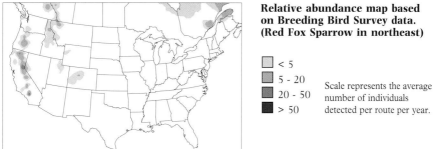

Relative abundance map based on Breeding Bird Survey data. (Red Fox Sparrow in northeast)

☐ < 5
▨ 5 - 20
▩ 20 - 50
■ > 50

Scale represents the average number of individuals detected per route per year.

the female alone probably incubates, but both parents feed the young. They are rarely parasitized by cowbirds.

RANGE: *Breeds* from w (Dillingham, Ekwok), c (Denali Park, Livengood) and n Alaska (Anaktuvuk Pass, Colville R., Porcupine R.), n Yukon, nw (Mackenzie Delta, Anderson) and e-c Mackenzie, sw Keewatin, n Manitoba, n Ontario, n Quebec (Great Whale R., Kuujjuaq), and n Labrador (Nachvak) south to n British Columbia (Dease Lake), n and c Alberta (Peace R.), c Saskatchewan (Nipawin), c Manitoba (Ilford, Gillam), n Ontario (s to Albany R., Moosonee, Little Abitibi R.), se and s-c Quebec (Hannah Bay, Schefferville, Gaspé Peninsula, Anticosti and Magdalen Is.), Newfoundland, nw New Brunswick, Prince Edward I., Nova Scotia (Cape Breton, e coast), extreme nw Maine.

Winters from e and s Minnesota, s Wisconsin, s Michigan, s Ontario, sw Quebec, New Brunswick (very rare), Nova Scotia (occasional), and s Newfoundland south to Florida, the Gulf Coast and s Texas. Rare but regular on west coast, from Washington to s California (principally in the interior). Most winter east of the Great Plains, from Iowa south to e Texas, and New Jersey south to Georgia. Casual or accidental in Bermuda, Greenland, Iceland (Nov), and Europe (Ireland, Germany, Italy; records Apr–June). This is one of the earliest sparrows to migrate in the spring, and last to arrive in the fall.

HISTORY: The Red Fox Sparrow was first described in 1786 by the German biologist, Blasius Merrem. Harry Swarth (1920) wrote: 'Type specimen was presented to the Museum or to Merrem by a Hessian officer. This would indicate that it was a winter specimen taken somewhere between Boston and Charleston and possibly between New York and Washington.' The AOU Check-list, however, gives the type locality as Quebec. Merrem named this species *Fringilla iliaca*. The name 'iliaca' is apparently from the Latin *ilia* referring to the groin or lower intestine, or loosely to the flanks. Seemingly, Merrem derived this name from that of the European thrush, the Redwing (*Turdus iliacus*), which has rusty flanks, and bares a superficial resemblance to the Red Fox Sparrow. In 1837, William Swainson coined the name *Passerella* for the fox sparrows, the diminutive of *Passer*, hence 'little sparrow,' a singularly inappropriate name for these, which are among the largest of the American sparrows. In Audubon's time, Red Fox Sparrows apparently were popular cage birds. Audubon writes: 'Many of these birds are frequently offered for sale in the markets of Charleston, they being easily caught in "figure-of-four traps!" Their price is usually ten or twelve cents each. I saw many in the aviaries of my friends . . .' Because most Red Fox Sparrows nest in remote areas in the far north, little is known about changes in their populations. Clear-cutting in some areas would create rank brush suitable for fox sparrows, so they may have benefited from recent habitat changes in the north.

GEOGRAPHIC VARIATION: Two subspecies are generally listed, the Eastern Fox Sparrow (*P.i. iliaca*) and the Yukon Fox Sparrow (*P.i. zaboria*) (Alaska to Manitoba), which tends to be grayer, especially in the head, and with a browner malar stripe and ventral streaking. Most, if not all eastern fox sparrows have gray in their crown and nape, and many are extensively gray. These two subspecies cannot be satisfactorily separated in the field, and probably not in the hand, although extremely gray birds are doubtless from the western part of the range.

MEASUREMENTS: (10 males): wing 86–92 (89), tail 67–74 (70), tarsus 24.1–25.4 (24.9), exposed culmen 10.7–13.0 (12.5), depth of bill at base 9.1–10.4 (9.9); (7 females): wing 84–88 (86), tail 67–73 (69), tarsus 23.1–25.4 (24.9), exposed culmen 10.7–12.2 (11.7), bill depth 9.1–10.2 (9.4) (Ridgway 1901).

Mass: 36.9 g (29.6–49.0) (Clench and Leberman 1978).

References: Threlfall and Blacquiere (1982), Zink (1994).

39 **Sooty Fox Sparrow** *Passerella unalaschcensis* [585a] PLATE 15

D. BEADLE.

IDENTIFICATION: 15.5–18.5 cm (*c.* 6–7.5 in), males slightly larger; sexes similar in coloration.

Sooty Fox Sparrows are large and very dark brown, with extensive dark brown streaking and spotting on underparts. They often look rather large-headed and small-billed.

Similar species: Other fox sparrows are similar in size, but are not so dark in coloration. Sooty Fox Sparrows have little if any gray in their plumage, although some have a gray wash on their face and upper back; although variable, none show conspicuous rustiness, although the uppertail-coverts, tertials, and coverts may be dark rusty brown. The side of the face is nearly uniformly brown in the lores and submoustachial areas. The dark, evenly colored head allows the pale eye crescents (one above, one below) to be quite noticeable.

Adult—*Head:* crown uniformly dark brown to nearly black; side of face unpatterned with a few beige flecks sometimes evident in submoustachial stripe and lores; ***back:*** nape and mantle dark brown to nearly black and unstreaked; ***rump*** and uppertail-coverts dull rufous-brown to dark rufous-brown; ***tail:*** dull rufous-brown to dark rufous-brown and unpatterned; ***wing:*** brown or dark brown with some hint of rust in scapulars, tertials, and coverts, no wing-bars; ***underparts:*** chin and throat whitish, flecked — often extensively — with brown or dark brown; breast and flanks heavily streaked or spotted with triangular brown or dark brown spots, often showing a collar of spots, followed by a pale band, then a dark patch below that; belly whitish, often spotted; ***bill:*** upper mandible dusky to dark; lower mandible paler, usually orange-yellow at base; ***legs:*** brownish; ***iris:*** dark brown.

First-fall and winter (July–Sept) resemble adults.

Juveniles (June–July) like adults, but pale areas on underparts buff or dark buff, rather than whitish.

VOICE: The song is a loud series of rather staccato notes rising and falling on different pitches, *she she shu tu-you tu-you*; many of the notes are slurred or buzzy. The common call is a loud *tik* or *thik*, or a sharp *zitt*.

HABITS: Territorial males sing from an exposed twig high in a bush, the top of a tree, or an exposed dead branch. When not singing, they are difficult to see. Sooty Fox Sparrows seldom fly long distances, but flit from bush to bush in jerky flight, often flicking their tail. They forage on the ground. In winter they are found singly or in small groups, although they do not tend to flock and are quite responsive to spishing.

HABITAT: Sooty Fox Sparrows are found in dense thickets, most commonly deciduous thickets (willow, alder), often along creeks or at the edge of bogs or ponds. In winter in California they are found in chaparral, often in fairly dry chaparral but especially in dense arborescent chaparral, or dense understory of oak woodlands. In southern British Columbia, they like dense understory, often Himalayan blackberry.

BREEDING: *Nest* is a bulky structure of small twigs, leaves, moss, and grasses, lined with finer grasses, and sometimes hair or feathers; it is generally placed in a crotch in bushes (up to 4 m), but sometimes on the ground. Nesting takes place from early May through June. *Eggs*, 3 or 4, are pale bluish green or greenish gray, boldly spotted or blotched with brown. *Incubation*, probably 12–14 days; the female alone probably incubates, but both parents feed the young. Not reported as a host for cowbirds.

RANGE: *Breeds* from Aleutian Is., west to Unalaska, Shumagin, Semidi, Kodiak and Middleton Is., Alaska Peninsula, Iliamna L., and Cook Inlet, south along the coast to British Columbia (including Queen Charlotte Is.) to nw Washington (Destruction and Lopez Is., nw Olympic Peninsula).

Winters from se Alaska and coastal British Columbia, south to nw Baja California, and se Arizona (Chiricahua Mountains; rare). Very rare on Bering Sea Is. (Pribilofs, Nunivak), n Alaska (Barrow) and Russia (Chukchi Peninsula); accidental in Japan.

HISTORY: The English ornithologist John Latham was the first to describe the 'Unalashka Bunting,' in 1782. At that time in his career, Latham thought Latin names to be superfluous, and thus it was not until 1788 that Johann Friedrich Gmelin named the Sooty Fox Sparrow *Emberiza unalaschcensis* in his 13th Edition of *Systema naturae*. Audubon named fox sparrows collected from the 'shores of the Columbia R.' near Fort Vancouver, Washington, *Plectrophanes Townsendi*, in honor of John Kirk Townsend, their collector. The subspecies breeding in southeastern Alaska and the Queen Charlotte Is. today carries the name *townsendi*.

GEOGRAPHIC VARIATION: Six subspecies are generally recognized: Shumagin fox sparrow (*P. u. unalaschcensis*) (which breeds on Aleutian, Shumagin, and Semidi Is., and Alaska Peninsula); Kodiak fox sparrow (*P. u. insularis*) (Kodiak and adjacent Is.); Valdez fox sparrow (*P. u. sinuosa*) (Prince William Sound, Kenai Peninsula, Middleton I.); Yakutat fox sparrow (*P.u. annectens*) (Yakutat Bay); Townsend's fox sparrow (*P. u. townsendi*) (s coastal Alaska, Queen Charlotte Is.); and sooty fox sparrow (*P. u. fuliginosa*) (mainland coast of British Columbia, Vancouver I., nw Washington). These subspecies differ clinally in size and coloration. The sparrows from the Aleutians and sw Alaska are relatively larger, larger billed, lighter brown, with less ventral spotting than those from the Yakutat Bay south. The southernmost birds from coastal s Alaska and British Columbia are very dark, appearing nearly black with very heavy ventral spotting; even the belly is spotted with dark brown. The populations in s British Columbia are probably resident; those from the Aleutian Is., Kodiak I., and Kenai Peninsula winter the farthest south, in southern California, and in general the northern populations leapfrog the southern ones during southward migration and wintering.

MEASUREMENTS: (8 males, Alaska Peninsula): wing 81–85 (84), tail 73–81 (76), tarsus 25.0–26.0 (25.3), exposed culmen 12.0, depth of bill at base 9.5–10.5 (10.0); (10 males, Kodiak I., Alaska): wing 78–86 (82), tail 71–79 (74), tarsus 24.0–27.0 (25.2), exposed culmen 12.0–13.0 (12.3), bill depth 9.5–11.0 (10.3); (10 males, Prince William Sound, Alaska): wing 78–84 (81), tail 68–76 (73), tarsus 23.5–25.0 (24.4), exposed culmen 11.2–13.0 (12.2), bill depth 9.2–10.5 (9.9); (9 males, Yakutat, Alaska): wing 80–83 (81), tail 67–76 (73), tarsus 23.5–25.0 (24.7), exposed culmen 11.0–12.5 (11.8), bill depth 9.0–10.0 (9.4); (10 males Admiralty and Baranof Is., Alaska): wing 75–81 (79), tail 67–74 (71), tarsus 24.0–26.0 (25.0), exposed culmen 10.8–12.2 (11.6), bill depth 8.5–9.5 (9.1) (Swarth 1920).

(10 males, s Alaska): wing 77–84 (81), tail 67–74 (71), tarsus 24.4–26.7 (25.4), exposed culmen 11.2–12.5 (11.9), bill depth 7.4–8.1 (7.9); (7 females, s Alaska): wing 75–82 (81), tail 66–77 (70), tarsus 23.3–25.2 (24.6), exposed culmen 10.4–12.5 (11.2), bill depth 7.6–8.6 (7.9) (Ridgway 1901).

Mass: (N=270) 31.5 g (25.3–42.1) (Berkeley, California; February, a.m.) (Linsdale and Sumner 1934).

References: Gabrielson and Lincoln (1959), Linsdale (1928), Linsdale and Sumner (1934), Swarth (1920), Zink (1994).

40 **Slate-colored Fox Sparrow**   PLATE 15
Passerella schistacea [585c]

IDENTIFICATION: 15–18 cm (*c.* 6–7 in), males slightly larger; sexes similar in coloration.

Slate-colored Fox Sparrows are large (though not for fox sparrows), with slate-colored head and back washed with brown, brown wings and rump, a rusty brown tail, pale lores, yellowish lower mandible, and breast and flanks heavily spotted with dark brown.

Similar species: The Red Fox Sparrow is much more rufous, especially in the rump and tail, with rufous spotting ventrally. Sooty Fox Sparrows are variable, but all have much browner backs, are generally darker in overall coloration, with more ventral spotting; the belly of Slate-colored Fox Sparrows is whitish and usually unspotted, whereas that of Sooty Fox Sparrows is often brown spotted or streaked. With the exception of Aleutian populations, Song Sparrows are smaller, and have a dark, smaller bill.

Adult—*Head:* dusky grayish or brownish gray; lores dark buff; ear-coverts brown, flecked with beige; malar stripe darker brown; ***back:*** nape and mantle brownish gray and unpatterned; ***rump*** and especially uppertail-coverts rusty brown; ***tail:*** rusty brown and unpatterned; ***wing:*** dull rusty brown; tertials and coverts rusty; median coverts may be buff-tipped, forming one indistinct wing-bar; ***underparts:*** chin and throat whitish, generally lightly flecked with dark brown; breast and flanks brown spotted, generally with a brown central breast spot; belly white and usually unspotted; ***bill:*** upper mandible grayish brown; lower mandible yellow, blue-gray (large-billed) often dusky at tip; ***legs*** and ***feet:*** pale brownish; ***iris:*** dark brown.

First-fall and winter (July–Sept) resemble adults, but upperparts more distinctly tinged with brown.

Juveniles (July–Aug) forehead, crown, and nape brownish gray, and perhaps rusty-tinged; lower back, rump and uppertail-coverts brown, faintly streaked, and becoming more rusty brown posteriorly, underparts light buffy, heavily spotted or streaked with brown, belly whitish; wing feathers gray-brown, coverts and tertials narrowly tipped with buff (no wing-bars). Molt before migrating.

VOICE: The song is clear and ringing, starting with two or three syllables on different pitches ***too-wheet-whoo tweek-tsuck-tseeka tsew!***, with every other note emphasized, or ***shree-wee shu-shu-shu-shu-shu wit-wit-wit***; several of the elements may have a buzzy quality, and many may have bunting-like warbles. Individual males sing two to five different songs, not singing the same song twice in a row. The song may closely resemble that of the Green-tailed Towhee, and song mimicry may be involved. The call is a distinctive metallic ***chink, chek***, or ***klink***, reminiscent of the call of the California Towhee or a faint ***seet*** or ***psippt***.

HABITS: On the breeding grounds, males sing persistently from brushy thickets, sometimes from an exposed perch, but also from the ground or low vegetation. Singing intensity is greatest in the morning and evening. Slate-colored Fox Sparrows are generally difficult to see. Females will give a broken-wing display near a nest. They feed principally on the ground where they scratch for seeds and insects. In winter, they usually are solitary or occur in small flocks.

HABITAT: Slate-colored Fox Sparrows nest in deciduous thickets (rose, willows, alders, aspen, birch, mountain whitethorn (*Ceanothus*), manzanita, bush chinquapin, bearberry, wild rose, gooseberry, or elderberry), and sometimes in thick, scrubby conifers (pine, spruce, fir), generally along streams. In winter, they are found in chaparral and streamside thickets..

BREEDING: *Nest* is a bulky deep cup of grass, twigs, moss, bark, and rootlets, lined with finer grass, hair, and sometimes feathers. Nests are commonly placed near the ground to up to 2 m in a bush (often *Ceanothus*), or in heather. Nesting takes place from mid-May through mid-July. ***Eggs***, usually 3–4, are pale greenish or bluish, thickly speckled with brown, reddish brown, or purple. ***Incubation***, probably 12–14 days; the female alone probably incubates, but both parents feed the young. They are occasionally parasitized by cowbirds.

RANGE: *Breeds* from sw and c interior British Columbia (Thutade L.), se British Columbia (Crowsnest Pass), sw Alberta (Banff, Waterton L.) south to mountains of s-c and sw British Columbia, c and e Washington, c and ne Oregon, se Idaho, w Montana, s to s-c Colorado, n–c Utah (Wasatch Mountains), Nevada (south to Esmeralda, Mineral and White Pine cos.), and from s-c Oregon (Siskiyouou Peak and Grayback Mountain), south to ne California (Warner Mountains), and in the Sierra Nevada to Tulare Co. and east to L. Tahoe, and in the west to Homboldt, Trinity, Mendocino, Glenn, and Lake cos., and locally in the mountains in Santa Barbara,

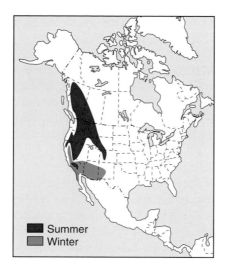

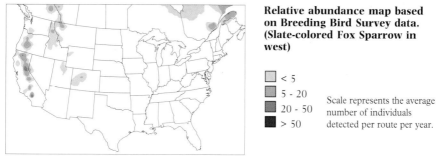

Relative abundance map based on Breeding Bird Survey data. (Slate-colored Fox Sparrow in west)

☐ < 5
▨ 5 - 20   Scale represents the average
▨ 20 - 50   number of individuals
■ > 50   detected per route per year.

Ventura, Kern, Los Angeles, Riverside (San Jacinto and Santa Rosa mountains) and San Bernardino cos., and probably in San Diego Co.

Winters from n interior California (Paine Creek; uncommon), coastal s California, s Nevada (rare), c Arizona (Hualapai and Kofa mountains; local), n New Mexico (occasional), south to n Baja California, s Arizona (Ajo, Chiricahua Mountains), n Sonora, and w Texas (El Paso).

HISTORY: Ironically, the type specimen of this western species was collected along the Platte R., 25 miles (40 km) east of the northeastern corner of Colorado, in the present state of Nebraska. It was described in 1858 by Spencer Fullerton Baird, and although the type is clearly a bird from along the Platte, the description seems to apply to birds from California. Baird later corrected this mistake, and applied the name *Passerella megarhynchus* to birds from Fort Tejon, California. Perhaps because Slate-colored Fox Sparrows and other fox sparrows have generally been considered to be a single species, the status of these birds east of the Rocky Mountains is unclear, but it is probable that they are at best uncommon in the western plains today.

Populations in the mountains of Oregon may be increasing slightly, but the data on this are not clear.

GEOGRAPHIC VARIATION: There are two groups of subspecies, the 'Thick-billed Fox Sparrows' and the 'Slate-colored Fox Sparrows'. These may soon be separated into different species, but are generally similar in appearance, differing principally in bill size. Individuals of these different groups hybridize fairly frequently in eastern California (Warner and White mountains, Mono L.) and western Nevada (Walker R. Range).

Five or six subspecies of Slate-colored Fox Sparrows have been generally recognized, but most of these are but poorly differentiated. The northernmost, *P. s. altivagans*, breeds from the interior of c British Columbia south to s British Columbia where it grades into *P. s. schistacea*. *P. s. altivagans* has been put with the Red Fox Sparrows, but vocal and biochemical evidence indicates that it belongs with the Slate-colored Fox Sparrows. It has a brown unstreaked back. The other subspecies closely resemble *P. s. schistacea* with brownish gray or slaty crown and back, with dull rusty brown wings, uppertail-coverts and tail. Birds from the mountains near Mono Lake (*P. s. monoensis*) appear to hybridize with Thick-billed Fox Sparrows.

MEASUREMENTS: (10 males, Pine Forest Mountains, Nevada): wing 78–85 (80), tail 78–85 (81), tarsus 22.8–24.0 (23.4), exposed culmen 11.0–11.8 (11.5), depth of bill at base 8.8–10.2 (9.5) (Swarth 1920).

(15 males): wing 78–87 (82), tail 73–87 (80), tarsus 21.6–24.6 (23.4), exposed culmen 11.2–12.7 (12.2), depth of bill at base 8.9–10.4 (9.9); (5 females): wing 77–82 (80), tail (no data), tarsus 22.9–23.6 (23.4), exposed culmen 11.4–12.7 (11.9), bill depth 9.7–10.7 (10.2) (Ridgway 1901).

Mass: (no data available).

References: Martin (1977), Swarth (1920), Zink (1986, 1994).

Genus *Melospiza*

Sparrows of the genus *Melospiza* are rather small to large, with short rounded wings, rather long tails (nearly equal to or longer than the wing), rounded or double-rounded tails, and with the exception of adult Swamp Sparrows, conspicuously streaked, brownish plumage.

The three presently recognized species of *Melospiza* are all widespread in Canada and the United States. The Song Sparrow is one of the most widespread and geographically variable of North American birds.

Many ornithologists have merged *Melospiza* with *Passerella*, but molecular evidence shows that they are sufficiently different to warrant generic separation.

41 **Song Sparrow** *Melospiza melodia* [581]   **PLATE 16**

IDENTIFICATION: 12–17 cm (*c.* 5–7 in), males slightly larger; sexes similar in coloration.

The Song Sparrow is extremely geographically variable. It is rusty brown to dark brown in general coloration, with streaked back, flanks, and breast, the streaks often concentrated in the central breast spot. The throat is white or whitish, often somewhat brown spotted, and outlined by conspicuous dark malar stripes. The long and round tail is characteristically flopped to one side or pumped up and down in flight.

Similar species: Lincoln's sparrows are somewhat smaller, shorter-tailed, and more gracile, with thinly striped flanks and breast, usually without a conspicuous central spot, with a buffy cast to the flanks, breast and submoustachial stripe, grayish side of neck and supercilium, and gray central crown-stripe. Adult Swamp Sparrows generally have a conspicuously rusty cap, rusty cast to the wings, especially in the coverts, reddish buff flanks and inconspicuous ventral streaking. In juvenal plumages, the three *Melospiza* are very similar. In the east, Song Sparrows are larger (tail 60 mm or longer) with whitish submoustachial stripe, and relatively unstreaked crown, often with a paler median crown-stripe (see account of Lincoln's Sparrow). Savannah Sparrow often has a central breast spot, but has thinner, sharper striping, and a slimmer, often paler bill. It usually has yellow in the supercilium and obviously pink legs. Its flight is direct and stronger than that of the Song Sparrow, and its tail distinctly shorter. Fox sparrows are conspicuously larger (large Aleutian Song Sparrows do not migrate); Red Fox Sparrows are much more rufous and have gray in the crown.

Adult—*Head:* brown to light rusty (southwest), streaked, with paler brown or gray-brown median crown-stripe; supercilium pale in front of eye; gray to gray-brown behind the eye; eye-stripe brown; ear-coverts gray to gray-brown, edged with dark brown moustachial stripe; submoustachial stripe pale; malar stripe dark brown; throat white or whitish, with or without (southwest; Rocky Mountains) brown spotting; head markings on birds from coastal British Columbia and Alaska are indistinct, with birds appearing to have nearly uniformly dark brown heads, somewhat paler in the supercilium, submoustachial stripe, and throat; ***back:*** brown to rusty brown (southwest) with centers of feathers dark brown or rusty brown; brown streaking on back indistinct on north Pacific Coast, where birds appear to have nearly uniformly colored dark backs; ***rump:*** brown to rusty brown and streaked; ***tail:*** rusty brown (southwest) to brown or dark brown, relatively long and rounded or double rounded; ***wing:*** rust-brown to dark brown, often with rust-brown in greater coverts; ***underparts:*** chin and throat whitish, spotted or unspotted (southwest; Rocky Mountains) with brown; breast and flanks usually boldly streaked or spotted with spots concentrated into a usually conspicuous central spot; belly whitish and unspotted (except on north Pacific Coast); undertail-coverts whitish with darker centers; ***bill:*** dark brown to horn colored, lower mandible paler than upper, especially toward base; ***legs*** and ***feet:*** pale yellowish brown; ***iris:*** dark brown.

First-fall and winter*:* (July–Nov) resemble adults, but are buffier on breast and flanks.

Juveniles*:* (June–Aug) have a brown crown, with paler median stripe in most populations; back brown, with centers of feathers dark brown and appearing rather streaked; rump and tail brown to rusty brown; underparts like adults, but buffier and streaking somewhat thinner; birds from coastal British Columbia and Alaska have nearly uniform dark backs. Usually but not always molt before migrating.

VOICE: The song, though variable, is distinctive. It characteristically starts with a series of two to four loud, clear whistles on the same pitch, followed by a trill, often a buzzy trill, then several short notes, ***chrup chrup chee chee tceeeeeeee tzcu***, the ***chee chee*** higher and ***tzcu*** lower in pitch, or sometimes a Swamp Sparrow-like trill, followed by a buzzy trill and short notes, ***chril-chril-chril-chril-chril churzzzzzzzzzzzz tik-zp***. An individual generally sings several different songs, commonly singing one song several times, then switching to another. The call note is a distinctive ***tchenk***, ***tchip***, or ***chimp***, and often is a useful aid to identification. They also give an indistinctive ***tseep***, less often the ***chimp*** note, and a note that is a stuttering trill.

HABITS: On the breeding grounds, males sing persistently from an exposed perch or a telephone wire; flight-singing is rare. Individuals sing throughout the year, but infrequently in winter, and the winter song may be different from the summer one. Territorial birds sometimes sing at night. Although Song Sparrows tend to stay in dense vegetation, they are not generally difficult to see, and often respond vigorously

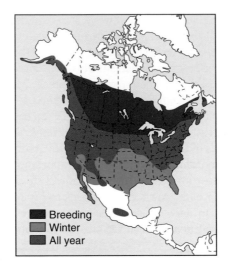

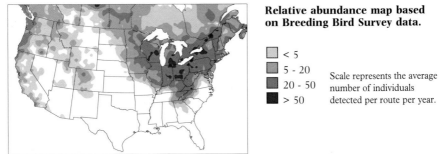

Relative abundance map based on Breeding Bird Survey data.

- ☐ < 5
- ☐ 5 - 20
- ☐ 20 - 50
- ■ > 50

Scale represents the average number of individuals detected per route per year.

to spishing. In winter, they are usually found in loose small flocks, often associated with other sparrows. Their flight is jerky, not strong and their long tail is characteristically flipped to one side and pumped in flight. In spring, territorial defense is vigorous, and chases frequent. Song Sparrows usually forage on the ground.

HABITAT: Except for the Aleutian Is. and coastal Alaskan populations, the habitat used by Song Sparrows is remarkably similar throughout their range. They are generally found in open brushy habitats, often along the borders of ponds or streams (invariably so in the southwest), abandoned pastures, thickets or woodland edge. In winter they also are found in tall weedy fields, marshes, moist ravines, and brush piles. In the Aleutians, they are found in beach grass just above the high tide line, in grassy areas near the beach amongst boulders and drift-wood, and in winter they feed on tidal mudflats. In the San Francisco Bay area they are resident in salt and brackish marshes with cordgrass, pickleweed and gumplant. On both coasts they are found in brackish marshes with cattails, sedges and pickleweed; they often forage on mudflats.

BREEDING: *Nest* is a bulky cup of leaves, strips of bark, weeds, and grass lined with finer grass, rootlets, and hair. Nests are commonly placed on the ground, among grasses, sedges, cattails and a variety of shrubs (myrtle, willow) and bushes, or low in a bush, small tree or rarely a cavity, or among cacti (Channel Is., California), to 3 m (12 ft); nests are placed low to the ground in clumps of pickleweed, stalks of cordgrass or in gumplant in saltmarshes. Nesting takes place from late Feb (California, late Mar in Ohio, mid-Apr in Ontario) into Aug. *Eggs,* usually 3–6 (most commonly 4, 3 in saltmarshes and Arizona), are glossy, pale green to greenish white, or blue through blue-green, speckled or blotched with reddish brown. *Incubation,* 10–14 days, young fledge in 7–14 days; the female alone incubates and (usually) builds the nest, but both parents feed the young. As many as three broods may be raised in a season. They are commonly parasitized by cowbirds.

RANGE: *Breeds* from Aleutian Is. (w to Attu Is.), Shumagin Is., Semidi Is., Amak and Middleton Is., Kodiak I. group, s Alaska (Cook Inlet, Kenai Peninsula, Cordova), s-c Yukon (Squanga L.), s Mackenzie (north to Great Slave L.), n Manitoba (Churchill), Akimiski I., Ontario, s Quebec (Lac Saint-Jean, St. Lawrence R., Anticosti and Madeleine Is.) and sw Newfoundland (Parsons Pond), south through Maritime Provinces to coastal and nw South Carolina, n Georgia (Athens, Atlanta, Rome), ne Alabama (DeKalb Co.), Tennessee, Missouri (Mississippi Lowlands, north of Missouri R.), perhaps formerly in n Arkansas, ne Kansas (Walcott), South Dakota, Nebraska (scarce south to Platte R.), Colorado, n New Mexico (Santa Fe, Taos), Arizona, and locally through the Mexican highlands from Durango to Michoacán and Puebla.

Winters from s Alaska (resident in the Aleutians, Kodiak I., Alaska Peninsula), c and s British Columbia, c Minnesota, s Ontario (north rarely to Thunder Bay, Ottawa), sw Quebec (rarely to Quebec), s New Brunswick, Prince Edward I., Nova Scotia and s Newfoundland (rarely) south to Florida (rare and irregular in south), the Gulf Coast, s Texas and New Mexico. Most winter at lower elevations, south of the Great Lakes, from Massachusetts, Ohio, Iowa, s Nebraska, Colorado and sw coastal British Columbia south to n Florida, c Texas and s California. Casual or accidental in Banks I. (Franklin Dist.), Bermuda, Bahamas, and nw Europe (Britain, Norway; records from Apr–June).

HISTORY: The Song Sparrow was first described by Alexander Wilson in 1810, who named it *Fringilla melodia.* Audubon called the species 'very abundant,' and it is today one of the commonest and most conspicuous of the sparrows in much of its range. In pre-colonial times, Song Sparrows were scarcer in the forested northeast than today. More recently, they have doubtless benefited from the abandonment of marginal farms in that region, and they thrive in suburban situations; their breeding range has spread southward in recent years into central North Carolina, southern Kentucky, and western Tennessee. Song Sparrows were locally common along permanent rivers in Arizona in the 1800s, but declined greatly there late in the 19th century as a consequence of drainage and the destruction of grasslands. Today, their populations seem to be relatively stable throughout most of their range.

GEOGRAPHIC VARIATION: Twenty-nine subspecies from north of Mexico are generally recognized. Eastern birds (including *Melospiza m. melodia*, *M. m. euphonia*, and *M. m. juddii*, which probably cannot be separated reliably, even in the hand), breeding west to the Rocky Mountains, are rich chocolate-brown, with the eastern-most perhaps somewhat more reddish brown in color; the east coastal *M. m. atlantica* is perhaps grayer. Rocky Mountain breeders (northeast Oregon, Montana, south to New Mexico, central Arizona [White Mountains]) (*M. m. montana*) are very like east-ern birds, but paler rusty gray in hue, with somewhat more slender bills. *M. m. samuelis* and *M. m. pusillula*, from the saltmarshes around San Francisco Bay, are small, slen-der-billed and dark in coloration; birds from the Channel Is. of California (the similar *M. m. micronyx*, *M. m. clementae*, and *M. m. graminea* [extinct]) are also small and slen-der-billed, but much paler, with back grayish, with brown streaking, and rusty greater coverts. Other Song Sparrows breeding from sw Oregon south through California (*M. m. cleonensis*, *M. m. gouldii*, *M. m. heermanni*, and *M. m. cooperi*), including those breeding around the brackish marshes around Suisun Bay (*M. m. maxillaris*), resem-ble eastern Song Sparrows but have darker ventral streaking, and are less rusty; in the hand they can be seen to have short wings. Birds from the Virgin R. in southwestern Utah, southeastern Nevada (Pahranagat Valley) (*M. m. fallax*), southern Arizona, and northwestern Sonora (*M. m. saltonis*) and Baja California (*M. m. rivularis*) are pale reddish brown, with feathers edged with pale gray, and less pale rusty spotting ven-trally. *M. m. saltonis* average paler than *M. m. fallax*.

Song Sparrows from the Aleutian Is. (*M. m. maxima*, *M. m. sanaka*) and Amak I. (*M. m. amaka*) are very large with long and relatively slender bills, dark, with a paler throat, breast with a band of chestnut streaks, and back dark brown with gray edges. Birds from southern Alaska, southern Yukon, British Columbia, Washington and Oregon (south to Coos Bay) (*M. m. caurina*, *M. m. rufina*, *M. m. kenaiensis*, *M. m. insignis*, *M. m. inexpectata*, *M. m. morphna* and *M. m. merrilli*) are smaller, very dark with inconspicuously patterned backs, but are somewhat more brightly colored below than Aleutian birds, although very heavily streaked on the breast, flanks, and even the belly. Birds from south-central British Columbia, eastern Washington, Idaho, and northeastern Oregon are paler below and can be dark rusty brown on the back; these grade into *M. m. montana*.

MEASUREMENTS: See table.

Mass: (238 males) 21.0 g (18.2–29.8), (176 females) 20.5 g (11.9–26.10) (Pennsylvania); 42.4 g (40.2–45.7) (Aleutian Is., Alaska); 18.8 g (San Francisco Bay, California) (Dunning 1993); (12 males) 46.1 (41.7–53.0) (outer Aleutian Is.) (Alaska Museum).

References: Aldrich (1984), Marshall (1948a), (1948b), (1964b), Zink and Dittmann (1993).

Measurements of Male Song Sparrows (*Melospiza melodia*) of 7 different subspecies[a]

Subspecies[c] (Sex)	N	Wing Length		Tail Length		Tarsus Length		Exposed Culmen		Bill Depth[b]	
		Mean	Range	Mean	Range	Mean	Range	Mean	Range	Mean	Range
M. m. melodia (M)	41	67	63–71	67	62–71	21.8	20.3–23.4	12.5	11.4–13.2	8.1	7.9–8.9
M. m. melodia (F)	36	65	61–71	64	56–70	21.3	20.1–22.4	12.2	11.4–13.0	7.9	7.6–8.6
M. m. montana (M)	39	69	66–74	70	64–77	22.4	21.3–23.4	12.2	11.2–14.0	7.4	6.9–7.9
M. m. montana (F)	30	66	62–70	67	62–73	22.4	20.8–22.9	11.9	10.4–12.7	7.1	6.9–8.1
M. m. fallax (M)	15	67	65–69	69	66–71	21.3	20.1–22.1	12.5	11.2–12.7	7.3	7.1–7.4
M. m. fallax (F)	12	64	63–67	66	61–71	20.6	20.1–21.1	11.9	11.4–12.2	6.9	6.9–7.1
M. m. cooperi (M)	23	63	58–68	63	56–86	21.8	20.3–22.6	12.2	11.2–13.2	7.5	7.4–7.9
M. m. cooperi (F)	4	61	58–63	63	63–64	21.8	21.3–22.6	12.2	11.9–12.5	7.4	–
M. m. samuelis (M)	22	61	56–64	59	53–62	21.1	19.8–22.4	12.2	10.9–12.7	6.9	6.6–7.4
M. m. samuelis (F)	11	58	56–60	58	53–60	20.6	19.8–21.8	11.9	11.4–12.5	6.9	6.4–7.4
M. m. morphna (M)	20	68	65–71	66	61–73	22.9	21.6–23.6	13.0	11.9–13.7	7.1	6.9–7.6
M. m. morphna (F)	13	65	62–69	63	58–68	22.6	21.8–23.6	12.5	11.4–13.2	7.1	6.4–7.6
M. m. maxima and sauaka (M)	16	85	82–87	83	78–87	27.9	26.9–29.2	16.3	15.0–18.0	8.4	7.6–9.1
M. m. maxima and sauaka (F)	12	81	78–85	78	71–82	27.2	25.9–27.9	16.0	14.7–17.0	8.1	7.6–8.6

[a](Ridgway 1901); [b]at base; [c]consult text for approximate geographical regions

42 **Lincoln's Sparrow** *Melospiza lincolnii* [583]   Plate 17

D. BEADLE ·

IDENTIFICATION: 11.5–14.5 cm (*c.* 4.5–6 in), males slightly larger; sexes similar in coloration.

Lincoln's is a medium-sized sparrow, with a rather short tail, a broad gray supercilium and median crown-stripe, and a thinly streaked, buffy breast and flanks.

Similar species: The Song Sparrow is generally larger with a longer tail; the breast spotting of the Song Sparrow is bolder, and although Lincoln's Sparrow may have a central breast spot, this is generally more pronounced on Song Sparrows; Song Sparrows have a conspicuous brown malar stripe, whereas the malar stripe of Lincoln's Sparrows is thin. The buffy, thinly streaked breast and flanks, and grayish face (supercilium and side of neck) of Lincoln's Sparrow are distinctive. Savannah Sparrows, which generally occur in open fields, not tangles or thickets where Lincoln's Sparrows are likely to be found, lack the buffy breast, have a yellowish, not gray supercilium, and have a shorter notched tail. Juvenile *Melospiza* are very difficult to separate. Song Sparrows are larger than the other two (wing length 60 mm or longer), and have a white malar stripe; Lincoln's and Swamp sparrows have buffy or buffy white malar stripes. Lincoln's Sparrows show some gray or buff streaking in the crown; Swamp Sparrows often appear to have unstreaked, black crowns. Lincoln's Sparrows have some streaking in the chin and throat, but Swamp Sparrows may have this as well. Swamp Sparrows consistently have more rusty edgings of their coverts and tertials, but this too is variable. In the hand, Lincoln's Sparrows often have gray mouth lining, and Swamp Sparrows yellow lining, but this is variable.

Adult—*Head:* crown brown or rusty brown, with a gray median crown-stripe; supercilium and side of neck gray; ear-coverts brownish, outlined with darker brown; moustachial and malar stripes brown; submoustachial stripe buffy ochre; chin and throat buffy white, thinly streaked with dark brown; ***back:*** nape, mantle, and scapulars buffy olive, sharply streaked with black; ***rump:*** olive and brown streaked; ***tail:*** grayish brown, middle rectrices with brown centers; ***wing:*** brown, sometimes with slightly rusty edged to greater coverts and tertials; ***underparts:*** throat whitish or buffy white, thinly flecked or streaked with dark brown; breast and flanks buffy ochre, thinly streaked with dark brown, and sometimes with a median breast spot; belly whitish; undertail-coverts buffy with brown centers; ***bill:*** horn colored, lower mandible slightly yellowish; ***legs:*** brownish; ***iris:*** brown.

First-fall and winter: (July–May) resemble adults, but more buffy, with markings less sharply defined.

Juveniles: (July–mid-Sept) resemble adults, but crown brown or grayish brown streaked, and supercilium brownish; edges of coverts and tertials may be somewhat rusty.

VOICE: The song is sweet and gurgling, and has the quality of Purple Finch or House Wren songs: ***churr-churr-churr-wee-wee-wee-wee-wah-wah***, or ***ootle ootle weetle weetle eeteeteetyaytoo***. Occasionally a flight song is given. The call note is a variable sharp ***tep*** or ***chip***, or a faint ***tsick, tschuck***, or ***tit***, or a buzzy ***zzeeet***.

HABITS: On the breeding grounds, singing males are inconspicuous as they sing from dense thickets. The adults around the nest are nervous, flitting in and out of sight, uttering rapid ***chips***, and will run away from the nest. In migration and winter, they occur in dense low cover, and rarely far from cover, and do not seem to flock. They are generally said to be skulkers, but respond well to spishing, and usually are not hard to see.

HABITAT: Lincoln's Sparrows breed in boggy areas with stunted tamarack, black spruce, and low willows and alders, willow thickets, and cut-over areas where there is dense vegetation. In winter, they are often found in moist areas, tangles, brushy edges of ponds, dense weedy fields with ragweed, frostweed, etc.

BREEDING: ***Nest*** is placed on the ground in a well-concealed shallow depression. The nest is a fragile cup of sedges and grasses and dead leaves, lined with finer grasses and sometimes hair. The female alone builds the nest. Nesting begins in late May to mid-June, and continues into July. ***Eggs***, 3–6, usually 4 or 5, are greenish white, spotted with reddish brown. ***Incubation***, about 13 days; female alone incubates; both parents feed the young, but feeding is done principally by the female when the young are in the nest; young leave the nest after 12 days; apparently double-brooded. The species is infrequently parasitized by cowbirds.

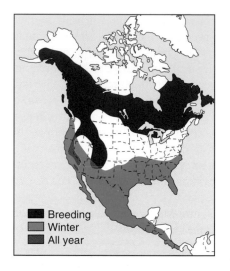

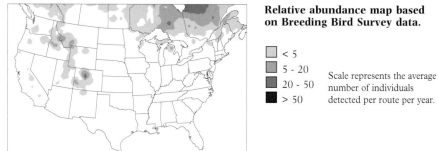

Relative abundance map based on Breeding Bird Survey data.

- ☐ < 5
- ☐ 5 - 20
- ☐ 20 - 50
- ■ > 50

Scale represents the average number of individuals detected per route per year.

RANGE: *Breeds* from w and c Alaska (Kobuk and Yukon valleys; Iliamna L.), c Yukon (Forty Mile) w-c and se Mackenzie (Inuvik, Yellowknife), n Saskatchewan, n Manitoba (Churchill), n Ontario, Belcher Is., Quebec (north to Kuujjuarapik, Kuujjuaq, Kangiqsualujjuaq), south to s California (in mountains, south to s Tulare Co. and San Jacinto Mountains), w-c Nevada (Carson Range), c Idaho, Utah (mountains), e-c Arizona (White Mountains), n New Mexico (San Juan and Sangre de Christo ranges; Taos), w half of Colorado, Wyoming, w Montana, se and c Alberta (Waterton Lakes, Red Deer, Camrose), c Saskatchewan (Prince Albert), Manitoba (absent in sw), se Minnesota (south to n Pine Co.), n Wisconsin, n Michigan (south to Clare and Sanilac cos.), s Ontario (rare south of Canadian Shield), New York (Adirondack Mountains), s Vermont, w Massachusetts (Berkshire Mountains, rare), n New Hampshire, c Maine, New Brunswick, Prince Edward I., c Nova Scotia, and Newfoundland.

Winters uncommonly from sw British Columbia, w Washington, and Oregon, and n California, s Nevada, sw Utah, Arizona, c New Mexico, Oklahoma, e Kansas (rare), c Missouri, s Kentucky, coastal Virginia, North Carolina (rare), and n Georgia, south to Florida, the Gulf Coast, Texas to Costa Rica (rare), and Panama (rare), and rarely south to the Bahamas, Cuba, Jamaica and Puerto Rico. Most common in winter in Texas, s New Mexico, Arizona, and s California. Casual or very rare in winter north to s Alaska, Colorado, Wisconsin (rare), Michigan (rare), s Ontario, Massachusetts, and Nova Scotia.

HISTORY: In his *Birds of America*, Audubon wrote: 'We had been in Labrador nearly three weeks before this Finch was discovered. One morning while the sun was doing his best to enliven the gloomy aspect of the country, I chanced to enter one of those singular small valleys here and there to be seen.' There he heard '. . . the sweet notes of this bird as they came thrilling on the sense, surpassing in vigour those of any American Finch with which I am acquainted, and forming a song which seemed a compound of those of the Canary and Wood-lark of Europe. I immediately shouted to my companions, who were not far distant. They came, and we all followed the songster as it flitted from one bush to another to evade our pursuit. No sooner would it alight than it renewed its song; but we found more wildness in this species than in any other inhabiting the same country, and it was with difficulty that we at last procured it. Chance placed my young companion, Thomas Lincoln, in a situation where he saw it alight within shot, and with his usual unerring aim, he cut short its career.' Later, Audubon named it in honor of its collector. It seems unlikely that there have been significant changes in the status of Lincoln's Sparrow in recent times as they breed in habitats that are little exploited by humans. In recent years, their numbers have increased slightly in both the east and west, with highest breeding densities recorded in Quebec and Nova Scotia.

GEOGRAPHIC VARIATION: Three subspecies are generally recognized: the Eastern Lincoln's Sparrow (*M. l. lincolnii*); Montane Lincoln's Sparrow (*M. l. alticola*); and the Northwestern Lincoln's Sparrow (*M. l. gracilis*). *M. l. alticola*, which breeds in the mountains of Montana and Oregon southward, averages somewhat larger than *M. l. lincolnii* or *M. l. gracilis*, and is said to be somewhat darker on the back, but it is not clear that this is so. This subspecies is not recognized by many ornithologists, and certainly could not be identified in the field. *M. l. gracilis*, which breeds along coastal Alaska and central British Columbia, is somewhat smaller than *M. l. lincolnii*, and similar in coloration to *M. l. alticola*.

MEASUREMENTS: (17 males): wing 57–67 (63), tail 53–62 (58), tarsus 19.8–21.8 (20.8), exposed culmen 10.4–11.9 (11.2), bill depth at base 5.8–7.1 (6.4); (14 females): wing 55–62 (59), tail 51–59 (54), tarsus 18.8–20.6 (19.8), exposed culmen 9.7–11.7 (10.7), bill depth 5.6–6.1 (5.8) (Ridgway 1901).

Mass: (N=76) 18.6 g (14.8–24.0) (Pennsylvania, May) (Clench and Leberman 1978).

Reference: Rimmer (1986).

43 **Swamp Sparrow** *Melospiza georgiana* [584]   PLATE 17

IDENTIFICATION: 12–15 cm (*c.* 5–6 in), males slightly larger; sexes similar in coloration.

Swamp Sparrow is a dark, medium-sized sparrow, with a rusty crown, rusty wings, black streaks on back, grayish supercilium and ear-coverts separated by a brown eyestripe, grayish unstreaked or faintly streaked breast, whitish throat, and slightly rusty buff flanks. The rusty crown is variable, and often brownish, with a brownish or grayish median crown-stripe, especially in fall and winter.

Similar species: Swamp Sparrows are more likely to be confused with Lincoln's Sparrows, especially in fall and winter, than any of the other rusty-capped sparrows. Juvenile *Melospiza* sparrows are very difficult to separate in the field. See Lincoln's Sparrow account.

Adult—*Head:* forehead black, crown rusty, sometimes streaked with blackish, divided by a more or less distinct grayish or buffy brown median stripe; supercilium, lores, and ear-coverts grayish, the supercilium often being paler above and in front of the eye; eye and moustachial stripes dark brown or black, outlining the gray ear-coverts; submoustachial stripe thin and pale; malar stripe thin and dark; throat whitish and unstreaked or lightly streaked; ***back:*** nape grayish, or grayish brown; mantle and scapulars light brown broadly streaked with black, some broadly edged with buff; ***rump:*** rusty brown, streaked with dark brown, with median rectrices with dark brown centers; ***tail:*** rusty brown; ***wing:*** brown with the exposed edges of the coverts

rusty, the inner edges black; ***underparts:*** chin and throat whitish or white, sometimes flecked with brown; breast grayish or grayish brown, sometimes with slight
streaking; flanks rusty beige, and thinly streaked; belly white; undertail-coverts
whitish with brown centers; ***bill:*** upper mandible dark brown; lower mandible yellowish with a brownish tip, or brown in young birds; ***legs*** and ***feet:*** brown; ***iris:***
brown.

First-winter (Aug–Mar) resemble adults, but the nape, supercilium, and ear-coverts
are buffy brown rather than grayish, and the crown is dark brown, heavily streaked,
with little or no rusty.

Juveniles (July–mid-Sept) resemble adults, but underparts streaked; crown blackish
or darkly streaked; facial markings pale brown rather than gray; usually some rusty
in coverts.

VOICE: The song is a musical trill on a single pitch, ***weet-weet-weet-weet-weet-
weet***, resembling that of the Chipping Sparrow, but not so dry, slower and louder,
and somewhat more variable. They alternate trills of different tempos. During the
nesting season, Swamp Sparrows may start to sing before dawn, and continue into
the night, and occasionally give a flight song. Some sing in the autumn, and
occasionally in the winter, usually not from an exposed perch. The call note is a
distinctive metallic ***chink*** or ***chip***.

HABITS: Territorial Swamp Sparrows sing persistently, usually from an exposed
perch, in a cattail or small bush. They characteristically fly only short distances, but
territorial chases can be common. In winter, they are found in dense vegetation, often
in low, open and wet areas, commonly at the edge of a pond or a flooded field. They
are not difficult to flush, and respond readily to spishing.

HABITAT: Swamp Sparrows nest in marshes, open bogs, and pond margins with
emergent vegetation such as cattail, bulrushes, willows, alders, or leather-leaf. In both
the breeding and winter seasons, they may be found in saltmarshes, but are more
generally found in fresh water.

BREEDING: ***Nest*** is almost never on the ground, but rather about 0.3 m high, in cattails, or shrubs over water, or in sedge tussocks. The nest is a bulky cup of grass, lined
with finer grasses, and rarely hair or rootlets; it is usually concealed from above;
ground nests have short tunnels leading to them. The female probably builds the
nest. Nesting begins in mid-Apr and continues through July. ***Eggs***, 3–6, usually 4–5,
are pale blue or greenish blue, and are speckled with brown or purple. ***Incubation***,
less than 14 days; the female alone incubates; young leave the nest after 10–12 days.
Some males are polygynous. Swamp Sparrows are parasitized by cowbirds.

RANGE: ***Breeds*** s Alaska (Anchorage, singing; rare), w-c and s Mackenzie
(Norman Wells, Yellowknife), n Saskatchewan, n Manitoba (Churchill), n Ontario,

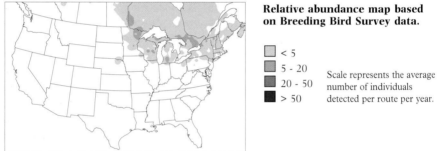

Relative abundance map based on Breeding Bird Survey data.

▢ < 5	
▨ 5 - 20	Scale represents the average
▧ 20 - 50	number of individuals
■ > 50	detected per route per year.

Quebec (north to Kuujjuarapik, s Labrador (Goose Bay) and Newfoundland, south through Yukon and e British Columbia (Peace R. area, Nelson), Alberta (south to Olds, Vermillion), c Saskatchewan (south to Emma L.), e North and South Dakota, and Nebraska, Missouri (formerly), Manitoba (except in sw), Minnesota, n and c (scarce) Illinois, c Indiana (s to Marion Co.), c Ohio, c West Virginia (south to Greenbrier Co.), and Maryland (common in Allegheny Mountains; local on marshes on the Nanticoke R. near Vienna, and Elk R. near Elkton).

Winters rarely Alberta (Calgary), e Nebraska, Kansas (rare in west), Iowa, Illinois, s Indiana, Great Lakes region, east to Massachusetts (uncommon), south to Florida, the Gulf Coast, and Texas, irregularly south to Tamaulipas, San Luis Potosí, and Jalisco. Casual or rare in se and s-c Alaska (Ketchikan, Middleton I.), w British Columbia, Washington, Oregon, California (principally along the coast in the fall and winter), s Arizona, s New Mexico, Bermuda, and Bahamas (possible). Winters most commonly in lowlands south and east of Iowa and Texas. Reported uncommonly in winter north to Minnesota, Wisconsin (regular in south), Michigan, s Ontario, sw Quebec, and the Maritime Provinces.

HISTORY: The Swamp Sparrow was called the 'reed sparrow' by the early American naturalist, William Bartram. Later, it was formally described by the British ornithologist John Latham in 1790. Because the specimen upon which he based his description came from Georgia, he named the species *Fringilla georgiana*. In 1811, Alexander Wilson redescribed the species as *Fringilla palustris*, the Swamp Sparrow.

Historically, Swamp Sparrows were probably abundant in suitable habitat, which in the northeast was probably primarily restricted to the marshy borders of rivers, beaver ponds, and bogs. In some areas, the clearing of forests may have created additional patches of suitable habitat for the species; this apparently happened in New Hampshire, where its range has apparently increased since earlier times. However, the draining of marshes has adversely affected numbers in many areas. This is probably why it declined after 1940 in northwestern Ohio and southern Ontario. Recently, numbers have nearly tripled in Michigan where Swamp Sparrows have apparently benefited from the rise in the level of the Great Lakes.

GEOGRAPHIC VARIATION: Three subspecies are generally recognized: Southern (or Eastern) Swamp Sparrow, *M. g. georgiana*; Northern (or Western) Swamp Sparrow *M. g. ericrypta*; and Coastal Plain Swamp Sparrow, *M. g. nigrescens*. *M. g. ericrypta* resembles *M. g. georgiana*, but is slightly paler above, with less rusty in the wings; the two show clinal variation, and grade into each other, and cannot be separated in the field. *M. g. nigrescens* differs from the others (at least in breeding plumage) by having a much broader black band on the forehead, and the black streaking on the back, especially on the nape and mantle, is distinctly heavier. It is apparently locally resident along the Atlantic Coast from New Jersey south to Maryland.

MEASUREMENTS: (8 males): wing 58–66 (62), tail 55–64 (59), tarsus 21.3–22.1 (21.6), exposed culmen 10.9–11.9 (11.7), depth of bill at base 6.1–6.4 (6.2); (8 females): wing 58–62 (59), tail 52–61 (56), tarsus 20.3–22.1 (21.3), exposed culmen 10.7–11.9 (11.2), bill depth 5.8–6.1 (6.0) (Ridgway 1901).

Mass: (N=76) 18.6 g (14.8–24.0) (Pennsylvania, May) (Clench and Leberman 1978).

Reference: Bond and Stewart (1951).

Genus *Zonotrichia*

Four of the five species of *Zonotrichia* are found north of Mexico; the Neotropical Rufous-collared Sparrow (*Zonotrichia capensis*) breeds in the Greater Antilles, Hispaniola, and the highlands of southern Mexico, Central America and South America, where it is the most widespread and abundant sparrow.

Zonotrichias are medium large to large sparrows with large conical bills. In all species the tail is about the same length as the wing, and rounded or slightly double-rounded. The wing is rather long and pointed (6th, 7th, or 8th primary longest). They are typically monomorphic in coloration, although males may be somewhat more brightly colored than females. In all, males average slightly larger than females.

Zonotrichias characteristically breed in woodland edge or tall shrubby habitats. The eastern White-throated Sparrow may breed in fairly dense woods, and Harris's Sparrow may nest some distance from woodland edge. They nest on or near the ground, and the nest is commonly placed near the base of a small shrub or tree. Their flight is direct, and with the exception of some west coast populations of White-crowned Sparrows, all are migratory.

There are several reports of hybrids between the White-throated Sparrow and 'Slate-colored' Junco, suggesting a close affinity with the genus *Junco*. Vocally *Zonotrichia* resemble each other with songs that contain clear whistled elements, unlike other sparrows. They may also be closely allied with the Eurasian genus *Emberiza*, as they bear a superficial resemblance to some species.

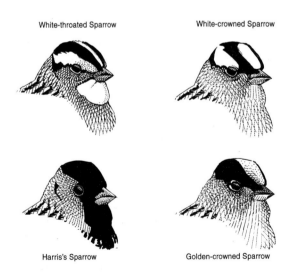

White-throated Sparrow   White-crowned Sparrow

Harris's Sparrow   Golden-crowned Sparrow

44 **White-throated Sparrow**
Zonotrichia albicollis [558]

PLATE 19

D. BEADLE 95

IDENTIFICATION: 15–17 cm (*c*. 6–7 in), males slightly larger; sexes similar in coloration.

The White-throated Sparrow is a fairly large sparrow, with a pale or white supercilium, which is yellow in front of the eye (supraloral spot), pale or white median crown-stripe, pale or white throat abruptly delimited against unmarked or slightly streaked gray breast, and brown or rusty brown.

Similar species: The White-crowned Sparrow is generally grayer, especially on the nape, and the back is not as brown as the White-throated Sparrow; the White-crowned has a yellow or pinkish, not horn colored bill, and although the throat is pale gray, it is not white, and the color does not contrast sharply with the gray on the upper breast. Except in juvenal plumage, White-crowned Sparrows never have streaking on their breast, which some White-throats may have. First winter White-crowned Sparrows have rusty brown crown stripes.

Adult—*Head:* polymorphic with median crown-stripe and supercilium either both white or both pale brownish tan; lateral crown and eye-stripes dark chocolate brown to black, generally darker in white morph birds; ear-coverts and lores gray; sub-moustachial stripe faint or absent; ***back*** and scapulars brown or rusty brown streaked with dark brown or black, the feathers edged with beige; ***rump:*** gray-brown with faint streaks; ***tail:*** long, brown, and slightly notched; ***wing:*** brown, with median and greater coverts tipped with whitish, forming two narrow wing-bars, the anterior one more distinct than the posterior one; innermost greater coverts and tertials edged with rusty brown; **underparts:** throat white or dull white, sharply delimited against gray breast, which may be faintly streaked; flanks light brown and faintly streaked; belly dull white and unmarked; **bill:** upper mandible horn colored; lower mandible paler; **legs:** pale pinkish brown; **iris:** brown to reddish brown. Sexes similar, but female coloration generally duller than male.

First-fall and winter (July–Feb) similar in coloration to more dull-colored females, but even duller, with beige instead of white on head and throat, and throat patch not so sharply delimited; gray of chest with indistinct streaking.

Juveniles (late June–early Aug) median crown-stripe indistinct, yellow in supercilium reduced or absent, forehead, crown and nape chestnut-brown, streaked with black; chin and throat whitish, flaked with dusky, with dark moustachial stripe; breast and flanks heavily streaked with dark brown; belly and undertail-coverts white and generally unmarked.

Nestlings: pale clove-brown.

VOICE: The song is a clear, loud whistle, characteristically starting with a lower whistle followed by three or four higher wavering elements; less frequently the first element is the highest, followed by a lower one, then by three yet lower ones. The song almost always has at least one change in pitch, and may have up to three. The most common note is a distinctive **tseet**; they may also give a quiet **tip** note or a louder **pink** alarm call.

HABITS: On the breeding grounds, males sing persistently, commonly from a perch, but not often an exposed one, and often from a conifer. They start singing early in the morning, but sing only occasionally during the middle of the day; there is another period of active singing near dusk; sometimes sings at night. The members of a pair are almost always different colormorphs. They sing occasionally in winter. In winter, they are generally found in loose flocks or small groups, sometimes in mixed species flocks. When flushed, they may fly up into a small nearby tree where they are easily seen. They are easy to spish up.

HABITAT: The White-throated Sparrow is a brushland bird at all seasons. They most commonly breed in semi-open mixed woods, commonly where spruce, balsam fir, birch, and aspen predominate, but may also breed in hemlocks, northern white-cedar, tamarack-alder, and white pine swamps, conifer plantations, and bogs. In winter they are often found in dense deciduous thickets or brush piles, often in woodland edge or in a woodland clearing.

BREEDING: Nest is placed near or on the ground (to 3 m) in areas of small trees, interspersed with low vegetation (commonly beaked hazel and blueberries in Ontario). The nest, which is well concealed in shrubs, and may be under mats of dead vegetation or a fallen log, is a cup of coarse grass, twigs, needles, and wood

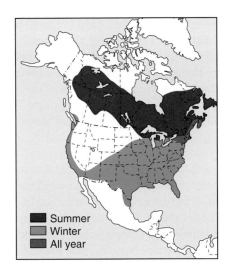

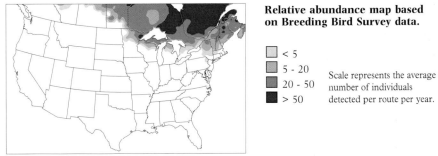

Relative abundance map based on Breeding Bird Survey data.

☐ < 5
☐ 5 - 20
▨ 20 - 50
■ > 50

Scale represents the average number of individuals detected per route per year.

chips, lined with fine grasses, rootlets and hair. The female alone builds the nest. Nesting takes place from late May through early July, with a peak in early to mid-June; rarely double-brooded. *Eggs,* 3–7, usually 4, bluish, heavily marked with brown or reddish brown spots and blotches. *Incubation,* 11–14 days; female alone broods, but both parents feed the young; young fledge in 7–12 days (usually 8–9). Rarely parasitized by cowbirds. The species is apparently monogamous.

RANGE: *Breeds* mainly east of the Rocky Mountains, from se Yukon, w-c and s Mackenzie (rarely wanders north to Coppermine), c and n Saskatchewan, Manitoba (except in extreme ne and sw), n Manitoba (Churchill), n Ontario, and c Quebec, south to s-c Alberta (west of Calgary), s Saskatchewan (Qu'Appelle Valley, Moose Mountain), n-c North Dakota (Turtle Mountains, Pembina Hills), n and e Minnesota (south to Anoka Co.), c Wisconsin, c Michigan, s Ontario (rare south of the Canadian Shield), New York (uncommon in south, Long I.), Vermont, New Hampshire, Maine, Massachusetts (uncommon in southeast), and n Pennsylvania.

Winters from s Maritimes, sw Quebec, s Ontario (rarely), s Michigan, s Wisconsin, s Minnesota (rarely), e South Dakota (rarely), and Colorado (uncommon and local), Utah (rare and local), south to s Florida and the Gulf Coast, n Tamaulipas, Nuevo León, s Texas, New Mexico, s Arizona; on the Pacific coast (where uncommon) from s British Columbia south through California to n Baja California. Winters principally in the southeast, north and west to e Kansas. Casual, Coats I., NWT, Baffin I., and casual but regular in Alaska (any season), and in Europe (including Iceland, the British Isles, The Netherlands, Denmark, Sweden, Finland, and Gibraltar; most records from the spring).

HISTORY: The first description of the White-throated Sparrow appeared in 1760 in George Edward's *Gleanings of Natural History*, and was based on a specimen from 'Pensilvania' (Philadelphia). Johann Friedrich Gmelin used this as the basis of naming the species *Fringilla albicollis* in the 13th Edition of *Systema naturae* (1789). Audubon writes: 'It is a plump bird, fattening almost to excess, whilst in Louisiana, and affords delicious eating, for which purpose many are killed with *blow-guns*. These instruments — should you not have seen them — are prepared by the Indians, who cut the straightest canes, perforating them by forcing a hickory rod through the internal partitions which intersect this species of bamboo . . . With these blow-guns or pipes, several species of birds are killed in large quantities; and the Indians sometimes procure even squirrels by the means of them.'

White-throated Sparrows were abundant in colonial times, and remain so today. As they prefer forest-edge habitats, they have benefited from some forestry practices, although their numbers decline as forests regenerate, or are cleared for agriculture. In New England and New York, white-throats have locally expanded their breeding range into lowland sites in recent years. Their numbers appear to decline following severe winters.

GEOGRAPHIC VARIATION: No subspecies have been described. Hybrids with White-crowned and Golden-crowned sparrows, and 'Slate-colored' juncos (several records and specimens) have been described.

MEASUREMENTS: (7 males): wing 72–77 (75), tail 71–76 (73), tarsus 22.9–24.6 (23.6), exposed culmen 10.7–12.2 (11.4), depth of bill at base 7.6–8.1 (7.9); (7 females): wing 60–73 (71), tail 68–74 (70), tarsus 22.4–23.9 (23.1), exposed culmen 11.2–11.7 (11.4), bill depth 7.4–7.9 (7.6) (Ridgway 1901).

Mass: (N=1884) 25.9 g (19.0–35.4) (Pennsylvania) (Dunning 1993).

Reference: Falls and Kopachena (1994).

45 **Golden-crowned Sparrow**   PLATE 18

Zonotrichia atricapilla [557]

IDENTIFICATION: 15–18 cm (*c.* 6–7 in), males slightly larger; sexes similar in coloration.

The Golden-crowned Sparrow is a fairly large sparrow with a yellow crown, bordered by a heavy black line in summer (Mar–July), with the crown-stripes indistinct in winter.

Similar species: The crown color separates the Golden-crowned Sparrow from the other *Zonotrichias*, which it otherwise resembles. Some, perhaps mostly first-year birds, resemble first-year White-crowned Sparrows, but the lateral crown-stripes are brown with yellow spot in the center of the crown above the bill (White-crown has a buffy median crown-stripe), supercilium is light gray-brown (not buffy), and ear-coverts are gray (not buffy); bill dusky (not yellowish or pinkish) and most have yellowish lores. White-crowned Sparrows are in general warm buffy in color whereas Golden-crowned Sparrows are brown. Golden-crowned Sparrow has a rather dull, unmarked face, and lacks a strong eyeline, making the dark eye stand out; White-crowned Sparrow has a strong eyeline. Golden-crowned Sparrow's head looks round in profile, whereas White-crowned Sparrow's often show a peak behind the eye. The dull, brown winter or immature may be mistaken for a female House Sparrow if seen from behind.

Adult—*Head:* blackish brown sides of crown become brown behind the head; median crown-stripe is broad and yellow; it becomes light gray rather abruptly toward the back of the head; lores yellow or gray; ear-coverts gray; nape brownish gray, with or without faint streaking; ***back:*** grayish olive-brown, with back and scapulars broadly streaked with brownish black, suffused with rusty brown; ***rump:*** grayish brown; ***tail:*** long, brown, slightly notched; ***wing:*** brown with chestnut-brown or brown greater and median coverts tipped with white, forming two wing-bars; outer webs of greater coverts and tertials more or less chestnut-brown; **underparts:** throat, side of neck and breast gray, becoming paler on belly, and buffy on flanks; **bill:** dark, with upper mandible darker than lower mandible; **legs:** pale brownish; **iris:** brown.

Adults in winter have a duller head pattern than in summer, with lateral crown-stripes brown. This plumage is quite variable.

First-winter (Aug–Mar) variable, and not separable from all adults. Median crown-stripe indistinct, but with some yellow or yellow-brown between the lores; the head markings become more distinct with age. There is a partial pre-alternate molt in the species.

Juveniles (June–July) forehead and lateral crown-stripes brown, median crown-stripe buff, extending posteriorly; entire crown streaked with black; nape with tinge of rusty brown; **back:** streaked with black and buffy brown; **rump:** and uppertail-coverts brown; **wing:** dark gray, edged with buffy white, tertials and greater coverts edged with rust and tipped with buffy white; chin and throat whitish, flecked in dark brown; sides of throat, breast and flanks cream colored and heavily streaked with black; belly paler and spotted with black.

VOICE: The song characteristically consists of three clearly whistled descending notes, in a minor key, sometimes followed by a quiet trill; the song is sometimes transcribed as 'three blind mice,' or 'oh dear me'). The song is given year round, though infrequently in winter. Rarely there are variations (such as the reversal of the second and third notes or the addition of a fourth note). They also give a hard, loud slurred **chink** or **chip** note and a sharp **tizeet** note.

HABITS: On the breeding grounds, males sing persistently from an exposed perch, often a dwarf willow or alder, or tall weed (cow parsnip). They sing throughout the day. In winter, Golden-crowned Sparrows are generally found in loose flocks or small groups, and are commonly found with White-crowned Sparrows. Although Golden-crowned tend to prefer moister and denser areas than White-crowned, there is considerable overlap in wintering habitat. They do not tend to fly far when flushed but move from bush to bush; the juveniles are hard to see. They are easy to spish up.

HABITAT: On the breeding grounds, they are found in rank deciduous thickets, commonly alders and willows, or dwarf conifers, near timberline, often along hillsides or along ravines, and in similar habitats near sea level. In winter, they occur in thickets and weed patches along rivers, fence rows, or in dense brushy margins of cultivated fields.

BREEDING: Nest is placed on the ground, at the base of a small shrub (commonly alder) or bush under overhanging vegetation, or rarely on a low branch. The nest is a bulky cup of dry grass, ferns, leaves, bark, and twigs lined with fine grasses, hair, and feathers. The female alone probably builds the nest. Nesting takes place from late

May through early August. **Eggs**, 3–5, usually 5, pale green, heavily mottled with brown. **Incubation**, unknown; female alone probably broods, but both parents feed the young; fledging age not known. Not known as a host for cowbirds.

RANGE: *Breeds* in w and n-c Alaska (north to Wales, Kobuk) and c Yukon (Ogilvie Mountains, Kluane), and probably sw Mackenzie (Nahanni Park), the Alaska Peninsula (common) and Aleutians (to Unimak Is.) and Shumagin Is., south (especially in Coast Ranges) to s British Columbia (Okanagan Valley, southern Vancouver Is.) and extreme nw Washington and sw Alberta (Banff).

Winters from s Alaska (west to Kodiak) and s British Columbia, south (mainly west of the Cascades and Sierra Nevada) to s Baja California; rare in winter east of the Sierra Nevada, from Colorado, Kansas, and Utah south to n Sonora and w Texas. Very rare in east where reported regularly from Ontario and along the east coast from Nova Scotia south to Florida. Most common in winter along the west coast from Oregon south to northern Baja California.

In ***migration*** occurs rarely in Pribilofs, w Aleutians, and s Alberta and Saskatchewan, and Kansas. Accidental in spring (May) and fall (Sept–Oct) on Wrangel I. and Chukchi Peninsula, Russia, and Japan.

HISTORY: John Latham first described the Golden-crowned Sparrow in his *General Synopsis of Birds* (1781). At that time Latham thought Latin names unnecessary and named this species a variety of the Black-crowned Bunting from Nootka Sound, which was said to be from the Sandwich Is. In the 13th Edition of *Systema naturae* (1789), Johann Friedrich Gmelin named the species *Emberiza atricapilla*, on the basis of Latham's description. There is little information on changes of its status, but clearing of forests in its breeding range may have increased the amount of dense thicket habitat that it prefers.

GEOGRAPHIC VARIATION: None has been described. Hybrids with White-crowned and White-throated sparrows have been reported.

MEASUREMENTS: (7 males): wing 76–83 (80), tail 73–83 (76), tarsus 23.4–25.6 (24.4), exposed culmen 11.2–13.2 (12.2), bill depth 7.9–8.1 (8.0); (7 females): wing 74–81 (78), tail 69–83 (76), tarsus 23.4–24.9 (24.1), culmen 11.4–12.7 (11.9), bill depth 7.6–7.9 (7.7) (Ridgway 1901).

Mass: (N=542) 26.5 g (21.2–36.5) (Berkeley, California; March) (Linsdale and Sumner 1934).

Reference: Linsdale and Sumner (1934).

46 **White-crowned Sparrow**   PLATE 19
Zonotrichia leucophrys [554]

IDENTIFICATION: 14–17 cm (*c.* 5.5–7 in), males slightly larger; sexes similar in coloration.

The White-crowned is a fairly large sparrow. Adults are distinguished from other sparrows by the black and white striped head, grayish breast and bill color (yellowish to reddish pink); first winter birds (before Feb; some west coast birds retain some of the rusty crown feathers into the first summer) resemble adults in color pattern, but are warm, rusty beige where the adults are black, and pale buffy where the adults are whitish.

Similar species: First-winter birds (before Feb) resemble first-winter Golden-crowned Sparrows, but are more pallid in coloration, with a distinct buffy median crown-stripe and rusty brown lateral crown-stripes; bill pinkish or yellowish; dorsal streaking light rusty brown, not brownish as in Golden-crowned Sparrow; resemble American Tree and Rufous-crowned sparrows in general coloration, but are easily separable.

Adult—*Head:* a broad, white median crown-stripe extends to just behind the bill to the back of head; black lateral crown-stripes join over top of bill; supercilium white, extending to the eye (eastern and western mountain populations) or to the base of bill (western and west coast populations); eye-stripe and lores black (white in western and west coast birds); chin, throat, ear-coverts, and nape gray, with some brown in the nape; may have a faint dark malar stripe (west coast); **back:** mantle feathers with dark rusty brown or brown (west coast) centers and beige edges, making back appear streaked; scapulars grayish brown, broadly edged in pale brown in fresh plumage; tertials dark brown, broadly edged with pale brown; **rump:** grayish brown, lightly streaked; **wing:** brown, with tips of median and greater coverts white, forming two conspicuous wing-bars; **underparts:** unstreaked and grayish, paler on chin and belly than on breast and flanks; **tail:** long, slightly notched; **bill:** pinkish, reddish pink, yellow-orange to pinkish orange (northwest) or yellowish (Pacific Coast); **legs:** yellowish; **iris:** dark brown.

First-winter (July–Feb, Mar) like adults, but median crown-stripe, supercilium, and chin pale buff, lateral crown-stripes and eye-stripe light rusty brown, belly suffused with buff. Head markings become black and white by Apr in most populations, but brown feathers are retained through the first year in Pacific Coast populations.

Juveniles (June–Aug) like young in first fall, but forehead and crown pale and streaked with black; back and rump streaked; primaries edged with buff; secondaries and tertials edged with dull rust; chin, throat, breast and flanks pale and heavily streaked with black; belly and undertail-coverts unstreaked. Some west coast individuals retain this plumage into November.

VOICE: The song is variable with many regional dialects, but distinctive. In the east and north it is characteristically two (one to four) clearly whistled notes, the second slightly lower than the first, followed by three descending buzzy or husky notes, **dear-dear buzz buzz buzz**. Along the Pacific Coast, the song usually starts with a long, clearly whistled note that is higher pitched than the rest of the song, and is followed by two to four notes that may be clear, buzzy or warbled; the song may be the best way to distinguish west coast breeding birds from northern migrants. The commonest call note is a hard **pink, tsit** or **zink** (geographically variable), or a thin **seep**; around the nest adults use a warning **tip** or **tsit** note.

HABITS: On the breeding grounds, males sing persistently throughout the day from an exposed perch on a dwarf spruce, tamarack, willow or birch, or from a rock. They also frequently sing at night, and occasionally sing in winter. In winter White-crowns are generally found in loose flocks or small groups, sometimes in mixed flocks, often with other *Zonotrichia*. They forage on the ground, usually in fairly open areas. When flushed, they commonly fly up into a small nearby tree or hedgerow, and are easily seen. White-crowns are easy to spish up.

HABITAT: In northern and montane habitats, White-crowned Sparrows are birds of open stunted trees (conifers, willows, or birch), where they are often a common and conspicuous species. On the Pacific Coast, from central California to British

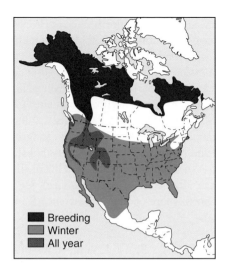

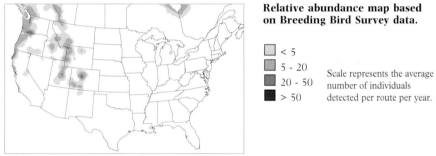

Relative abundance map based on Breeding Bird Survey data.

- ☐ < 5
- ▨ 5 - 20
- ▨ 20 - 50
- ■ > 50

Scale represents the average number of individuals detected per route per year.

Columbia, they breed commonly in deciduous thickets along the coast and in urban gardens. In winter White-crowns occur in brushy areas, hedgerows, woodland edges, multiflora rose, and gardens. They tend to occupy more open habitats than either White-throated or Golden-crowned sparrows.

BREEDING: *Nest* is placed on the ground, often at the base of a small bush, or low in bushes (to 3 m; one reported 12 m high). The nest is a bulky cup of coarse grass, twigs, bark shreds, moss and lichens, lined with fine grass, hair, feathers or rootlets, commonly concealed in grass clumps, mossy hummocks, or slightly under rocks. The female alone builds the nest. Nesting begins in Mar (Pacific Coast) or June (north), and continues through July; may raise 2–3 broods on the Pacific Coast. *Eggs*, 2–6, usually 3 on the Pacific Coast and 4–5 in the north, pale greenish blue, spotted and splotched with brown. *Incubation*, 12–14 days; female alone broods, but male may feed female on nest and both parents feed young; young fledge in 9–11 days. The species is occasionally polygynous. Along the Pacific Coast, the species is frequently parasitized by cowbirds.

RANGE: *Breeds* from w and n Alaska (north slope of Brooks range, Barrow [rare]), n Yukon, n Mackenzie, c Keewatin, n Manitoba, n Quebec, Labrador, and nw Newfoundland, south to s Alaska, the Alaska Peninsula (west to Izembek Bay), Kodiak I., south in mountains and coastal areas (but absent along the n and c coast of British Columbia and Queen Charlotte Is.) to s California (to Santa Barbara Co., San Bernardino Mountains), n Nevada (Ruby Mountains, Carson Range, Diamond Mountains), n and e-c Arizona (White and San Francisco mountains, North Rim of Grand Canyon; uncommon), n New Mexico (Jemez, Sangre de Cristo and Culebra mountains), se Alberta and sw Saskatchewan (Cypress Hills), n Saskatchewan (Lake Athabasca, Reindeer L.), n Manitoba (south to Gillam, Ilford), n Ontario (Fort Severn, Hawley L., Cape Henrietta Maria, Moosonee), s-c Quebec (Schefferville) southeast to the outer north shore of the St. Lawrence R., and nw Newfoundland (south to Flowers Cove).

Winters from c Alaska (casual), s British Columbia, Washington, Idaho, Wyoming, South Dakota (rare), Minnesota (rare), southern Ontario (uncommon), and Nova Scotia (rare) south to s Baja California, Michoacán, Querétaro, San Luis Potosí, Tamaulipas, s Texas, Gulf Coast to Florida (uncommon and local) and Georgia (uncommon). Most common in winter west of the 100th meridian from s-c Texas to Colorado and California, south into n Mexico and Baja California. Accidental or casual in Japan, Little Diomede and Wrangel islands, islands in the Bering Sea, the Aleutians (Shemya in Sept), the Arctic Is., Greenland, Britain (May), France (Aug), The Netherlands (Dec–Feb), and western Germany, and, in winter, in the Bahama Is., Cuba and Jamaica.

HISTORY: The White-crowned Sparrow was first described by the German naturalist Johann Reinhold Forster (after whom Forster's Tern was named) in *An account of the birds sent from Hudson's Bay* (1772), on the basis of specimens from the Severn R. in northwestern Ontario, and Fort Albany, on the west coast of James Bay. He named the species *Emberiza leucophrys* (white-eyebrowed bunting). Forster also first described the Eskimo Curlew in this paper. Two of the subspecies of White-crowned Sparrows were named after 19th century American naturalists, Thomas Nuttall and William Gambel, who were active in western ornithology. Thomas Nuttall was an English naturalist who came to North America at the age of 22, where he ultimately became a full-time naturalist. He both traveled and published extensively. William Gambel was born in Philadelphia in 1823. At the age of 15, he accompanied Nuttall on an 11-month trip to the southeastern United States, and later on other expeditions. In 1849, after a short but productive life, he died on the Feather R. in California. In 1840, Thomas Nuttall described and named *Fringilla gambelii* (= *Z. l. gambelii*) on the basis of birds from Walla Walla, Washington. In 1899, Robert Ridgway named *Zonotrichia leucophrys nuttalli* in honor of Nuttall.

Eastern and northern populations of White-crowned Sparrows nest in habitats that have been little disturbed by humans, and there is no reason to suspect that their numbers have been significantly affected. In the 1980s, they declined in abundance in Utah, Colorado, the southern Rocky Mountains, and Sierra Nevada, but increased in Montana, Wyoming, Nevada, and Newfoundland. White-crowned Sparrows remain common in suitable habitat along the Pacific Coast.

GEOGRAPHIC VARIATION: Five subspecies are generally recognized: the Eastern White-crowned Sparrow (*Z. l. leucophrys*); Gambel's Sparrow (*Z. l. gambelii*); Mountain White-crowned Sparrow (*Z. l. oriantha*); Puget Sound White-crowned Sparrow (*Z. l. pugetensis*); and Nuttall's White-crowned Sparrow (*Z. l. nuttalli*). *Z. l. leucophrys* and *Z. l. oriantha* differ from the others in that the supercilium from the eye to the bill is black rather than white, and the bill is pink (rather than orange-pink or yellow). The underparts of *Z. l. oriantha* average paler than those of *Z. l. leucophrys*; the two cannot be separated in the field, and some workers do not recognize *Z. l. oriantha*. *Z. l. gambelii* is slightly larger than *Z. l. leucophrys*, with a yellow-orange or orange-pink bill; the white supercilium in this subspecies and the following two goes to the bill. *Z. l. nuttalli* and *Z. l. pugetensis* are similar; the former tend to have relatively shorter wings (in migratory populations, the primaries extend well beyond the secondaries and tertials); they differ from *Z. l. gambelii* by having a dull yellow bill, yellow in the bend of the wing, and overall darker and duller coloration, with back stripes brown rather than rusty brown and back lacking gray. *Z. l. leucophrys* breeds in the northeast. It intergrades with *Z. l. gambelii*, which breeds in the northwest, along the southern coast of Hudson Bay. *Z. l. gambelii* intergrades with *Z. l. oriantha* in the mountains of southern Alberta. *Z. l. oriantha* breeds in the mountains from southern Alberta and Montana south to central Arizona and northwestern New Mexico, and winters at lower elevations, and south to central Mexico; its breeding range does not overlap *Z. l. leucophrys*. *Z. l. pugetensis* breeds from southwestern British Columbia, west of the Cascade Range to northwestern California, and winters from British Columbia to southern California; it is replaced by *Z. l. nuttalli*, which is resident from the coast of central western California south to Santa Barbara Co. In *Z. l. nuttalli* some of the black and white feathers of the crown are admixed with brown and tan feathers from the first basic plumage in the first summer.

Hybrids with Harris's, White-throated, Golden-crowned, and Song sparrows have been reported.

MEASUREMENTS: Eastern White-crowned Sparrow (13 males): wing 76–83 (80), tail 68–82 (75), tarsus 22.1–23.9 (23.4), exposed culmen 10.9–11.9 (11.4), bill depth at base 7.1–8.4 (7.6); (13 females): wing 73–81 (77), tail 68–76 (72), tarsus 21.3–24.4 (23.1), culmen 10.4–11.9 (11.2), bill depth 7.1–8.1 (7.4). [probably including *Z. l. oriantha* which are nearly the same size].

Gambel's Sparrow (7 males): wing 76–83 (79), tail 66–74 (71), tarsus 21.3–23.6 (22.9), culmen 9.9–11.2 (10.7), bill depth 7.1–7.4 (7.3); (7 females): wing 74–83 (76), tail 67–74 (70), tarsus 21.8–22.4 (22.1), culmen 9.9–10.9 (10.7), bill depth 6.9–7.1 (7.1).

Coastal Sparrows [probably including *Z. l. nuttalli* and *Z. l. pugetensis*] (7 males): wing 72–75 (74), tail 68–75 (72), tarsus 22.4–24.4 (23.4), culmen 10.4–11.9 (11.2), bill depth 7.4–7.6 (7.5); (7 females): wing 68–77 (69), tail 64–69 (66), tarsus 22.1–23.9 (22.9), culmen 9.9–11.9 (11.2), bill depth 7.4–7.6 (7.5) (Ridgway 1901).

Mass: (N=162) 29.4 g (21.6–38.5) (Pennsylvania); *Z. l. gambelii* (N=50) 25.5 g (21.0–28.5) (California); *Z. l. nuttalli* (N=50) 32.0 g (27.0–35.5) (California); *Z. l. pugetensis* (N=50) 25.3 g (21.4–29.1) (California); *Z. l. oriantha* (N=50) 28.4 g (23.3–33.7) (Oregon) (Dunning 1993). (24 males) 29.8 g (28.0–33.3), (20 females) 28.2 g (25.0–32.0) (Kuujjuaq, Quebec; July); (16 males) 28.1 g (26.4–30.0), (9 females) 30.3 g (26.5–33.3) (Churchill and Gillam, Manitoba; June); (22 males) 25.4 g (23.5–28.5), (18 females) 23.9 g (22.1–26.6) (Inuvik, Northwest Territories) (Rising, unpublished).

References: Banks (1964), Dunn *et al.* (1995), Graber (1955).

47 **Harris's Sparrow** *Zonotrichia querula* [553]   PLATE 18

D. BEADLE 94.

IDENTIFICATION: 16–19 cm (*c*. 6.5–7.4 in), males somewhat larger; males somewhat brighter in coloration.

Harris's Sparrow is a large sparrow. In breeding plumage the black face and cap and large pink bill are diagnostic. In first-winter plumage, the white chin and throat are dark brown flecked, with a necklace of dark brown feathers across the breast; crown is brown and streaked, with light brown lores and eye line.

Similar species: This is a distinctive species. The black on the throat and breast separates Harris's Sparrow from the other *Zonotrichia*; first-winter Harris's may lack black on the throat, but the ochre on the side of the face is distinctive. Harris's Sparrows are obviously larger than most other sparrows.

Adult—*Head:* crown, face, chin and throat black, extending back to eye; eye-stripe behind eye and ear-coverts brownish buffy, becoming grayish on ear-coverts and side of neck and pale next to the black throat patch; black spot or patch at back of ear-coverts; ***back:*** hindneck and nape brownish; back and scapulars brown, broadly streaked with brownish black; ***rump:*** brownish; ***wing:*** brown; median and greater coverts edged in white or buffy white, forming two wing-bars; ***tail:*** brown, slightly notched; ***underparts:*** breast and flanks white, flecked with dark brown; belly white; ***bill:*** pink; ***legs*** and ***feet:*** light brown; ***iris:*** brown.

First-winter (Aug–Apr) like adult, but crown mostly brown, flecked with dark brown or black feathers; brown around bill and side of face; chin and throat white; malar stripe dark brown connecting to a dark brown necklace on upper breast; most dull-plumaged winter birds are probably first-winter birds.

Juveniles (July–Aug) forehead and crown heavily streaked with black; side of head creamy buff, with some black streaking; back of head and nape dull chestnut and mottled with dark; back streaked and mottled, rump grayer and mottled with black; wings blackish, with feathers narrowly edged with buff; median and greater coverts narrowly edged in white, making two narrow wing-bars; chin and throat white, spotted with black; center of breast with a conspicuous black spot; chest and flanks buffy white and heavily streaked; belly white.

VOICE: The song is one to several clear whistled notes on the same minor key, often followed by other notes that may be higher or lower, sometimes ending with a slow trill. Call a distinctive series of musical tinkling notes. Note a loud *chip* or *wink*.

HABITS: On the breeding grounds, males sing persistently, often from the top of a spruce tree or an exposed rock. In winter, they are generally found in loose flocks or small groups, sometimes in mixed flocks. They rarely sing in winter. When flushed, they often fly into a small tree or bush and are easily seen. They are easy to spish up.

HABITAT: On the breeding ground, they are found in open spruce often near the spruce tundra border, or woodland edge, or in burns. Nests may be some distance from nearest woods. In winter, they are found in weedy fields, hedgerows, low brush or the edge of deciduous woods.

BREEDING: *Nest* is placed on the ground, well concealed in reindeer moss and other vegetation (Labrador tea) or small trees (commonly birch, alder, or spruce), never far from a conifer stand. The nest is a bulky cup of dead grass, rootlets, and sometimes mosses, lined with finer grass and sedges, and sometimes caribou hair. Nesting takes place from mid-June through early July; the female alone appears to build the nest. *Eggs*, 3–5, usually 4, pale green, heavily splotched with brown. *Incubation*, 13–14 days. The female alone incubates, but both sexes feed the young.

RANGE: *Breeds* from Mackenzie (Inuvik, eastern Mackenzie Delta, Great Bear Lake, Coppermine, Bathurst Inlet), s Keewatin (Aberdeen and Nueltin lakes), n Manitoba (Churchill), and nw Ontario (Fort Severn) south to eastern Great Slave Lake, northwestern Saskatchewan (Hasballa and Milton lakes) and n-c Manitoba (Gillam).

Winters from se Alaska (Juneau, Ketchikan), s British Columbia (rare), s Idaho (very rare), n Utah (rare but regular), n Colorado, s Saskatchewan (rare), s Manitoba (rare), Iowa (common in west, uncommon in east), sw Minnesota, Illinois (rare) and sw Ontario (rare), rarely south through Washington and Oregon to s California (mostly east of the Sierra Nevada), s Nevada, s Utah, s New Mexico, s Texas, nw Louisiana, Arkansas and w Tennessee. Commonest in winter in c Kansas, c Oklahoma, and n-c Texas. Very rare in migration and winter in c and n Alaska and coastal Washington and California, s Arizona, and throughout e United States, from Newfoundland south to Florida.

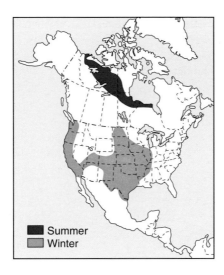

HISTORY: Edward Harris was a wealthy amateur naturalist and friend and benefactor of Audubon who accompanied Audubon on his Gulf Coast expedition and later on his Missouri R. expedition. It was on the latter, on 4 May, 1843, below the Black Snake Hills, near present-day St. Joseph, Missouri, that Harris shot a sparrow with a black crown and throat and a pink bill that Audubon was convinced was a new species. Audubon wrote in his journal: 'I am truly proud to name it *Fringilla Harrisii*, in honor of one of the best friends I have in this world.' Thomas Nuttall, however, had collected the first specimen of Harris's Sparrow on 28 April, 1834, near Independence, Missouri, as he was ascending the Missouri R. with Townsend. Although he did not publish a description until 1840, Nuttall's name *Fringilla querula* (the plaintive finch, presumably after its song) has priority. Audubon's common name, however, instead of Nuttall's 'Mourning Finch' has become established.

Because Harris's Sparrow breeds only in isolated areas of northern Canada, it is unlikely that there have been significant disturbances to its breeding habitat. Christmas Bird Count data indicate no change in status between 1970 and 1990, although there has been some expansion of wintering range both to the north and west since 1930.

GEOGRAPHIC VARIATION: None described. Hybrids with White-crowned and White-throated sparrows have been recorded.

MEASUREMENTS: (41 males from NWT): wing 86 (SD=2.2), tarsus 23.8 (0.7), culmen from nostril 9.5 (0.4), mass 37.4 g (2.0); (40 females from NWT): wing 81 (1.9), tarsus 22.7 (0.8), culmen from nostril 9.4 (0.4), mass 33.7 g (2.2) (Norment and Shackleton).

Mass: (19 males from Kansas) 38.8 g (36.8–41.7); (19 females from Kansas) 33.7 g (31.4–36.3) (Dunning 1993).

Reference: Norment and Shackleton (1993).

Genus *Junco*

Although juncos are highly variable in plumage, currently only three or four species are recognized. Two of these, the Dark-eyed Junco (*Junco hyemalis*) and the Yellow-eyed Junco (*J. phaeonotus*) are found north of Mexico. The Volcano Junco (*J. vulcani*) is found in the highlands of Costa Rica, and the Guadalupe Junco (*J. insularis*) on Guadalupe Island, Mexico. Yellow-eyed Juncos are generally divided into five sub-species, one of which occurs north of Mexico. Dark-eyed Juncos are divided into 14 subspecies, all of which occur north of Mexico; the Guadalupe Junco is often put in this species. The 21 forms of juncos are geographically complementary, and in the past several different species have been recognized. In this book the phenotypically distinctive subspecies or groups of subspecies are described separately to facilitate understanding the diversity of this group.

With the exception of the Volcano Junco, juncos have white lateral tail feathers, are predominantly gray or gray and pinkish and white in coloration, and are unstreaked as adults. They breed at high latitudes or altitudes and, again with the exception of the Volcano Junco, are characteristic birds of coniferous or mixed forests, although they can be found in other habitats. Although many populations are migratory, and they leave regions with extreme winter conditions, they are among the hardiest of the sparrows — reflected in the common vernacular name for the group, 'snowbird.' For the most part, even resident populations tend to form wandering flocks in winter. Adult juncos undergo a complete molt before migrating; in the fall, the fresh feathers are often tinged with buff or brown, making even predominantly gray forms brownish in hue. Juvenile juncos molt their body plumage and most coverts before migrating, but retain their wing feathers, greater coverts, and often tail feathers for the first year. First-year juncos are generally duller in coloration than adults.

Because juncos as a group are adapted to boreal conditions, it is generally speculated that they arose in the north. During glacial advances we could speculate that they were pushed southward, and boreal conditions in southwestern and central American highlands would extend into lowland areas, allowing colonization of these areas by juncos. As the glaciers retreated, populations of juncos became isolated in these high-land areas, and differentiated. Alternatively, some have suggested a southern origin for Juncos, with the Volcano Junco perhaps linking them with *Zonotrichia*. In many ways the Volcano Junco seems out of place in this genus, and it has been suggested that they are more closely related with other sparrows, perhaps the *Zonotrichia*. There are several records of hybrids between the 'Slate-colored' (Dark-eyed) Junco and the White-throated Sparrow (*Z. albicollis*) — perhaps indicating that these genera are closely allied; there are chromosomal similarities between them. There is, as well, a Chinese bird, the Fukien Slaty Bunting (*Latoucheornis siemsseni*) which is similar in general appearance to the Slate-colored Junco, but no one has investigated their relationships rigorously.

48 **Dark-eyed Junco** *Junco hyemalis* [567]   **PLATES 20 & 21**

D. BEADLE 95.

IDENTIFICATION: 13–17 cm (*c.* 5–6.5 in), males slightly larger than females; males generally more brightly colored than females. Five distinctive types (groups of subspecies) are treated separately.

'Slate-colored Junco' (*J. h. hyemalis*) [567]

The 'Slate-colored' Junco is slate-gray, except for having a white belly and white outertail feathers; the gray is darkest on head. The bill is pink. Females and first-year birds are paler and often have considerable brown in their plumage, especially in back and flanks.

Similar species: 'Oregon' juncos have a dark gray or gray head, with contrasting brown or brownish gray back and pinkish brown on the flanks; the gray on the throat and flanks of the slate-colored junco is concave — forms an inverted U on the breast — whereas the Oregon junco has a convex hood. These forms intergrade with each other in the northwest, and intermediate individuals occur. The 'White-winged' junco is larger, usually has two white wing-bars, and always has more white in the tail (some individuals of several subspecies of Dark-eyed Junco, including slate-colored juncos have white wing-bars).

Adult male—*Head:* neck, chest, upper breast, sides, flanks and upperparts plain slate-color, darker on head, paler on rump and sides; ***tail:*** outer rectrix (6th) white, with extensive white on 5th, and some on 4th; ***wing:*** slate-gray; ***underparts:*** belly, lower breast, and undertail-coverts white; ***bill:*** pink, sometimes dusky at tip; ***legs:*** dark pinkish brown; ***feet:*** darker; ***iris:*** dark brown.

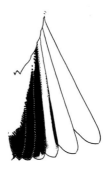

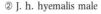

① J. h. hyemalis female ② J. h. hyemalis male ③ Male maximum white

Adult female, like adult male, but slate-color lighter, sometimes decidedly so, and less white in tail.

First-winter (Aug–Mar) like adult, but grays dull, and head, and especially breast, flanks, back and rump washed with brown, often pinkish brown; eye grayish brown, becoming darker with age; females browner than males, with wide brown edging on tertials.

Juveniles (June–Aug) crown, back, and rump brown, sometimes slightly rufescent on back, streaked, or mottled with dark brown; throat, breast, and flanks buffy or buffy gray, streaked with dark brown, belly and undertail-coverts unmarked white; legs pinkish.

VOICE: The song is usually a simple trill on one pitch, like Chipping Sparrow, but more musical; occasionally changes in pitch. The song is occasionally given year round, though most commonly in spring (Feb–June, depending on latitude) and rarely in winter. The calls are a simple *tit tit tit* or a smacking *tack tack tack*, the latter distinctive.

HABITS: On the breeding grounds, males sing persistently, especially early in the season, from an exposed perch, often from near the top of a conifer, a snag, or tall dead tree. In winter, they are generally found in loose flocks or small groups, and may flock with other sparrows, often in open woods, or in weedy areas at the edge of woods, hedgerows, or fields. They do not tend to fly far when flushed, and are easy to see. They respond to spishing.

HABITAT: On the breeding grounds, they are found in a variety of woods, but especially in open woods, cut-over areas, plantations, commonly but not necessarily in coniferous or mixed woods; in the north, they may occur in urban parklands and gardens. In the Allegheny Mountains they are found at 700–900 m, and are most common in brushy edge habitats; farther south in the Appalachians they nest up to 1350 m. In northeastern Ohio, they nest in cool hemlock ravines and mature

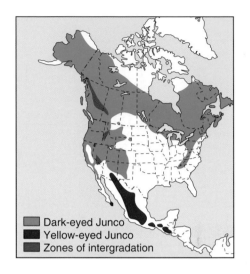

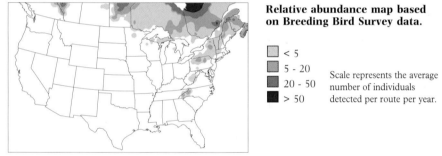

Relative abundance map based on Breeding Bird Survey data.

- < 5
- 5 - 20
- 20 - 50
- > 50

Scale represents the average number of individuals detected per route per year.

beech–maple forest. In the north, they are more strictly birds of coniferous woods, and are especially common in young jack pines.

BREEDING: *Nest* is usually built on the ground and well concealed under vegetation, and often placed beside rocks, logs, or roots. Occasionally, nests are built in low trees on ledges, in river banks, or in niches in buildings. The nest is a cup of grasses or rootlets, lined with fine grasses or hair. The female alone probably builds the nest. Nesting takes place from May through July, later in north than south; probably double-brooded in the south. *Eggs*, 3–6, grayish or pale bluish white, speckled or splotched with brown or reddish brown. *Incubation*, 11–13 days; female alone broods, but both parents feed; young leave nest at 9–13 days. Parasitized by cowbirds.

RANGE: *Breeds* from w (Nondalton, Katmai Park) and nw (Kobuk) Alaska, n Yukon, nw and c Mackenzie, s Keewatin, n Manitoba and Ontario, Quebec and Labrador (n to the tree line) and Newfoundland south to s-c Alaska, ne British Columbia, sw Alberta, c Saskatchewan, s Manitoba, c Minnesota, se Wisconsin, c

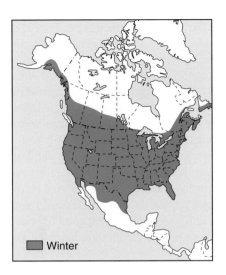

Winter

Michigan, s Ontario, ne Ohio, n Pennsylvania, south in mountains to se New York, w and c Massachusetts, w Connecticut, ne West Virginia, w Maryland, w Virginia, w North Carolina, e Kentucky, e Tennessee, sw South Carolina, and n Georgia.

Winters from s Canada and Newfoundland south to Florida (rare in the south), Alabama, Louisiana (uncommon in south), Texas, Tamaulipas, c Chihuahua, n Sonora and n Baja California. It is commonest east of c Kansas and Texas, and south of Canada and n Minnesota, and uncommon along the west coast and south and west of n New Mexico. Most of the slate-colored juncos wintering in coastal British Columbia appear to be Cassiar Slate-colored Juncos. Rare, but probably regular in Russia (Chukchi Peninsula, Wrangel I.), islands in the Bering Sea, Banks, Southampton and Baffin Is.; casual or accidental in Bermuda, the Bahama Is., Jamaica, and Europe (Britain, The Netherlands, Norway, Poland, Gibraltar; most records in winter and spring).

HISTORY: Carl Linnaeus, the great Swedish botanist, first described and named the 'Slate-colored Junco' in the 10th Edition of his *Systema naturae* (1758), basing his description on Mark Catesby's The Snow-bird, *Passer nivalis*, one of several birds described and illustrated in his *Natural History of Carolina* (1731). Linnaeus called this species *Fringilla hyemalis*, or 'winter finch,' as Catesby knew of this species only from the winter. The name *Junco* was coined by Johann Wagler for the Yellow-eyed Junco. The name is based on the Latin *juncus*, a rush — an inappropriate name for these birds, which are rarely found in rushes!

It has always been a common bird; Audubon wrote that '. . . there is not a person in the Union who does not know the little Snow-bird . . .' and it today remains one of our most familiar winter sparrows. Recently, numbers of juncos have declined somewhat in New Brunswick and New Hampshire, perhaps reflecting habitat loss.

GEOGRAPHIC VARIATION: Three of the subspecies of Dark-eyed Juncos are put in the 'Slate-colored' Junco complex, the northern Slate-colored Junco (*J. h. hyemalis*), the Appalachian Carolina Junco (*J. h. carolinensis*), and the northwestern Cassiar Slate-colored Junco (*J. h. cismontanus*). The hood of Carolina Juncos is a uniform light gray, whereas in Slate-colored Juncos it is generally darker; females of both tend to have lighter hoods. Carolina Juncos may have a dark spot on the base of the upper bill, which may be bluish in color. Carolina Juncos breed from western Virginia and southern West Virginia southward, and are probably non-migratory, but move to lower elevations in winter. Juncos from western Maryland, northern West Virginia, Pennsylvania and southern New York are intermediate between *J. h. hyemalis* and *J. h. carolinensis*. Cassiar Juncos breed east of the coastal ranges from central Yukon southeast to north-central and eastern British Columbia and west-central Alberta. These birds represent a stable population of apparent hybrids between Slate-colored and 'Oregon' juncos (*J. h. oreganus*), and they are intermediate in coloration between the two. Males have darker heads, the edge of the slate on the breast convex instead of concave; females have flanks washed with pink or brown, rather than gray. Most of the Slate-colored Juncos wintering in coastal British Columbia appear to be *J. h. cismontanus*.

MEASUREMENTS: (see table).

Mass: (data from western Pennsylvania): 1016 males (March) 16.4–25.4 g (20.6), 213 females (March) 14.3–23.4 g (19.1); 418 males (October) 14.3–23.1 g (19.5); 169 females 14.4–21.2 g (18.2) (Clench and Leberman 1978).

'White-winged Junco' (*Junco hyemalis aikeni*) [566]

IDENTIFICATION: A large junco with a large bill, an important diagnostic feature. 'White-winged' Juncos are like 'Slate-colored' Juncos, but the slate color is lighter, the greater and median secondary coverts are usually white-tipped, forming two distinct wing-bars, and outer three tail feathers (6th, 5th, 4th rectrices) are largely white, with white usually present on the 3rd.

Similar species: Slate-colored Juncos are smaller, and rarely have white on the 3rd rectrix or white wing-bars. Other juncos usually lack white wing-bars, and have pink or reddish in their plumage.

Adult—See above. White-winged Juncos are less sexually dimorphic in both size and color than other juncos.

First-winter (Aug–Mar) like adults, but more or less tinged with light grayish brown, especially on back.

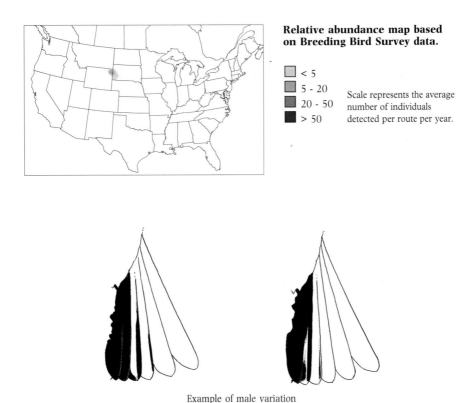

Relative abundance map based on Breeding Bird Survey data.

☐ < 5
▨ 5 - 20
▧ 20 - 50
■ > 50

Scale represents the average number of individuals detected per route per year.

Example of male variation

Juveniles (July–Aug) like Slate-colored Junco, but with white wing-bars and three outer tail feathers white.

VOICE: The song is like Slate-colored Junco; the **chip** calls are said to be more musical than those of the Slate-colored Junco.

HABITS: On the breeding grounds, males sing from an exposed perch, typically a pine tree. In fall and winter, the birds form small flocks that frequently forage on ground; other species, especially other juncos, may join them.

HABITAT: White-winged juncos are most common in pine forests, but may also be found in spruce or aspen. In winter, they are found in brushy habitats, around feeders, but avoid open grassland.

BREEDING: *Nest* is placed on the ground, commonly under logs, roots, rock ledges, or in artificial sites (cans; roof tiles). Nests are probably like those of other juncos, and built by both parents. Nesting takes place in June and early July. *Eggs*, 3–4, white or creamy white, speckled with brown or cinnamon-brown. *Incubation*, about

12 days; female alone probably broods, but both parents feed the young; young fledge in about 12 days. Occasional host for cowbirds.

RANGE: *Breeds* from se Montana (Rosebud Mountains, Lone Pine Hills), ne Wyoming (Bear Lodge Mountains, Sundance, Black Hills), South Dakota (Black Hills, Harding, and Shannon cos.), and nw Nebraska (Sioux Co.).

Winters in the Black Hills (chiefly at lower elevations) s through Colorado (chiefly in foothills) to n-c New Mexico, and n Arizona (Flagstaff; sporadic), and e to c South Dakota, w and c Kansas (regular, but not common), w and c Oklahoma (principally in Panhandle) and n Texas (Briscoe Co.; one record). Records from Missouri and Ontario apparently are of aberrant white-winged slate-colored juncos; white-winged juncos have been reported from Tennessee.

HISTORY: Charles Aiken, a pioneer ornithologist from Colorado Springs, collected the first specimens of the White-winged Junco near Fountain, Colorado, where they are fairly common in winter. In 1873, Robert Ridgway named the bird *Junco hyemalis* var. *aikeni* in his honor.

GEOGRAPHIC VARIATION: None described. Rarely hybridizes with 'pink -sided' juncos in southeastern Montana (Powder R. Co.), and a hybrid individual has been collected in Colorado in winter.

MEASUREMENTS: (see table); no data on weight.

'Gray-headed Junco' (*Junco hyemalis caniceps s.l.)* [569]

IDENTIFICATION: 'Gray-headed' Juncos are fairly large, dark-eyed and gray-headed sparrows. The head, wings, rump, and tail are gray, with black around the eye and lores; lower mandible yellow, upper mandible yellow or gray (varies geographically); back is a bright rusty red, the red usually confined to the interscapular region; their throat, breast, and flanks pale gray, without a line of demarcation between the breast and flanks; outer three tail feathers partly or completely white. Females are slightly duller in color than males, sometimes with somewhat less white in tail.

Similar species: Yellow-eyed Juncos are similar in general coloration, but have a bright yellow iris; Yellow-eyed also has rust-edged greater coverts and tertials. Oregon and pink-sided Juncos have throat that contrasts with the flank color, and usually darker gray heads.

Adult—See above.

First-winter (Aug–Mar) like adults, but the grays are paler, and less strongly contrasting with the white of the belly; flanks more or less tinged with buff; reddish brown of back duller; bill somewhat darker, and dusky at tip.

① Male   ② Female

Juveniles (July–Sept) head buffy brown, streaked with brown; back and rump bright rusty red, streaked with dark brown; rump buffy, streaked with black; rectrices dark gray, with outer two white; underparts buffy, streaked with dark brown on throat, breast and flanks; belly whitish; legs yellowish.

VOICE: Song and calls like those of other Dark-eyed Juncos, but perhaps more varied than that of the Slate-colored Junco.

HABITS: As with other juncos, males sing persistently from an exposed perch near the top of a tall tree, often the top of a conifer, during the nesting season. Singing occurs from Feb through July, and is most intense during nesting — after mid-Mar. In winter, in the southern part of their range, some males apparently stay on or near their breeding territories, but most form flocks, often with other juncos. They feed almost exclusively on the ground.

HABITAT: Gray-headed Juncos are found in the mountains, generally above 1800 m, and are often found in conifers (spruce, Douglas-fir, ponderosa and lodge-pole pines, and fir), but also in aspen, oak, and mountain mahogany. They are more likely to be found in rather arid woodlands than the other Dark-eyed Juncos. In winter, they are found along the lower edges of coniferous forests, brushy ravines with scrub oak, mountain mahogany, and hawthorn, sagebrush, and weeds, but not generally in open fields.

BREEDING: *Nest* is a cup of coarse grasses or rootlets, lined with finer grass or hair. It is commonly placed on the ground, perhaps in a depression, and often under a rock or small shrub or bush (bearberry, juniper buffaloberry), but may be placed low in a tree, or under the eaves of a house; nesting commences in late Mar in the south, and late Apr or May farther north; they are probably double-brooded, at least in the southern part of their range. *Eggs*, 3–5, are white or pale bluish white, speckled or spotted with buffy brown or rusty brown. *Incubation*, probably 11–12 days; female alone probably incubates, but both parents feed the young. Parasitized by cowbirds.

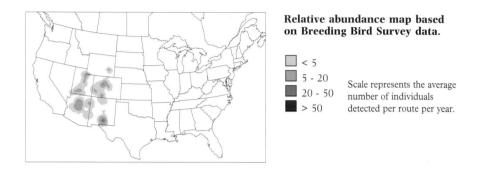

**Relative abundance map based
on Breeding Bird Survey data.**

☐ < 5
☐ 5 - 20   Scale represents the average
■ 20 - 50   number of individuals
■ > 50   detected per route per year.

RANGE: *Breeds* from s Idaho, n Nevada (Santa Rosa Mountains), c Nevada (Ruby Mountains), sw Nevada (Grapevine Mountains), n Utah (Unita Mountains), n-c Colorado (Medicine Bow Range), s through c and w New Mexico to Catron Co. and w Texas (Guadalupe Mountains), c Arizona (White Mountains, Mogollon Plateau), and west to se California (White and Inyo mountains, Clark Mountain).

Winters at lower elevations in breeding range, s through w Texas, Arizona, and s California, n to Santa Barbara Co. (rare to uncommon), to n Sinaloa, Chihuahua and n Durango. Rare in Western Plains (e Montana, s-c Nebraska, Kansas, Oklahoma, principally in Panhandle). Casual in British Columbia, Ontario.

HISTORY: The Gray-headed Junco was first described by Samuel Washington Woodhouse in 1853 as *Struthus caniceps*, the 'gray-headed snow finch.' As a youth, Woodhouse knew Nuttall, Gambel, and Cassin at the Philadelphia Academy of Sciences. After obtaining a degree in medicine, he became surgeon and naturalist in the U.S. Army, and made several excursions to the American west.

GEOGRAPHIC VARIATION: The Gray-headed Junco consists of two subspecies, the northern *J. h. caniceps*, and the southern *J. h. dorsalis*. These intergrade in north-central Arizona and east-central New Mexico. Typically, *J. h. caniceps* have a darker gray head and throat than *J. h. dorsalis; J h. caniceps* have a flesh-colored upper mandible, whereas that of *J. h. dorsalis* is dark. Northern birds, on average, have smaller bills. *J. h. caniceps* hybridizes with pink-sided juncos in northern Utah (Wasatch Mountains, Woodruff, Garden City), southern Wyoming (Fort Bridger, Wind R. and Big Horn mountains), northern Nevada (Jarbridge Mountains), and southern Idaho (Swan L.), and with Oregon juncos in southwestern Nevada (Charleston and Sheep mountains; Pine Forest Mountains), southwestern Nevada (Grapevine Mountains) and eastern California (White and Inyo mountains, Clark Mountain).

MEASUREMENTS: (see table).

Mass: 21.8 g (18.0–26.0) (Arizona) (Dunning 1993).

Reference: Miller (1941).

'Pink-sided Junco' (*Junco hyemalis mearnsi*)

IDENTIFICATION: The 'Pink-sided' Junco is like the Slate-colored Junco, but head and breast gray, with pinkish brown cinnamon flanks, back dull brown.

Similar species: White-winged Junco is gray-backed, has white in wings, more white in tail, and no pink in flanks. Head not so dark as that of 'Oregon' juncos (*J. h. 'oreganus'*), which also tends to have pinkish back, and browner flanks; Pink-sided Junco has contrasting black lores which makes it look pale-gray headed with a black mask, a contrast not so noticeable in female Oregon Juncos. The pink flanks, convex bib pattern, and brown back separate it from slate-colored junco. The chestnut-brown on the back of the Gray-headed Junco (*J. h. caniceps*) is much more distinct.

Adult—See above.

First-winter (Aug–Mar) like adult.

Juveniles (July–Aug) like slate-colored junco, but back browner, or cinnamon-brown.

VOICE: The song is like that of other Dark-eyed Juncos.

HABITS: Like other juncos, on the breeding grounds, males sing from exposed perches, most commonly pines. In fall and winter, they are found in loose flocks, commonly with other kinds of juncos and other species. They sometimes jump into the air to catch insects.

HABITAT: On the breeding grounds, they are most commonly found at the edge of pine woods, but also will nest in other edge situations, in spruce, aspen, or mountain mahogany. In winter, they are often in thickets and shrublands at lower elevations, and are common around feeders.

BREEDING: *Nest* is usually placed on the ground, often under a stone or other object, or at the base of a flower. The nest is a cup of dry grass or stems and pine needles, lined with finer grass or hair. Usually only the female builds the nest. Nesting takes place from June through early Sept, usually June and early July. *Eggs*, 3–4, usually 4, dull white or greenish white, spotted or blotched with reddish brown or lavender. *Incubation*, and fledging not known, but probably like other juncos. Cowbird parasitism not reported.

① Male   ② Female

RANGE: **_Breeds_** from se Alberta and sw Saskatchewan (Cypress Hills), and n-c Montana (w to Madison Co. and e to Big Horn Mountains), e Idaho (Preston), nw Wyoming (Wind R. and Teton mountains), and s to se Idaho.

Winters from Utah, Wyoming, w and c Nebraska s to n Sonora, c Chihuahua, and w Texas, and rarely to California (especially the lower Colorado R. Valley); has been reported e to Nova Scotia (Sable I.).

HISTORY: The Pink-sided Junco was described by Robert Ridgway in 1897 on the basis of material from Fort Bridger, Wyoming, provided by Edgar Alexander Mearns, an army surgeon and ornithologist who was a founding member of the American Ornithologists Union.

GEOGRAPHIC VARIATION: None described; hybridizes with gray-headed junco in northern Utah Summit Co. (Uinta Mountains) southern Wyoming (Rattlesnake and Casper mountains), and southern Idaho (Cassia Co.); rarely hybridizes with white-winged junco in southeastern Wyoming (Powder R. Co.).

MEASUREMENTS: (see table).

Mass: (N=221) 18.2 g (15.5–26.0) (Arizona) (Dunning 1993).

'Oregon Junco' (*Junco hyemalis oreganus* in part) [567.1]

IDENTIFICATION: Adult male Oregon Juncos have a dark gray to black hood, with a convex bib on their breast, dark chestnut back and scapulars, and rusty brown flanks. Females are slightly duller, with grayer hoods, often brown on the nape and hindneck.

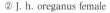

① J. h. mearnsi male   ② J. h. oreganus female   ③ J. h. oreganus male

Similar species: Oregon Juncos can generally be separated from Pink-sided Juncos by their darker hoods and browner flanks, although female Oregon Juncos are confused with Pink-sided Juncos (see that account). Gray-headed Juncos have gray heads with grayish white underparts, redder back, and grayish flanks.

Adult—See above.

First-winter (July–Apr) like adults, but males show less color contrast.

Juveniles (June–Aug) forehead and crown brown, profusely streaked with dark brown; back, rump, and uppertail-coverts rusty, streaked with darker brown; tail dark brown with two lateral rectrices white; wings blackish, with coverts tipped with whitish or buffy white, forming two whitish wing-bars; throat and breast heavily streaked; flanks strongly tinged with buffy; belly white or buffy white.

VOICE: Vocalizations are similar to those of other Dark-eyed Juncos.

HABITS: Like other juncos, males sing persistently from an exposed perch. In winter, they are found in flocks, often with other juncos or birds.

HABITAT: Oregon Juncos generally breed in open coniferous forests, moist redwood canyons, dry pine forests in the California interior, aspens, compact low conifers at timberline, heavy but arid live oak, oak-madroño associations, digger and Coulter pine forests, Monterey cypress, eucalyptus, and along the coast in city parks and gardens. Migrating and wintering juncos may be found in a variety of habitats, including chaparral, fence rows, piñon–juniper woods, sagebrush, brush, urban gardens.

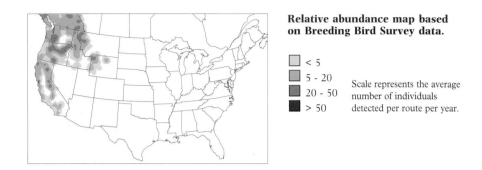

Relative abundance map based on Breeding Bird Survey data.

☐ < 5
▨ 5 - 20   Scale represents the average
▦ 20 - 50   number of individuals
■ > 50   detected per route per year.

BREEDING: *Nest* is usually placed on the ground at the base of a shrub or under an overhanging bank, rock, or root, and is usually near water; occasionally in a small tree, with nests placed in lodgepole pines or Douglas-fir as high as 3 m (20 ft). The nest is a neatly woven cup of grasses or rootlets, lined with finer grasses or hairs. Probably the female alone builds the nest. Egg-laying takes place from late Mar through late July, commencing earlier in the south and at lower elevations than in the north. ***Eggs***, 3–5, usually 4, white, sometimes tinged with green, and spotted or blotched with reddish brown. ***Incubation***, about 13 days; female alone broods, but both parents feed the young; young fledge in 11–14 days. A host for cowbirds.

RANGE: *Breeds* from se Alaska (Yakutat, Haines) s along coast, and from the c interior British Columbia (Takla L., McGregor R.) and extreme w Alberta (Yellowhead Pass, Banff) s through the interior of British Columbia, n and c-w Idaho, nw Montana, Washington, Oregon, extreme w Nevada (Galena Creek), and in mountains through California and n Baja California.

Winters resident or partly resident throughout much of its range, but many populations move to low elevations in winter. Found from s Alaska, s British Columbia, n Idaho, w Montana, Wyoming, and South Dakota s to n Baja California, n Sonora, c Chihuahua and c Texas. Reported regularly, but rarely e of the Great Plains, to Nova Scotia, Massachusetts, West Virginia, and Tennessee. Accidental on St. Lawrence I., Alaska (January).

HISTORY: The Oregon Junco was first described by John Kirk Townsend in 1837. It was one of many new species collected by him and Thomas Nuttall on their Columbia R. expedition near Fort Vancouver, Washington.

GEOGRAPHIC VARIATION: Five subspecies of 'Oregon' Juncos from north of Mexico are delimited, the Oregon junco (*J. h. oreganus*), which breeds in southeast Alaska south to central coastal British Columbia, the Montana junco (*J. h. montanus*), which breeds in the interior of British Columbia, Washington, western Idaho and Montana, and Oregon, Shufeldt's junco (*J. h. shufeldti*), which breeds from south-

western British Columbia, south along the coast to central California, Thurber's
junco (*J. h. thurberi*), which breeds from the southern interior Oregon, south to
northern Baja California, and Point Pinos junco (*J. h. pinosus*), which is resident in
the coastal hills of central California, from Golden Gate south to southern San
Benito and Monterey cos. Variation in size and color among these Oregon Juncos is
clinal: *oreganus* generally have more reddish backs than *montanus*, which are quite
variable in back color; *shufeldti* resemble *montanus* in color, but average brighter in
color and smaller; *thurberi* has a lighter, more pinkish red back than *shufeldti*; and
pinosus has a ruddier back and sides than *thurberi*. Individual birds probably cannot
be safely assigned to subspecies. Oregon Juncos hybridize with Slate-colored Junco
in south-central Yukon (Carcross) and northwestern British Columbia (Bennett City,
Atlin, Telegraph Creek), eastern British Columbia and western Alberta (Jasper Park,
Yellowhead and Moose passes), and with Gray-headed Junco in southern Nevada
(Grapevine Mountains) and se California (White and Inyo mountains, Clark
Mountain).

MEASUREMENTS: (see table). Weight [no data available].

Measurements of adult juncos from breeding grounds (data from Miller 1941)

Population	sex	wing [a]	tail [b]	bill length [c]	bill depth [d]	tarsus [e]	toe length [f]
Slate-colored (northern)	m	78 (104)[g]	69 (104)	8.0 (92)	6.0 (89)	20.6 (116)	8.3 (113)
	f	74 (50)	66 (48)	8.0 (53)	5.9 (41)	20.3 (57)	8.2 (57)
Slate-colored (Appalachian)	m	80 (79)	72 (79)	8.4 (76)	6.2 (76)	21.1 (93)	8.6 (93)
	f	76 (42)	69 (40)	8.3 (38)	6.2 (31)	20.9 (37)	8.5 (47)
Slate-colored (Atlin, Stikine BC)	m	79 (46)	70 (44)	8.1 (34)	5.9 (36)	20.4 (51)	8.2 (51)
	f	74 (40)	65 (38)	8.1 (32)	5.9 (30)	20.3 (40)	8.1 (40)
White-winged	m	88 (50)	80 (50)	8.9 (50)	7.2 (49)	21.1 (50)	8.4 (47)
	f	83 (38)	77 (35)	8.8 (35)	7.2 (35)	20.8 (36)	8.1 (36)
Pink-sided	m	81 (74)	73 (73)	8.2 (64)	6.2 (54)	20.1 (74)	8.0 (66)
	f	77 (46)	70 (45)	8.0 (43)	6.1 (38)	19.8 (44)	8.0 (44)
Oregon (interior BC, WA, OR)	m	79 (141)	70 (141)	8.3 (125)	6.0 (125)	19.9 (150)	8.0 (150)
	f	74 (51)	66 (51)	8.0 (55)	5.9 (52)	20.0 (58)	7.9 (60)
Oregon (coastal BC, WA, OR)	m	76 (64)	67 (56)	8.2 (63)	5.9 (57)	19.8 (67)	8.0 (67)
	f	72 (24)	63 (24)	8.0 (23)	5.8 (22)	19.6 (24)	8.0 (25)
Oregon (coastal AK, BC)	m	75 (74)	66 (74)	8.2 (71)	5.8 (64)	20.7 (75)	8.4 (75)
	f	71 (38)	63 (35)	8.2 (33)	5.8 (33)	20.4 (38)	8.2 (39)
Oregon (s OR, CA)	m	77 (86)	69 (86)	8.0 (84)	5.6 (81)	19.6 (95)	8.1 (95)
	f	73 (48)	65 (42)	7.8 (42)	5.6 (43)	19.4 (49)	8.0 (49)

Measurements of adult juncos from breeding grounds (data from Miller 1941) (*continued*)

Population	sex	wing[a]	tail[b]	bill length[c]	bill depth[d]	tarsus[e]	toe length[f]
Oregon	m	72 (62)	64 (62)	8.1 (58)	5.7 (58)	19.8 (67)	8.0 (67)
(c coastal CA)	f	69 (40)	61 (41)	8.1 (36)	5.8 (32)	19.6 (41)	7.8 (39)
Gray-headed	m	82 (95)	77 (87)	8.9 (101)	6.8 (98)	20.9 (103)	8.5 (87)
(southern)	f	78 (47)	.73 (43)	8.8 (48)	6.7 (46)	20.7 (50)	8.3 (51)
Gray-headed	m	82 (159)	74 (145)	8.4 (154)	6.3 (137)	20.3 (157)	–
(northern)	f	77 (81)	70 (72)	8.2 (82)	6.3 (82)	20.0 (81)	–
Yellow-eyed	m	79 (113)	75 (111)	8.4 (105)	6.3 (89)	20.9 (117)	8.6 (114)
	f	75 (78)	72 (71)	8.5 (59)	6.5 (52)	21.0 (77)	8.4 (78)

[a]cord (mm); [b]longest feather from base; [c]nostril to tip; [d]at base; [e]to last undivided scute; [f]without claw; [g]mean (sample size)

49 **Yellow-eyed Junco** *Junco phaenotus* [570]   PLATE 21

IDENTIFICATION: 14–16 cm (*c.* 5.5–6.5 in), males slightly larger; sexes similar in coloration.

Yellow-eyed Juncos have a gray head, with black lores and around eye, yellow iris, black upper mandible, yellowish lower mandible, rusty red back, rusty outer webs of greater coverts and tertials, a light gray throat, flanks, and rump, and a gray tail with white outer feathers.

Similar species: Southern gray-headed juncos have similar bill color, but have a dark iris, and no rusty in coverts or tertials; Yellow-eyed Juncos are paler on the rump, throat and belly.

Adult—*Head* and nape gray; black in lores and around the eye; ***back:*** mantle rusty red; ***rump:*** pale; ***tail:*** rectrices gray, with lateral two (rarely three) white; ***wing:*** gray, greater coverts and tertials edged with cinnamon-rufous; ***underparts:*** chin, throat, breast, flanks, and belly pale gray to white; ***bill:*** upper mandible blackish, lower mandible yellow; ***legs:*** yellowish, toes darker; ***iris:*** bright yellow.

First-winter (Sept–Dec) like adults, but paler in color, throat almost white, with iris olive-gray to grayish yellow.

Juveniles (June–Oct) forehead, crown, and nape gray, streaked with black; lores and area around eye black, ear-coverts gray; back rusty red, streaked with black; scapulars

Sexes similar – spine variations shown

gray, streaked with black; rump and uppertail-coverts gray, and faintly streaked; rectrices black, with extensive white in outer two; wings dark, with tertials and greater coverts edged with chestnut; no wing-bars; breast and flanks grayish, streaked with black, belly and undertail-coverts dull white.

VOICE: The song characteristically consists of three parts of contrasting rhythm and pitch *chip chip chip wheedle wheedle kee kee kee kee kee*. It has also been described as being Chipping Sparrow like, but lower pitched. The notes are a sharp *chip* or a softer *tsspt*, softer and less blunt than those of Dark-eyed Juncos.

HABITS: Territorial males sing from an exposed perch, as high as 20 m, often from a pine tree. They feed on the ground, often scratching for food among pine needles; they 'shuffle' rather than hop. Although resident, they may move to lower elevations in winter. However, they do not tend to flock with other juncos or sparrows, but are found in family-sized groups.

HABITAT: Yellow-eyed Juncos are found in montane conifer and pine-oak forests, from 1850 to 2500 m, usually above 2000 m. They generally feed in understory, in brush or thickets, scratching in litter for insects and seeds; they are common around picnic sites.

BREEDING: *Nest* is a cup of woven coarse grasses lined with fine grass and hair, often deer hair. They are usually placed on the ground, commonly under a piece of bark, stone, or in a tuft of grass; occasionally nests are placed in trees, as high as 5 m. Nesting takes place from mid- to late Apr through May; the female alone builds the nest. *Eggs*, 3–5, usually 3–4, are grayish white or pale bluish white, spotted or splotched with buffy brown. *Incubation*, 15? days; females alone incubate; both parents feed the young. Parasitism by cowbirds not recorded.

RANGE: *Resident* from sw New Mexico (Big Hatchet, Animas and Peloncillo mountains) and se Arizona (Santa Rita, Santa Catalina, Pinal and Graham mountains) s to Chihuahua, n-c Coahuila, Nuevo León, sw Tamaulipas, Oaxaca, w Veracruz, Chiapas,

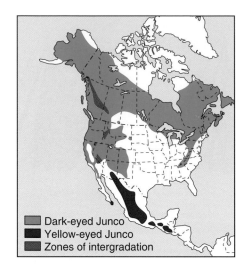

Dark-eyed Junco
Yellow-eyed Junco
Zones of intergradation

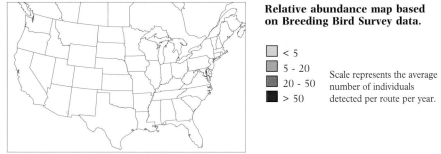

Relative abundance map based on Breeding Bird Survey data.

< 5
5 - 20
20 - 50
> 50

Scale represents the average number of individuals detected per route per year.

and w Guatemala; also Cape district of Baja California. Has been recorded out of breeding range in Arizona (Whetstone Mountains) and may wander somewhat.

HISTORY: The Yellow-eyed Junco was first described on the basis of material from Mexico, and named in 1831 by Johan Georg Wagler, a Professor and Director of the Zoological Museum of Munich. Wagler's promising career was cut short when, at the age of 32, he was killed by a stray shot while hunting.

GEOGRAPHIC VARIATION: None reported north of Mexico. *J. p. palliatus* breeds in U.S. and northern Mexico; *J. p. phaenotus* breeds in the s Mexican highlands, and averages darker gray and buff. Baird's Junco (*J. p. bairdi*), of s Baja California, Chiapas Junco (*J. p. fulvescens*) and Guatemala Junco (*J. p. alticola*) are sometimes considered separate species.

MEASUREMENTS: (see table).

Reference: Miller (1941).

Genus *Calcarius*

All four species in the genus *Calcarius* breed in North America, and one, the Lapland Longspur, is circumpolar in its distribution. Longspurs are medium-sized terrestrial sparrows with long, pointed wings, relatively small bills, and a long and slender hind claw (the 'longspur'), and are strongly sexually dimorphic in plumage color. They all commonly give larking flight-songs, and are gregarious in migration and winter. McCown's Longspur differs from the others by having a larger and relatively thicker bill, a relatively shorter tail, and a somewhat shorter spur. Consequently it has been put in a monotypic genus *Rhynchophanes* by some workers. However, because it has hybridized with Chestnut-collared Longspurs, and otherwise is quite longspur-like, today most ornithologists include it in *Calcarius*. Longspurs are all strong flyers, and consequently frequently wander from their usual ranges in migration.

The relationships of the longspurs to other sparrows are not clear. Because of the males' bright display plumage, and the pronounced sexual dimorphism, they superficially resemble many of the Eurasian buntings (*Emberiza*), and probably partly for this reason are placed close to them in lists. Some molecular data suggest that they are neither particularly close to *Emberiza* nor other American emberizids.

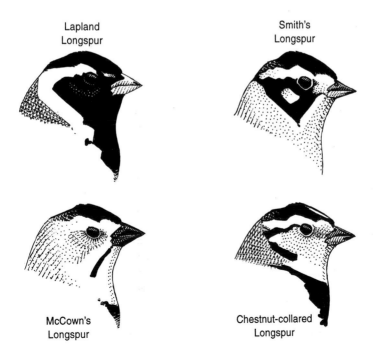

Lapland Longspur

Smith's Longspur

McCown's Longspur

Chestnut-collared Longspur

50 **McCown's Longspur**

Calcarius mccownii [539]

IDENTIFICATION: 13–15 cm (*c.* 5–6 in), males slightly larger; sexes differ in coloration.

The facial pattern of breeding male McCown's longspurs is striking: they have a black cap, malar stripe, and breast band, and whitish side of face and throat and a large pinkish bill. Their median coverts are rusty, giving them a rusty shoulder, and they flash a lot of white in their tail when flushed. Females are similarly patterned, but have little or no black markings, and are grayish rather than white on the face and throat. In winter their feathers are tipped with buff (although there is a limited prealternate molt, they essentially wear into their breeding plumage). McCown's Longspur's tail pattern is distinctive: the outermost rectrix is nearly pure white, the middle two brown, and the others tipped with brown, making an inverted 'T' pattern in flight.

Similar species: Although in breeding plumage, the longspurs are relatively easy to separate, identification can be more difficult in winter. Juvenile McCown's Longspurs have a lightly streaked breast, but in winter they are the only longspur with an unstreaked breast. Although ventral streaking is faint on some other wintering longspurs, Lapland Longspurs always show streaking on their flanks. McCown's Longspur usually shows some chestnut on the lesser and median coverts, and appears to be pale, relative to others. The mantle streaking is not so distinct as that on other longspurs. When flushed, McCown's Longspur shows a lot of white in the tail, separating it from either Smith's or Lapland longspurs; if well seen, the tail pattern can also be used to separate it from Chestnut-collared Longspur. McCown's Longspur has a pinkish bill with a dark tip, but other longspurs may be similarly

Adult male

colored. Relative to other longspurs, especially the Chestnut-collared Longspur, McCown's Longspur appears to be large-billed and chunky, long-winged and short-tailed. In contrast, Chestnut-collared Longspur is small and delicate looking, and seems to have relatively short wings, as well as faint streaking on the breast; males usually show chestnut in their collar and black on the breast and belly (male Lapland Longspurs may also show chestnut in their collar and black on their breast). Smith's Longspurs are a warm rusty buff overall, especially on their underparts; other longspurs arc usually white-bellied. Vesper Sparrows also show white in their tail and have rusty lesser coverts, but are streaked below, have a thin white eye-ring, and do not act like longspurs.

Summer male (May–Aug)—*Head:* forehead and anterior part of crown black (depending on wear, feathers may be buff-tipped); supercilium, supraocular spot, and lores white; ear-coverts white under and behind eye, gray toward neck; malar stripe black, throat white; *back:* nape gray, with brownish streaks; mantle, scapulars, and tertials brown, with pale edges; *rump* and uppertail-coverts grayish, with darker centers; uppertail-coverts long, extending half way down tail; *tail:* middle two rectrices brown; outermost rectrices white; others brown-tipped, with brown variably extending up the outer web somewhat more on the innermost white rectrices; *wing:* grayish brown, anterior lesser coverts gray, posterior lesser coverts and median coverts chestnut; greater coverts and secondaries broadly, but not distinctly edged with white; inner webs of wing feathers whitish, making underside of the wing appear white; *underparts:* chin and throat white; breast with a crescent-shaped broad black band; belly and flanks grayish white; undertail-coverts white; *bill:* black; *legs* and *feet:* grayish brown; *iris:* brown or black.

Adult male in winter (Sept–Apr) like summer male, but black areas on head concealed by brown tips, and on breast by buffy tips.

Adult female (May–Aug)—*Head:* crown grayish brown, with indistinct brown streaks; supercilium whitish buff; ear-coverts whitish buff becoming brown toward

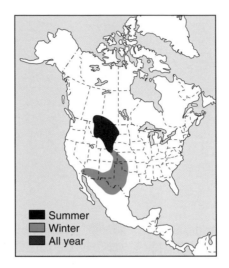

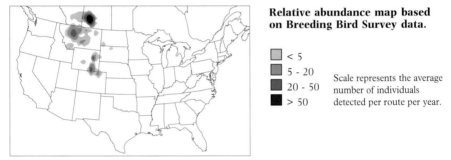

Relative abundance map based on Breeding Bird Survey data.

- < 5
- 5 - 20
- 20 - 50
- > 50

Scale represents the average number of individuals detected per route per year.

neck; malar and eyeline stripes grayish brown; **back:** brown with dark brown centers to mantle feathers giving back a streaked appearance; **rump** and uppertail-coverts brown; **tail:** pattern same as adult male; **underparts:** throat buffy pale gray, breast band grayish white, belly pale; **wing:** brown with varying amounts of cinnamon in lesser and median coverts (apparently varies with age), inner webs of wing feathers whitish; **bill:** pinkish or light brown, with dark tip; **legs** and **feet:** brownish; **iris:** black.

Female in winter (Sept–Apr) like summer female, but feathers edged with buffy, and streaks on back less distinct.

First-winter (after Aug) resemble adults, but are less brightly colored and buffier; females in their first year have little chestnut in the wing.

Juveniles (May–Aug) resemble females in winter, but are distinctly streaked on the breast and flanks.

VOICE: Territorial males sing a distinctive, warbling, musical song, *see see see mee see me hear me hear me see.* The song is frequently sung during an elaborate, stiff-winged aerial display flight, but may be sung from a fence, rock, or the ground; females have been reported to sing. During flight, they give a dry rattle, *chip-pur-r-r-r.* Call notes are a two-noted *prit-tup*, or a single *whit.*

HABITAT: McCown's Longspurs are birds of the sparse, dry high plains, typically in places where heavily grazed shortgrass (buffalo grass) is interspersed with cactus (prickly pear) and scattered shrubs. Unlike Chestnut-sided Longspurs, they frequently forage in fallow fields. In winter, they are found in shortgrass pastures or bare dirt fields.

HABITS: The aerial display flight of the male is striking. With slow, stiff wing-beats, the male rises to 20 m high, singing, and gliding back down to the ground. The display is much like that of the Lark Bunting (or Yellow-breasted Chat or mockingbird, for that matter). During courtship on the ground, either sex will raise one or both wings, displaying the white wing linings. Territorial males chase intruders from their territory, and occasionally chase females. In winter, they tend to be found in flocks, often with other longspurs (especially Chestnut-collared), and even more often with Horned Larks. When on the ground, they may crouch down into a depression where they are difficult to see, and the flock flushes explosively when approached. In spite of their preferred open, shortgrass habitat, they can be difficult to see.

BREEDING: *Nest* is placed in a depression in the ground, often beside a clump of grass or brush (rabbit brush, horsebrush, Coronilla). The nest is a cup of dried grasses and weed stems, lined with finer grasses and sometimes hair. Nesting begins late Apr (Colorado) and early May, and continues through July. The species is often double-brooded. *Eggs*, 2–6, usually 3–4, are white to grayish white, boldly spotted with dark brown; the female alone builds the nest. *Incubation*, 12 days; female alone incubates, although the male may shelter the young after they are one day old; the young fledge after about 10 days; both parents feed the young. The species is occasionally parasitized by cowbirds. McCown's Longspur is apparently monogamous.

RANGE: *Breeds* from s Alberta (north to Hanna, Youngstown and west to Lethbridge, Vulcan), sw and s-c Saskatchewan (north to Rosetown, Davidson, Regina), south through w North Dakota, w and n-c South Dakota, Montana, and extreme se Idaho (probable), to w Nebraska (Sioux Co.), and n-c Colorado (Washington, Weld, Larimer cos.). Formerly bred to ne North Dakota, sw Minnesota, and south to the Oklahoma Panhandle.

Winters from se California (Imperial Valley and s Mojave Desert [Lancaster]; rare), c and especially se Arizona, s and e New Mexico, e Colorado (very rare), and w Kansas (sporadic), south through c Oklahoma, s-c Texas to ne Sonora, Chihuahua, w Coahuila, and n Durango. Most common in winter in sw Texas and Nevada.

In *migration* the species is rare throughout California, but commonest along the s coast. Casual to rare in s Oregon (Harney and Klamath cos.), s British Columbia (Chilliwack, Newgate), n-c Alberta (Lesser Slave Lake), n Saskatchewan (Hanson Lake Road), e Kansas, Missouri (winter; one specimen), Illinois, Indiana, Massachusetts (January; banded), e Texas, and Louisiana (New Orleans, Jefferson Davis Parish).

HISTORY: After graduating from West Point in 1840, Captain John Porter McCown was ordered to assist in the transportation of Indians to the Indian Territory. Later he served in the Mexican War under General Winfield Scott. In late spring 1851, while near San Antonio, Texas, McCown collected the first two specimens of McCown's Longspurs, which were in a flock of Horned Larks, and sent them to George Lawrence, who named them in his honor. When the Civil War broke out, McCown, a native of Tennessee, resigned his commission and joined the Confederate Army. After the war, he retired to Arkansas.

It seems clear that not only has this species declined in abundance greatly since 1900, but also that its range has become smaller. At the turn of the century, McCown's Longspur bred south to western Oklahoma and east to northeastern North Dakota and southwestern Minnesota. The reasons for this are not clear. Certainly the habitat of the Great Plains has been significantly modified, but McCown's Longspurs seem to do best in arid, overgrazed pastures — of which there is today an abundance. Historically, however, fires were a part of the prairie ecology, and these are more strictly controlled today than in the past. This, as well as widespread use of herbicides, pesticides, and fertilizers may have been deleterious to them.

GEOGRAPHIC VARIATION: None described. There is a record of a hybrid Chestnut-collared × McCown's Longspur.

MEASUREMENTS: (6 males): wing 89–94 (91), tail 49–56 (53), tarsus 19.1–20.8 (19.6), exposed culmen 11.2–13.2 (11.9), bill depth at base (2 specimens; 8.1); (7 females): wing 80–87 (84), tail 46–50 (48), tarsus 18.0–19.8 (19.1), exposed culmen 10.7–11.9 (11.2), bill depth 7.6–8.4 (8.1) (Ridgway 1901).

Mass: (21 breeding males) 25.4 g, (14 breeding females) 25.0 g (n-c Colorado). (87 males) 26.7 g, (48 females) 24.7 g (With 1994).

Reference: With (1994).

Winter Longspurs at a glance

Characteristic	McCown's	Lapland	Smith's	Chestnut-collared
Bill	Stout; pink with dark tip	Dark or pinkish with dusky tip	Horn with dusky tip	Pinkish with dusty tip
Facial pattern	Indistinct, with pale supercilium	Ear-coverts distinctly outlined; malar stripe dark	Ear-coverts distinctly outlined, showing pale interior spot	Indistinct: malar may be brownish
Nape	Pale brown or grayish; indistinctly streaked	Dark brown; may show rust	Buffy tan; thin streaks	Pale brown; may show rust
Breast, flanks, and belly	Pale; unstreaked; may show black; white belly	Whitish; streaked; white belly	Buffy; lightly streaked; buffy belly	Pale buff; lightly streaked or blackish flecked; pale buff belly
Primary projection beyond tertials	Long (short tailed)	Long	Long	Short
Coverts	Medians rusty in males; light buff in females	Brown greaters edged with rusty	Lessers and medians white edged or white	Brown; may show white lessers
Tail	White extensive	White limited to outer 2 feathers	White limited to outer 2 feathers	White extensive

51 **Lapland Longspur** *Calcarius lapponicus* [536] PLATES **23 & 24**

D.BEADLE 94.

IDENTIFICATION: 13.5–17 cm (*c.* 5.5–7 in), males slightly larger; sexes differ in coloration.

Longspurs are large, strong-flying sparrows. Breeding male Lapland Longspurs have a black face, outlined with a buffy white or white supercilium and post-auricular stripe that runs to the upper breast, a bright rusty back of crown and nape, and a bright yellow bill with a black tip. Females have a pale buffy supercilium and ear-coverts, which are outlined by blackish eyeline and moustachial stripes; the pale side of neck is highlighted by a narrow rusty collar. There is a crescent-shaped black bib surrounding the white throat.

Similar species: Breeding males are distinctive. Females are darker and more brightly marked than Smith's Longspurs, which are buffy overall, and lack the black-ish crown, malar, eyeline, and breast markings of female Lapland Longspurs. For wintering longspurs see McCown's Longspur. Laplands, like McCown's and Smith's, are long-winged, but more distinctly streaked on the breast and flanks, and have a white (not buffy) belly. Laplands are generally more brightly colored than Smith's or McCown's, sometimes with rusty in their coverts and tertials.

Summer male (May–Aug)—**Head:** crown black, flecked with varying amounts of buff or pale buff; side of face and throat black; supraloral spot may have some flecks of buff; eye-stripe wide and bright pale buffy or white, connecting with a bright buffy post-auricular stripe that runs to the upper breast; **back:** nape and side of neck rusty or rufous, variously flecked with buff (depending on wear); mantle brown with blackish centers, and variously edged with pale buff, giving back a streaked appear-ance; **rump** and uppertail-coverts blackish brown to brown with broad pale buffy edges; **tail:** outer two rectrices blackish, with white on the outer webs, and at the tip

Adult male

of the inner webs; other rectrices blackish; ***wing:*** brown, with indistinct pale edges to feathers; coverts and scapulars with buffy brown edges; ***underparts:*** chin, throat and breast black, with varying amounts of white on the sides of the breast; flanks white, with black streaking; lower breast and belly white; undertail-coverts white; ***bill:*** bright yellow, with black tip; ***legs*** and ***feet:*** black; ***iris:*** black.

Adult male in winter (Sept–Apr) the black on the head is confined to the crown, the posterior and lower borders of the ear-coverts, and a patch on the chest, and is obscured by the pale brownish tips to the feathers; although there is a limited pre-alternate molt, the birds essentially wear into summer plumage, so become progressively more brightly colored toward the end of the winter. The throat is whitish, the rusty collar is somewhat obscured by buffy feather tips, and the bill dull orange.

Adult female (May–Aug) resembles adult male, but has brownish ear-coverts, bordered with black, a white throat and less rust in the collar.

Female in winter (Sept–Apr) resembles male in winter, but may be somewhat duller, and the neck often without a trace of rust.

Juveniles (June–July) crown, back, and rump dark brown, with broad pale or rusty edges to feathers; throat and breast streaked with brown; belly pale buff; greater coverts and tertial broadly edged with rufous buff; tail pattern as in adults.

VOICE: The song of the Lapland Longspur is a variable, almost squeaky, melodious ***churtle churtle seerilee-seerilee-serrilee seetle-we-we-you***, first rising slightly, then descending slightly. The song is often given during a flight display during which the male will rise 3–15 m and glide back to earth with his wings held above his back. The sharp rattle, ***pit-tic***, or ***pit-tic-tic***, is frequently given in flight; this rattle is similar to that of Smith's Longspur, but unlike Smith's rattle, Laplands intersperse rattles with ***teu*** notes. Other notes are a sharp ***pzeet***, or ***pit-zweet***, or ***pist-czur-a***,

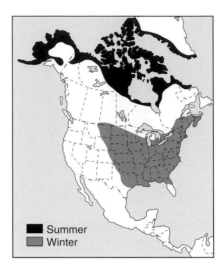

and a plaintive, musical *teu*, or **beew**, also often given in flight, or intermixed with the song.

HABITAT: The Lapland Longspur is generally the commonest bird of the high Arctic where it can be found in a variety of tundra habitats, avoiding only the wettest tundra, and dry, well-drained areas. Where Lapland Longspurs co-occur with Smith's Longspur, the two species may overlap, but Smith's seem to prefer wetter areas. Lapland Longspurs are most common in fairly wet tundra, rather thickly vegetated upland areas, and in the sedge ('grassy') margins of streams, around tundra ponds, and hummocks of sedges in marshes. In migration and winter, they can be found in fallow fields, short pastures, and along beaches.

HABITS: Males arrive on the breeding grounds shortly before females and, weather permitting, start to defend and advertise a territory. They commonly give a flight-song, and chase intruders from their territory, but also will sing from a rock or the top of a sedge tussock, or even a telephone wire. During courtship, the pair engages in reciprocal chasing. When flushed from the nest, the female may give a distraction display, alarm notes, or both, but usually does not fly far from the nest. In migration and winter, the species characteristically forms large flocks, sometimes of apparently over a million individuals. Especially in the east, where they are not particularly common, Lapland Longspurs are often found with pipits, Horned Larks, and Snow Buntings, although the longspurs generally stay together in these mixed flocks. In the mid-west, it has been my experience that they usually are found in flocks of only Lapland Longspurs; in the high plains and southwest, they may be found with other longspurs, and in the west often with Horned Larks. When flushed, smaller flocks will fly around a field, and drop back into the short vegetation, often not far from where they took off. If one moves slowly, one can often approach the flock closely, and sometimes walk into it. The longspurs are, nonetheless, surprisingly difficult to see well when on the ground.

BREEDING: *Nest* is placed in a depression in the ground, often beside a small hummock of sedge or moss. The nest is a cup of rather coarse sedge, lined with finer sedges, grasses, feathers (commonly ptarmigan), or hair (often caribou). Nesting begins in late May and continues through early July. *Eggs,* 1–6, usually 5, are pale greenish white, heavily splotched and spotted with brown, often with black scrawls. The female alone builds the nest. *Incubation,* 10–14 days; female alone incubates; young fledge after 8–10 days (earlier if disturbed); both parents feed the young. The species is rarely polygynous.

RANGE: *Breeds* from w and n Alaska (including islands in Bering Sea, Alaska Peninsula, and Aleutians), n Yukon, Banks, Prince Patrick (Mould Bay), Melville (Winter Harbor), Bathurst and c Ellesmere (Lake Hazen) Island south to c Alaska (Mt. McKinley, Talkeetna Mountains, Middleton I.), n Yukon (south to Ogilvie Mountains), n Mackenzie, s Keewatin (Nueltin L.), n Manitoba (Churchill), n Ontario (Winisk, Cape Henrietta Maria), James Bay (Twin Is.), n Quebec (south to Fort George, Cape Jones, Kuujjuaq) and Labrador (south along coast to Cape Harrison). Also found in northern Eurasia (where they are called Lapland Buntings).

Winters from coastal Alaska (rare), s British Columbia (Okanagan Valley, very rare), se Alberta (Milk R.), s Saskatchewan, c and s Minnesota, c Wisconsin, c Michigan, s Ontario (north to Kingston), s Quebec (north to Lac Saint-Jean), New Brunswick, Prince Edward I., and Nova Scotia, irregularly south through c Montana, c Wyoming, and e Colorado, to e and c Texas (irregularly common in Panhandle and in northeast, uncommon south to Austin, San Antonio, Houston), Louisiana (irregularly abundant to common in north and southwest; rare elsewhere), Alabama (abundant to common in Tennessee Valley, Black Belt), and to n Florida (Panhandle, ne coast; rare). Uncommon to rare in the east.

Irregular in winter in northern part of range; regular, but uncommon, in west, south to s California; very rare on the coast of Alaska in winter. Commonest in winter in the central plains, where winter wheat is grown, and irregularly in Arkansas, and northern Louisiana and Alabama. Casual in Mexico.

Regular in Oregon and California in migration, especially in fall.

HISTORY: The great Swedish naturalist, Carolus Linnaeus, named the Lapland Longspur *Fringilla lapponica* in the 10th edition of his *Systema Naturae,* in 1758. As a young man, Linnaeus had done field work in Lapland, where he certainly became familiar with this longspur. Linnaean genera are much more inclusive than those used by contemporary ornithologists (he recognized a total of only 512 genera of animals in 1758), and he put many birds with finch-like bills in the genus *Fringilla,* today used only for the chaffinches and some of their closest relatives. *Emberiza*, another Linnaean genus, would have been more appropriate for the Lapland Longspur.

Audubon first encountered this species in Kentucky, in February 1819. He wrote, 'I saw immense flocks scattered over the open grounds on the elevated grassy banks of the Ohio. Having my gun with me, as usual, I procured more than sixty in a few minutes. . . . Although in rather poor condition, we found them excellent eating.' His description of their behavior shows him to have been a keen observer of longspurs: 'In their movements they resemble the Snow Bunting. They run and hop [I have not seen them hop. — JR] on the ground with ease and celerity, many making toward a tuft of withered grass the same time, to search for the few seeds that may yet be procured around or beneath it, and all the while uttering a repetition of *chirps*, in a rather low and plaintive accent. When on the wing . . . they formed into compact bodies, wheeled and cut to and fro through the air, now high, now low, in the manner of Larks, alighting suddenly, and perhaps immediately flying off again to renew their curious evolutions. At times flocks composed of hundreds would settle on the top-rails of fences, or on the lower large branches of trees in the fields; but on such occasions they appeared as much discontented as the Snow Buntings are, when they also alight on trees, fences, or houses.'

In migration and winter, the abundance of Lapland Longspurs shows much year-to-year variation at most localities, doubtless reflecting variation in the severity of the weather, and the availability of food. This makes it difficult to assess long-term changes in their numbers. Their breeding habitat, however, has been little altered by human activity, and in spite of the fact that unseasonably severe weather often results in the death of thousands of these birds, their numbers probably are not declining.

GEOGRAPHIC VARIATION: Three North American subspecies generally are recognized. *C. l. lapponicus* breeds in the eastern Canadian Arctic and northern Eurasia. *C. l. alascensis* breeds in the western Canadian Arctic and Alaska, including the islands in the Bering Sea. Although there appears to be some clinal variation in color, with western Arctic birds being paler than eastern ones, these subspecies are poorly marked, and cannot be differentiated in the field. *C. l. coloratus* of the Commander (Komandorskiye) Is., Kamchatka, and northwestern Siberia, breeds, or has bred, occasionally on Attu I., in the Aleutian Is., Alaska, but is less common than *C. l. alascensis* there. *C. l. coloratus* is darker than *lapponicus* with a dark back and wing-coverts, and the black on the upper breast extends to flanks.

MEASUREMENTS: *C. l. lapponicus* (16 males): wing 90–101 (96), tail 60–67 (63), tarsus 20.6–22.6 (21.8), exposed culmen 10.4–12.2 (11.4), bill depth at base 6.1–7.1 (6.9); (9 females): wing 88–92 (90), tail 58–65 (61), tarsus 20.6–22.4 (21.1), exposed culmen 10.4–11.4 (10.7), bill depth 6.1–7.4 (6.6).

C. l. alascensis (22 males): 91–100 (96), tail 58–68 (63), tarsus 20.6–22.6 (21.8), exposed culmen 10.4–12.5 (11.7), bill depth 6.6–7.4 (6.9); (24 females): wing 86–93 (89), tail 56–63 (58), tarsus 20.3–22.3 (21.3), exposed culmen 10.2–11.9 (10.9), bill depth 5.8–7.1 (6.6) (Ridgway 1901).

Mass: (N=68) 27.3 g (23.5–32.5) (Alaska) (Dunning 1993).

52 **Smith's Longspur** *Calcarius pictus* [537]   PLATES **23 & 24**

IDENTIFICATION: 14–17 cm (*c.* 5.5–7 in), males slightly larger; sexes differ in coloration.

Smith's Longspurs are medium-sized sparrows, with a rich buffy tan nape, chin, breast, and belly. In summer males have a black crown and a broad, white supercilium and white ear-coverts, boldly outlined in black; females are similarly patterned, but are brown where the males are black, buffy tan where the males are white, and have thin, brown streaks on their breast; both sexes have nearly all white outer two tail feathers. All wintering birds resemble breeding females.

Similar species: At all times of the year, Smith's Longspur can be distinguished from the other longspurs by the nearly uniform buffy tan plumage. McCown's and Chestnut-sided longspurs show much more white in the tail; Lapland somewhat less. The flight rattle of Smith's Longspur is not intermixed with the single plaintive **beew** notes, as in Lapland Longspurs.

Summer male (May–Aug)—**Head:** forehead and crown dark brown or black (depending on extent of wear), often flecked with white toward the back of the crown; supercilium, lores, and supraloral spot white; ear-coverts white, boldly outlined by a wide, black post-ocular and moustachial stripes, and boldly edged with black toward neck; malar stripe white; **back:** nape bright buffy, back and **rump** black, with feathers edged with bright buff, making back appear streaked; **tail:** blackish brown, with lateral two rectrices mostly white; **wing:** brown, anterior lesser coverts black, posterior lesser coverts white, median and greater coverts narrowly edged with whitish, forming one or two indistinct wing-bars; **underparts:** uniformly warm ochraceous buff; **bill:** dusky, with darker tip and brownish yellow base; **legs** and **feet:** pale to dark brown; **iris:** brown.

Adult male

Adult male in winter (Sept–Apr) the black on the head is replaced by streaked brown, and the throat and breast are thinly streaked; otherwise like summer males, but the median and greater coverts are more distinctly tipped white. The summer plumage is obtained through wear and a rather extensive pre-alternate molt, more extensive than in other longspurs.

Summer female (May–Aug)—***Head:*** patterned as summer male, but crown dark brown, flecked with buff; supercilium, lores, and ear-coverts light buffy brown, boldly edged with dark brown; ***back*** and ***rump:*** dark brown, with broad buffy edges to feathers; ***tail:*** dark brown, with lateral two rectrices mostly white; ***wing:*** brown with posterior lesser coverts white, and edges of median and greater coverts tipped in pale buff; ***underparts:*** uniformly ochraceous buff, with breast thinly streaked with brown; ***bill:*** dusky, with darker tip and brownish yellow base; ***legs*** and ***feet:*** brown; ***iris:*** brown.

Female in winter (Sept–Apr) like winter male, but paler, and without black and pure white on lesser coverts.

Juveniles (July–Sept) similar to adults in winter, but perhaps somewhat more heavily streaked on throat and breast; young apparently complete their postjuvenal molt south of the breeding grounds.

VOICE: The male's song is somewhat like that of a Chestnut-sided or Yellow warbler, ***ta ta tee twe twe twee-werr-tee we chew.*** The first notes are weak, and the song increases in strength to the emphatic ***we chew*** at the end. The call is a staccato rattle-call, ***tic-tic-tic-tic***, that is like the similar call of the Lapland Longspur; this may be given on the ground, and is commonly given in flight, both on the breeding grounds and in migration and winter. They also give a sneezy ***syn*** call.

HABITAT: In summer, Smith's Longspurs breed in a band of subarctic moist tundra at the edge of the tree-line, where they are characteristically found in sedges,

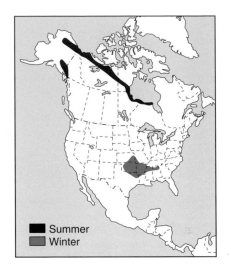

interspersed with clumps of heaths, tamaracks, and scattered dwarf spruce. In migration and winter they can be found in fallow fields, but are more commonly found in shortgrass prairie (often where three-awn grass (*Aristida*) is common), golf courses, and airports.

HABITS: Smith's Longspurs arrive on their breeding grounds later than Laplands. Males start to sing almost immediately upon arrival. When the females are laying, males frequently chase each other, often giving the rattle call. No territories or pair bonds in the usual sense are formed, as females will copulate with 1–3 males for each clutch, and similarly each male with 1–3 females.

In migration and winter, they form fairly tight flocks. Such flocks are often rather large, consisting of around 200 individuals, and usually confined to Smith's Longspurs, although occasionally including a few other longspurs or Snow Buntings. Smith's Longspurs run, rather than hop, and often will run a short distance before taking flight.

BREEDING: *Nest* is placed in a depression in the ground beside relatively dry hummocks, rhododendrons, or birches, or among sedges. The nest is a cup of woven sedges and grasses, lined with hair, lichens, or feathers (often ptarmigan feathers). Nesting begins in early June at Churchill, Manitoba, and may continue through early July. The female alone builds the nest. *Eggs*, 4–6, usually 4, are pale brownish or greenish, marked with dark purple-brown lines, spots, or blotches. *Incubation,* 11–12 days; female alone incubates, although the male may brood for a short time; the young fledge after 7–9 days; the female and her mate or mates feed the young. The species is not parasitized by cowbirds. Smith's Longspurs are polygynandrous (each adult has one to several mates).

RANGE: *Breeds* from n and e-c Alaska (Anaktuvuk Pass, Susitna R. highlands, Wrangell Mountains region) and adjacent Yukon (Kluane) and British Columbia (Chilkat Pass), east across n Yukon (Herschel I.), n Mackenzie (Caribou Hills, Little Carcajou L., Anderson R., Coppermine), s Keewatin, ne Manitoba (Churchill), and n Ontario (Fort Severn, Winisk, Cape Henrietta Maria).

Winters from w Missouri (very rare), Kansas (regular in s Flint Hills; rare elsewhere), south through Oklahoma (fairly common in central part of state; apparently declining in the Panhandle), Arkansas (particularly in northwest, Mississippi Alluvial Plain), and w Tennessee (Shelby Co.) south to n Alabama (rare), Louisiana (nw, very rare), and northern Texas Panhandle, ne Texas (scarce but regular), casually south to Edwards Plateau and Houston.

In *migration* Smith's Longspurs pass through w Ontario, Wisconsin (very rare), w-c and sw Minnesota (very rare), Missouri (uncommon in spring; rare in fall), Illinois (common in spring, rare in fall), Indiana (rare), and Ohio (more common in spring than fall). Probably commonest in winter in c Oklahoma.

Vagrant east to the east coast [Nova Scotia (Aug, Oct), Massachusetts (Oct), Connecticut, New York, New Jersey, Maryland, North Carolina (Dec), and South Carolina (Dec, Feb); 1880s], and west to Arizona (White Mountains, Apr), Nevada (fall), and coastal California (Sept, Oct).

HISTORY: The first specimen taken of Smith's Longspur was taken by John Richardson at Carlton House, Saskatchewan, in April, 1827, where it was '. . . associating with the Lapland Buntings on the banks of the Saskatchewan . . . '. On the basis of this individual, Swainson and Richardson, in their *Fauna Boreali-Americana* (1831), first described Smith's Longspur, *Emberiza picta*, and gave it the English name of 'painted bunting.' In 1839, Audubon, not knowing of Richardson's specimen, named this longspur *Plectrophanes Smithii*, on the basis of specimens collected near Edwardsville, Illinois by his friends Edward Harris and John Bell. Gideon B. Smith was a friend of Audubon's from Baltimore, '. . . who has done much for science.' Bell wrote Audubon that 'We found these birds very abundant on the low prairie, near a lake in Illinois . . .'. Bell noted that ' . . . they run very nimbly . . .', and that 'they utter a sharp *click*, repeated several times in quick succession, and move off with an easy undulating motion, for a short distance, and alight very suddenly . . . seeming to fall as it were perpendicularly for several feet to the ground. They seemed to prefer the spots where the grass was shortest.'

Although Swainson and Richardson's Latin name *picta* has priority over Audubon's *Smithii*, the common name 'Smith's Longspur' has remained.

GEOGRAPHIC VARIATION: None described.

MEASUREMENTS: (7 males): wing 86–96 (92), tail 59–69 (63), tarsus 19.8–20.3

(20.1), exposed culmen 10.2–11.2 (10.7), bill depth at base 5.8–6.4 (6.1); (6 females): wing 87–90 (88), tail 55–59 (58), tarsus 20.1–20.6 (20.3), exposed culmen 10.2–11.4 (10.9), bill depth 5.8–6.4 (6.1) (Ridgway 1901).

Mass: (26 males) 28.1 g (24.1–31.1), (11 females) 25.9 g (23.8–28.9) (Manitoba); (22 males) 28.5 g (25.5–31.8), 24.3 g (22.0–26.9) (Anaktuvuk Pass, Alaska) (Briskie 1993a, b).

References: Briskie (1993a, b), Houston and Street (1959).

53 **Chestnut-collared Longspur**   Plates **22 & 24**
Calcarius ornatus [538]

IDENTIFICATION: 12–15 cm (*c.* 4.5–6 in), males slightly larger; sexes differ in coloration.

Male Chestnut-collared Longspurs in breeding plumage are unmistakable: the black chest and belly are distinctive, and at a distance displaying males initially look like small blackbirds; individuals have varying amounts of chestnut in the breast and belly, but this appears dark at a distance. They also have a bright ochre face, black crown and stripe behind the eye, white supercilium, a black spot or line on the side of the face, a conspicuous chestnut collar, and show a lot of white in the tail. Females are plain brown, with no black or white on the head but a pale buff supercilium, the chestnut collar obscure, and dark on the breast and belly greatly reduced or absent. They have faint brown streaking on the breast, and the same tail pattern as males.

Similar species: The facial pattern of breeding male Chestnut-collared Longspurs resembles that of Smith's Longspurs, but the Chestnut-collared lacks the black moustachial stripe of Smith's. They have a broad, chestnut collar. Breeding females are variable, but may show some black ventrally, perhaps quite a lot, and there is often a hint of rust in the collar. Breeding female McCown's are paler and grayer below — and larger.

In winter, both McCown's and Chestnut-collared longspurs show a lot of white in the tail, more than the other longspurs. McCown's has more white, but this can be difficult to see. See the account of McCown's Longspur for more details. Winter male Chestnut-collareds may show a white spot on the shoulder (posterior lesser coverts, contrasting with the black anterior lesser coverts).

Summer male (Apr–Aug)—**Head:** crown black, with a white spot in middle at back; eye-stripe (behind eye), and spot on the lower part of ear-coverts black;

Adult male

supercilium white; lores, side of face and throat pale yellow ochre; **back:** nape chestnut; back and **rump** brown, with feathers broadly to narrowly edged (depending on wear) with pale buff; **tail:** outer two rectrices (5th and 6th) mostly white; rectrices 2, 3, and 4 white, with dark tips; middle pair of rectrices brown and pointed; **underparts:** chin and throat pale ochre buff; breast, flanks, and belly black (tipped with beige in unworn birds), often flecked with varying amounts of dark chestnut; lower belly and undertail-coverts white; **wing:** brown, with greater coverts and tertials broadly edged with buff; anterior lesser coverts black; posterior lesser coverts white; **bill:** flesh colored, darker on upper bill and tip; **legs** and **feet:** brown to black; **iris:** brown.

Adult male in winter (Aug–Apr) like summer males, but black of head and breast, and chestnut of neck obscured by brownish or dull buffy tips to feathers (they wear into summer plumage).

Adult female (Apr–Aug)—**Head:** crown beige, thinly streaked with dark brown; supercilium and lores pale buff; side of face brown, thinly streaked with darker brown; **back** and **rump** brown (nape may be tinged with chestnut), thinly streaked with darker brown; **tail:** pattern as in male, but lighter brown; **wing:** brown, with greater coverts and tertials broadly edged with buff; anterior lesser coverts black; posterior lesser coverts white; **underparts:** throat buffy; breast, flanks, and belly buffy gray, thinly streaked with brown, usually with varying amounts of dark brown to blackish feathers; undertail-coverts buffy; **bill:** pale flesh colored, with darker tip; **legs** and **feet:** brownish; **iris:** brown.

Female in winter (Sept–Mar) like summer female, but feathers tipped with buffy.

Juveniles (July–Aug) crown and back dark brown, with feathers edged with pale buff; throat pale buffy gray, lightly speckled with brown; chest and flanks buffy, streaked with brown; belly paler, and lightly streaked; tail pattern as in adults; bill gray brown; legs and feet flesh colored.

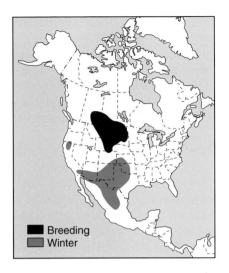

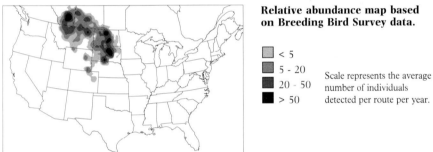

Relative abundance map based on Breeding Bird Survey data.

▨ < 5	
▨ 5 - 20	Scale represents the average
▨ 20 - 50	number of individuals
■ > 50	detected per route per year.

VOICE: The song of the Chestnut-collared Longspur is musical, and has the quality of the song of the Western Meadowlark. It generally lasts 2–3 s, and contains 7–8 phrases, each made up of several notes. The song becomes buzzy toward the end. The flight call is a distinctive *til-lip* or *cheed-lup*, the first syllable accented. The alarm note is a whistled *wheer*, or a staccato, rattling *tri-ri-rip*.

HABITAT: Chestnut-collared Longspurs nest in mixed grassland and in northern fescue. They can be found in moderately grazed grasslands and poor fields, and generally are found in moister, and somewhat denser vegetation than McCown's Longspurs. Unlike McCown's Longspurs, they do not nest in cultivated fields, but will sometimes nest in recently mowed sites. In suitable habitat, they may nest in rather high density and are perhaps loosely colonial. In winter they are found in short or tall grass and mowed alfalfa.

HABITS: Territorial males are frequently involved in chases, and do a lot of flight-singing, although less than McCown's Longspurs. Displaying males will rise from the ground with rapidly beating wings, circle and sing, then drop back to the ground. Breeding males characteristically sit on top of a tall bunch of grass, a weed or small bush, where they are distinctive; they often sing from these perches. Females are more difficult to see. They usually walk away from the nest before flying, and may give a distraction display that involves showing the white in the tail. In winter, Chestnut-collared Longspurs are usually found in small flocks, often confined to the species only but sometimes containing other longspurs and Horned Larks.

BREEDING: *Nest* is placed on the ground, often in a clump of grass, and often beside a stone. The nest is a cup of dried grasses, lined with finer grasses and sometimes feathers and hair. Nesting begins in May and continues through early July; the species is apparently double-brooded. *Eggs*, 3–6, usually 3–5, are creamy white, spotted or scrawled with browns or purplish browns; the female alone builds the nest. *Incubation*, 12–13 days; female alone incubates; young fledge in 9–11 days. The species is occasionally parasitized by cowbirds. Chestnut-collared Longspurs are apparently monogamous.

RANGE: *Breeds* from se Alberta (west to Lethbridge, Calgary; north to Sullivan L., Czar) and s Saskatchewan (south of Bigger, Burke L., Quill L., east to s Manitoba (Brandon, Winnipeg), North Dakota (uncommon in east), w Minnesota (Clay and Traverse cos.), south through c and e Montana, e Wyoming and South Dakota (except for se) to se Colorado (Weld and Washington cos.), and occasionally to western Nebraska (Sioux and Kimball cos.; formerly Cherry and Holt cos.).

Winters from s California (rare, but sometimes in flocks of more than 40), ne California (very uncommon), s Arizona (abundant in se), s New Mexico (common), rarely north to se Colorado (Baca Co.; very rare), and sw Kansas (probable; rare), Oklahoma (uncommon to common in c and w, rare in east), Texas (locally fairly common in nw), Arkansas (casual), and nw Louisiana (casual), south to n Sonora, w Coahuila, and on the Mexican Plateau to Zacatecas and Aguascalientes. Commonest in winter in se Arizona, sw New Mexico, c Oklahoma, and n-c and nw Texas. Recorded once in winter in e Missouri (St. Charles Airport), and in s Nevada (Las Vegas). Vagrant north to n Alberta, n Manitoba (Churchill), east to Newfoundland, New Brunswick, Nova Scotia, Maine, Massachusetts (4 records), New York (4 records), Maryland, Virginia, w Florida (Tallahassee, possibly Dade Co.), and west to British Columbia (several records), Washington (2 records), and ne Oregon (2 records).

In *migration* throughout California (especially s California, and nw coast, very rare in spring), s Oregon (very rare), eastern Colorado (casual in spring in western valleys), and Missouri (very rare, most records in spring), Illinois (very rare, no fall records), and Ontario (2 records, spring).

HISTORY: The first specimen of Chestnut-collared Longspur was collected by John Kirk Townsend in the spring of 1834, from along the Platte R. in western Nebraska.

This is just one of several new species discovered by Townsend and his companion, Thomas Nuttall on their expedition to the west coast.

Chestnut-collared Longspurs have decreased substantially in abundance in recent times, presumably as a consequence of the destruction of much of their prairie habitat. In the late 1800s they were a common breeding species in western Kansas, where they no longer nest, and their numbers have been substantially reduced in western Minnesota, where they used to be abundant, and in Saskatchewan. They nonetheless still breed in high density in places where suitable habitat remains.

GEOGRAPHIC VARIATION: None described. There is a record of a hybrid McCown's × Chestnut-collared Longspur.

MEASUREMENTS: (15 males): wing 81–90 (85), tail 51–61 (56), tarsus 18.8–20.6 (19.8), exposed culmen 9.7–11.2 (10.4), bill depth at base (two specimens) 5.8 and 6.4; (10 females): wing 75–85 (80), tail 48–57 (52), tarsus 18.3–21.1 (19.6), exposed culmen 9.9–10.9 (10.4), bill depth 5.6–6.1 (5.8) (Ridgway 1901).

Mass: (N=20) 18.9 g (10.8–20.9) (Arizona) (Dunning 1993).

Genus *Emberiza*

The 38 or so species of *Emberiza* all breed in the Old World, from Northern Europe to Asia and Africa. Of the seven species that have been reported in North America, only the Rustic Bunting occurs regularly, and it is quite rare.

This is a variable genus. Many of the species are brightly colored and sexually dimorphic in coloration, but some are rather plain and monomorphic. All of the species that have been reported in North America, except for the Gray Bunting, show white in the tail when in flight. In Alaska, a sparrow with white in its tail is probably a longspur, but worth a close look. *Emberiza* are often said to be closely related to *Calcarius*, but there seems to be little supportive evidence.

54 **Pine Bunting** *Emberiza leucocephalos* [2883]   PLATE 26

D.BEADLE.

IDENTIFICATION: 16.5 cm (*c.* 7 in), males slightly larger; sexes differ in coloration.

Pine Buntings are large, rather long-tailed sparrows, the largest of the *Emberiza* that reach North America. Adult males have a distinctive head pattern, with a white cheek and crown, black lateral crown-stripes, a broad chestnut stripe through the eye, and a chestnut chin and throat. Adult females have a less distinct facial pattern, with a pale supercilium, grayish ear-coverts with a pale spot near the posterior edge, and brownish or rusty brown streaks on the breast and flanks. Males in the first winter are like adults, but are less brightly colored, and have a streaked crown, and rusty streaks on their underparts.

Similar species: Female Reed Buntings are similar to female Pine Buntings, but have brownish ear-coverts, without the light spot, and have a paler supercilium and submoustachial stripe, and a darker malar stripe. Female Rustic Buntings are similar, but are more brightly patterned, with rustier markings on the breast and flanks. Female and winter Smith's Longspurs are buffier in hue, and not so heavily streaked below. None of the North American sparrows (with the exception of the juncos, Vesper Sparrow, and longspurs) have conspicuous white in the tail.

Adult male (Feb–Aug)—***Head:*** forehead, lateral crown-stripes, and back of neck black; remainder of crown and nape white; eyeline stripe and lores broad, and brick red, contrasting with white ear-coverts, which are narrowly edged with black on both upper and lower margins; side of neck with a narrow pale or white streak; ***back:***

mantle light rufous-cinnamon, streaked with dark brown; ***rump*** and uppertail-coverts deep rufous-cinnamon, slightly mottled with pale buff; ***tail:*** brownish black; outer rectrices edged with white on inner webs toward tip; outermost rectrix edged with white, with black toward base and tip; ***wing:*** grayish black, edged with cinnamon-rufous; coverts edged with cinnamon-rufous; ***underparts:*** chin and throat brick red, contrasting with the white ear-coverts and a white band across the upper breast; breast and flanks rusty; belly whitish; ***bill:*** upper mandible slate-gray to brownish black; lower mandible pale horn color; ***legs:*** pale flesh-brown; ***iris:*** dark brown.

Male in winter (Sept–Jan) similar to males in summer, but the feathers are tipped with brown, obscuring the cinnamon and white markings on the head; they have a thin eye-ring. First-winter males are duller in coloration than adult males. There is a partial facial molt in Feb–Mar, but otherwise males wear into summer plumage.

Adult female (May–Sept)—***Head:*** forehead brown with cinnamon mottling; crown streaked with pale buff and dark brown; supercilium and lores pale; eye-stripe dark brown, ear-coverts grayish brown, edged with dark brown, and with a pale spot on the back margin; submoustachial stripe whitish, malar dark; throat whitish; ***back, wings,*** and ***tail*** similar to adult male; ***underparts:*** chin and throat pale, breast and flanks streaked with chestnut; belly white; soft parts colored as in males.

Female in winter (Sept–Apr) like adult males, but duller in coloration.

Juveniles like females but duller in coloration, with a dull cinnamon rump and streaked back.

VOICE: The song is long and repetitious, and resembles that of the Yellowhammer; it is described as ***sri-sri-sri-sri-sri-zyyh***. There is considerable variation, and an individual may sing several different song types. A ***tsik, tic,*** or ***twik*** note is given both when perched and in flight.

HABITS: In the breeding season, territorial males sing from the tops of small trees (birches). In winter, they are often in flocks, but only single birds have been reported in North America.

HABITAT: In the breeding season, Pine Buntings nest in the edge of sparse forests and clearings, with overgrown bushes.

RANGE: *Breeds* in the Palearctic, from Finland east to nw Siberia. *Winters* in s China. Fall migration is Aug–Nov; spring migration is Mar–June. Reported twice from Attu, Aleutian Is., Alaska: 19 Nov 1985 (male); 6 Oct 1993 (first-year male).

GEOGRAPHIC VARIATION: None in our area; *E. l. leucocephalos* is the subspecies that has been found in North America. Hybridizes freely with the Yellowhammer (*E. citrinella*) where their ranges overlap in western Siberia.

MEASUREMENTS: (males): wing 88–100 (94; N=39), tail 68–83 (75; N=27), tarsus 17.6–20.8 (19.5; N=27); culmen from skull 13.2–15.4 (14.5; N=27); (females): wing 84–95 (89; N=17), tail 64–75 (69; N=10), tarsus 18.8–19.8 (19.5; N=10), culmen 13.3–15.5 (14.2; N=10) (Cramp and Perrins 1994).

Mass: (7 males) 28.4 g (26.0–33.5); (4 females) 24.6 g (24.0–25.8) (sw Siberia, summer) (Cramp and Perrins 1994).

References: Cramp and Perrins (1994), Kessel and Gibson (unpublished).

55 **Little Bunting** *Emberiza pusilla* [535.2]   PLATE **25**

D. BEADLE.

IDENTIFICATION: 13–14 cm (*c.* 5–5.5 in), males slightly larger; sexes differ in coloration.

The Little Bunting is a small bunting with a flat forehead, a small, sharply pointed bill, short neck, short legs, and a short tail. In profile, the upper mandible is flat or slightly concave. The dull chestnut cheeks and median crown-stripe of adults, and the thin eye-ring are distinctive.

Similar species: The combination of the small size, bill shape and eye-ring separate Little Bunting from female Reed Buntings, which can be similar to female Pine Buntings. The Reed Bunting has a thicker bill, which appears to be relatively shorter than Little Bunting's, and the upper mandible is slightly convex in profile. Little Bunting has a rather small head, with a flat forehead; Reed Buntings have a larger, more rounded head. Little Buntings have short legs and short, rectangular tails; Reed Buntings have longer tails (this may not be obvious), and they frequently spread their tails. Rustic Buntings are similar in shape, but larger, have a more rounded head, and often show a ragged crest (Little Bunting can show this). Little Buntings have a broad chestnut or buffy central crown-stripe, whereas Rustic Buntings have a thin pale buffy stripe. The facial markings of the Rustic Bunting are sharper than those of Little Bunting, and Little Bunting has buffy cinnamon ear-coverts and lores. The

Variation amongst males

pale spot at the back of the ear-coverts is bright in Rustic Bunting, and obscure in Little Bunting.

Adult (May–Aug)—***Head:*** median crown-stripe, ear-coverts, and lores cinnamon-buff, the latter narrowly outlined with dark brown eyeline and moustachial stripes; posterior border of ear-coverts dark brown, often with a pale spot at the back; lateral crown-stripes dark brown; supercilium pale cinnamon-buff, paler than ear-coverts; ***back, rump,*** and uppertail-coverts brownish, and dark brown streaks; ***tail:*** brownish black; outer rectrices mostly white, with some dark brown on inside and tip; variable, but little white in the second outermost rectrix; ***wing:*** brownish, edged with buff; median and greater coverts edged with pale buff, forming two wing-bars; ***underparts:*** chin and upper throat buffy; lower throat whitish; breast and flanks brown streaked; belly whitish; ***bill:*** upper mandible grayish black, with cutting edges paler; lower mandible pale flesh pink (fall) to dull gray with a pink tinge (spring); ***legs:*** pale reddish flesh; ***iris:*** red-brown or dark brown (gray-brown in first fall).

Fall and winter (Sept–Apr) similar to adults, but warmer in hues, with streaking less sharply defined.

Juveniles like females but more yellowish buff, stripes on the head indistinct, and ventral streaking more extensive.

VOICE: The song is quiet and sweet, consists of buzzy phrases and clicks, such as ***srri zee srri see sip sip sip zrree dz-oo dz-oo***. Migrants give paired hard, sharp ***tik tik***, ***tzik tzik***, or ***pick pick*** notes.

HABITS: The flight of the Little Bunting is light and fast, like a small finch, but not undulating. On the ground it creeps, and nervously flicks its wings. In migration it often forms flocks, but North American records are of single birds. Territorial males sing from the tops of small trees.

HABITAT: Little Buntings breed in moist shrubby tundra, in willows along rivers through the boreal forest, or in open forests. In western Siberia they are often in dwarf birch or spruce, and in northern Russia in alders and willows in river valleys. In winter they are found in shortgrass on hillsides and in plains.

RANGE: ***Breeds*** in the Palearctic, from n Finland east to n Siberia, south to Lake Biakal and the Sea of Okhostsk. ***Winters*** in e Asia, south to n Burma, and east to n India, and rarely continental Europe, the British Isles, North Africa, and the Philippines. Fall migration is Aug–Nov; spring migration is Mar-May. There are three records for North America, an immature found aboard ship in the Chukchi Sea, 280 km nw of Icy Cape, Alaska, on 6 Sept 1970, and an immature male collected at Shemya I., Aleutian Is., Alaska, on 8 Sept 1977. One was seen at Point Loma, San Diego Co., California (Oct).

GEOGRAPHIC VARIATION: None described.

MEASUREMENTS: (males): wing 69–76 (72; N=30), tail 51–58 (55; N=11), tarsus 16.5–18.2 (17.5; N=9), culmen from skull 11.6–13.4 (12.4; N=11); (females): wing 67–70 (69; N=13), tail 46–55 (52; N=9), tarsus 17.0–18.4 (17.7; N=7), culmen 11.2–12.6 (11.6; N=9) (Cramp and Perrins 1994).

Mass: (N=10) 13.0 g (11.0–14.0) (India) (Dunning 1993).

References: Cramp and Perrins (1994), Kessel and Gibson (1976).

56 **Rustic Bunting** *Emberiza rustica* [535.1]   PLATE **25**

D·BEADLE.

IDENTIFICATION: 14.5–15.5 cm (*c.* 6 in), males slightly larger; sexes differ in coloration.

Rustic Buntings are medium-sized sparrows with white underparts and bold rusty spots or streaks on their breast. Adult males have a black head, with a grayish white median crown-stripe, a white spot on the nape, a white supercilium, and a white spot on the back of the black ear-coverts. Females and first-winter birds are similarly patterned, but with brown on the crown and grayish brown ear-coverts. Juveniles may be less rusty on the breast.

Similar species: Female Reed Buntings are similar to female Rustic Buntings, but are not rusty, and lack the light spots on the nape and ear-coverts. The bill of Reed Buntings appears to be relatively blunt, not sharp like that of Rustic and Little buntings. Little Buntings are small, short-legged, and have a flat forehead; Rustic Buntings have a peaked crown; the rump of Little Bunting is brownish, whereas that of Rustic Bunting is rusty brown. Red Fox Sparrows are red, but are much larger, lack black on the head, and like most of the North American sparrows (with the exception of the juncos, Vesper Sparrow, and longspurs) lack conspicuous white in the tail.

Adult male (Feb–Aug)—***Head:*** black mottled with brown in unworn birds; median crown-stripe usually grayish white; white spot on nape; supercilium white;

Variations

supraloral spot and ear-coverts black, with a white spot on the back of the coverts; submoustachial stripe bold and white; malar stripe rusty, extending to bill; throat white; ***back:*** nape rusty, with a white spot at the back of the head; mantle rusty, streaked with dark brown; ***rump*** and uppertail-coverts deep rufous-cinnamon; ***tail:*** blackish; outer rectrices edged with white on inner webs toward tip; outermost rectrix (6th) mostly white, with black toward base and tip, 5th rectrix with white on the inner web toward the tip; ***wing:*** dark brown, with secondaries and tertials edged with cinnamon-rufous; middle and greater coverts white-tipped, forming two wing-bars; ***underparts:*** chin and throat white, contrasting with bright rusty streaks, often forming a band across the upper breast; flanks rusty streaked; belly white; ***bill:*** pinkish gray at base, dark gray at tip; ***legs:*** pale flesh brown; ***iris:*** dark brown.

Male in winter (Sept–Jan) similar to males in summer, but the feathers are tipped with brown, obscuring the black markings on the head. First-winter males probably are duller in coloration than adult males. There is a partial head molt in March, but otherwise males wear into summer plumage.

Adult female (May–Sept) similar to males, but duller, with the nape spot inconspicuous, and black markings brown to dark brown.

Female in winter (Sept–Apr) like adult females, but duller in coloration; the supercilium and submoustachial stripes are buffy.

Juveniles like females but duller and buffier in coloration.

VOICE: The song is a short, clear, and melodious ***dudeleu-deluu-delee***. It has the melancholy quality of that of the Lapland Longspur. The flight call is a double ***tic tic***, like that of the Little Bunting, or ***tic tic tic***; a faint ***tsip*** is given in flight.

HABITS: On the breeding grounds, male Rustic Buntings sing from an exposed perch, with their crown raised; singing begins in spring migration. When agitated, they raise their crown and flick their tail. When flushed from the ground, they fly up into trees. Their flight is quick, and slightly undulating. In migration and winter, Rustic Buntings are gregarious, and flocks of up to five birds have been recorded in Alaska, although many records are of single birds..

HABITAT: Breeds in low bushes in wet tundra, and in open coniferous forests, streamside thickets. In winter, Rustic Buntings are found in bushy areas, grasslands, open woods, and cultivated fields.

RANGE: *Breeds* in the Palearctic, from n Scandinavia east to n Siberia. *Winters* in China, Japan, and Commander (Komandorskiye) Is. (rare). Fall migration is Aug–Nov; spring migration is Mar–June. Rare in spring migration in w and c Aleutian Is. (mid-May through June, and very rare in fall migration (mid-Sept through Oct); casual on St. Lawrence I. (June), and in winter in interior Alaska (Fairbanks). Casual south to British Columbia (Queen Charlotte Is.: Queen Charlotte City, Oct, Masset, Aug; Vancouver I.: Jordan R., Nov [wintered]; Tofino [wintered]), Washington (Kent Ponds, King Co. [two records; wintered], Oregon (Multnomah Co., Nov; Lane Co., Apr), and to California (Humboldt Co., Jan; Kern Co., Nov; San Mateo Co., Nov).

GEOGRAPHIC VARIATION: None in our area. The Siberian subspecies *E. r. lati-fascia* is doubtless the one that strays to North America. The geographic variation in this species is slight, but Siberian birds are said to have black, rather than brownish black caps and ear-coverts, and more rufous in the tail.

MEASUREMENTS: (males): wing 78–83 (81; N=18), tail 48–59 (55; N=16), tarsus 18.8–20.3 (19.4; N=13), culmen from skull 11.6–14.9 (13.7; N=19); (females): wing 73–81 (78; N=10), tail 49–57 (54; N=7), tarsus 18.4–19.7 (19.1; N=15), culmen 12.0–15.0 (13.6; N=12) (Cramp and Perrins 1994).

Mass: (54 adult males) 21.0 g (17.7–24.3); (35 adult females) 20.1 g (18.0–22.9) (Japan, Oct–Nov) (Cramp and Perrins 1994).

References: Cramp and Perrins (1994), Kessel and Gibson (1976).

57 **Yellow-breasted Bunting**   PLATE **25**
Emberiza aureola [535.6]

D. BEADLE .

IDENTIFICATION: 14–15 cm (*c.* 5.5–6 in), males slightly larger; sexes differ in coloration.

Yellow-breasted Buntings are brightly colored, medium-sized sparrows. Males are unmistakable. Females have dark rusty brown lateral crown-stripes, and a paler buffy median crown-stripe, and a prominent whitish supercilium and yellow supraloral spot; they have a streaked breast and flanks, and most have a yellowish wash to their underparts; the ear-coverts are buffy, outlined with brown, and with a pale spot toward the upper back.

Similar species: Males in all plumages are bright yellow below, with a dark chestnut band across their breast, white lesser and median coverts, forming a white patch on the wing; they are unmistakable. Females resemble some of the other female *Emberiza*, but are distinctly yellowish in hue, have a conspicuous pale supercilium, and the back is streaked with brown and buff. Females in winter superficially resemble wintering bobolinks, which are substantially larger. Yellow-breasted Buntings appear to be rather chunky and short-tailed.

Adult male (Feb–Aug)—**Head:** face black, with a dark chestnut nape extending variably onto the crown; **back** and **rump:** dark chestnut with variable black streaks (the back tends to be darker in eastern birds); **tail:** brown-black edged with rust, white on outer two rectrices; **wing:** dark brown; secondaries and tertials edged in chestnut; lesser and median coverts white, greater coverts tipped in white, forming a wing-bar; **underparts:** chin and upper throat black; lower throat bright yellow, with

a dark chestnut (sometimes black) breast-band; breast and belly otherwise bright yellow, becoming paler toward tail, with chestnut streaking on the flanks; undertail-coverts buffy white; *bill:* upper mandible dark horn colored, with a paler cutting edge, lower mandible pale pink; *legs:* pink or straw colored; *iris:* dark. First-year males resemble winter males, but have some black on their throat.

Male in winter (Sept–Apr) similar to males in summer, but the feathers are tipped with buff, somewhat obscuring the bright colors; the throat is yellow. There is a partial facial molt in Mar–May, but otherwise males wear into summer plumage. First-winter males resemble females.

Adult females (May–Sept) *Head:* lateral crown-stripes dark brown, separated by a narrow pale median crown-stripe; supercilium is broad, and nearly white above the eye; supraloral spot yellow; ear-coverts buffy, outlined with a dark eye and moustachial stripes, with a pale spot on the brown back margin of the coverts; *back:* nape grayish brown, mantle streaked with brown and buff; *wing:* brown, with tips of median and greater coverts tipped in buff, forming two wing-bars; tertials are edged and tipped with buff or chestnut; *underparts:* washed with yellow, paler on throat and toward tail, thinly streaked with brown on breast and flanks; *tail:* brown, with white in outer two rectrices; soft part colors like males.

Female in winter (Sept–Apr) like females in summer, but duller.

Juveniles like females but duller.

VOICE: The song is short and melodious, written as ***tyy-tyy-tsyy-tsyy-tsitsi-tuu*** or ***tsiu-tsiu-tsiu vue-vue tsia-tsia trip-trip***. A hard ***tsik*** or ***thip*** note may be given in rapid succession when the bird is perched or in flight. There is also a soft ***tsee*** note.

HABITS: Yellow-breasted Buntings are gregarious outside the breeding season, but only single birds have been reported from North America. When flushed from the ground, they will fly up into a bush or tree, if available.

HABITAT: Yellow-breasted Buntings nest in wet streamside thickets of willow and birch, interspersed with grass, or in damp sedge meadows with sparse shrubs. In winter they are found in grassland, hedgerows, and gardens.

RANGE: *Breeds* in the Palearctic, from c Finland east to ne Siberia (Kamchatka, Commander [Komandorskiye] Is.), and Japan.

Winters from ne India east to se Asia, and occasionally to Great Britain, w Europe, and the Philippines. Fall migration is July–Sept; spring migration is Apr–June. There are four records for Alaska: a first-spring male was seen on St. Lawrence, Alaska, 26–27 June 1978; an adult male was collected at Attu I., Aleutian Is., 26 May 1988; a female was seen at Buldir I., Aleutians, 20–25 June 1988; and an adult male was seen at Buldir on 13 June 1990.

GEOGRAPHIC VARIATION: None in our area. The specimen was identified as *E. a. ornata*, which breeds in eastern Siberia and Japan. *E. a. ornata* tends to be darker on the back, has deeper yellow underparts, and a blacker (often black) bar on the chest than birds from the western Palearctic.

MEASUREMENTS: (males): wing 73–81 (78; N=19), tail 53–59 (55; N=18), tarsus 20.0–21.5 (20.9; N=12), culmen from skull 13.6–15.2 (14.4; N=19); (females): wing 72–76 (74; N=8), tail 51–56 (53; N=10), tarsus 19.5–20.8 (20.3; N=6), culmen 13.5–14.5 (14.0; N=8) (Cramp and Perrins 1994).

Mass: (8 males) 21.6 g (20.5–22.5); (5 females) 21.3 g (20.5–22.5) (se Siberia) (Cramp and Perrins 1994).

Reference: Cramp and Perrins (1994).

58 **Gray Bunting** *Emberiza variabilis* [535.3]   **PLATE 25**

D. BEADLE .

IDENTIFICATION: 14–17 cm (*c.* 5.5–7 in), males slightly larger; sexes differ in coloration.

Gray Bunting males are nearly uniformly gray, with a large, sharp, pale yellowish or pinkish bill. Females are brown, with a pale supercilium, extensive ventral streaking, and a bright rusty tail. Neither sex has white in the tail.

Similar species: Males are unmistakable; they may resemble 'Slate-colored' Juncos, but juncos have a white belly and conspicuous white in the tail. Females resemble other female *Emberiza*, but lack the white in the tail, and have a rusty tail.

Adult male—uniformly gray, with indistinct black streaking on the back and belly; **bill:** upper mandible pale horn colored; lower mandible yellowish or pinkish, darker toward tip; **legs:** dull pink; **iris:** dark.

First-winter male grayish on the face and belly, which is lightly streaked with rusty and perhaps black; back rusty and streaked with brown; crown pale rusty gray.

Adult female—Head: forehead and crown dark chestnut with a pale median crown-stripe; supercilium and lores pale; eye-stripe brown, ear-coverts pale brown, thinly edged with darker brown; submoustachial stripe whitish; malar stripe thin and dark; throat whitish; **back:** buffy brown, streaked with brown; **rump** and **tail:** bright rusty, with no white in tail; **wing:** brown, with edges of secondaries rusty; median and greater coverts dark and white-tipped, forming two wing-bars; **underparts:**

chin and throat pale, breast and flanks streaked with pale chestnut brown; belly white, faintly washed with yellowish buff; soft parts colored as in males.

Female in winter like adult males, but probably duller in coloration.

Juveniles resemble females, but are more heavily streaked below.

VOICE: The song is described as a series of loud fluty notes, a short ***vouee-tseeve-tseeve***. The call note is a soft ***tsik***.

HABITS: In migration and winter, Gray Buntings are typically found in pairs or flocks, but the North American records are of single birds. In their natural habitat, they are apparently difficult to see.

HABITAT: The Gray Bunting breeds in coniferous and mixed forests and thickets of dwarf bamboo, principally in hilly country. In winter they are found in hill forests with dense understory.

RANGE: ***Breeds*** in the Palearctic, on se Kamchatka Peninsula, Kuril I., s Sakhalin I., and locally in c Honshu and Hokkaido.

Winters in Japan and Ryukyu Is. There are two North American records, both from the Aleutian Is.: an adult male collected at Shemya I. (18 May 1977), and an immature male at Attu I., 29 May 1980.

GEOGRAPHIC VARIATION: None described.

MEASUREMENTS: None available.

Mass: The male collected at Shemya I. weighed 26.6 g.

Reference: Kessel and Gibson (1976).

59 **Pallas's Bunting** *Emberiza pallasi* [535.4]   PLATE **26**

D. BEADLE.

IDENTIFICATION: 13–15 cm (*c.* 5–6 in), males slightly larger; sexes differ in coloration.

The breeding male Pallas's Bunting has a black head, with a broad contrasting white submoustachial stripe and nape, and a blackish tail, contrasting with a whitish rump; they are unmistakable; males in winter are similar, but the black feathers of the head are tipped with brown. Females are pale in hue, with a pale supercilium, faint breast streaking, and a pink lower mandible.

Similar species: Males are similar in pattern to male Reed Buntings, but are much paler overall, with a whitish rather than a gray rump. The coverts and secondaries of Reed Buntings are edged in rust; those of Pallas's Bunting are pale. Female Reed Buntings are similar to female Pallas's Buntings, but darker in hue, with a more pronounced brown malar streak, and more ventral streaking. As in males, the coverts and secondaries of Reed Buntings are edged with rust; those of Pallas's Buntings are pale buff. The ear-coverts of Reed Buntings are darker and less uniformly colored than those of Pallas's. The back streaking is more striking on Pallas's Bunting than on Reed Bunting. In winter, female Pallas's Buntings have no or only faint streaking on their crown, whereas Reed Buntings usually show distinct lateral crown-stripes. The

upper mandible of Pallas's Bunting is nearly straight, and there is a distinct contrast between the dark upper mandible and the pale pinkish lower mandible (the bill is usually all black in breeding males); the upper mandible of Reed Bunting is slightly convex, and the bluish gray lower mandible contrasts little with the upper.

Adult male (May–Aug)—***Head:*** black, with bold white submoustachial stripes and a white collar; ***back:*** nape white; mantle pale buff to whitish, boldly striped with black; ***rump:*** white and unpatterned; uppertail-coverts pale and faintly streaked; ***wing:*** dark brown, with pale edges to secondaries; tertials with black centers; lesser coverts bluish gray; median and greater coverts are tipped with white or buff, forming two wing-bars; ***tail:*** black; outermost rectrix (6th) mostly white; 5th with white at the tip of the inner web; wing grayish black, edged with cinnamon-rufous; coverts edged with cinnamon-rufous; ***underparts:*** chin and throat black; breast, belly, and undertail-coverts buffy white to white; ***bill:*** upper mandible grayish black; lower mandible pinkish gray; bill of breeding males black; ***legs:*** flesh-brown or light brown; ***iris:*** brown or dark brown.

Male in winter (Sept–May) similar to males in summer, but the feathers are tipped with brown, obscuring the black and white markings on the head. First-winter males are duller in coloration than adult males. Although there may be a limited face molt, males wear into summer plumage.

Adult female (May–Sept)—***Head:*** crown pale brown, with faint streaks; supercilium and lores pale buff; ear-coverts buff, faintly outlined with pale brown; submoustachial stripe pale buff; malar stripe thin, brown; ***back:*** brown, with sharp brown streaks; ***wing:*** brown, with edges of median and greater coverts whitish buff, forming two wing-bars; ***tail:*** brown, patterned like male's; ***underparts:*** chin, throat, breast, flanks, and belly pale with faint or no streaking on the flanks; soft parts colored as in males. Winter females are slightly buffier.

Juveniles like females but duller in coloration, with a dull cinnamon rump and streaked back.

VOICE: The song is a soft trill, ***chi chi chi chi chi***, or a cricket-like ***tsisi tsisi tsisi tsisi***. The call is a quiet ***tsiup*** or ***tsee-see***.

HABITS: Pallas's Buntings are found singly or in flocks, in bushes or on the ground. North American records have been of single birds.

HABITAT: Breeds in cool, dry areas in overgrown thickets and dry tundra, including mountain tundra.

RANGE: ***Breeds*** in the e Palearctic, from Siberia south to w and ne China, Tibet, and Manchuria. Winters in China and Korea. Fall migration is in Aug–Oct; spring migration early Mar through mid-May. Three records (all spring) from Alaska: Barrow, 11 June 1968 (adult male); St. Lawrence I., 28 May 1973 (adult male); Buldir I., Aleutian Is., June 1992 (female).

GEOGRAPHIC VARIATION: None in our area; *P. pallasi polaris* of Siberia is probably the race that occurs in Alaska. Eastern birds are paler than western ones.

MEASUREMENTS: (10 males): wing 71–77 (74), tail 57–65 (61), tarsus 17.5–19.0 (18.2), culmen from skull 10.8–12.5 (11.5); (9 females): wing 68–73 (70); tail 57–62 (59), tarsus 17.3–18.9 (18.2), culmen 10.6–12.0 (11.4) (Cramp and Perrins 1994).

Mass: (8 males) 14.6 g (13.9–15.3); (3 females) 14.2 g (13.6–16.4) (nw Siberia) (Cramp and Perrins 1994).

References: Cramp and Perrins (1994), Kessel and Gibson (1976, unpublished).

60 **Reed Bunting** *Emberiza schoeniclus* [535.5]   **PLATE 26**

D. BEADLE.

IDENTIFICATION: 15–16.5 cm (*c.* 6–6.5 in), males slightly larger; sexes differ in coloration.

Breeding male Reed Buntings are unmistakable; they have a black head, with a broad contrasting white submoustachial stripe and nape, a dark back, streaked with black, a gray rump, and a blackish tail, white in the outer two rectrices. Males in winter are similar, but black of head is less distinct. Females are brown, with broad, pale or whitish supercilium and submoustachial streaks, the latter outlined by a thin brown moustachial stripe and a broad brown malar stripe, streaked breast and flanks, and white outer tail feathers.

Similar species: Males are similar in pattern to male Pallas's Buntings, but are much darker overall, with a gray rather than whitish rump that does not contrast strongly with the back and tail colors. The coverts and secondaries of Reed Buntings are edged in rust; those of Pallas's Bunting are pale. Female Reed Buntings are similar to female Pallas's Buntings, but darker in hue, with a more pronounced brown malar streak, and more ventral streaking. As in males, the coverts and secondaries of Reed Buntings are edged with rust; those of Pallas's Buntings are pale buff. The ear-coverts of Reed Buntings are darker and less uniformly colored than those of Pallas's. The back streaking is more striking on Pallas's Bunting than on Reed Bunting. There is, however, considerable geographic variation in Reed Buntings, and eastern Siberian birds are paler (more like Pallas's Buntings) than western ones, and the females have a rustier crown, and less ventral streaking. In winter, female Pallas's Buntings have

no or only faint streaking on their crown, whereas Reed Buntings usually show distinct lateral crown-stripes. The upper mandible of Pallas's Bunting is nearly straight, and there is a distinct contrast between the dark upper mandible and the pale pinkish lower mandible (the bill is usually all black in breeding males); the upper mandible of Reed Bunting is slightly convex, and the bluish gray lower mandible contrasts little with the upper.

Adult male (May–Aug)—***Head:*** black, with bold white submoustachial stripes and a white collar; ***back:*** nape white; mantle brown to rusty brown, boldly striped with black; ***rump*** and uppertail-coverts with a few dark streaks; ***wing:*** dark brown, with rusty edges to secondaries; tertials with black centers; lesser coverts rusty; median and greater coverts are dark brown to black edged with rust and tipped with buff, forming indistinct wing-bars; ***tail:*** black; outermost rectrix (6th) mostly white; 5th with considerable white in the inner web; ***underparts:*** chin and throat black; breast, belly, and undertail-coverts white; ***bill:*** upper mandible grayish black; lower mandible pinkish gray or pinkish brown; ***legs:*** pinkish brown or brown; ***iris:*** brown or dark brown.

Male in winter (Sept–May) similar to males in summer, but the feathers are tipped with brown, slightly obscuring the black and white markings on the head. First-winter males are duller in coloration than adult males. Although there may be a limited face molt, males wear into summer plumage.

Adult female (May–Sept)—***Head:*** lateral crown-stripes light rusty brown; median crown-stripe buff-brown, with faint streaks; supercilium and lores pale buff; ear-coverts brownish buff, outlined with pale brown; submoustachial stripe pale buff; malar stripe broad and dark brown; ***back:*** brown, with sharp brown streaks; ***rump:*** pale brown, with darker centers to feathers; ***wing:*** brown; lesser coverts rusty; edges of median and greater coverts and tertials rusty; ***tail:*** brown, patterned like male's; ***underparts:*** chin, throat, breast, flanks, and belly pale with faint or no streaking on the flanks; soft parts colored as in males. Winter females are slightly buffier.

Juveniles like females but duller in coloration, with a dull cinnamon rump and streaked back.

VOICE: The song is a short, rather disjointed staccato repeated loud trill, ***shree-shree-teeree-teeree***, or ***tsee tsee tsea tsisirr***, that is described as squeaky or tinkling. The call note is a distinct ***tzween***, rising at the end, a soft ***tseek-tseek***, or a short ***bzree***.

HABITS: Reed Buntings typically are found in pairs or in flocks, in bushes or on the ground. North American records have been of single birds. Breeding males typically sing from a high point in their territories; they are easy to approach and see.

HABITAT: Breeds in reeds and thickets along streams and around lakes. In winter it is found in marshes and pastures.

RANGE: ***Breeds*** from the British Isles, Scandinavia, n Russia and n Siberia south to the Mediterranean region, Iran, s Siberia, Kamchatka and n Japan.

Winters from the southern part of the breeding range south to nw India, ne China, and s Japan.

Casual in spring migration in the w Aleutian Is., Alaska (6 records, from 22 May–4 June).

GEOGRAPHIC VARIATION: None in our area; *P. s. pyrrhulina* of southeastern Siberia west to Kamchatka, and south to Manchuria and Japan is the race that has been collected in Alaska. *P. s. pyrrhulina* is paler in coloration than birds from western Europe, with the crown of the female somewhat rufous, and reduced breast streaking.

MEASUREMENTS: wing 78–86 (84; N=18), tarsus 20.3–21.8 (20.9; N=7), culmen from skull 11.2–12.5 (11.8; N=7); (adult females): wing 76–81 (79; N=15) (Japan) (Cramp and Perrins 1994).

Mass: (47 males) 22.5 g (19.8–26.5); (42 females) 20.3 g (17.3–23.0) (Japan) (Cramp and Perrins 1994).

References: Cramp and Perrins (1994), Flint *et al.* (1984), Kessel and Gibson (1976, unpublished).

61 **Snow Bunting** *Plectrophenax nivalis* [534]   **PLATE 27**

IDENTIFICATION: 15–19 cm (*c.* 6–7.5 in), males slightly larger; sexes differ in coloration.

The Snow Bunting is a large, chunky bunting, with a white or dusky head and belly, black-tipped white wings, black back, and white edges to its tail.

Similar species: In all plumages, Snow Buntings are unmistakable. McKay's Bunting is much whiter: male McKay's Buntings have a white back and rump, little black in their tail, and usually no black in the bend of their wings. Females have a whitish rather than a brownish back, with little black in the tail. 'Partial albinos' of other species may show a lot of white in their plumage, and have confused some observers.

Summer male (Apr–Aug)—**Head:** white, sometimes with some black in the crown; **back:** black, sometimes mottled with brown; **rump:** black, mottled with white; uppertail-coverts white; **tail:** outer three rectrices white, thinly tipped with black on the outer web; other rectrices with little white; **wing:** greater coverts, innermost secondaries, alula, and scapulars black; primaries black with white bases; median and lesser coverts white; **underparts:** white; **bill:** black; **legs** and **feet:** brown to black; **iris:** black.

Adult male in winter (Sept–Apr) like summer males, but the white areas are washed with pale rusty brown, particularly on the nape, crown, ear-coverts, and breast; black feathers on back and tail are edged with frosty brown; bill yellowish. Although there is a limited pre-alternate molt of the face feathers, adults wear into breeding plumage.

① Adult male   ② Adult female   ③ Juvenile/first-winter

First-winter male like adult males, but the juvenal wing, greater coverts, and tail feathers are retained, and they may have darker wings, and are more buffy on the crown, back, and underparts than adults.

Adult female (Apr–Aug) like adult males, but the crown is more likely to be dusky, and the black areas duller, often brownish.

Female in winter (Sept–Apr) like winter males.

First-winter female like adults, but with darker secondaries, a buffier head and browner underparts.

Juveniles (July–Aug) crown, back, and breast mottled grayish brown; back black, edged with buff; rump rusty brown; flanks pinkish; belly white; white on wings and tail as in adults; bill yellowish.

VOICE: The song of the Snow Bunting is a short, but musical, ***turee turee turee turiwee***, or ***sir plee si-chee whee-cher***. This is often given during an elaborate flight-song during which the male rises up to 15 m, then glides into the wind with his wings held in a 'V' above his body. Most of the singing takes place as he descends, and after he is on the ground. The call notes have been written as ***chee***, or a high-pitched ***tweet***, or a hard ***stirrp***.

HABITAT: Snow Buntings breed in the high Arctic in sparse, dry, rocky areas, such as shores, mountain slopes, and outcrops. In migration and winter they are characteristically found in fields, pastures, roadsides, and along the shore.

HABITS: In winter, Snow Buntings are usually found in flocks, often fairly large ones. As they move through a field, they appear to 'roll' along, like blowing snow, as birds toward the back of the flock leap-frog over those in the front. Although they usually stay on the ground, they not infrequently will fly into a tree or land on fences

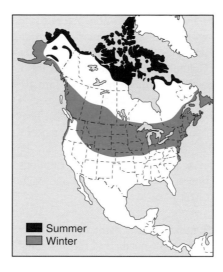

or telephone wires. Particularly where they are uncommon, they may associate with other species, such as Horned Larks and longspurs, but where they are common, they are more often in pure flocks. On the ground, they run rather than hop, and their flight is undulating. Flocks of males arrive on the breeding grounds well before females. As the weather gets warmer, they establish territories. Chases, fights, and flight-singing is common. During the molt in late summer Snow Buntings become quieter and more secretive; some can barely fly at this time.

BREEDING: *Nests* are placed on the ground, often in a crevice in rocks or frost-heaved peat, but sometimes in the open. The nest is a large thick-walled bulky cup of dried sedges, grasses, lichens, roots, leaves, and mosses lined with finer grasses and sometimes feathers, hair, and willow down. Nesting begins in late May and continues through July; the species is occasionally double-brooded. ***Eggs*,** 3–9, usually 4–7, are quite variable, but generally greenish or bluish, spotted, blotched, or scrawled with brown; the female alone builds the nest. ***Incubation*,** 10–15 days; female alone incubates; young fledge in 10–17 days. Both male and female Snow Buntings are occasionally bigamous.

RANGE: Circumpolar. In North America, ***breeds*** n Alaska and from w and sw Alaska (St. Lawrence and Nunivak islands, Pribilof Is., Aleutian Is., Alaska Peninsula, Shumagin Is., Kodiak I.), south in the mountains to s Alaska, nw British Columbia (Chilkat Pass), nw and c-e Mackenzie, c and se Keewatin (south to Eskimo Point), Hudson Bay (Nastapoka Is., Belcher Is.), n Quebec, and n Labrador (south perhaps to Nain). Snow Buntings are regularly seen in n Manitoba (Churchill) and n Ontario in summer, but are not known to breed that far south.

Resident in the Pribilof and Aleutian islands.

Winters from w Alaska, nw British Columbia across southern Canada, north to c Alberta, c Saskatchewan, s Manitoba, s Ontario (Thunder Bay, L. Nipissing, s Quebec (Aylmer, L. Saint-Jean, La Tabatière), and s Labrador (Battle Harbour), south through British Columbia, along the coast to nw California (rare), and e Washington, Oregon (fairly common in northeast; rare elsewhere), Idaho, n Utah (rare), n Colorado, n Kansas (rare), c Illinois, n Indiana, c Ohio, Pennsylvania, and south along the coast to North Carolina (Kitty Hawk). They are very rare or casual in winter south to s California (Kern Co.), Arizona, Nevada, ne New Mexico, e Texas, nw and c Oklahoma, Arkansas (2 records), Tennessee, c Mississippi, c Alabama, South Carolina, and ne Florida. Snow Buntings are irregular in winter, but are generally commonest in s Saskatchewan and Manitoba, the north-central States, and around the Great Lakes.

HISTORY: The Snow Bunting was first named *Emberiza nivalis,* 'snowy bunting,' in 1758 by Linnaeus. This, the most northerly breeding songbird, was doubtless well known by the great Swedish botanist and naturalist for, as a young man, he did extensive field work in Lapland.

It is difficult to assess historical changes in the abundance of Snow Buntings because they are irregular in their distribution, the irregularities probably reflecting different climatic conditions from year to year. In the 1800s Audubon said that they were found from Nova Scotia to Kentucky, where he saw them annually while he lived there. He called the species 'abundant.' Snow Buntings certainly are not abundant in Kentucky today, where they are considered to be rare transients and winter visitors. Nonetheless, human disturbance to their breeding grounds must have been negligible, and the clearing of forests and tall prairies would seem to have benefited them on their wintering grounds. If Audubon's account is accurate, perhaps the change in the abundance as far south as Kentucky reflects climatic amelioration.

GEOGRAPHIC VARIATION: *P. n. nivalis* is circumpolar in distribution. *P. n. townsendi,* which breeds on the Pribilof Is., the Aleutian Is., east to the tip of the Alaska, the Shumagin Is., Nunivak I., and on the Commander (Komandorskiye) Is., and Kamchatka, is larger than *P. n. nivalis,* but identical in coloration.

MEASUREMENTS: North America: (37 males): wing 106–116 (110), tail 61–74 (66), tarsus 20.6–23.1 (21.8), exposed culmen 9.7–11.4 (10.4), bill depth at base 5.8–6.9 (6.4); (17 females): wing 99–104 (102), tail 61–67 (64), tarsus 20.3–22.4 (21.3), exposed culmen 9.7–10.9 (10.2), bill depth 5.6–6.9 (6.1).

Bering Sea area: (22 males): wing 109–120 (113), tail 66–74 (71), tarsus 21.8–24.4 (23.1), exposed culmen 12.2–13.5 (12.7), bill depth 6.4–7.1 (6.6); (12 females): wing 103–116 (107), tail 62–69 (65), tarsus 20.8–23.4 (22.6), exposed culmen 10.9–13.5 (12.2), bill depth 6.1–6.9 (6.6) (Ridgway 1901).

Mass: (N=35) 42.2 g (34.0–56.0) (Alaska) (Dunning 1993).

62 **McKay's Bunting** *Plectrophenax hyperboreus* [535] PLATE **27**

IDENTIFICATION: 15–19 cm (*c.* 6–7.5 in), males slightly larger; sexes differ in coloration.

McKay's Bunting is a large, chunky sparrow that is white except for the wing-tips, and the tip of the center of the tail. Females have some dark mottling on the back.

Similar species: McKay's Bunting is much whiter than Snow Bunting: male McKay's Buntings have a white back and rump, little black in their tail, and no black in the bend of their wings. Females have a whitish rather than a brownish back, with little black in the tail. Juveniles are similar to juvenile Snow Buntings, and not separable with certainty.

Summer male (Apr–Aug)—*Head:* white; *back:* white, rarely with a few narrow black streaks, and the posterior scapulars with black blotches; *rump:* white; uppertail-coverts white; *tail:* outer four rectrices white; middle two to four rectrices black-tipped; *wing:* white, with tips of outer five primaries black; tertials black; alula white, sometimes with some black; *underparts:* white; *bill:* black; *legs* and *feet:* brown to black; *iris:* black.

Winter male (Sept–Apr) variable, but like summer males, but the crown, ear-coverts and breast are lightly washed with pale rusty brown; black feathers on back and tail are lightly edged with frosty brown; bill yellowish or pinkish. Adults apparently wear into breeding plumage.

① Adult male   ② Adult male or female   ③ First-winter male
(minimum black)   (maximum black)   or female

Adult female (Apr–Aug) like adult males, but the crown may be dusky, and the back narrowly streaked with black; the alula is black. The middle two rectrices are dusky to the base; the others may be dusky on the inner webs.

Female in winter (Sept–Apr) like winter males, but average darker; variable.

First-winter female like adults, but with darker secondaries, a buffier head and browner underparts.

Juveniles (July–Aug) crown, back, and breast mottled grayish brown; back black, edged with buff; rump rusty brown; flanks pinkish; belly white; white on wings and tail as in adults; bill yellowish. They are paler on average than Snow Bunting juveniles.

VOICE: The song has been described as a loud and sweet flute-like warble, like the song of the Western Meadowlark, but shorter. Both the songs and calls resemble those of the Snow Bunting.

HABITAT: McKay's Bunting breeds in upland, rocky tundra. In winter they occur principally along the coast.

HABITS: The behavior of McKay's Bunting is doubtless much like that of the Snow Bunting, but little has been written about it. Flight-singing occurs.

BREEDING: *Nest* is placed on the ground, often in a crevice in rocks or in hollow logs. The nest is a large thick-walled bulky cup of dried grasses, lined with finer grasses and sometimes feathers, hair, and willow down. Nesting begins in June. *Eggs*, about 5, are greenish and dotted with pale brown; probably the female alone builds the nest. *Incubation*, no information.

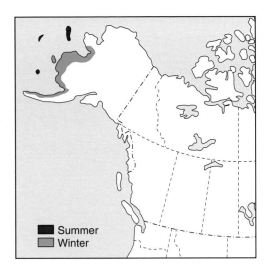

RANGE: ***Breeds*** on islands in the Bering Sea (Hall and St. Mathew islands, and occasionally in the Pribilof Is. and on St. Lawrence I.).

Winters along the coast of the Bering Sea in w Alaska (including Nunivak I.), from Nome south and west to Cold Bay. It has been reported north of the Bering Strait at Kotzebue in winter. They are casual in winter to the Aleutians (Adak, Unalaska), and south-coastal Alaska (Kodiak I., Homer). Casual south to Washington (Ocean Shores, Dec) and Oregon (Columbia R., Feb–Mar).

HISTORY: The first specimens of this little-known bunting were taken in 1879, by E. W. Nelson (after whom Nelson's Sharp-tailed Sparrow is named), from St. Michael, along Norton Sound, and Nulato on the Yukon R. Nelson commented on the differences between these specimens and the more common Snow Bunting, but did not suspect that they were a different species. Working under the harsh conditions of western Alaska, Nelson returned to Washington, then moved to the southwest because of tuberculosis. When Robert Ridgway described McKay's Snowflake as a new species in 1884, no ornithologist had yet seen or collected it on its breeding grounds. Ridgway named this species in honor of Charles Leslie McKay, who died before he became 28 while doing field work in Alaska. He was reported to have perished during a storm, but there was a rumor that foul play was involved. McKay collected specimens of the new bunting at Nushagak, and these, as well as those collected by Nelson, were used by Ridgway in describing the species. Charles H. Townsend was the first ornithologist to visit Hall I., and he collected adult and juvenile McKay's Buntings there in September, 1885.

McKay's Buntings are reported regularly from the Pribilof Is., but only rarely nest there; some *Plectrophenax* from the Pribilofs appear to be hybrids.

GEOGRAPHIC VARIATION: None described. McKay's Bunting apparently hybridizes with Snow Bunting on St. Lawrence I. and the Pribilof Is.

MEASUREMENTS: North America: (13 males): wing 110–119 (114), tail 66–75 (71), tarsus 21.1–23.6 (22.4), exposed culmen 11.2–12.7 (12.2), bill depth at base 6.4–7.4 (6.9); (14 females): wing 104–109 (107), tail 64–69 (67), tarsus 20.8–23.1 (21.8), exposed culmen 10.7–11.7 (11.2), bill depth 6.1–6.9 (6.4) (Ridgway 1901).

Mass: (N=11) 54.5 g (38.0–62.0) (Alaska) (Dunning 1993). (3 breeding males: 41, 44, and 45 g; 1 breeding female: 41.5 g; Alaska Museum.)

Reference: Kessel and Gibson (1976).

LIST OF PLATES

1 **Olive Sparrow** *Arremonops rufivirgatus*

   a   ***Adult:*** A chunky, secretive species. Note dull olive upperparts, pale olive-gray head and underparts and olive-brown flanks. Distinctive head pattern shows cinnamon-brown lateral crown-stripes, pale grayish supercilium and thin dusky eye-line. Bill grayish-pink.

   b   ***Juvenile:*** Generally buffier than adult, especially on face and breast. Sides of neck, breast and flanks sparsely streaked dusky brown. Greater and median coverts edged buff forming two obscure wing-bars.

2 **Green-tailed Towhee** *Pipilo chlorurus*

   a   ***Adult winter or first-winter:*** Unmistakable. Distinctive head pattern shows reddish chestnut crown, dark gray forehead, gray face offset by white supraloral patch and submoustachial stripe and blackish lores and malar stripe. Upperparts dull olive heavily washed grayish. Wings and tail edged bright yellow-green. Underparts whitish with gray breast and cinnamon-brown flanks.

   b   ***Adult in summer plumage:*** Similar to above except upperparts are a purer olive tone.

   c   ***Juvenile:*** Quite different from adult. Crown dull brown streaked black. Sides of neck, breast and flanks boldly streaked blackish. Upperparts buff and brown boldly streaked blackish. Edging to wing-coverts and tertials buff. Primaries, secondaries and tail edged bright yellow-green.

   d   ***Juvenile molting into first-winter plumage:*** This individual is molting in some olive scapulars and gray breast feathers.

Olive Sparrow

1a

1b

Green-tailed Towhee

2a

2d

2b

2c

3 Eastern Towhee *Pipilo erythrophthalmus*

a ***Adult male* Pipilo e. erythrophthalmus — *Eastern Towhee:*** Upper-parts and hood black contrasting with rusty orange flanks, white belly and rich buff undertail-coverts. On closed wing white speculum and edges to outer primaries and tertials. Iris red.

b ***Adult female:*** Similar pattern to male but with upperparts and hood warm brown rather than black.

c ***Adult male:*** Southeastern form with whitish iris.

d ***First-summer male:*** Very similar to adult male but note contrast between worn and brown-looking primaries and secondaries (and some coverts) and black rest of wing.

e ***Juvenile male molting into first-winter plumage:*** Obviously highly variable. This individual is mostly in juvenile plumage with bold black streaking on upperparts, breast and flanks and buff tips to wing coverts. Note some black feathering on face and scapulars and some orange on flanks. Iris brown.

f ***Adult female* Pipilo e. erythrophthalmus *in flight:*** Mostly brown with extensive white in tail, white speculum and whitish edges to outer primaries and tertials.

4 Spotted Towhee *Pipilo maculatus*

a ***Adult male* Pipilo m. curtatus — *Spotted Towhee:*** Unmistakable. Similar to Eastern Towhee but with variable white spotting on mantle and scapulars forming distinct lateral stripes. Note also different wing pattern with white tips to coverts and lack of speculum.

b ***Adult female:*** Similar to male but with upperparts and hood slaty-gray rather than black.

c ***Adult female* Pipilo m. curtatus *in flight:*** Compare with Eastern Towhee. Note slaty-gray upperparts, two white wing-bars and lack of speculum.

d ***Juvenile male:*** Upperparts and head brown lightly streaked darker. Some buffy spotting on scapulars. Underparts pale buff streaked dusky. Wings with two buffy bars, edges to tertials and outer primaries.

Eastern Towhee

3a

3b

3c

3d

3f

3e

4c

4d

4b

Spotted Towhee

4a

5 California Towhee *Pipilo crissalis*

a   *Adult:* Quite drab gray-brown upperparts with grayish underparts. Breast and flanks washed brown with contrastingly rusty cinnamon undertail-coverts. Head with grayish supercilium and ear-coverts and buffy cinnamon loral area and throat. Throat bordered with dusky streaks.

b   *Juvenile:* Differs from adult in having breast and flanks lightly streaked dusky brown. Lores and throat paler buff. Two narrow buffy wing-bars.

6 Canyon Towhee *Pipilo fuscus*

a   *Adult:* Much paler and grayer than California Towhee. Upperparts and face grayish tinged brown with contrasting rusty crown. Supraloral, submoustachial and throat areas pale buff. Throat bordered with dark streaks with dusky smudge on centre of breast. Underparts gray, paler on belly, with contrasting rusty cinnamon undertail-coverts.

b   *Juvenile:* Differs from adult in having breast and flanks boldly streaked dusky brown. Crown and ear-coverts 'warm' brown. Wings with two narrow buffy bars.

7 Abert's Towhee *Pipilo aberti*

a   *Adult:* Overall a 'warmer' looking bird than the preceding two species. Upperparts brown washed gray contrasting with buffy cinnamon underparts. Undertail-coverts brighter rusty cinnamon. Distinctive head pattern shows blackish loral area extending around bill to chin and malar area. Supraloral pale gray.

b   *Juvenile:* Similar to adult but breast and flanks lightly streaked brown. Pale buffy supraloral, warmer brown upperparts and wide buffy cinnamon wing-bars.

California Towhee

5a

5b

Canyon Towhee

6b

6a

7b

7a

Abert's Towhee

8 **White-collared Seedeater** *Sporophila torqueola*

    a   *Adult male* **Sporophila t. sharpei:** Very small. Stubby bill with convex culmen. Note blackish head with white lower eye-crescent. Throat and malar area are white contrasting with pale buff underparts. Variable dusky breast mottling. Upperparts dark grayish brown streaked darker. Wings and tail black. Wings with two whitish wing-bars and variable white 'speculum' at base of primaries.

    b   *Adult female:* Bicolored appearance. Generally brownish above and buffy below. Wings dark brown with two buff wing-bars. This individual lacks the 'speculum' patch.

    c   *First-winter male:* Similar to female but wings are black with whitish or buff wing-bars.

9 **Yellow-faced Grassquit** *Tiaris olivacea*

    a   *Adult male* **Tiaris o. olivacea:** Very small. Stubby bill with straight culmen. Basically olive above and grayish below. Head pattern distinct. Short supercilium, lower eye-crescent and throat bright rich yellow. Face and breast black. Slight variation between races.

    b   *Adult female:* Similar but duller than male. Shows only a trace of the male head pattern. Shorter supercilium, eye-crescent and chin pale lemon yellow. Face and throat/breast mottled dusky-gray.

    c   *First-winter male:* Similar to female but head pattern approaching that of adult male in color intensity and demarcation.

10 **Black-faced Grassquit** *Tiaris bicolor*

    a   *Adult male:* Very small. Stubby bill with straight culmen. Quite dark-looking. Face, breast and belly sooty black. Upperparts and crown dull olive. Flanks and undertail-coverts grayish. Bill mostly dark gray, pinkish on cutting edges.

    b   *Adult female:* Head and upperparts dull olive. Underparts pale grayish washed olive on breast and flanks. Bill with pinkish lower mandible.

    c   *First-winter male:* Similar to female except variable blackish mottling on face, throat and breast.

White-collared Seedeater

8c

8b

8a

Yellow-faced Grassquit

9c

9b

9a

Black-faced Grassquit

10c

10b

10a

12 Botteri's Sparrow *Aimophila botterii*

a   *Adult* **Aimophila b. arizonae** *in fresh plumage:* A large, hefty-billed *Aimophila*. Upperparts mostly brown with feathers showing black line down center and edged gray. Uppertail-coverts similar. Head with brown crown and post-ocular, grayish ear-coverts and pale buff supercilium and malar area. Wings mostly brown with diffuse paler edges to coverts but note broad tertials black edged brown. Underparts whitish suffused buff on breast and flanks — unmarked. Large bill grayish horn.

b   *Adult* **A. b. texana** *in fresh plumage:* Overall pattern similar to *arizonae* but much grayer on upperparts and head and with underparts paler with grayish buff wash on breast and flanks. On all Botteri's note greenish yellow tinge to lesser wing-coverts and yellow bend of wing.

c   *Adult* **A. b. arizonae** *in flight — worn plumage:* Appears bulky and laboured in flight. In worn plumage looks very drab and brown but notice streaked back, blackish tertials and black stripe down center of central tail. Abrasion and sun-bleaching may result in outer tail appearing pale and buffy.

d   *Adult* **A. b. arizonae** *in worn plumage:* This late summer individual is heavily abraded and sun-bleached. Most gray and buff fringes are lost and the bird is basically drab brown above and pale buffy gray below. Note blackish central streaks to mantle feathers and uppertail-coverts and shape of head and bill.

e   *Juvenile* **A. b. arizonae:** Upperparts buff-brown streaked black. Head mostly buffy with black centers to crown feathers and brown ear-coverts. Underparts buffy, slightly paler on throat and belly with dusky brown streaking on breast and flanks.

13 Cassin's Sparrow *Aimophila cassinii*

a   *Adult in fresh plumage:* Slightly smaller than Botteri's with proportionally smaller bill and slight crested appearance. Upperparts with feathers brown, broadly edged gray with black subterminal crescents and bars. Uppertail-coverts similar. Tail has central feathers pale and conspicuously 'laddered' with black. Head mostly gray with brown crown, post-ocular and crescent on lower edge of ear-coverts. Wings have coverts and tertials edged pale gray. Underparts pale gray but note brown spotting on sides of breast and rear flanks.

b   *Adult in worn plumage:* Differs from similarly worn Botteri's in lack-black streaked upperparts; instead shows some dusky crossbars, having a brown crescent on lower edge of ear-coverts and displaying some dusky spotting on rear flanks. Note also bill and head shape.

c   *Adult in flight — fresh plumage:* The tail pattern is distinctive in this plumage. It is mostly blackish with white outer web to outer feathers and pale grayish tips to most feathers. The central pair are buffy and 'laddered' with black along the centre.

d   *Adult in flight — worn plumage:* The tail pattern described above is largely lost due to abrasion. However, the central feathers should still appear paler than the rest of the tail. Otherwise can look very similar to Botteri's in this state of wear.

e   *Juvenile:* Upperparts similar pattern to adult but edged buff. Underparts whitish, washed buff on breast with dusky brown streaking on breast and flanks.

Botteri's Sparrow

12a

12b

12c

12d

12e

13a

13b

13c

13d

13e

Cassin's Sparrow

11 Bachman's Sparrow *Aimophila aestivalis*

a *Adult* **Aimophila a. aestivalis:** A chunky *Aimophila* with a large bill; not dissimilar to Botteri's Sparrow. Upperparts gray with black-and-chestnut feather centres. Head mostly buffy gray with dull chestnut lateral crown and post-ocular stripes. Wings mostly chestnut with gray edges but note broad tertials black edged whitish. Underparts pale gray with buffy gray wash on breast and flanks. Sides of breast show limited chestnut streaking.

b *Adult* **A. a. aestivalis:** Another view showing underparts more clearly. *A. a. bachmani* is very similar.

c *Adult* **A. a. illinoensis *(breeds Indiana and Illinois south to E Texas)*:** Much more rufescent on upperparts with dark chestnut feather centres. Head has rufous-chestnut lateral crown and post-ocular stripes contrasting with pale buff supercilium and submoustachial and buffy gray ear-coverts. Underparts are pale buff streaked rufous on breast-sides.

d *Juvenile* **A. a. aestivalis:** Overall quite buffy with black streaking on back and crown. Wings with rufous and buff feather edges to coverts tertials. Underparts buff, paler on belly with dusky spotting and streaking on neck, breast, and flanks.

14 Rufous-winged Sparrow *Aimophila carpalis*

a *Adult in fresh plumage:* A medium-sized, slim *Aimophila*. Upperparts grayish brown with narrow dusky streaking. Rump grayer. Head mostly pale gray with conspicuous rusty crown and post-ocular stripe. Whitish submoustachial bordered with short dusky moustachial and malar. Wings show buff edges to coverts and tertials and have rusty lesser coverts (usually mostly hidden). Underparts mostly pale gray.

b *Juvenile:* Differs from adult in having crown brown streaked dusky, usually with grayish central stripe. Ear-coverts are brown and underparts whitish, washed buff on breast with dusky streaking on breast and flanks.

15 Rufous-crowned Sparrow *Aimophila ruficeps*

a *Adult* **Aimophila r. scottii *(Texas)*:** A fairly robust *Aimophila*. Grayish brown upperparts with chestnut feather centers. Head mostly gray with contrasting rufous crown and post-ocular and white supraloral, eye-ring and submoustachial. Dusky malar stripe. Underparts pale gray, whiter throat and belly.

b *Adult* **A. r. ruficeps *(Sierra Nevada, California)*:** Smaller and darker than *scottii* and *eremoeca*. Upperparts streaked brown and black. Head has buffy gray cast and is less contrasty. Underparts are dull, sullied buffy gray, whiter on throat and belly.

c *Adult* **A. r. eremoeca *(Great Plains to SW New Mexico)*:** Very similar to *scottii* (many individuals cannot be accurately attributed to race) but averages purer ashy gray on upperparts and head with paler rufous crown edged with gray.

d *Juvenile* **A. r. scottii:** Upperparts buffy brown streaked darker. Crown brown. Underparts pale buffy gray streaked dusky gray on breast and flanks. Wings with buffy edges to coverts forming two narrow bars.

Bachman's Sparrow

11a

11c

11b

11d

14a

14b

Rufous-winged Sparrow

15a

15b

Rufous-crowned Sparrow

15c

15d

16 American Tree Sparrow *Spizella arborea*

a **Adult S. a. arborea *in summer plumage:*** Note rusty crown and post-ocular stripe. Bill with dark upper and yellow lower mandible. Upperparts a variegated pattern of buff, chestnut and black, white wing-bars, underparts whitish with rusty sides to breast.

b **First-winter *(Dec):*** Similar to above but 'warmer' overall with more extensive buffy brown on flanks and buffier edges to mantle. Note the dark smudge on breast center.

c **Juvenile:** Pale grayish white on face and neck with extensive dusky streaking on head, neck-sides and breast.

d **Adult S. a. ochracea *in summer plumage (breeds Alaska and Yukon to SW British Columbia):*** Differs from *arborea* in distinct 'hoare-frosted' plumage with wider white wing-bars and tertial edges.

20 Field Sparrow *Spizella pusilla*

a **Adult S. p. pusilla:** Note rusty crown and post-ocular stripe. Pale eye-ring usually obvious. Pinkish bill, grayish white underparts with rusty sides to breast and white wing-bars create distinctive look.

b **First-winter *(Oct):*** Similar to above but 'warmer' overall. Buffy supercilium, breast and flanks and browner ear-coverts.

c **Juvenile:** Paler and grayer on head, lacking the rusty crown. Underparts with buffy wash across breast and sparse dusky streaking. Wing-bars buffy.

d **Adult S. p. arenacea *(breeds east to Minnesota, central Kansas and Oklahoma):*** Much paler than *pusilla*; grayer on head, lacking the rusty post-ocular, whiter on underparts with buff smudge on breast sides.

21 Worthen's Sparrow *Spizella wortheni*

a **Adult:** Similar to a Field Sparrow. Note rufous cap, gray forehead and face, obvious whitish eye-ring, pink bill, indistinct buffy wing-bars, dark legs and gray rump.

22 Black-chinned Sparrow *Spizella atrogularis*

a **Adult male S. a. cana *(breeds southern California):*** Note gray head rump and underparts, extensive black around base of bill and on chin/throat, and richly colored buff and chestnut mantle and wings.

b **Adult female:** Similar to male but generally lacks the black head markings.

c **Juvenile:** Similar to adult female but head and breast washed brownish with indistinct dusky striations on breast and flanks.

d **Adult male S. a. evura *(breeds east of Sierra Nevada east to W Texas):*** Larger and somewhat paler than *cana*.

American Tree Sparrow

16c

16a

16b

16d

20a

20c **Field Sparrow**

20d

20b

Worthen's Sparrow

21a

22b

22c

22a

22d

Black-chinned Sparrow

17 **Chipping Sparrow** *Spizella passerina*

a   *Adult S. p. passerina in summer plumage:* Distinctive head pattern with long, narrow white supercilium, chestnut crown and black-bordered white forehead. Rump obviously gray. Bill black.

b   *Adult in summer plumage head-on:* Pattern distinctive.

c   *Adult in winter plumage (Dec):* Similar to above except crown streaked black, ear-coverts brown and supercilium, breast and flanks washed buff. Bill with pinkish lower mandible.

d   *First-winter (Oct):* Generally 'warmer' overall with buffy head, breast and flanks, crown brown streaked black — sometimes with buffy gray central stripe. Bill mostly flesh-pink.

e   *First-winter head-on:* Similar to, but less distinct than Clay-colored Sparrow — see below.

f   *First-winter in flight:* Grayish rump usually obvious.

g   *Juvenile:* Similar to first winter but with conspicuously streaked underparts and sides of neck. Rump can be brownish gray.

18 **Clay-colored Sparrow** *Spizella pallida*

a   *Adult in summer plumage:* Note especially the distinctive head pattern together with gray collar, brownish rump and buff wash across breast.

b   *Adult in summer plumage head-on:* The white central crown-stripe and supercilium together with the dark bordered buffy brown ear-coverts are diagnostic.

c   *First-winter (Oct):* Similar to adult but generally 'warmer' overall. Buff wash to crown-stripe, supercilium, breast and flanks.

d   *First-winter in flight:* Rump brown: generally buffer overall than Chipping and Brewer's Sparrows.

e   *Juvenile:* As first winter except distinct dusky streaking on breast and flanks and sides of neck. Head markings slightly less distinct.

19 **Brewer's Sparrow** *Spizella breweri*

a   *Adult S. b. breweri:* Buffy gray overall appearance. Head with streaked crown and noticeable whitish eye-ring. Upperparts narrowly streaked blackish. Underparts whitish with grayish buff wash across breast.

b   *Adult head-on:* Note especially streaked crown (lacking paler central stripe) and whitish eye-ring.

c   *Adult/First-winter in flight:* Buffy gray overall with no obvious features. Rump gray-brown.

d   *Juvenile:* Similar to adult but with dense dusky brown streaking on breast, flanks and neck-sides.

e   *Adult S. b. taverneri 'Timberline Sparrow' (breeds Yukon, NW British Columbia to W Alberta):* Similar to *breweri* but 'colder' and grayer with bold black streaking on upperparts. Underparts whiter.

f   *Juvenile taverneri:* Similar to *breweri* but more boldly streaked with black on upperparts and underparts.

Chipping Sparrow

17b 17a 17e 17d 17f 17c 17g

Clay-colored Sparrow

18b 18a 18e 18d 18c

Brewer's Sparrow

19b 19a 19c 19f 19e 19d

23 Vesper Sparrow *Pooecetes gramineus*

a   *Adult P. g. gramineus:* A chunky sparrow with very short primary extension beyond long tertials. Upperparts gray-brown streaked darker. Distinct head pattern with white eye-ring and white submoustachial contrasting with black malar. Underparts whitish narrowly streaked dusky on breast and flanks. Chestnut lesser coverts are distinctive but often hidden.

b   *Adult in flight:* Basically brown and streaky but note extensive white in outer two tail feathers and chestnut lesser wing-coverts.

c   *Juvenile:* Paler than adult, especially on head and neck. Neck, head, breast and flanks narrowly streaked blackish.

d   *Adult Pooecetes g. confinis:* Similar to *gramineus* but somewhat paler and grayer on upperparts and with finer, sparse streaking on underparts.

24 Lark Sparrow *Chondestes grammacus*

a   *Adult C. g. strigatus:* A chunky, heavy-billed sparrow. Head pattern is striking; chestnut lateral crown-stripes and ear-coverts contrast with white and buff supercilium, buff crown-stripe, white submoustachial and lower ocular area and black malar. Otherwise buffy-brown above, streaked darker and pale gray below with buff wash on flanks and dark smudge on breast center. Wings show two buffy bars and speculum.

b   *Adult in flight:* Note especially striking amount of white in tail, almost forming a terminal band.

c   *Juvenile:* Similar to adult but head pattern much reduced with chestnut replaced with brown. Crown is streaked darker. Underparts are whitish with breast and flanks spotted and streaked dusky.

29 Lark Bunting *Calamospiza melanocorys*

a   *Adult male in summer plumage:* A hefty, large-billed sparrow. Unmistakable. Mostly black, grayer on mantle with large white panel on wing-coverts and tertials. Bill blue-gray.

b   *Adult male molting into summer plumage (Mar–Apr):* Obviously highly variable. This individual has molted-in much new black feathering on head and body. Molting individuals can appear somewhat untidy.

c   *Adult male in winter plumage:* Upperparts grayish brown streaked black. Head with crown brown streaked black, brown ear-coverts, buffy supercilium and black throat. Underparts whitish variably mottled and streaked black. Wings as summer male but inner greater coverts and tertials are edged buff.

d   *Adult or first-winter female:* Upperparts buffy brown streaked dusky. Head with complex pattern of buff and brown with whitish supraloral, eye-ring and submoustachial. Underparts whitish streaked brown on breast and flanks. Closed wing with whitish panel on outer coverts.

e   *Adult female in flight:* Appear tubby and short-tailed. Note buffy-white wing panel and white tips to tail feathers forming terminal bar.

f   *Juvenile:* Similar to female but scaly-looking on mantle and underpart with fine streaking on neck and breast. Bill pinkish with dark tip.

Vesper Sparrow

23a

23b

23c

23d

Lark Sparrow

24a

24b

24c

Lark Bunting

29a

29b

29e

29c

29d

29f

BLACK-THROATED, SAGE, BELL'S AND
FIVE-STRIPED SPARROWS

PLATE 10

25 Black-throated Sparrow *Amphispiza bilineata*

a **Adult Amphispiza b. bilineata *(breeds central Texas):*** Upperparts mostly grayish tinged brown on lower back and rump. Distinctive head pattern with gray crown and nape, narrow white supercilium edged black, gray ear-coverts shading to black on lores, and white submoustachial contrasting with black throat and upper breast. Wings brown with coverts and tertials edged paler. Underparts pale gray, darker on breast.

b ***Juvenile* A. b. bilineata:** Quite different from adult. Upperparts brown streaked darker. Head with grayish brown crown and ear-coverts contrasting with whitish supercilium and throat. Wings brown with distinct buffy bars. Underparts white streaked dusky brown on breast and flanks.

c ***Adult* A. b. bilineata *in flight:*** Grayish brown above with distinctive black, white and gray head pattern. Note black tail with whitish outer web to outer feathers.

d ***Adult* A. b. deserticola *(breeds Oregon, Wyoming and W Colorado south):*** Same overall pattern as *bilineata* but averages slightly larger and paler with more extensive brown wash to upperparts and nape.

27 Sage Sparrow *Amphispiza nevadensis*

a ***Adult* Amphispiza n. nevadensis:** Upperparts sandy grayish brown very narrowly streaked dusky brown. Head purer gray with contrasting white supraloral, eye-crescents and submoustachial and dusky malar stripe. Wings brown with buff edges to coverts and rusty tinge to tertials. Underparts whitish with some suffused brown streaking on flanks and a dark smudge on center of breast. Bill mostly dark horn.

b ***Adult* A. n. nevadensis *in flight:*** Note sandy-colored upperparts and gray head contrasting with mostly blackish tail. Outer web of outer tail feathers may be white in fresh birds.

c ***Juvenile* A. n. nevadensis:** Buffy brown above with bold black streaking. Crown and ear-coverts gray-brown streaked darker. Wings show two 'spotted' whitish bars. Underparts are buffy white with dense black streaking on breast and flanks. Bill with pale base to lower mandible.

d ***Adult* A. n. canescens *(breeds central California):*** Overall pattern same as *nevadensis* but more richly colored with darker ear-coverts, blacker malar stripe, more rufescent wings and darker streaking on breast-sides and flanks.

26 Bell's Sparrow *Amphispiza belli*

a ***Adult* Amphispiza b. belli:** Somewhat smaller and smaller-billed than Sage Sparrow. Overall pattern is similar to Sage but note much darker deep brown upperparts and darker gray head. The malar is black contrasting with the white submoustachial. Wings are dark brown with conspicuous buffy edges to coverts and tertials. White underparts are washed cinnamon-brown on flanks with blackish streaking on breast-sides and flanks and blackish smudge on breast center.

28 Five-striped Sparrow *Amphispiza quinquestriata*

a ***Adult:*** An attractive dark sparrow restricted to SE Arizona. Upperparts nape and crown are rich rusty brown, tinged gray. Head has distinctive black-and-white pattern. Wings rich brown with paler buffy edges to coverts and tertials. Underparts are mostly mid-gray with whiter throat and belly and blackish smudge on breast center.

b ***Adult in flight:*** Appears mostly dark rich brown with contrasting black tail. Whitish outer web to outer tail feathers may be visible on fresh birds.

Black-throated Sparrow

25a

25c

25b

25d

Sage Sparrow

27b

27a

Bell's Sparrow

26a

27c

27d

28b

28a

Five-striped Sparrow

30 Savannah Sparrow *Passerculus sandwichensis*

a   ***Adult* Passerculus s. mediogrisus *in fresh plumage (widespread in East):***
Typical Savannah Sparrow. Upperparts brown, streaked black with bold pale
'braces.' Head shows whitish central crown-stripe and variable yellow suffusion on
supraloral (often more extensive). Wings mostly brown with buff edges to coverts
and often a rufous panel on tertials and secondaries. Underparts white narrowly
streaked blackish. Tail with whitish outer web to outer feathers (often noticeable
in flight).

b   ***Juvenile* Passerculus s. mediogrisus:** Overall much buffier than adult. Upperparts,
neck and underparts profusely streaked blackish. Wings with broader buff edges to
coverts.

c   ***Adult* Passerculus s. sandwichensis *(breeds Aleutian Is., Alaska):*** Much larger
than *mediogrisus* and typically paler overall. Note 'colder' grayer plumage and whiter
'braces' on mantle.

d   ***Adult* Passerculus s. labradorius:** Very similar to typical *mediogrisus* but tends to be
darker, more rufescent, brown on upperparts and has underparts more boldly streaked
black. Occurs in the NE region.

e   ***Adult* Passerculus s. nevadensis:** Typical of mid-western races. Appears paler and
buffier than typical *mediogrisus*. Supraloral and face tend to be buffy yellow. However,
note there is much variation in this region and many individuals cannot be reliably
identified as to race.

f   ***Adult* Passerculus s. nevadensis:** Very similar to *alaudinus* but even paler. Note
especially whitish supercilium and restricted, narrow brown streaking on breast. Again
caution is advised due to intergradation.

g   ***Adult* Passerculus s. rostratus — *Large billed Savannah Sparrow (winter
visitor to Salton Sea and coastal S California):*** Large with very large bill. Grayish
brown upperparts streaked dusky. Lacks yellow on supraloral. Underparts whitish
streaked brown. Essentially unmistakable in its limited range.

h   ***Adult* Passerculus s. beldingi — *Belding's Savannah Sparrow (breeds
California saltmarshes):*** Small, dark and heavily streaked. Upperparts dark brown
streaked black. Yellow supraloral. Underparts white with bold, thick black streaking
right down to belly.

i   ***Adult* Passerculus s. princeps — *Ipswich Sparrow (breeds Sable I., Nova
Scotia):*** Large and conspicuously pale. Upperparts grayish brown, streaked dusky
with prominent whitish 'braces' on mantle. Pale yellow supraloral. Wings mostly pale
rust with pale buff edges to coverts and tertials. Underparts white with narrow rusty
brown streaking on breast and flanks. Distinctive in its limited range.

Savannah Sparrow

30a

30b

30c

30d

30e

30f

30g

30h

30i

33 Henslow's Sparrow *Ammodramus henslowii*

a **Adult in slightly worn plumage — early summer:** A large-billed, flat-crowned *Ammodramus*. Upperparts scaly-looking due to pale buff fringes. Head and collar pale olive with black lateral crown-stripes, post-ocular and edges to rich buff submoustachial. Wings mostly chestnut. Underparts white, washed buff on breast with narrow black streaking on breast and flanks. Bill pink with dark culmen.

b **Adult in flight:** Note extensive chestnut in back and wings contrasting with olive collar and black-and-olive head pattern.

c **First-winter or adult in fresh plumage:** As adult summer except brighter looking with broader pale fringes to upperparts and wing-coverts. Note pale buff central crown-stripe.

d **Juvenile:** Paler overall than adult with broad buff fringes to feathers on upperparts and wing-coverts. Head mostly buffy olive with similar, though more diffuse, pattern as adult. Underparts white, washed buff on breast with limited black spotting on breast-sides.

32 Grasshopper Sparrow *Ammodramus savannarum*

a **Adult Ammodramus s. pratensis (eastern region) — in fresh plumage:** A beautifully marked *Ammodramus*. Upperparts black-and-chestnut with buff feather edges forming 'braces' (buff edges of mantle feathers). Head mostly buffy with black lateral crown and post-ocular. Central crown-stripe is pale buff and the supraloral is tinged rich ochraceous. Wings show two buffy bars and broad buff edges to tertials. Underparts pale buff with ochraceous streaking on breast-sides.

b **Adult A. s. pratensis in flight:** Very 'quail-like.' Note complex pattern of black-and-chestnut and gray-and-buff on upperparts and two pale buff wing-bars. Lesser wing-coverts tinged green.

c **Adult A. s. pratensis in worn plumage — mid-summer:** Feather wear causes buff fringes to abrade and sun-bleaching results in a paler, browner version of above.

d **Juvenile A. s. pratensis:** Differs from adult in having scaly-looking upperparts and wing-coverts, whiter supercilium, face and underparts, warm brown ear-coverts and light blackish streaking on breast.

e **Adult A. s. ammolegus (south-east Arizona):** Similar to *pratensis* but is more rufous, especially on scapulars and wing-coverts, and shows distinct chestnut streaking on breast-sides and flanks.

f **Adult A. s. floridanus (Florida):** Differs from other races in being darker and grayer on upperparts with broader black feather-centers.

g **Adult A. s. perpallidus (widespread):** Very similar to *pratensis* but is somewhat paler overall with paler ash-gray and buff edges to back feathers and paler buff underparts.

31 Baird's Sparrow *Ammodramus bairdii*

a **Adult in fresh plumage:** A chunky *Ammodramus*. Upperparts black and chestnut with broad pale buff fringes or 'braces.' Head and collar mostly buff with fine black streaking on lateral crown and neck. Ear-coverts brown edged black with ochraceous supraloral. Underparts white with sparse blackish streaking on breast.

b **Adult — detail showing crown and nape:** Note the rich ochraceous patch on central crown and upper nape; this tends to become more obvious with wear.

c **Adult in flight:** Lacks the spiky-tailed effect common to other Ammodramus. The pale buff 'braces' and edges to wing-coverts and tertials are usually obvious. The outer webs of the outer tail feathers can appear whitish (not unlike Savannah Sparrow).

d **Juvenile:** Differs from adult in being very scaly-looking on upperparts and wing-coverts. Underparts white, washed buff on breast with blackish streaking on breast and flanks.

Henslow's Sparrow

33a
33b
33d
33c
32b
32a
32d
32c
Grasshopper
Sparrow
32g
32f
32e
31c
31a
31b
31d

Baird's Sparrow

34 LeConte's Sparrow *Ammodramus leconteii*

a *Adult in early summer:* Distinctive. Upperparts buffy with black streaking contrasting with ash-gray collar streaked chestnut. Head shows black lateral crown and post-ocular stripe contrasting with whitish crown-stripe and rich buff supercilium and malar region. Underparts white washed buff on breast and flanks with limited black streaking on breast sides and along flanks.

b *Adult — detail showing crown and nape:* Note the gray collar and ear-coverts, and black, white, and buff head pattern.

c *Adult in flight:* Note the sharply pointed tail feathers typical of the genus. LeConte's look pale and stripy in flight. Note buff edges to wing-coverts and tertials.

d *First-winter or adult in fresh plumage:* As summer adult except brighter looking with more chestnut in feather centers on mantle and scapulars. Some individuals may retain some juvenile streaking on breast.

e *Juvenile in fresh plumage:* Overall buffy, browner on mantle with bold black streaking on back. Lacks the gray collar and white crown-stripe of adult. Narrow dusky streaking across breast and along flanks. Note dusky smudge on lower edge of ear-coverts.

f *Juvenile in worn plumage (Oct — some birds migrate in this plumage):* Similar to above but variably worn and paler with somewhat less streaking on underparts.

35 Saltmarsh Sharp-tailed Sparrow *Ammodramus caudacutus*

a *Adult Ammodramus c. caudacutus:* Upperparts olive-brown streaked dusky with whitish 'braces' (white edges to mantle feathers). Head shows gray central crown contrasting with black-streaked chestnut lateral stripes. Ear-coverts gray surrounded by rich buff supercilium and malar region. Wings mostly brown but note whitish edges to tertials. Underparts white, washed pale buff on breast with bold blackish streaking on breast and flanks.

b *Adult A. c. caudacutus — detail showing crown and nape:* Note mid-gray collar, central crown and ear-coverts.

c *Adult A. c. caudacutus in flight:* Darker than LeConte's in flight. Note olive-brown upperparts, whitish 'braces,' and extensive dull chestnut-brown in wings.

d *Juvenile A. c. caudacutus:* Buffy brown upperparts boldly streaked black. Collar rich brown. Crown and ear-coverts dusky-brown with buff supercilium and face. Underparts buff washed rich ochraceous on breast. Breast and flanks narrowly streaked dusky.

36 Nelson's Sharp-tailed Sparrow *Ammodramus nelsoni*

a *Adult Ammodramus n. nelsoni:* Differs from Saltmarsh Sharp-tailed in having rich ochraceous wash across breast and along flanks with much reduced and diffused dusky streaking on breast-sides. Upperparts, especially collar, are brighter and grayer and 'braces' whiter.

b *Juvenile A. n. nelsoni:* Similar to Saltmarsh Sharp-tailed but overall brighter and more ochraceous, especially on underparts. Some dusky streaking may be present on breast-sides.

c *Adult A. n. subvirgatus:* A 'washed-out' version of *A. n. nelsoni*. The upperparts are grayer and less sharply defined and the underparts are paler with very diffused streaking.

LeConte's Sparrow

34b

34a

34c

34e

34f

34d

Saltmarsh Sharp-tailed Sparrow

35b

35a

35c

35d

36c

36b

36a

Nelson's Sharp-tailed Sparrow

37 **Seaside Sparrow** *Ammodramus maritimus*

a   *Adult* **Ammodramus m. maritimus** — *Northern Seaside Sparrow:* A chunky, spike-billed *Ammodramus* restricted to coastal saltmarshes. Mostly grayish with contrasting yellow supraloral and whitish submoustachial and throat. Wings are olive-brown. Underparts are pale gray with bold dusky gray streaking.

b   *Adult* **A. m. maritimus** *in flight:* Note dingy gray upperparts streaked darker. Wings and tail are dull olive-brown.

c   *Juvenile* **A. m. maritimus:** Quite different from adult. Upperparts are brown boldly streaked black. Head shows mostly black crown, buffy face contrasting with brown ear-coverts and thin dark malar stripe. Wings show two narrow buffy bars. Underparts mostly buff streaked dusky on breast and flanks.

d   *Adult* **A. m. macgillivraii** — *MacGillivray's Seaside Sparrow:* Very similar to *maritimus;* many individuals cannot be safely differentiated. Note ochraceous wash to submoustachial and breast and flanks (matched by some first-winter *maritimus).*

e   *Adult* **A. m. mirabilis** — *Cape Sable Seaside Sparrow:* Note distinct olive tones on head and upperparts. Mantle streaked black with pale gray 'braces' (edges of mantle feathers). Wings mostly olive-brown with pale edges to coverts and tertials. Underparts whitish with bold blackish streaking.

f   *Adult* **A. m. nigrescens** — *Dusky Seaside Sparrow:* Extinct. Upperparts gray-brown boldly streaked black. Wings with brown edges to feathers. Underparts white with sharply defined black streaking. The pied appearance is offset by yellow supraloral and bend of wing.

g   *Adult* **A. m. peninsulae** — *Scott's Seaside Sparrow:* Dark olive-brown upperparts with indistinct dusky streaking. Underparts gray with paler belly. Wings contrastingly dull chestnut brown.

h   *Adult* **A. m. sennetti** — *Texas Seaside Sparrow:* Similar to a 'washed-out' version of *fisheri* (see below) although with more olive tones on head, wings and tail and with grayer streaking on underparts.

i   *Adult* **A. m. fisheri** — *Louisiana Seaside Sparrow:* Very richly marked. Upperparts gray streaked black with pale 'braces.' Head with blackish ear-coverts and lateral crown-stripes and rich ochraceous wash on supercilium and submoustachial. Underparts whitish with rich ochraceous wash on breast and flanks and bold blackish streaking.

Seaside Sparrow

37a

37b

37c

37d

37e

37f

37g

37h

37i

38 **Red Fox Sparrow** *Passerella (iliaca) iliaca*

    a   *Adult P. i. iliaca (breeds central and north Alaska across northern provinces to eastern Canada):* Note predominantly rusty red and gray plumage and especially the bright rufous rump and tail.

    b   *Juvenile P. i. iliaca:* Gray-brown mantle with dusky fringes to feathers giving barred effect; dark brown malar and denser spotting and streaking on underparts.

    c   *Adult P. i. iliaca in flight:* The bright rufous rump and tail are usually obvious; note also extensive rust color in wings.

39 **Sooty Fox Sparrow** *Passerella (iliaca) unalaschcensis*

    a   *Adult P. u. fuliginosa (breeds coastal British Columbia to NW Washington):* The darkest subspecies in this group; note very dark, dusky brown upperparts and extensive and dense dusky spotting and streaking on underparts.

    b   *Juvenile P. u. fuliginosa:* Similar to adult except underparts are mostly buffy with dense brown blotches and streaking.

    c   *Adult P. u. unalaschcensis (breeds Aleutian Is. and Alaska Peninsula):* One of the paler subspecies of this group; upperparts chocolate brown, grayer on supraloral and auriculars; whitish underparts with quite heavy brown spotting and streaking.

    d   *Adult P. u. unalaschcensis in flight:* Fairly uniform brown in appearance with no rufous in tail (*fuliginosa* similar but much darker).

40 **Slate-colored Fox Sparrow** *Passerella (iliaca) schistacea*

    a   *Adult P. s. altivagans (breeds interior central to southern British Columbia):* Intermediate between *P. i. iliaca* and *P. s. schistacea;* note uniform brown mantle, gray face and neck, whitish supraloral and whitish underparts spotted and streaked brown. The tail shows quite noticeable dull rufous fringes.

    b   *Adult P. s. altivagans in flight:* The moderately rufous tail contrasts with the uniform brown back and gray neck and head.

    c   *Adult P. s. schistacea (breeds southern British Columbia to south-central Colorado and Nevada):* The smallest billed subspecies in this group; note slaty gray head and mantle (often washed with brown), brown, tinged rufous, tail and whitish underparts sparsely spotted and streaked brown.

40 **"Thick-billed" Fox Sparrow** *Passerella (iliaca) megarhyncha*

    d   *Adult P. m. megarhyncha (breeds in the Sierras):* Generally the largest billed subspecies in this group; note the grossly swollen effect of the bill, uniform slaty gray mantle and head (sometimes washed with brown), and the whitish underparts sparsely spotted and streaked brown.

    e   *Adult P. m. megarhyncha in flight:* Note brown wings and tail contrast with slaty gray mantle and head. However, note that *P. s. schistacea* is very similar in appearance.

Red Fox Sparrow

38c

38b

38a

Sooty Fox Sparrow

39d

39b

39c

39a

**Slate-colored
Fox Sparrow**

40b

40e

40a

40d

40c

**"Thick-billed"
Fox Sparrow**

41 Song Sparrow *Melospiza melodia*

a **Adult Melospiza m. melodia — *fresh plumage, early spring (widespread in the East)*:** Upperparts brown, streaked black with gray edges to feathers. Head mostly grayish with brown lateral crown- and eye-stripes and whitish supraloral and submoustachial. Broad malar stripe black. Wings and tail mostly dull chestnut tinged rusty. Wing-coverts and tertials edges buff. Underparts whitish washed brown on flanks with bold blackish streaking on breast and flanks. A variable black smudge is usually evident on center of breast.

b **Adult M. m. melodia — *worn plumage, mid-summer*:** Feather abrasion and sun-bleaching wears away gray and buff feather edges and reduces bird to the dull individual shown.

c **Juvenile M. m. melodia:** Overall buffer than adult with bold blackish streaking on back, neck and underparts. Head pattern is more diffuse than adult and note the quite bold eye-ring. Wings and tail are brighter chestnut and wing-coverts are edged buff.

d **Adult M. m. sanaka *(east Aleutian Is., Alaska)*:** Very large. Upperparts gray with chestnut streaking. Head gray and chestnut with bold white supraloral and submoustachial. Underparts gray, paler on belly and boldly streaked chestnut.

e **Adult M. m. morphna *(British Columbia — California)*:** Smaller and more rufescent than Aleutian races. Upperparts dark chestnut streaked black becoming grayer on head. Underparts gray, paler on throat and belly and densely streaked with dull chestnut.

f **Juvenile M. m. morphna:** Overall very dark-looking. Dark chestnut above and mostly grayish on head and underparts. Densely streaked and mottled dusky on upper and underparts.

g **Adult M m. inexpectata *(Alaska, British Columbia and Yukon)*:** Similar size as *morphna* but plumage more reminiscent of *sanaka*. Streaking on upper and underparts blacker and supraloral and submoustachial whiter than either race.

h **Adult M. m. samuelis *(north San Fransisco Bay)*:** Along with *pusillula* (below) are small, slender-billed saltmarsh dwelling birds. Both are quite dark brown above (*pusillula* averages grayer) and white below with bold black streaking on breast and flanks.

i **Adult M. m. pusillula *(south San Francisco Bay)*:** See *samuelis* (above).

j **Adult M. m. heermani *(central California)*:** Similar to typical Eastern *melodia* but is 'warmer' with buffy edges to back feathers and buffier suffusion to flanks.

k **Adult M. m. montana *(Rocky Mountains)*:** Similar to *melodia* but averages paler and distinctly more grayish on upperparts and head. Underparts white, tinged buff with brown streaking on breast and flanks.

l **Adult M. m. clementae *(Santa Rosa Is. — California)*:** Overall very pale with ash-gray upperparts narrowly streaked dusky. Wings are pale chestnut with buff edges to coverts and tertials and underparts are white with narrow blackish streaking.

m **Adult M. m. saltonis *(SE California — W. Arizona)*:** Strikingly pale. Upperparts ash-gray, streaked rusty. Wings mostly pale rust with buff edges. Underparts white, tinged buff with pale rusty streaking.

Song Sparrow

41a

41b

41c

41d

41e

41f

41g

41j

41h

41i

41l

41k

41m

43 Swamp Sparrow *Melospiza georgiana*

a **Adult M. g. georgiana *in summer plumage:*** Note bright rusty crown contrasting with gray face and neck sides. Narrow blackish eye-stripe and malar. Mantle boldly striped black and buff contrasting with bright rusty scapulars and wings. Underparts pale gray, darker on breast, and washed buffy brown on flanks.

b ***Adult in worn plumage (mid-summer):*** Obviously variable but can appear quite drab (as shown). Rusty and buff feather edges worn away.

c ***First-winter:*** Similar to adult but with streaked crown, brownish ear-coverts, supraloral and malar region washed buff. Breast gray variably striated darker and flanks extensively washed cinnamon-brown.

d ***Adult in winter plumage:*** Very similar to summer adult but with streaked crown, brown tinge to ear-coverts and more extensive buff on flanks.

e ***Juvenile:*** Crown dusky black. Upperparts, wing-coverts and tertials edged buff. Face and breast buffy with neck, breast and flanks boldly streaked dusky-brown. Throat is whitish, unmarked.

42 Lincoln's Sparrow *Melospiza lincolnii*

a **Adult M. l. lincolnii:** A beautifully plumaged species. Note gray supercilium and crown-stripe contrasting with brown lateral crown-stripes. Ear-coverts are brown edged black. Submoustachial is bright buff. Upperparts are gray-brown with black streaking. Underparts are whitish, washed buff on breast and flanks with fine blackish streaking on breast and flanks.

b ***First-winter:*** Very similar to adult but averages buffier overall with buffy brown tinge to face and collar.

c ***Juvenile:*** Very similar to juvenile Swamp Sparrow. Differs in having brown crown finely streaked black, buffier ear-coverts and whitish throat lightly spotted dusky. On average the underparts are more boldly streaked but this is highly variable.

Swamp Sparrow

43a

43c

43b

43e

43d

Lincoln's Sparrow

42a

42b

42c

45 Golden-crowned Sparrow *Zonotrichia atricapilla*

a *Adult summer:* Upperparts brown streaked blackish. Striking head pattern: sides of crown black, grayish on lores, with broad central crown area yellow becoming pale gray towards rear. Face and underparts pale gray, paler on throat and belly and washed brown on flanks. Wings show two narrow whitish bars. Bill dusky with pinkish lower mandible.

b *Adult winter:* Very similar to above but generally duller, especially on the head. Head pattern variable but usually shows yellow forecrown and blackish supraloral area. Face and underparts sullied with brown.

c *First-winter:* Similar to winter adult but usually duller with variable head pattern. Extent and tone of yellow on forecrown varies; some birds hardly show any. The supraloral area is usually duskier than the rest of the rather plain head. Note the grayish, slightly bicolored bill.

d *Juvenile:* Somewhat paler on the head and underparts with extensive dusky streaking on neck-sides, breast and flanks. Usually just a hint of yellow on the forecrown, which is usually invaded by dusky streaks.

47 Harris's Sparrow *Zonotrichia querula*

a *Adult summer:* A large, handsome sparrow. Unmistakable. Striking head pattern with crown, face, and bib black contrasting with pale gray ear-coverts and neck-sides. Note black lower edge to ear-coverts. Large bill bright pink. Upperparts are buffy brown, streaked black. White underparts are relieved by black streaking along flanks.

b *Adult winter:* Very similar to summer adult except that the head pattern is more diffuse with buffy brown ear-coverts and black crown feathers edged buff and scaly-looking. Bib usually all-black but can show some white on throat. Otherwise flanks often with buffy brown suffusion.

c *First-winter:* Not dissimilar to winter adult except throat is white with variable amount of black across upper breast. Head is mostly buff with black crown feathers broadly edged buff and scaly-looking. Note chestnut crescent on lower edge of ear-coverts. Underparts are white, washed buffy brown on flanks with chestnut suffusion on breast-sides. Flanks are streaked dusky. Bill pinkish.

d *Juvenile:* Buffier overall than first-winter bird with extensive black streaking on neck-sides, breast and flanks. Crown brown, streaked black. Bill pinkish.

Golden-crowned Sparrow

45a

45b

45d

45c

47a

47b

47d

47c

Harris's Sparrow

44 White-throated Sparrow *Zonotrichia albicollis*

a **Adult 'white stripe' morph:** Unmistakable. Upperparts rusty brown with darker streaking. Head pattern distinctive: white central crown-stripe bordered by black lateral stripes, white supercilium and bright yellow supraloral, black eye-stripe, mid-gray face and upper breast surround the white throat and malar area. Wings russet-brown with two whitish bars. Underparts pale gray tinged brown on flanks.

b **Adult 'tan stripe' morph:** Virtually identical to above except head pattern duller with sullied buff crown-stripe and supercilium, brown lateral crown-stripes streaked black, paler yellow supraloral and more developed malar stripe. Underparts are often sullied with brown and slightly striated darker on breast and flanks.

c **First-winter showing some retained juvenile plumage:** Similar to the 'tan stripe' individual described above but shows retained juvenile streaking on underparts. Birds in this plumage can be seen on migration in October.

d **Juvenile:** As adult 'tan stripe' but shows paler gray neck streaked dusky, less distinct head pattern, more pronounced dusky streaking on underparts and wing-coverts edged buff.

46 White-crowned Sparrow *Zonotrichia leucophrys*

a **Adult Zonotrichia l. leucophrys (breeds NE Canada):** Upperparts ash-gray and buff streaked black and chestnut. Head mostly mid-gray with striking black-and-white striped crown. Note black lores. Wings show white tips to coverts and tertials. Underparts mostly gray, paler on belly and tinged brown on flanks. Bill is reddish pink with darker culmen. *Z. l. oriantha* (breeds Western mountains) is very similar.

b **Juvenile Z. l. leucophrys:** Upperparts buffy streaked darker. Head pattern is less distinct with some streaking on neck. Underparts pale gray heavily streaked dusky on breast and flanks. Wings show buffy edges to coverts and tertials.

c **First-winter Z. l. leucophrys:** Head pattern similar to adult except black-and-white replaced by chestnut-and-buff, and ear-coverts washed brown. Upperparts are buffier and flanks moderately suffused brown.

d **First-winter Z. l. leucophrys/gambelii intergrade:** Obviously variable but some individuals can show pale supraloral with sullied dusky loral stripe as shown.

e **First-winter Z. l. gambelii (breeds Alaska to central Canada):** Typically shows clean pale gray supraloral area. The bill varies from yellow-orange to orange with dusky tip.

f **First-winter Z. l. nuttalli (breeds coastal central California):** Also shows pale gray supraloral area. Note the more well-developed dusky malar stripe. Bill usually pale lemon yellow with dusky tip. Note *Z. i. pugetensis* (breeds coastal British Columbia to n. California) is very similar.

g **Adult Z. l. gambelii:** Very similar to *leucophrys* but note clean, pale gray loral area, cleaner, grayer edges to mantle feathers and paler orange-yellow bill.

h **Adult Z. l. nuttalli:** This and *pugetensis* are smaller and browner than the other races. Upperparts are buffy brown with some brown suffusion on nape. The loral area is pale gray. The underparts show a stronger brownish suffusion on the flanks. Note the pale yellow bill and some yellow at the bend of wing (usually hidden). The shorter primary extension is usually evident on this pair of subspecies.

White-throated Sparrow

44a

44b

44c

44d

46a

46b

46c

46f

46e

46d

46g

46h

White-crowned Sparrow

48 Dark-eyed Junco *Junco hyemalis*

a **Adult male J. h. hyemalis 'Slate-colored Junco' (widespread in east):** Upperparts, hood and flanks dark slate-gray. Belly and undertail-coverts white. Note concave lower edge to gray hood. Bill pale pink.

b **Adult male in flight:** Note extensive white in three outer tail feathers and very dark overall appearance.

c **Adult female:** Somewhat paler than adult male with variable brown wash on head and upperparts. Wing-coverts and tertials sometimes edged paler gray.

d **Juvenile:** Generally quite dark overall. Note extensive dense dusky streaking on mantle, head, breast and flanks. Wing-coverts edged buff. Pale eye-ring may be present. Bill pink with dusky tip and culmen.

e **First-winter male:** Similar to adult male except head and back variably suffused brown. Wing-coverts and, especially, tertials are edged brown.

f **First-winter female:** Note especially the strong brownish suffusion to whole of hood and upperparts. Flanks are washed buffy brown and wing-coverts and tertials edged buff. Note — there is much individual variation and some birds cannot be reliably aged and sexed in the field.

g **Adult male J. h. hyemalis (Ontario, winter):** A variant showing bold white wing-bars. See *J. h. aikeni* below.

h **Adult male J. h. aikeni 'White-winged Junco' (breeds SE Montana, NE Wyoming, S Dakota to NW Nebraska):** Larger and paler than 'Slate-colored' Junco. Note bold white wing-bars and pale tertial edges.

i **Adult male in flight:** Note extensive amount of white in tail; usually four outermost feathers are mostly white. Also appears paler gray on upperparts with obvious white wing-bars and paler tertial edges.

j **Adult male J. h. oreganus 'Oregon Junco' (breeds SE Alaska through California):** Unmistakable. Blackish hood contrasting with chestnut back, whitish underparts and pinkish rusty flanks.

k **Adult male in flight:** Combination of black hood and chestnut back is unique. This subspecies has the least amount of white in the tail.

l **Adult female:** Duller version of male. The hood is gray suffused with brown on crown and nape.

m **Juvenile:** Generally paler and 'warmer' than 'Slate-colored Junco.' Hood and upperparts cinnamon-brown. Extensive dusky streaking on back, head, breast and flanks. Wing-coverts and tertials edged buff.

Dark-eyed Junco

48b

48a

48d

48e

48c

48f

48i

48g

48h

48k

48m

48j

48l

48 Dark-eyed Junco *Junco hyemalis (continued)*

n *Adult* Junco h. mearnsi 'Pink-sided Junco' *(breeds SE Alberta to SW Saskatchewan south to SE Idaho):* Sexes similar. Quite distinctive with dull brown back, mid-gray hood and dark lores. Underparts white with bright pinkish cinnamon sides to breast and flanks. Wings gray with brown edged inner greater coverts and tertials.

o *Adult* J. h. mearnsi *in flight:* Note outer three tail feathers largely white.

p *First-winter female* J. h. cismontanus *(breeds central British Columbia):* Very drab. Upperparts grayish brown shading to clearer gray on throat and upper breast. Note concave lower edge to hood. Flanks washed brown.

q *First-winter female* J. h. oreganus 'Oregon Junco':* Upperparts brown. Hood gray-brown mottled pale gray and buff. Note convex lower edge to hood. Flanks and breast-sides rusty cinnamon.

r *Adult male* J. h. caniceps 'Gray-headed Junco' *(breeds Rocky Mountains.):* Distinctive. Bright rusty-red mantle contrasts with gray scapulars. Hood and underparts mid-gray, paler on belly. Lores blackish. Wings mostly gray. Bill is all pale pink in this northern race.

s *Adult male* J. h. caniceps *in flight:* Overall gray with rusty triangle on mantle. Note extensive white in outer three tail feathers.

t *Juvenile* J. h. caniceps: Back, crown, and ear-coverts brown streaked dusky. Underparts whitish, washed buff on breast with extensive dusky streaking on breast and flanks.

u *Adult male* J. h. dorsalis 'Gray-headed Junco' *(breeds N-C Arizona, C New Mexico to E-C Arizona, S New Mexico and W Texas):* Very similar to *caniceps* (which it replaces southwards) although paler overall with a larger, bicolored bill.

49 Yellow-eyed Junco *Junco phaenotus*

a *Adult* Junco p. palliatus *(breeds SE Arizona to SW New Mexico):* Unmistakable in its limited range. Rusty red back contrasts with mid-gray hood. Throat and underparts pale gray. Wings mostly gray with rusty edges to inner greater coverts and tertials. Black loral area highlights the pale yellow-orange iris. Bill bicolored.

b *Adult in flight:* Rusty red in back and wings contrasts with gray head and rump. White in tail restricted largely to outer two feathers.

c *First-winter:* Similar to adult but note pale tips to greater coverts and tertials. Iris color variable — can be pale gray.

d *Juvenile:* Very similar to juvenile Gray-headed Junco (above) but note pale iris, rustier back and whiter underparts crisply streaked dusky.

Dark-eyed Junco

48o

48n

48p

48q

48r

48s

48t

48u

Yellow-eyed Junco

49a

49b

49c

49d

50 McCown's Longspur *Calcarius mccownii*

a **Adult male summer:** Stocky build with hefty bill, long wings and short tail. Pale gray face contrasts with black crown and moustachial stripe. Upperparts grayish buff narrowly streaked blackish. Underparts whitish with thick black breast-band and mottled gray flanks. Closed wing shows chestnut lesser and median coverts. Bill black.

b **Adult male summer in flight:** Note especially extensive white in tail and chestnut median and lesser wing-coverts. McCown's appears very long winged in flight.

c **Adult female summer:** Differs from male in having more subdued head pattern, scaly, grayish breast and reduced chestnut in wing-coverts.

d **First-winter male:** Very pale and sandy-looking. Upperparts and crown buffy streaked blackish. Ear-coverts buff outlined brown. Underparts whitish, tinged buff with variable blackish breast-band. Wings show chestnut lesser and median coverts broadly edged buff. Bill pinkish.

e **First-winter male in flight:** Note pale sandy appearance with extensive white in tail and some chestnut on shoulders.

f **First-winter female:** Very similar to first winter male but lacks any black on breast and has greatly reduced (or no) chestnut in wing-coverts.

g **Juvenile:** Similar to winter birds but has upperparts appearing scaly and neck and breast spotted and streaked dusky brown. Bill pinkish with dark tip and culmen.

53 Chestnut-collared Longspur *Calcarius ornatus*

a **Adult male summer:** Smaller and more neatly proportioned than McCown's. Unmistakable. Distinctive black-and-white head pattern contrasting with yellow-ochre face and chin and chestnut nape. Upperparts buffy brown streaked darker. Underparts mostly sooty black, white on lower belly and undertail-coverts. Closed wing shows white bar on otherwise black lesser coverts. Bill pinkish-gray with dusky tip.

b **Adult male summer in flight:** Note extensive white in tail, chestnut nape and black-and-white lesser wing-coverts.

c **Adult female summer:** Mostly buffy brown streaked darker on upperparts. Streaked crown contrasts with whitish supercilium. Underparts pale buff lightly striated brown on flanks and with variable amount of blackish scaling on breast. Lacks obvious white bar on lesser coverts.

d **Adult male summer:** Some individuals show variable amounts of chestnut admixed with the black on the underparts (quite extensive here).

e **First-winter male:** A muted version of adult male. Buffy face and supercilium, brown crown streaked black, and reduced chestnut on nape. Underparts appear scaly due to broad buffy fringes to black feathers.

f **First-winter female:** Very similar to adult female but lacks any black on breast and averages heavier streaking on breast-sides and flanks.

g **Juvenile:** Similar to young female but appears scaly on back and has neck and breast streaked with dusky brown.

McCown's Longspur

50b

50a

50c

50e

50g

50d

50f

53b

53a

Chestnut-collared Longspur

53c

53d

53g

53e

53f

52 **Smith's Longspur** *Calcarius pictus*

a   *Adult male in breeding plumage:* A neatly proportioned, relatively small-billed longspur. Note distinctive head pattern — crown black, supercilium and lores white and ear-coverts black with white centre and border on lower edge. Upperparts brown, streaked blackish. Underparts and collar variably buffy orange. Closed wing shows white bar on lesser coverts (sometimes obscured).

b   *Adult male in flight:* Note white on outer two tail feathers. Buffy collar; black and white head and white bar on inner lesser coverts.

c   *Adult female in breeding plumage:* A 'washed-out' version of male. Head pattern diffused with black and white replaced by brown and buff. Underparts pale buff with variable cinnamon streaking on breast sides. White on lesser coverts usually reduced.

d   *First-winter male:* Similar to adult female but decidedly 'warmer.' Upperparts show distinct pale buffy 'braces' (edges of mantle feathers) on mantle. Underparts show variable brownish cinnamon streaking on breast and flanks. Inner lesser coverts with broad white edges (more obvious in flight).

e   *Juvenile:* Similar to first-winter bird but with bolder dusky streaking on neck, breast and flanks. Greater coverts and tertials edged rufous.

51 **Lapland Longspur** *Calcarius lapponicus*

a   *Adult male in breeding plumage (slightly worn):* Unmistakable. Head pattern distinctive with black crown, face and upper breast, white post-ocular stripe extending down to breast sides, and bright rufous-chestnut nape. Upperparts with pale 'braces' on mantle. Underparts white with thick black streaking along flanks. Bill pale.

b   *Adult male in flight:* Reduced white in outer two tail feathers. Chestnut nape, black and white head and relatively plain wings.

c   *Adult male molting into breeding plumage — late March:* Similar to above but with mottled black and white face and breast. In this plumage not unlike adult female.

d   *Adult female in breeding plumage:* Differs from male in having reduced chestnut on nape, blackish crown with whitish coronal patch, brown ear-coverts boldly edged blackish, white supercilium extending around to malar area and throat, and finer dusky streaking on flanks.

e   *First-winter male:* Similar to adult female but much 'warmer' overall. Face and supercilium distinctly buffy. Greater wing-coverts and tertials edged bright rufous forming panel in closed wing. Bill pinkish to brick-red.

f   *First-winter female:* Very similar to above; many individuals cannot be reliably sexed in the field. Averages buffier on underparts with sparse streaking on breast and flanks.

g   *Juvenile:* Similar to first-winter birds but decidedly paler on upperparts with bold blackish streaking on neck, breast and flanks.

Smith's Longspur

52b
52a
52c
52e
52d

Lapland Longspur
51a
51c
51b
51e
51d
51f
51g

50 **McCown's Longspur** *Calcarius mccownii*

a   *First-winter male:* Distinctive flight silhouette; the longest-winged shortest-tailed longspur. Note extensive white in tail. Overall quite pale and sandy-colored with dark streaking on back and crown. Underparts whitish with some dark mottling on breast (not visible here). The median wing-coverts have distinctive chestnut centers.

b   *First-winter female:* Very similar to above but median coverts have dark brown and black centers.

c   *Open tail:* Shows more white than any other longspur. Black is reduced to a narrow terminal bar.

d   *Closed tail:* Even here the extensive white is still quite obvious.

53 **Chestnut-collared Longspur** *Calcarius ornatus*

a   *First-winter male:* Proportionally shorter-winged and longer-tailed than McCown's. Shows extensive white in tail. Overall buffy brown with blackish streaking on upperparts and crown. Underparts whitish with quite extensive scaling on breast and belly (hardly visible here). Nape usually with pale chestnut on sides. Lesser wing-coverts black with white bar on inner edge.

b   *First-winter female:* Very similar to above but lacks the chestnut on nape and has lesser wing-coverts blackish with buffy gray edges.

c   *Open tail:* Shows extensive white. Black appears as a triangle.

d   *Closed tail:* Appears mostly dark with white flashes on sides (basal two-thirds).

52 **Smith's Longspur** *Calcarius pictus*

a   *First-winter male:* Similar shape to Chestnut-collared but with proportionally longer tail. Tail with outer two feathers largely white. Buffier and 'warmer' than other longspurs. Back is boldly streaked blackish with pale buff 'braces' (edges of mantle feathers). Underparts buff. Lesser wing-coverts blackish, edged buff with variable white bar on inner edge.

b   *First-winter female:* Similar to above but pattern on lesser wing-coverts more diffuse, lacking white bar on inner edge.

c   *Open tail:* Outer two feathers largely white with variable dark stripes on outer webs.

d   *Closed tail:* Appears mostly dark with narrow white edge just visible.

51 **Lapland Longspur** *Calcarius lapponicus*

a   *First-winter male:* Shape not dissimilar to Smith's but proportionally shorter-tailed. Tail with least amount of white amongst the longspurs. Upperparts brown streaked blackish with pale buff 'braces.' Some pale chestnut is usually evident on nape. Underparts whitish with dark streaking on breast (hardly visible here). Greater wing-coverts and tertials show distinctive reddish chestnut edges.

b   *First-winter female:* Very similar to above but usually shows little or no chestnut on nape.

c   *Open tail:* Outer two feathers variably black and white. Outermost mostly white with dark stripe on outer web.

d   *Closed tail:* Appears mostly dark with very narrow white edge barely visible.

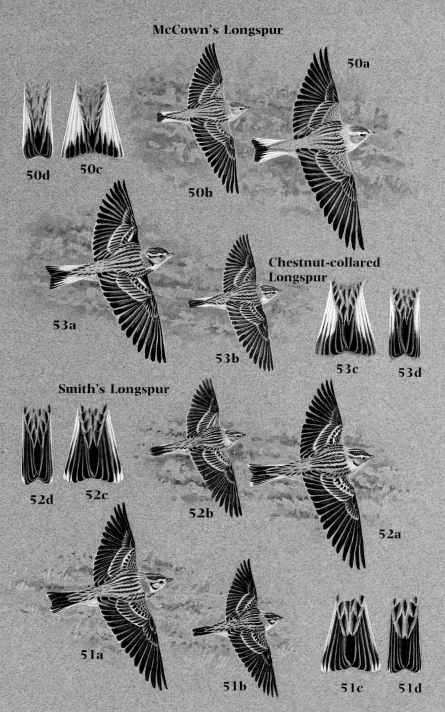

McCown's Longspur

50a

50d   50c

50b

Chestnut-collared
Longspur

53a

53b

53c   53d

Smith's Longspur

52d   52c

52b

52a

51a

51b

51c   51d

Lapland Longspur

55 **Little Bunting** *Emberiza pusilla*

a *Adult:* A small, compact bunting. Note particularly distinctive head pattern with chestnut crown bordered with black lateral stripes, buffy white supercilium variably rufous on supraloral, chestnut ear-coverts bordered black with whitish spot at rear edge. This bright individual shows some buff on malar area and chin.

b *Adult or first-winter:* A duller individual than above. All birds have buffy brown upperparts streaked blackish and whitish underparts narrowly striated black on breast and flanks.

56 **Rustic Bunting** *Emberiza rustica*

a *Adult male summer:* Unmistakable. Black and white head pattern unique. Upperparts buff-brown streaked black with chestnut scapulars, nape and rump. Underparts white with bold rusty malar and streaking on breast and flanks. Closed wing shows two whitish bars.

b *Adult female summer:* A dull version of the male. The head pattern in particular is less distinct with crown brown streaked black and ear-coverts brown edged blackish.

c *First-winter male:* Very similar to adult female but tends to be tinged buff on supercilium and submoustachial. The scapulars, nape and rump are chestnut edged buff and less distinct than on adult birds.

58 **Gray Bunting** *Emberiza variabilis*

a *Adult male:* Overall mid-gray variably darker on face. Upperparts streaked black. Closed wings have brown and olive fringes. Stout bill yellowish with darker culmen.

b *Adult female:* Very different from male. Upperparts buffy streaked darker with contrasting chestnut rump and tail edges. Head shows pale buff supercilium and submoustachial contrasting with brown ear-coverts. Underparts whitish narrowly streaked brown on breast and flanks.

c *First-winter male:* Highly variable. Upperparts much like female but head and underparts more like adult male, usually with some brown on lateral crown and ear-coverts and brown streaking on breast and flanks.

57 **Yellow-breasted Bunting** *Emberiza aureola*

a *Adult male summer:* Combination of largely chestnut upperparts, black face and mostly yellow underparts distinctive. Note also chestnut breast-band and large white patch on lesser and median wing-coverts.

b *Adult female:* Upperparts brown streaked black with paler 'braces' (edges of mantle feathers). Head shows broad whitish supercilium washed yellow on supraloral, greyish ear-coverts outlined black with pale spot at rear edge and gray-tinged nape. Underparts pale yellow with narrow streaking on breast sides. Wings show broad white fringes to median coverts.

c *Juvenile/First-winter:* Similar to female but buffier overall, lacking yellow tones. Mantle shows distinct pale 'braces.' Underparts are variably streaked dusky on breast and flanks.

Little Bunting

55a

55b

Rustic Bunting

56a

56b

56c

Gray Bunting

58a

58c

58b

57b

57a

57c

Yellow-breasted Bunting

59 Pallas's Bunting *Emberiza pallasi*

a   ***Adult male summer:*** Head and bib black with contrasting white submoustachial and collar. Upperparts pale buff streaked black with white 'braces' (edges of mantle feathers) and whitish rump. Underparts whitish, almost unmarked. Closed wing lacks any rusty tones and shows two whitish bars and blue-gray lesser coverts. Bill usually blackish.

b   ***Adult male summer — detail of head:*** Note white submoustachial stripe.

c   ***Adult male winter:*** Similar to summer male except head mostly brown and throat variably whitish. Bill paler on lower mandible.

d   ***Adult female:*** Head shows pale supercilium, buffy ear-coverts and brown crown narrowly streaked dusky. Brown malar stripe contrasts with otherwise whitish underparts.

e   ***First-winter:*** Very similar to adult female. Averages buffier with less distinct supercilium, dark brown lower edge to ear-coverts and more distinct streaking on breast sides. Bill with pinkish lower mandible.

60 Reed Bunting *Emberiza schoeniclus*

a   ***Adult male summer E. s. pyrrhulina:*** Larger than Pallas's Bunting with convex culmen. Overall pattern similar to Pallas's but note gray rump and pale rufous tones in closed wing. Lesser coverts are always rufous.

b   ***Adult male winter:*** Similar to summer male except head mixed black and brown and throat variably whitish. Submoustachial and collar tinged buff.

c   ***Adult female:*** Similar to Pallas's Bunting in overall pattern but note rufous in wing and darker lateral crown-stripes.

d   ***First-winter:*** Again, note rufous in wing, darker lateral crown-stripes (Pallas's shows a uniform brown crown) and strongly convex culmen.

54 Pine Bunting *Emberiza leucocephalos*

a   ***Adult male summer:*** Unmistakable. Note distinctive black, white and chestnut head pattern. Upperparts brown streaked black with chestnut rump. Underparts largely chestnut on breast and flanks with white crescent across upper breast.

b   ***Adult female:*** Differs from male in less distinct head pattern. Note pale supercilium, grayish ear-coverts, edged black and with pale spot on rear edge and blackish malar. Underparts streaked brown on breast and flanks.

c   ***First-winter male:*** Not dissimilar to adult male but head pattern more diffuse with streaked crown. Breast and flanks streaked chestnut.

Pallas's Bunting

59c

59b

59d

59a

59e

60b

Reed Bunting

60c

60a

60d

Pine Bunting

54a

54b

54c

61 **Snow Bunting** *Plectrophenax nivalis*

a   *Adult male summer (slightly worn):* Unmistakable. Head and underparts white, mantle and scapulars black. Tail black with extensive white in outer feathers. Wings mostly white with black alula and outer primaries and tertials. Bill black.

b   *Adult female summer:* Duller than male. Back grayish-brown streaked black, crown buffy streaked blackish, ear-coverts washed buffy gray and underparts white. Wings show reduced amount of white.

c   *Juvenile:* Mouse-gray above streaked darker on back. Pale eye-ring. Underparts grayish, mottled darker on breast and paler on belly. Wings show broad rusty fringes to tertials and reduced white panel.

d   *Adult male winter:* Variable. Usually with bright buff-cinnamon crown and ear-coverts. Upperparts buffy brown with black centers to feathers. Face and underparts white with cinnamon breast sides. Wings with broad rusty fringes to tertials and extensive white panel. Bill yellowish.

e   *Adult male molting (early April):* Essentially as summer male but with back feathers still edged buffy and appearing quite scaly.

f   *First-winter male:* Similar to adult male winter but has less white in wings. Note especially black in primary coverts; this is variable.

g   *Female winter:* Very similar to first-winter male but tends to be a bit darker and buffier and shows much reduced white in wing.

h   *Adult male summer in flight:* Pied appearance. Basically white with black back, outer primaries, alula and central tail.

i   *Adult male winter in flight:* Similar to above but back buff-brown streaked black and crown and ear-coverts cinnamon-brown.

j   *Adult female summer in flight:* Back grayish streaked black, crown buff streaked black. Much reduced white in wings — mostly edges to coverts and secondaries.

k   *First-winter male in flight:* Very similar to adult winter male but with black on primary coverts and tips to outer secondaries.

l   *Female winter in flight:* Variable and difficult to age. Note reduced amount of white in wing — edges to coverts and secondaries.

62 **McKay's Bunting** *Plectrophenax hyperboreus*

a   *Adult male summer:* Unmistakable. Mostly white with variable amounts of black on scapulars, tertials, outer primaries and central tail. This individual is at the 'maximum black' end of the scale. Bill black.

b   *Adult female summer:* Similar to male but with back streaked black. Crown is narrowly streaked black and there is some buffy suffusion on ear-coverts, breast and tertial edges. Alula is black.

c   *Adult male winter:* Differs from summer male in having variable buffy cinnamon suffusion to crown, ear-coverts and back. Back is variably streaked dusky. Bill yellowish.

d   *Winter female or first-winter male:* Highly variable, similar to above but with bolder streaking on back, rusty fringes to tertials and some black on primary coverts.

e   *Adult male summer in flight:* Mostly white. Black outer primaries, some scapulars, tertials and central tail feathers.

f   *Adult male winter in flight:* Similar to above but buffy suffusion to crown and back.

g   *Winter female or first-winter male in flight:* Highly variable. Some black on primary coverts and alula. Back streaked black and more black in tail.

Snow Bunting

61a
61h
61j
61l
61i
61k
61b
61c
61e
61f
61d
61g

62a
62e
62f
McKay's
Bunting
62g
62d
62b
62c

REFERENCES

Aldrich, J.W. 1984. *Ecogeographical variation in size and proportions of song sparrows* (Melospiza melodia). Ornithol. Monogr. No. 35, American Ornithologists' Union, Washington, D.C.

American Ornithologists' Union 1957. *Check-list of North American birds*, 5th ed. Am. Ornithol. Union, Washington, D.C.

American Ornithologists' Union 1983. *Check-list of North American birds*, 6th ed. Am. Ornithol. Union, Lawrence, KS.

Audubon, J.J. 1967. *The Birds of America.* Dover Publs., New York (reprint).

Austin, Jr., O.L. (ed) 1968. *Life histories of North American cardinals, buntings, towhees, finches, sparrows, and allies.* Bull. 237 U.S. Nat. Mus. parts 2 and 3.

Banks, R.C. 1964. Geographic variation in the White-crowned Sparrow, *Zonotrichia leucophrys. Univ. California Publs. Zool* **70**:1–123.

Bond, G.M. and R.E. Stewart 1951. A new Swamp Sparrow from the Maryland coastal plain. *Wilson Bull.* **63**:38–40.

Borror, D.J. 1975. Songs of the Rufous-sided Towhee. *Condor* **77**:183–195.

Bradley, R.A. 1977. Geographic variation in the song of Belding's Savannah Sparrow (*Passerculus sandwichensis beldingi*). *Bull. Florida State Mus. Biol. Sci.* **22**:57–99.

Briskie, J.V. 1993a. Anatomical adaptation to sperm competition in Smith's Longspurs and other polygynandrous passerines. *Auk* **110**:875–888.

Briskie, J.V. 1993b. Smith's Longspur (*Calcarius pictus*). In *The Birds of North America*, No. 34 (A. Poole, P. Stettenheim, and F. Gill, eds). Acad. Nat. Sci., Philadelphia, and Amer. Ornithol. Union, Washington, D.C.

Burns, K.J. and S.J. Hackett. 1993. Nest and nest-site characteristics of a western population of Fox Sparrow (*Passerella iliaca*). *Southwestern Natrl.* **38**:277–279.

Carey, M., D.E. Burhans, and D.A. Nelson 1994. Field Sparrow (*Spizella pusilla*). In *The Birds of North America*, No. 103 (A. Poole and F. Gill, eds). Philadelphia: The Academy of Natural Sciences; Washington, D.C.: The American Ornithologists' Union.

Cartwright, B.W., T.M. Shortt, and R.D. Harris 1937. Baird's Sparrow. *Trans. Royal Canadian Institute*, **21**:153–197.

Chilton, G., M.C. Baker, C.D. Barrentine, and M.A. Cunningham 1995. White-crowned Sparrow (*Zonotrichia leucophrys*). In *The Birds of North America*, No. 183 (A. Poole and F. Gill, eds). The Academy of Natural Sciences, Philadelphia, and the American Ornithologists' Union, Washington, D.C.

Clench, M.H. and R.C. Leberman 1978. Weights of 151 species of Pennsylvania birds analyzed by month, age, and sex. *Bull. Carnegie Mus. Nat. Hist.* **5**:1–85.

Cramp, S. and C.M. Perrins (eds) 1994. *Handbook of the Birds of Europe and the Middle East and North Africa. The Birds of the Western Palearctic*, Vol. IX. Oxford Univ. Press, Oxford, U.K.

Davis, J. 1951. Distribution and variation of the brown towhees. *Univ. California Publs. Zool.* **52**:1–120.

Dickinson, Jr. J.C. 1952. Geographic variation in the Red-eyed Towhee of the eastern United States. *Bull. Mus. Comp. Zool.* **107**:272–352.

Dixon, C.L. 1978. Breeding biology of the Savannah Sparrow on Kent Island. *Auk* **95**:235–246.

Dunn, J.L., K.L. Garrett, and J.K. Alderfer 1995. White-crowned Sparrow subspecies: Identification and distribution. *Birding* **27**:183–200.

Dunning, J.B. 1993. Bachman's Sparrow (*Aimophila aestivalis*). In *The Birds of North America*, No. 38 (A. Poole, P. Stettenheim, and F. Gill, eds). Philadelphia: The Academy of Natural Sciences; Washington, D.C.: The American Ornithologists' Union.

Falls, J.B. and J.G. Kopachena 1994. White-throated Sparrow (*Zonotrichia albicollis*). In *The Birds of North America*, No. 128 (A. Poole and F. Gill, eds). Philadelphia: The Academy of Natural Sciences; Washington, D.C.: The American Ornithologists' Union.

Flint, V.E. 1984. A field guide to birds of the USSR. Princeton University Press, Princeton.

Gabrielson, I.N. and F.C. Lincoln 1959. *The Birds of Alaska*. Wildlife Management Institute, Washington, D.C.

Gibson, D.D. and B. Kessel 1992. Seventy-four new avian taxa documented in Alaska 1976–1991. *Condor* **94**:454–467.

Graber, R.R. 1955. Taxonomic and Adaptive Features of the Juvenal Plumage in North American Sparrows. Ph.D. Thesis, Univ. Oklahoma, Norman, Oklahoma.

Greenlaw, J. 1993. Behavioral and morphological diversification in Sharp-tailed Sparrows (*Ammodramus caudacutus*) of the Atlantic Coast. *Auk* **110**:286–303.

Greenlaw, J. and J.D. Rising 1994. Sharp-tailed Sparrow (*Ammodramus caudacutus*). In *The Birds of North America*, No. 112 (A. Poole and F. Gill, eds). Philadelphia: The Academy of Natural Sciences; Washington, D.C.: The American Ornithologists' Union.

Groschupf, K. 1992. Five-striped Sparrow (*Amphispiza quinquestriata*). In *The Birds of North America*, No. 21 (A. Poole, P. Stettenheim, and F. Gill, eds). Philadelphia: The Academy of Natural Sciences; Washington, D.C.: The American Ornithologists' Union.

Harrison, C. 1978. *A field guide to the nests, eggs and nestlings of North American birds.* W. Collins and Sons, London.

Houston, C.S. and M.G. Street 1959. *The Birds of the Saskatchewan River: Carlton to Cumberland.* Special Publ. No. 2, Saskatchewan Nat. Hist. Soc. Regina, Sask.

Hyde, A.S. 1939. The life history of Henslow's Sparrow, *Passerherbulus henslowi* (Audubon). Misc. Publ. No. 41, Univ. Michigan, Ann Arbor.

Johnson, N.K. and J.A. Marten 1992. Macrogeographic patterns of morphometric and genetic variation in the Sage Sparrow complex. *Condor* **94**:1–19.

Kaufman, K. 1990. *Advanced birding.* Houghton Mifflin Co., Boston, MA.

Kessel, B. and D.D. Gibson 1976. Status and distribution of Alaska birds. Studies Avian Biol. No. 1, Cooper Ornithol. Soc., Lawrence, Kansas.

Knapton, R.W. 1994. Clay-colored Sparrow (*Spizella pallida*). In *The Birds of North America*, No. 120 (A. Poole and F. Gill, eds). Philadelphia: The Academy of Natural Sciences; Washington, D.C.: The American Ornithologists' Union.

Linsdale, J.M. 1928. Variation in the Fox Sparrow (*Passerella iliaca*) with reference to natural history and osteology. *Univ. California Publs. Zool.* **30**:251–392.

Linsdale, J.M. and E.L. Sumner 1934. Winter weights of Golden-crowned and Fox sparrows. *Condor* **36**:107–112.

Marshall, J.T. Jr. 1948a. Ecological races of song sparrows in the San Francisco Bay region. Part I. Habitat and abundance. *Condor* **50**:193–215.

Marshall, J.T. Jr. 1948b. Ecological races of song sparrows in the San Francisco Bay region. Part II. Geographic variation. *Condor* **50**:233–256.

Marshall, J.T. Jr. 1964a. Voice in communication and relationships among brown towhees. *Condor* **66**:345–356.

Marshall, J.T. Jr. 1964b. The song sparrows of the Mexican plateau. *Auk* **81**:448–451.

Martin, D.J. 1977. Songs of the Fox Sparrow. I. Structure of song and its comparison with song in other Emberizidae. *Condor* **79**:209–221.

Mearns, B. and R. Mearns 1988. *Biographies for Birdwatchers*. Academic Press, London.

Mearns, B. and R. Mearns 1992. *Audubon to Xantus*. Academic Press, London.

Mengel, R.M. 1965. *The birds of Kentucky*. Ornithol. Monogr. No. 3, American Ornithologists' Union, Lawrence, KS.

Miller, A.H. 1929. A new race of Black-chinned Sparrow from the San Francisco Bay district. *Condor* **31**:205–207.

Miller, A.H. 1941. Speciation in the avian genus Junco. *Univ. California Publs. Zool.* **44**:173–434.

Murry, B.G. Jr. 1969. A comparative study of LeConte's and Sharp-tailed Sparrows. *Auk* **86**:199–231.

Naugler, C.T. 1993. American Tree Sparrow (*Spizella arborea*). In *The Birds of North America*, No. 37 (A. Poole, P. Stettenheim, and F. Gill, eds). Philadelphia: The Academy of Natural Sciences; Washington, D.C.: The American Ornithologists' Union.

Norment, C.J. and S.A. Shackleton 1993. Harris' Sparrow (*Zonotrichia querula*). In *The Birds of North America*, No. 64 (A. Poole and F. Gill, eds). Philadelphia: The Academy of Natural Sciences; Washington, D.C.: The American Ornithologists' Union.

Oberholser, H.C. 1974. *The Bird Life of Texas*. Univ. Texas Press, Austin.

Paynter, Jr. R.A. 1978. Biology and evolution of the avian genus *Atlapetes* (Emberizinae). *Bull. Mus. Comp. Zool* **148**:323–369.

Post, W. and J.S. Greenlaw 1994. Seaside Sparrow (*Ammodramus maritimus*). In *The Birds of North America*, No. 127 (A. Poole and F. Gill eds). Philadelphia: The Academy of Natural Sciences; Washington, D.C.: The American Ornithologists' Union.

Potter, P.E. 1971. Territorial behavior in Savannah Sparrows in southeastern Michigan. *Wilson Bull.* **84**:48–59.

Price, J., S. Droege, and A. Price 1995. *The Summer Atlas of North American Birds*. Academic Press, London.

Pyle, P., S.N.G. Howell, R.P. Yunick, and D.F. DeSante 1987. *Identification Guide to North American Passerines*. Slate Creek Press, Bolinas, California.

Pyle, P. and D. Sibley 1992. Juvenal-plumaged LeConte's Sparrows on migration. *Birding* **24**:70–76.

Quay, T.L., J.B. Funderburg Jr., D.S. Lee, E.F. Potter, and C.S. Robbins 1983. *The Seaside Sparrow, Its Biology and Management*. Occ. Papers North Carolina Biol. Survey, 1983–5.

Ridgway, R. 1901. *The Birds of North and Middle America:* Part 1. Bull. 50, U.S. Nat. Mus., Washington, D.C.

Rimmer, C.C. 1986. Identification of juvenile Lincoln's and swamp sparrow. *J. Field Ornithol.* **57**:114–125.

Rising, J.D. 1988. Geographic variation in sex ratios and body size in wintering flocks of Savannah Sparrows (*Passerculus sandwichensis*). *Wilson Bull.* **100**:183–203.

Rising, J.D. and J.C. Avise 1993. Application of genealogical-concordance principles to the taxonomy and evolutionary history of the Sharp-tailed Sparrows (*Ammodramus caudacutus*). *Auk* **110**:844–856.

Robertson, W.B. Jr. and G.E. Woolfenden 1992. Florida Bird Species. Special Publ. No. 6, Florida Ornith. Soc., Gainesville, Florida.

Schulenberg, J.H., G.L. Horak, M.D. Schwilling, and E.J. Finck 1994. Nesting of Henslow's Sparrow in Osage County, Kansas. *Bull. Kansas Ornithol. Soc.* **44**:25–28.

Shane, T.G. 1974. The nest site selection behavior of the Lark Bunting, *Calamospiza melanocorys*. M. Sci. thesis, Kansas State University, Manhattan.

Sibley, C.G. 1950. Species formation in the red-eyed towhees of Mexico. *Univ. California Publs. Zool.* **50**:109–194.

Sibley, C.G. and D.A. West 1959. Hybridization in the Rufous-sided Towhees of the Great Plains. *Auk* **76**:326–338.

Stobo, W.T. and I.A. McLaren 1975. The Ipswich Sparrow. *Proc. Nova Scotia Inst. Sci.* **27**:1–105.

Sutton, G.M. 1935. The juvenal plumage and postjuvenal molt in several species of Michigan sparrows. Bull. No. 3, Cranbrook Inst. Sci., Bloomfield Hills, Michigan.

Sutton, G.M. 1936. The postjuvenal molt of the Grasshopper Sparrow. Occ. Papers Mus. Zool., Univ. Michigan, No. 336.

Swarth, H.S. 1920. Revision of the avian genus Passerella, with special reference to the distribution and migration of the races in California. *Univ. Cal. Publs. Zool.* **21**:75–224.

Swarth, H. and Brooks, A. 1925. The Timberline Sparrow. A new species from northwestern Canada. *Condor* **27**:27–69.

Threlfall, W. and J.R. Blacquiere 1982. Breeding biology of the Fox Sparrow in Newfoundland. J. Field Ornithol. **53**:235–239.

Tweit, R.C. and D.M. Finch 1994. Abert's Towhee (*Pipilo aberti*). In *The Birds of North America*, No. 111 (A. Poole and F. Gill, eds). Philadelphia: The Academy of Natural Sciences; Washington, D.C.: The American Ornithologists' Union.

Van Rossem, A.J. 1947. A synopsis of the Savannah Sparrows of northwestern Mexico. *Condor* **49**:97–107.

Weatherhead, P.J. 1979. Ecological correlates of monogamy in tundra-dwelling Savannah Sparrows. *Auk* **96**:391–401.

Webster, J.D. 1959. A revision of the Botteri Sparrow. *Condor* **61**:136–146.

Wege, D.C., S.N.G. Howell, and A.M. Sada 1993. The distribution and status of Worthen's Sparrow *Spizella untheni*: a review. *Bird Conservation International* **3**:211–220.

Wheelwright, N.T. and J.D. Rising 1993. Savannah Sparrow (*Passerculus sandwichensis*). In *The Birds of North America*, No. 45 (A. Poole and F. Gill, eds). Philadelphia: The Academy of Natural Sciences; Washington, D.C.: The American Ornithologists' Union.

Willoughby, E.J. 1991. Molt of the Genus *Spizella* (Passeriformes, Emberizidae) in relation to ecological factors affecting plumage wear. *Proc. Western Foundation Vert. Zool.* **4**:247–286.

With, K.A. 1994. McCown's Longspur (*Calcarius mccownii*). In *The Birds of North America*, No. 96 (A. Poole and F. Gill, eds). Philadelphia: The Academy of Natural Sciences; Washington, D.C.: The American Ornithologists' Union.

Wolf, L.L. 1977. Species relationships in the avian genus *Aimophila*. Ornith. Monogr. No. 23, American Ornithologists' Union, Lawrence, KS.

Woolfenden, G.E. 1956. Comparative breeding behavior of *Ammospiza caudacuta* and *A. maritima*. *Univ. Kansas Publ., Mus. Nat. Hist.* **10**:45–75.

Zembal, R., K.J. Kramer, R.J. Bransfield, and N. Gilbert 1988. A survey of Belding's Savannah Sparrows in California. *American Birds* **42**:1233–1236.

Zimmerman, J.L. 1988. Breeding season habitat selection by the Henslow's Sparrow (*Ammodramus henslowii*) in Kansas. *Wilson Bull.* **100**:17–24.

Zink, R.M. 1982. Patterns of genic and morphologic variation among sparrows in the genera *Zonotrichia, Melospiza, Junco,* and *Passerella*. *Condor* **84**:632–649.

Zink, R.M. 1986. Patterns and evolutionary significance of geographic variation in the Schistacea group of the fox sparrow (*Passerella iliaca*). Ornithol. Monogr. No. 40, American Ornithol. Union, Washington, D.C.

Zink, R.M. 1988. Evolution of Brown Towhees: allozymes, morphometrics and species limits. *Condor* **90**:72–82.

Zink, R.M. 1994. The geography of mitochondrial DNA variation, population structure, hybridization, and species limits in the fox sparrow (*Passerella iliaca*). *Evolution* **48**:96–111.

Zink, R.M. and J.C. Avise 1990. Patterns of mitochondrial DNA and allozyme evolution in the avian genus *Ammodramus*. *Syst. Zool.* **39**:148–161.

Zink, R.M. and D.L. Dittmann 1993. Gene flow, refugia, and evolution of geographic variation in the song sparrow (*Melospiza melodia*). *Evolution* **47**:717–729.

Zink, R.M., D.L. Dittman, S.W. Cardiff, and J.D. Rising 1991. Mitochondrial DNA variation and the taxonomic status of the large-billed savannah sparrow. *Condor* **93**:1016–1019.

REFERENCES USED FOR DISTRIBUTIONS

GENERAL

American Ornithologists' Union 1983. *Check-list of North American birds, 6th edition.* Allen Press, Lawrence, Kansas.

Cramp, S. and C.M. Perrins (eds) 1994. *Handbook of the Birds of Europe and the Middle East and North Africa.* Vol. 9 Buntings and New World Warblers. Oxford Univ. Press, Oxford, England.

Erskine, A.E. 1992. *Atlas of Breeding Birds of the Maritime Provinces.* Nova Scotia Museum, Halifax, Nova Scotia.

Godfrey, W.E. 1986. *The Birds of Canada.* Nat. Mus. Natural Sci., Ottawa, Canada.

Kantrud, H.A. and J.E. Roelle 1982. *Maps of Distribution and Abundance of Selected Species of Birds on Uncultivated Native Upland Grasslands and Shrubsteppe in the Northern Great Plains.* U.S. Dept. Interior, Washington, D.C.

Lewington, I., P. Alström, and P. Colston 1991. *A Field Guide to the Rare Birds of Britain and Europe.* Harper Collins Publ., Jersey, U.K.

Massey, J.A., S. Matsui, T. Suzuki, E.P. Swift, A. Hibi, N. Ichida, Y. Tsukamoto, and K. Sonobe 1982. *A Field Guide to the Birds of Japan.* Kodansha International, Tokyo.

Potter, E.F., J.E. Parnell, and R.P. Teulings. *Birds of the Carolinas.* Univ. North Carolina Press, Chapel Hill, North Carolina.

Portenko, L.A. 1989. *Birds of the Chukchi Peninsula and Wrangel Island.* Vol. 2. Smithsonian Institution Libraries, Washington, D.C.

Roberson, D. 1980. *Rare Birds of the West Coast.* Woodcock Publications, Pacific Grove, California.

Root, T. 1988. *Atlas of Wintering North American Birds.* Univ. Chicago Press, Chicago, Ill.

Ryser, F.A. Jr. 1985. *Birds of the Great Basin: A Natural History.* Univ. Nevada Press, Reno, Nevada.

Todd, W.E.C. 1963. *Birds of the Labrador Peninsula and Adjacent Areas.* Univ. Toronto Press, Toronto, Ontario.

REGIONAL: CANADA

Alberta:

Pinel, H.W., W.W. Smith, and C.R. Wershler 1993. *Alberta Birds, 1971–1980.* Vol. 2. Passerines. Prov. Mus. Alberta, Edmonton, Alberta.

Semenchuk, G.P. 1992. *The Atlas of Breeding Birds of Alberta.* Federation of Alberta Naturalists, Edmonton, Alberta.

British Columbia:

Cannings, R.A., R.J. Cannings, and S.G. Cannings 1987. *Birds of the Okanagan Valley, British Columbia.* Royal British Columbia Mus., Victoria, British Columbia.

Manitoba:

Knapton, R.W. 1979. *Birds of the Gainsborough-Lyleton region (Saskatchewan and Manitoba).* Special Publ. No. 10, Saskatchewan Hist. Soc., Regina, Saskatchewan.

New Brunswick:

Squires, W.A. 1976. *The Birds of New Brunswick.* Monogr. No. 7, New Brunswick Mus., Saint John, New Brunswick.

Newfoundland:

Austin, O.L. Jr. 1932. *The Birds of Newfoundland Labrador.* Memoir No. 7, Nuttall Ornithological Club, Cambridge, Massachusetts.

Peters, H.S. and T.D. Burleigh 1951. *The Birds of Newfoundland.* Dept. Nat. Resources, Prov. of Newfoundland, St. John's, Newfoundland.

Northwest Territories:

Manning, T.H., E.O. Höhn, and A.H. Macpherson 1956. *The Birds of Banks Island.* Bull. 143, Nat. Museum of Canada, Ottawa, Ontario.

Nova Scotia:

Tufts, R.W. 1986. *Birds of Nova Scotia, ed. 3.* Nova Scotia Mus., Halifax, Nova Scotia.

Ontario:

Cadman, M.D., P.F.J. Eagles, and F.M. Helleiner 1987. *Atlas of the Breeding Birds of Ontario.* Univ. Waterloo Press, Waterloo, Ontario.

James, R.D. 1991. *Annotated Checklist of the Birds of Ontario.* Life Sciences Misc. Publ., Royal Ontario Mus., Toronto, Ontario.

Peck, G.K. and R.D. James 1987. *Breeding Birds of Ontario: Nidiology and Distribution.* Vol. 2: Passerines. Life Sciences Misc. Publ., Royal Ontario Mus., Toronto, Ontario.

Speirs, J.M. 1985. *Birds of Ontario.* Natural Heritage/Natural History, Inc., Toronto, Ontario.

Saskatchewan:

Belcher, M. 1980. *Birds of Regina.* Special Publ. No. 12, Saskatchewan Nat. Hist. Soc., Regina.

Callin, E.M. 1980. *Birds of the Qu'Appelle, 1857–1979.* Special Publ. No. 13, Saskatchewan Nat. Hist. Soc., Regina, Saskatchewan.

Houston, C.S. and M.G. Street 1959. *The Birds of the Saskatchewan River: Carlton to Cumberland.* Special Publ. No. 2, Saskatchewan Nat. Hist. Soc., Regina, Saskatchewan.

Nero, R.W. 1967. *The Birds of Northeastern Saskatchewan.* Special Publ. No. 6, Saskatchewan Nat. Hist. Soc., Regina, Saskatchewan.

REGIONAL: UNITED STATES

Alabama:

Imhof, T.A. 1962. *Alabama Birds.* Univ. Alabama Press, University, Alabama.

Alaska:

Gabrielson, I.N. and F.C. Lincoln 1959. *The Birds of Alaska.* Wildlife Management Institute, Washington, D.C.

Gibson, D.D. and B. Kessel 1992. Seventy-four new avian taxa documented in Alaska. *Condor* **94**:454–467.

Kessel, B. and D.D. Gibson 1978. *Status and Distribution of Alaska Birds.* Studies Avian Biol. No. 1, Cooper Ornith. Soc., Lawrence, Kansas.

Williamson, F.S.L. and L.J. Peyton 1962. *Faunal Relationships of Birds in the Iliamna Lake Area, Alaska.* Biol. Paper No. 5, Univ. Alaska, Fairbanks, Alaska.

Arizona:

Davis, W.A. and S.M. Russell 1990. *Birds in Southeastern Arizona.* Tucson Audubon Soc., Tucson, Arizona.

Phillips, A., J. Marshall, and G. Monson 1964. *The Birds of Arizona.* Univ. Arizona Press, Tucson, Arizona.

Arkansas:

James, D.A. and J.C. Neal 1986. *Arkansas Birds: Their Distribution Abundance.* Univ. Arkansas Press, Fayetteville, Arkansas.

California:

Garrett, K. and J. Dunn 1981. *Birds of Southern California: Status and Distribution.* Los Angeles Audubon Soc., Los Angeles, California.

Small, A. 1994. *California Birds: Their Status and Distribution.* Ibis Publ. Co., Vista, California.

Unitt, P. 1984. *The Birds of San Diego County.* Memoir 13, San Diego Soc. Nat. Hist., San Diego, California.

Yocom, C.F. and S.W. Harris 1975. *Birds of Northwestern California.* Humboldt State Univ., Arcata, California.

Colorado:

Andrews, R. and R. Righter 1992. *Colorado Birds.* Denver Mus. Nat. Hist., Denver, Colorado.

Connecticut:

Bevier, L.R. 1994. *The Atlas of Breeding Birds of Connecticut.* Bull. 113, State Geol. and Nat. Hist. Survey of Connecticut, Hartford, Connecticut.

Delaware:

Hess, G.K., R.L. West, M.V. Barnhill III, and L.M. Fleming. In press. *Birds of Delaware.* Univ. Pittsburgh Press, Pittsburgh, Pennsylvania.

Florida:

Robertson, W.B. Jr. and G.E. Woolfenden 1992. *Florida Bird Species: An Annotated List.* Special Publ. No. 6, Florida Ornith. Soc., Gainesville, Florida.

Georgia:

Haney, J.C., P. Brisse, D.R. Jacobson, M.W. Oberle, and J.M. Paget 1986. *Annotated Checklist of Georgia Birds.* Occasional Publ. No. 10, Georgia Ornith. Soc., no site of publication designated.

Idaho:

Burleigh, T.D. 1972. *Birds of Idaho.* The Caxton Printers, Caldwell, Idaho.

Illinois:

Bohlen, H.D. 1989. *The Birds of Illinois.* Indiana University Press, Bloomington, Indiana.

Indiana:

Mumford, R.E. and C.E. Keller 1984. *The Birds of Indiana.* Indiana Univ. Press, Bloomington, Indiana.

Iowa:

Dinsmore, J.J., T.H. Kent, D. Koenig, P.C. Petersen, and D.M. Roosa 1984. *Iowa Birds.* Iowa State Univ. Press, Ames, Iowa.

Kansas:
Thompson, M.C. and C. Ely 1992. *Birds in Kansas, Vol. 2*. Univ. Kansas Press, Lawrence, Kansas.

Kentucky:
Mengel, R.M. 1965. *The Birds of Kentucky*. Ornith. Monogr. No. 3, American Ornithologists' Union, Lawrence, Kansas.
Monroe, B.L. Jr. 1994. *The Birds of Kentucky*. Indiana Univ. Press, Bloomington, Indiana.

Louisiana:
Lowery, G.H. Jr. 1955. *Louisiana Birds*. Louisiana State University Press, Baton Rouge, Louisiana.
Oberholser, H.C. 1938. *The Bird Life of Louisiana*. Bull. 28, Dept. Conservation, New Orleans, Louisiana.
Remsen, J.V. Jr., S.W. Cardiff, and D.L. Dittmann. In prep. *Birds of Louisiana*.

Maine:
Adamus, P.R. 1987. *Atlas of Breeding Birds in Maine 1978–1983*. Maine Dept. Inland Fisheries and Wildlife, Augusta, Maine.

Maryland:
Stewart, R.E. and C.S. Robbins 1958. *Birds of Maryland and the District of Columbia*. North American Fauna No. 62, U.S. Dept. Interior, Washington, D.C.

Massachusetts:
Veit, R.R. and W.R. Petersen 1993. *Birds of Massachusetts*. Massachusetts Audubon Soc., Lincoln, Massachusetts.

Michigan:
Brewer, R., G.A. McPeek, and R.J. Adams Jr. 1991. *The Atlas of Breeding Birds of Michigan*. Michigan State Univ. Press, East Lansing, Michigan.
Granlund, J., G.A. McPeek and R.J. Adams 1994. *The Birds of Michigan*. Indiana Univ. Press, Bloomington, Indiana.

Minnesota:
Janssen, R.B. 1992. *Birds in Minnesota*. Univ. Minnesota Press, Minneapolis, Minnesota.

Missouri:
Robbins, M.B. and D.A. Easterla 1992. *Birds of Missouri*. Univ. Missouri Press, Columbia, Missouri.

Montana:
McEneaney, T. 1993. *The Birder's Guide to Montana*. Falcon Press, Helena, Montana.

Nebraska:
Bray, T.E., B.K. Padelford, and W.R. Silcock 1986. *The Birds of Nebraska*. Publ. by authors, Bellevue, Nebraska.
Ducey, J.E. 1988. *Nebraska Birds: Breeding Status and Distribution*. Simmons-Boardman Books, Omaha, Nebraska.

Nevada:
Alcorn, J.R. 1988. *The Birds of Nevada*. Fairview West Publ., Fallon, Nevada.
Linsdale, J.M. 1936. *The Birds of Nevada*. Pacific Coast Avifauna No. 23, Univ. California, Berkeley, California.

New Hampshire:
Foss, C.R. 1994. *Atlas of Breeding Birds in New Hampshire*. Audubon Soc. of New Hampshire. Dover, New Hampshire.

New Jersey:
Leck, C.F. 1984. *The Status and Distribution of New Jersey's Birds*. Rutgers Univ. Press, New Brunswick, New Jersey.

Sibley, D. 1993. *The Birds of Cape May*. Cape May Bird Observatory, Cape May, New Jersey.

New Mexico:
Ligon, J.S. 1961. *New Mexico Birds*. Univ. New Mexico Press, Albuquerque, New Mexico.

New York:
Anderle, R.F. and J.R. Carroll 1988. *The Atlas of Breeding Birds in New York State*. Cornell Univ. Press, Ithaca, New York.

Bull, J. 1974. *Birds of New York State*. Doubleday, Garden City, New York.

North Carolina:
Pearson, T.G., C.S. Brimley, H.H. Brimley, D.L. Wray, and H.T. Davis 1959. *Birds of North Carolina, revised edition*. State Museum, Raleigh, North Carolina.

North Dakota:
Steward, R.E. 1975. *Breeding Birds of North Dakota*. Tri-College Center for Environmental Studies, Fargo, North Dakota.

Ohio:
Peterjohn, B.G. 1989. *The Birds of Ohio*. Indiana University Press, Bloomington, Indiana.

Peterjohn, B.G. and D.L. Rice 1991. *The Ohio Breeding Bird Atlas*. Ohio Dept. Nat. Res., Columbus, Ohio.

Oklahoma:
Baumgartner, F.M. and A.M. Baumgartner 1992. *Oklahoma Bird Life*. Univ. Oklahoma Press, Norman, Oklahoma.

Wood, D.S. and G.D. Schnell 1984. *Distributions of Oklahoma Birds*. Univ. Oklahoma Press, Norman, Oklahoma.

Oregon:
Gabrielson, I.N. and S.G. Jewett 1970. *Birds of the Pacific Northwest*. Dover Publs., New York.

Gillingan, J., M. Smith, D. Rogers, and A. Contreras (Eds) 1994. *Birds of Oregon: Status and Distribution*. Cinclus Publs., McMinnville, Oregon.

Pennsylvania:
Brauning, D.W. 1992. *Atlas of the Breeding Birds in Pennsylvania*. Univ. Pittsburgh Press, Pittsburgh, Pennsylvania.

Poole, E.L. 1964. *Pennsylvania Birds: An Annotated List*. Livingston Publ. Co., Narberth, Pennsylvania.

South Carolina:
Post, W. and S.A. Gauthreaux Jr. 1989. *Status and Distribution of South Carolina Birds*. Contribution No. 18, The Charleston Mus., Charleston, South Carolina.

Sprunt, A. Jr. and E.B. Chamberlain 1949. *South Carolina Bird Life*. Univ. South Carolina Press, Columbia, South Carolina.

South Dakota:
South Dakota Ornithologists' Union 1991. *The Birds of South Dakota*. Aberdeen, South
    Dakota.

Tennessee:
Robinson, J.C. 1990. *An Annotated Checklist of the Birds of Tennessee*. Univ. Tennessee Press,
    Knoxville, Tennessee.

Texas:
Kutac, E.A. 1989. *Birder's Guide to Texas*. Lone Star Books, Houston, Texas.
Oberholser, H.C. 1974. *The Bird Life of Texas*. Vol. 2. Univ. Texas Press, Austin, Texas.

Utah:
Behle, W.H. 1985. *Utah Birds: Geographic Distribution and Systematics*. Occasional Publ. No. 5,
    Utah Mus. Nat. Hist., Salt Lake City, Utah.
Behle, W.H., E.D. Sorensen, and C.M. White 1985. *Utah Birds: A Revised Checklist*. Occasional
    Publ. No. 4, Utah Mus. Nat. Hist., Salt Lake City, Utah.

Vermont:
Laughlin, S.B. and D.P. Kibbe 1985. *The Atlas of Breeding Birds of Vermont*. Univ. Press of New
    England, Hanover, New Hampshire.

Virginia:
Kain, T. 1987. *Virginia's Birdlife: An Annotated Checklist*. Virginia Avifauna No. 3, Virginia Soc.
    Ornithology, no site of publication designated.

Washington:
Jewett, S.G., W.P. Taylor, W.T. Shaw, and J.W. Aldrich 1953. *Birds of Washington State*. Univ.
    Washington Press, Seattle, Washington.

West Virginia:
Hall, G.A. 1983. *West Virginia Birds*. Carnegie Mus. Nat. Hist. Special Publ. No. 7, Pittsburgh,
    Pennsylvania.

Wisconsin:
Robbins, S.D. Jr. 1991. *Wisconsin Birdlife*. Univ. Wisconsin Press, Madison, Wisconsin.

Wyoming:
Scott, O.K. 1993. *A Birder's Guide to Wyoming*. American Birding Assn., Colorado Springs,
    Colorado.

REGIONAL: MEXICO
Howell, S.N.G. and S. Webb 1995. *The Birds of Mexico and Northern Central America*. Oxford
    Univ. Press, Oxford, England.
Van Rossem, A.J. 1945. *A Distributional Survey of the Birds of Sonora, Mexico*. Occasional
    Papers Mus. Zoology, Louisiana State Univ., Baton Rouge, Louisiana.

INDEX

Numbers in **bold** indicate the plate number in the color plate section which starts on page 295.